The Beginner's Guide to *Mathematica*® Version 4

The Beginner's Guide to *Mathematica*® Version 4

Jerry Glynn

MathWare
Urbana, IL

Theodore Gray

Wolfram Research, Inc.
Urbana, IL

CAMBRIDGE
UNIVERSITY PRESS

PUBLISHED BY THE PRESS SYNDICATE OF THE UNIVERSITY OF CAMBRIDGE
The Pitt Building, Trumpington Street, Cambridge, United Kingdom

CAMBRIDGE UNIVERSITY PRESS
The Edinburgh Building, Cambridge CB2 2RU, United Kingdom   http://www.cup.cam.ac.uk
40 West 20th Street, New York, NY 10011–4211, USA   http://www.cup.org
10 Stamford Road, Oakleigh, Melbourne 3166, Australia
Ruiz de Alarcón 13, 28014 Madrid, Spain

First published 2000

Printed in the United States of America

Typeset in Mathematica

A catalogue record for this book is available from the British Library

Library of Congress Cataloguing-in-Publication Data
Glynn, Jerry.
    The beginner's guide to Mathematica, version 4 / Jerry Glynn,
Theodore Gray.
        p.   cm.
    Includes bibliographical references and index.
      ISBN 0-521-77153-6 (hb) – ISBN 0-521-77769-0 (pb)
        1. Mathematica (Computer file) 2. Mathematics – Data pro-
cessing. I. Gray, Theodore W. II. Title.
QA76.95 .G552 2000
510′.285′5369 – dc21   99-050341

ISBN 0 521 77153 6 (hardback)
ISBN 0 521 77769 0 (paperback)

Table of Contents

Preface

This book is both a tutorial and a reference book. To use it as a tutorial, start at the beginning and read the chapters in sequence. You will get a good idea of what *Mathematica* Version 4 does, and will find things explained in a sensible order. To use it as a reference, scan the table of contents to find the question you want answered.

Although this book will get you started using *Mathematica*, it is not a complete reference book. You will need to refer to the on-line help system frequently: See <u>Chapter</u> 6 for information about the help system.

We are indebted to several people for help with this book:

Professor Eugene Nichols, for his suggestion to Jerry Glynn which turned into <u>Chapter</u> 60 (and then threatened to take over the whole book).

For reading early versions and making useful suggestions, Eva Gray, Kurt Peckman, Mike Rasberry, and Tom Sherlock.

For help with specific chapters, Rob Knapp and P.J. Hinton.

Alan Harvey, for making our work with Cambridge University Press pleasant and productive, and getting checks to us within milliseconds of our editor's bill.

For his patience and persistence in editing the manuscript and getting the authors to clarify their ideas, David Eisenman (who still feels strongly that Social Security payments should be indexed not to prices but to median income, and who *still* quite mistakenly believes that "data" is the plural of some word no one has ever heard of).

For cover and book design under pressure, Andre Kuzniarek.

Scott May, for suggesting <u>Chapter</u> 29, motivated by the hundreds of calls he has received from people who have had this problem; he also suggested the discussion of plotting 3-D points as a surface in <u>Chapter</u> 42.

And finally, the authors thank their wives Joyce Glynn and Jane Billman whose encouragement and good humor helped us when things got tough.

Chapter 1

What do I need to make *Mathematica* work on my computer?

Mathematica is a big program; fortunately computers are bigger. Until about mid-1998 it was necessary to discuss the question of whether a computer had enough memory, disk space, or processor speed to run *Mathematica*. This is no longer an issue for any new computer: If you buy it, it will run *Mathematica*. (Unless it's some kind of cellular phone pretending to be a computer, or a personal organizer pretending to be a computer, etc.)

To run *Mathematica* comfortably, you need 32MB of RAM and about 150MB of disk space, most of which is for the online documentation. A minimal installation without documentation requires 40MB of disk space; the documentation is still available directly from the CD-ROM, but it's less convenient because the CD must be in the drive, and access is slower.

In the Windows world, Windows 95, 98, 00, or NT is required.

In the Macintosh world, System 8 or later is required. (The Grape colored iMac is an especially wonderful machine to run *Mathematica* on, right out of the box.)

Mathematica is also available for a bewildering and ever-changing array of Unix workstation and mainframe computers. To find out today's menu, consult the Wolfram Research web site at http://www.wolfram.com.

Chapter **2**

Can I read the rest of this book without reading this chapter?

No. This is a short chapter, but if you don't read it you won't understand anything else in the whole book. As long as you promise to read this chapter, we promise not to be long-winded or to tell you anything that isn't essential.

Know your computer! Most people who drive expensive sports cars in crowded parking lots have learned to drive first. Likewise, it's a good idea to have spent a few days with your computer before using a program like *Mathematica*. You should be familiar with how to start ("launch") a program; use the mouse (if you have one) to edit text; scroll; work with windows and menus (if you have them). You should also be comfortable with the other basic operations of your particular brand of computer—write a few letters with your word processor; draw a picture with the mouse.

Capitalization! All of *Mathematica's* built-in names start with a capital letter: `Sin`, `Table`, `Factor`, `Integrate`, `Expand`, `Plot`, `Pi`, `E`, `I`, etc. Some have more have than one capital letter: `NestList`, `ContourPlot`, `ListDensityPlot`, etc. You must type these names exactly as shown, with the exact capitalization shown, or it won't work.

Square brackets! Functions and commands use square brackets, not parentheses: `Sin[x]`, `Factor[x² - 9]`. If you want to get a sensible answer, you can't say `Sin(x)` or `sin[x]` or `sin(x)`. It has to be exactly `Sin[x]`.

Use the Correct Key! After following the installation instructions that came with your copy of *Mathematica*, you will be faced with a blank notebook window. To enter an expression, just start typing. Try `2+2`. Then use the "action key" to tell *Mathematica* to carry out the evaluation. This key is different on different kinds of computers:

> **Macintosh:** Enter or Shift-Return. (Shift-Return means press the return key while holding down the shift key.)

> **Windows:** Shift-Enter. (Many DOS keyboards have two enter keys, but they both do the same thing.)

> **X-Windows:** Shift-Return. (X keyboards are highly variable: You'll have to figure out which key acts as the return key.)

Here is what a typical session with *Mathematica* might look like:

In[1]:= **2 + 2**

Out[1]= 4

The statement we typed is in **boldface** and labeled *In[1]*. *Mathematica's* result is printed in plain type and labeled *Out[1]* (all this happens automatically). In the rest of this book we're not going to show the *In/Out* labels because you rarely need to refer to them.

Notebooks and Cells! You will see "cell brackets" on the right-hand side of your window as you start entering text and doing evaluations:

Do not be alarmed; the cell brackets are quite useful, but you can ignore them at first. Just remember, if you want to start a new input line from scratch, scroll the window (if necessary) so you can see past the bottom of the last piece of text in the window, and click in the area below the last text. A horizontal line should appear across the whole width of the window. This is an indication that you can start typing.

Version 4! This book describes features of Version 4 of *Mathematica*. Although many of the topics we talk about will work in earlier versions (particularly Version 3), many of them will not. If you are currently using an older copy of *Mathematica*, it is worthwhile to get it upgraded.

You can't click on paper! In various places in this book you may notice underlined words, or sentences that say "click here to...". These represent hyperlinks that are, of course, useless in the printed version of the book. This book is principally intended as an interactive electronic document: The printed version is a subset of the full electronic version.

If you wish to purchase the electronic edition of this book, click here, or visit our web site at http://www.mathware.com/BeginnersGuide.

Chapter **3**

Why is *Mathematica* split into a front end and a kernel?

Mathematica is divided right down the middle into front end and kernel. These two parts are separate programs that communicate through a bi-directional data stream called *MathLink*.

The front end is the part of *Mathematica* that you interact with. It handles windows, menus, dialog boxes, text, typeset expressions, graphics, animations, sounds, palettes, notebooks, and cells.

The kernel carries out calculations that are presented to it by the front end.

There are several reasons for this organization:

- The kernel and front end can run on separate computers. For example, the front end may be running on a personal computer on your desk while the kernel is running on a large UNIX server in another building.

- The front end can connect to several kernels at the same time, sending and receiving calculations to all of them simultaneously. Multiple kernels allow you to carry out calculations in one kernel while waiting for a very long calculation in another kernel to finish.

- If something goes wrong with a calculation (for example, if it turns out to take an infinite amount of memory), you can shut down that kernel without affecting the front end or calculations running in other kernels.

- Because the kernel is a purely data-in/data-out program with no user interface, it is particularly easy to port to new computer systems. It is virtually identical regardless of what platform it is running on.

When you first start up *Mathematica* you are really starting just the front end. Only if you start a calculation with Shift-Return (or use a palette button that is set up to do a calculation) will a kernel be started. The first calculation you do will typically take quite a bit longer than you might expect: You are waiting for the kernel half of *Mathematica* to be launched.

■ For Software People

MathLink, the protocol used to communicate between the front end and kernel, is a documented public communications protocol. There is nothing magic about the way the front end and kernel use *MathLink*; any program can connect to either the *Mathematica* front end or the *Mathematica* kernel the same way they connect to each other.

Thus, software developers can use *Mathematica's* front end to drive virtually any system that accepts data as input and produces data as output. Likewise, any program that needs the services of a computational engine can call up the *Mathematica* kernel directly.

■ Using the kernel as a computational engine

Several packages are available from Wolfram Research that allow programs to use the *Mathematica* kernel as an embedded component. There are components that work with Microsoft Word and Excel, Fortner Research's Transform, and Xmath. Click http://www.wolfram.com/applications/index.html for more information (others may be available by the time you read this).

If you have your own front-end-like program and would like to connect it to the kernel, the *MathLink Developers Kit* allows you to do so quite easily.

■ Using the front end with other computational engines

The *Mathematica* front end can be connected directly to an alternate kernel. In this case, the non-*Mathematica* kernel must be programmed to respond to commands (*MathLink* packets) sent to it by the front end. After finishing whatever calculation it has been instructed to carry out, the alternate kernel sends back the results in the form of *MathLink* packets, which the front end displays.

The names and formats of the packets involved in this interchange are documented in the *MathLink Developers Kit*, available from Wolfram Research, Inc.

An option that can sometimes greatly simplify the connection is to use a *Mathematica* kernel as a buffer between the *Mathematica* front end and an alternate kernel. In this case, the front end and *Mathematica* kernel communicate in the ordinary way; the *Mathematica* kernel forwards calculation requests to the alternate kernel after processing them in some way. Likewise, it processes the results from the alternate kernel before forwarding them back to the front end for display. In this case, you can make up any protocol you like for communication between the *Mathematica* kernel and your alternate kernel (using *MathLink* as the transport layer).

A particularly clever use of the *Mathematica* kernel as a buffer is to translate 2-D typeset expressions from the front end into whatever format is most convenient for the alternate kernel, and to translate the alternate kernel's output back into 2-D typeset notations for display in the front end.

For example, if you had a fancy theorem-proving system that understands only a sort of pseudo-19th century linear syntax, you could use the beautiful typesetting available in the *Mathematica* front end to enter your queries and display your results.

Chapter **4**

How do I get the electronic version of this book?

If you want the electronic version of this book, you can buy and download it from http://www.mathware.com/BeginnersGuide. The download time will depend on your internet connection; with a 28.8K modem it will take about half an hour.

To order a CD-ROM version of the book, contact:

> **MathWare**
> P.O. Box 3025
> Urbana, IL 61803
> http://www.mathware.com
> info@mathware.com
> Phone: 800-255-2468
> FAX: 217-384-7043

After getting the files (and uncompressing them if your browser did not do this automatically), open the "AddOns" folder (directory) in your main *Mathematica* folder. It should contain a folder called "Autoload". Drag the "Beginner's Guide V4" folder into the "Autoload" folder. (On multi-user UNIX systems, you can install it in your home directory in ".Mathematica/AddOns/Autoload".)

After moving the folder, restart the *Mathematica* front end and choose "Rebuild Help Index" from the Help menu. This will incorporate the book into the Help Browser and include its index in the Master Index section (see Chapter 6 for more information about the Help Browser).

You can now use the book in several ways. If you want to read whole chapters (perhaps even in order) the easiest way is to open TableOfContents.nb using the **Open** command in the **File** menu. After selecting a chapter from the listing, click on the underlined word "Chapter", and that chapter will be opened automatically.

You can also read the book inside the Help Browser, by clicking on the "Add-Ons" radio button. You will then see an item "Beginner's Guide V4" in the first column: Click on it to get a listing of the parts and chapters in the book. This gives you the same listing as the table of contents file.

The Help Browser allows you to look at an index of this book mixed in with indices of the main *Mathematica* book, Reference Guide, and any other *Mathematica* books you may have installed. Click on the "Master Index" radio button in the Help Browser, then either scan the categories or type in the Lookup field to locate an index entry. When you click on an item, you will see the entries for that topic in all the currently available documentation and books. Using merged indices lets you get more than one perspective on the material, although we promise you that the material in The Beginner's Guide will, of course, be by far the most useful.

Chapter **5**

What's the difference between numerical and symbolic calculation?

In the last few years, people have gotten used to the idea that computers can do algebra and calculus, not just arithmetic. *Mathematica* is one of the programs that made this happen. What are the differences between numerical and symbolic computations?

Many programs (and calculators) can do numerical calculations like this:

>   **27 + 8**

>   35

Mathematica goes beyond this: It can do algebraic calculations, where the answer is not a number:

>   **27 x + 8 x**

>   35 x

With a numerical calculator we can work out the value of the following expression:

>   **(3 + 8)^5**

>   161051

In *Mathematica*, we can use symbolic variable names in place of the numbers **3** and **8**:

>   **(a + b)^5**

> $(a + b)^5$

and then get the multiplied-out form:

>   **Expand[(a + b)^5]**

> $a^5 + 5\,a^4\,b + 10\,a^3\,b^2 + 10\,a^2\,b^3 + 5\,a\,b^4 + b^5$

We can integrate the expression with respect to **a**:

$$\int (\mathbf{a} + \mathbf{b})^5 \, d\mathbf{a}$$

$$\frac{a^6}{6} + a^5 \, b + \frac{5 \, a^4 \, b^2}{2} + \frac{10 \, a^3 \, b^3}{3} + \frac{5 \, a^2 \, b^4}{2} + a \, b^5$$

Symbolic calculation does not just mean algebra or calculus. For example, *Mathematica* can compute all the permutations of a list of names (curly-brackets are used to indicate lists of items):

Permutations[{Jane, Addison, Trevor, Jessica}]

{{Jane, Addison, Trevor, Jessica}, {Jane, Addison, Jessica, Trevor},
{Jane, Trevor, Addison, Jessica}, {Jane, Trevor, Jessica, Addison},
{Jane, Jessica, Addison, Trevor}, {Jane, Jessica, Trevor, Addison},
{Addison, Jane, Trevor, Jessica}, {Addison, Jane, Jessica, Trevor},
{Addison, Trevor, Jane, Jessica}, {Addison, Trevor, Jessica, Jane},
{Addison, Jessica, Jane, Trevor}, {Addison, Jessica, Trevor, Jane},
{Trevor, Jane, Addison, Jessica}, {Trevor, Jane, Jessica, Addison},
{Trevor, Addison, Jane, Jessica}, {Trevor, Addison, Jessica, Jane},
{Trevor, Jessica, Jane, Addison}, {Trevor, Jessica, Addison, Jane},
{Jessica, Jane, Addison, Trevor}, {Jessica, Jane, Trevor, Addison},
{Jessica, Addison, Jane, Trevor}, {Jessica, Addison, Trevor, Jane},
{Jessica, Trevor, Jane, Addison}, {Jessica, Trevor, Addison, Jane}}

Symbolic calculation also applies to expressions involving only numbers. For example, in *Mathematica* we can do calculations involving fractions and get back exact answers:

$$\frac{1}{3} + \frac{2}{5}$$

$$\frac{11}{15}$$

We can compute numbers that are larger than most calculators could handle:

200 !

7886578673647905035523632139321850622951359776871732632947425331
2443594499634033429203042840119846239041772121389196388302576412
2790242637105061926624952829931113462857270763317237396988943941
2244562145166424025403329186413122742829485327752424240757390312
2403212574055795686602260319041703240623517008587961789222227811
9623703897374720000000000000000000000000000000000000000000000000
00

The ⁚ at the end of each line lets us know that the number continues on the next line.

Mathematica generally does not make approximations unless asked to. If we ask a calculator for the square root of 12, it has little choice but to give us a numerical approximation accurate to a few decimal places. If we ask *Mathematica*, it has the option of returning a symbolic result instead:

$\sqrt{12}$

$2\sqrt{3}$

Mathematica has rearranged the expression somewhat but has left it with a square root, since there is no better way to represent the answer without making an approximation.

If we want a numerical approximation, we can use the **N** function:

$\mathbf{N}\left[\sqrt{12}\right]$

3.464101615137754

Throughout the rest of this book you will learn about *Mathematica's* symbolic, numerical, graphical, and programming capabilities.

Chapter **6**

How do I ask *Mathematica* for help?

Mathematica Version 4 contains a very large volume of online documentation, almost 100MB of data: the full text of The Mathematica Book, function reference guide, Guide to Standard Packages, Getting Started documentation, and demos.

The best way to get help depends on the nature of the problem.

If you want more information about a specific function, say **NestList**, you can select it and choose "Find in Help..." in the Help menu (Command-Shift-F on the Macintosh, or F1 on Windows). This will give you the text of the reference guide entry for the selected function. For example, for **NestList**, you see:

On the other hand, if you are looking for a function to perform a certain task but don't know what it's called, you can browse around in the categories you see above. They are organized into logically related categories and subcategories, so the same function may appear in several different places if it can be used for different purposes.

For help with add-on packages, click on the "Add-Ons" radio button. You will get a list of help categories for the standard packages included with *Mathematica*, as well as help for any optional packages or books you may have installed. For example, if you have installed this book according to the instructions in Chapter 4, you will see "Beginner's Guide" listed under this category.

For help with menu commands, dialog boxes, etc., look in Getting Started and Other Information categories.

If you want to find information on a particular topic but don't know where it might be found, click on the Master Index radio button. You can read the alphabetical index, or type in a word to search for entries that match it. The Master Index covers the contents of the entire help system, including any optional packages/books you may have installed. For example, if you have installed this book, and you look up a given function name in the Master Index, you will see an entry for the Reference Guide section, an entry for The *Mathematica* Book, and, if we talk about the function, an entry for The Beginner's Guide.

Chapter **7**

How do I define constants and functions?

In this chapter we're going to define simple functions and constants. <u>Chapter</u> 56 and <u>Chapter</u> 58 describe how to define more-complicated functions.

To define a constant, use a single equals sign:

> **a = 5**
>
> 5

Once defined, you can use the constant anywhere you want:

> **a + 7**
>
> 12
>
> **a^2**
>
> 25

When defining a function, you need to remember only two important things:

- Use an underscore character after each argument name on the left-hand side (but not on the right-hand side).

- Use a **:=** in the middle.

(The reasons for these rules are explained in <u>Chapter</u> 56 and <u>Chapter</u> 58.)

Here is an example:

> **f[x_] := x^2**

This function can be applied to many different kinds of arguments. We can use it on a simple number:

```
f[5]
```

25

We can use it on an expression that evaluates to a number:

```
f[100!]
```

87097824890894800794165901619444858655697206439408401342159 3253 .
62433799963465833258779670963327549206446903807622196074763 642 .
89411435920190573960677507881394607489905331729758013432992 987 .
18476460737588943431348338296680151515628085416269176619573 749 .
31734536035195944960000000000000000000000000000000000000000 .
00000

We can use it on a symbolic expression:

```
f[a + b]
```

$(a + b)^2$

Note that there is no problem with variable name conflicts:

```
f[1 + x]
```

$(1 + x)^2$

```
f[f[1 + x]]
```

$(1 + x)^4$

We can plot the function:

```
Plot[f[x], {x, -2, 2}];
```

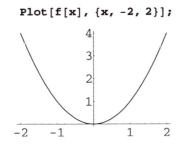

We can take the derivative of the function:

```
∂ₓ f[x]
```

2 x

In other words, we can use a defined function in all the same ways that we can use built-in functions.

When working a mathematical problem, it is often helpful to define some intermediate quantities. For example, we might want to define the volume of a cylinder as π times the radius squared times the height. We could define such a function this way:

> **CylinderVolume[radius_, height_] := π radius^2 height**

We can now use the function:

> **CylinderVolume[3, 5]**
>
> $45\,\pi$

Since we can include symbolic values in the arguments, we can, for example, specify units:

> **CylinderVolume[20 Yards, 12 Yards]**
>
> $4800\,\pi\,\text{Yards}^3$

If we want to see a decimal approximation of this quantity, we can use the **N** function:

> **N[CylinderVolume[20 Yards, 12 Yards]]**
>
> $15079.6\,\text{Yards}^3$

Including units is often very helpful, but seldom thought of. For an extensive example using units, see Chapter 73.

Chapter 8

How do I share notebooks with those who have different brands of computers?

There is no inherent problem transferring *Mathematica* notebook files from any brand of computer to any other. Whether you have a Macintosh, Windows, or Unix computer, notebook files are fully compatible.

Notebooks are plain, 7-bit ASCII text files; you can look at one in any ordinary text editor, and if you are familiar with *Mathematica* expression syntax, it will make sense to you.

To get a notebook from one brand of computer to another, you do, of course, need to have some means of transferring files, such as ftp, floppy disk, etc. Notebook files can be transferred in either "text" or "binary" mode; either will work equally well.

▪ Ways to make notebooks non-portable

It is possible to create notebook files that are not, in fact, fully portable. The two most common ways are to use fonts that do not exist on the other computer, or to use the PICT graphics format (which works only on the Macintosh) or Metafile format (which works only on Windows).

To avoid the font problem, you should either stick to a small number of common fonts or make sure the fonts you use are available where you want to transfer the notebook. If you use only style sheets that came with *Mathematica*, which include a good variety of fonts and styles, you will be safe. If a given font that you use is not available, *Mathematica* will substitute one that is.

The PICT/Metafile graphics problem usually happens when you paste a graphic into *Mathematica* from another program. Because the paste operation uses the platform-specific graphic format of the machine you are on, the result is a notebook that will work only on that platform. If you were to take a notebook with such a graphic to any other type of computer, the image would not be visible.

To avoid the PICT/Metafile problem, select the graphic(s) and choose the **Bitmap** command from the **Cell** menu, **Convert To** submenu. This will convert the graphic into a portable format that can be displayed on all platforms.

There is no analogous problem going from Unix computers to the Mac, because Unix computers do not have a standard graphics interchange format: Graphics pasted on these platforms are automatically stored as portable Bitmap format images.

■ Subtler incompatibilities

A notebook taken from one type of computer to another will usually look extremely similar. However, there are certain subtle ways in which the appearance may not be identical. These differences may become an issue in some cases.

Mathematica uses the fonts available on the host computer system. As discussed above, this means a font used by a notebook may not be available on the computer it is being displayed on, resulting in a substitution. However, even if the font *is* available, it may not be the *same* as the one with the same name on the original platform. For example, it is common for the "Times" font to have slightly different character widths on different platforms. This can affect the wordwrapping of lines of text, which in turn can affect the pagination of large printed documents. Particularly when one system is using Adobe Type 1 fonts while the other is using TrueType fonts, significant differences in font metrics can exist.

In many cases this is not a concern, but for someone trying to maintain a page number index while printing a book, font metric differences can be a major problem.

There is no easy solution to this problem. Consider distributing your work electronically instead, or stick to the same platform for editing and printing.

Chapter 9

What was new in V3.0?

Theo: The introduction of V3.0 was a major milestone in the development of *Mathematica*. It represented a fundamental change in the structure of the program, and introduced many new ideals. V4.0 is not another change of this magnitude. V4.0 represents an incremental improvement in the program, with some new ideas, new features, and improvements to existing features. We've included two chapters, one for things that were new in V3.0 and a second for things that are new in V4.0.

Jerry: What were the three most significant new things in Version 3?

Theo: What, only three? How can I possibly limit myself to only *three* new things?

Jerry: OK, how about only two?

Theo: Typesetting. Palettes. Help browser. The symbolic foundation of the front end.

■ Typesetting

Theo: Typesetting means that instead of:

```
Integrate[1 / (1 - x^3), x]
```

$$\frac{\text{ArcTan}[\frac{1 + 2\ x}{\text{Sqrt}[3]}]}{\text{Sqrt}[3]} - \frac{\text{Log}[-1 + x]}{3} + \frac{\text{Log}[1 + x + x^2]}{6}$$

you can do:

$$\int \frac{1}{1 - x^3}\,dx$$

$$\frac{\tan^{-1}\left(\frac{2x+1}{\sqrt{3}}\right)}{\sqrt{3}} - \frac{1}{3}\log(x - 1) + \frac{1}{6}\log(x^2 + x + 1)$$

Jerry: This is an obvious improvement. I'm sure it required at least 4×10^6 hours of programming. In particular, I notice that even the input is typeset.

Theo: Yes, typesetting represents many person-years of work, mainly by Neil Soiffer, the designer of the system. It's something no other system can do.

Jerry: *No* other system? Are you sure?

Theo: Yes, almost *no* other system. Some can do math with typeset output, and some can do typeset input but no (or hardly any) math. No other fully integrated system can do publication-quality typeset input and output for a full range of math and science expressions. Remarkably, this remains true even after all the years since the release of V3.0.

Jerry: Can't T$_E$X create equations like this?

Theo: Sure, but T$_E$X can't do math. Remember, what you see above is typed in interactively, in real time, and you get the output from the typeset input automatically just by typing Shift-Return. Nowhere in the process was there a cryptic series of input commands, as would be necessary in T$_E$X or Maple, for example.

Three chapters in this book discuss typeset input and output, for beginner (Chapter 16), intermediate (Chapter 17), and advanced (Chapter 18) users.

■ Palettes

Theo: This is a palette:

Jerry: Nice, I guess. They are like menus or toolbars, right?

Theo: Yes. You can use them to create typeset expressions like the ones above. A palette button might be programmed to expand a polynomial, solve an equation, make a plot, etc. They are also user-customizable, so you can create your own personal palettes.

Jerry: Of course *Mathematica* comes with a set of built-in palettes; I saw them in the **Palettes** submenu of the **File** menu.

Theo: Palettes are useful for beginning users of *Mathematica*, for advanced users doing things they don't normally do, and most importantly they are useful for creating custom versions of *Mathematica* where certain operations have been emphasized by placing them in palettes. You'll see examples of this in later chapters.

■ Help Browser

Theo: The Help Browser is an extensible, searchable full text help system. It has the entire *Mathematica* Book, reference guide, package documentation, and front end help in notebook form. Books in *Mathematica* form can be added to the Browser, and their tables of contents and even *indices* are automatically included. (Imagine that! A single compound index, mixing together the *Mathematica* Book and eight other books about interesting topics!)

For example, this very book can be installed in the Help Browser. At http://www.mathware.com/BeginnersGuide you will find the electronic version of this book available for downloading. Once installed, it becomes an integral part of your *Mathematica* system.

There are now a fair number of books available in this form.

■ Symbolic Foundation

Theo: Symbolic foundation means that all elements of the front end are based on the *Mathematica* language. For example, this sentence is represented as:

```
Cell[TextData[{
   StyleBox["Theo:",
     FontWeight->"Bold"],
   " Symbolic foundation means that all elements \
of the front end are based on the ",
   StyleBox["Mathematica",
     FontSlant->"Italic"],
   " language.  For example, this sentence is \
represented as:"
}], "Text"]
```

Jerry: Ack. This is an improvement?

Theo: You non-programmer types are all alike.

Jerry: Sure—not bald; don't wear funny shoes; go to sleep before 3AM.

Theo: The fact that all elements in the front end are based on *Mathematica* expressions is very valuable. Text, math expressions, graphics, palettes, whole Notebooks, user preference settings, all display options, etc., etc., are *all* represented as expressions in the *Mathematica* language. This means you can write *programs* to do things in the front end. Not "scripts" in some silly scripting language designed by a high school student, but real programs in a real language.

Jerry: I can see that you have strong feelings about this capability! My problem is that you haven't shown me an example yet that I care about.

Theo: Watch this!

```
Do[SetOptions[SelectedNotebook[], WindowSize →
    N[{400 + 200 Sin[i], 400 + 200 Sin[i]}]], {i, 0, 2 π, π / 5}];
```

Jerry: Thrilling, but how will the reader of the miserable paper version of this document get an idea of what just happened? (By the way, what did happen?)

Theo: `SelectedNotebook[]` is a function that represents the current notebook window (the one you're typing into). As with other *Mathematica* functions, a notebook object has many options. One of them is `WindowSize`, which represents the size of the window in points (one point equals $\frac{1}{72}$ inch). If you change the value of the `WindowSize` option using the standard `SetOptions` command, almost magically the window itself *changes size*.

In this case, we made the front notebook window, this one, grow and shrink in a sinusoidal way. There are not many programs that can do *that* in a single line of code. If you do find one, substitute `RiemannSiegelTheta` for `Sin`. There *definitely* aren't any other programs that can do that!

Jerry: Dear reader, you have just lived through a microcosm of the past twenty years of development in the computer industry: Talented, hard-working, software engineers create capabilities that impress the *hell* out of themselves but do not even begin to impress anyone else on earth.

Perhaps somewhere in here lurks a useful feature, but, sadly, I don't see it yet.

Theo: There are lots of potential uses of *Mathematica's* ability to resize windows under program control. For example, you might have some courseware that needs a collection of windows: a graphing window, some palettes, a help area, and a worksheet. You could write a program to arrange them optimally for any arbitrary screen size, instead of having to pick one static arrangement.

Jerry: How about a *better* example?

Theo: OK, automatic index generation. This book has a big fancy printed index, and a very fine electronic index full of hyperlinks. These indices were generated automatically using a fairly large *Mathematica* program that makes extensive use of the fact that the notebooks that make up the book are symbolic objects.

Jerry: That's a good example (finally).

Theo: This topic is discussed in greater detail in <u>Chapter</u> 62.

Chapter **10**

So, what's new in V4.0?

Theo: The introduction of V3.0 was a major milestone in the development of *Mathematica*. It represented a fundamental change in the structure of the program, and introduced many new ideas. V4.0 is not another change of this magnitude. V4.0 represents an incremental improvement in the program, with some new ideas, new features, and improvements to existing features. We've included two chapters, one for things that were new in V3.0 and a second for things that are new in V4.0.

■ Spell checker

Finally! *Mathematica* now has a professional-quality spell checker for Notebook documents. It's specially tuned to work well with text containing *Mathematica* commands. For more information about what makes this spell checker especially good for technical text, see Chapter 51.

■ Real-time 3-D Graphics

Finally! *Mathematica* can now rotate 3-D graphics in real time inside a Notebook document. Using OpenGL 3-D rendering technology, the Notebook interface now allows you to generate a 3-D graphic, then spin it around with the mouse. For more information, see Chapter 37.

■ Import/Export

In V4, *Mathematica* is able to import and export data in a variety of standard formats, including tables and image formats. This allows *Mathematica* to be used for amusing things such as image processing. There are several chapters dedicated to this topic, including Chapter 45 on image processing, Chapter 79 on importing data and Chapter 80 on exporting data.

■ Numerics

One of the most important improvements in V4.0 is the introduction of extremely fast and efficient numerical operations. Many existing features are now much faster and use much less memory, and sophisticated new numerical operations have been introduced.

Many of these improvements are the result of a new, more efficient internal representation for arrays of machine-precision floating point numbers and integers. Being able to store large arrays of numbers efficiently is crucial to many large numerical computations. The new representation also allows operations to be performed on the numbers much more quickly than was previously possible.

In addition, many new algorithms have been added or improved to make specific operations faster. For example, consider the Factorial function. Some of you may remember the days when 69! was special, because it was the largest factorial you could do on a calculator that only did 2-digit exponents in its scientific notation mode. Of course, these days 69! is child's play (and you get the exact answer):

69 !

171122452428141311372468338881272839092270544893520369393648040╲
9232572797541406474240000000000000000

While many people have gotten used to the idea that you can do 1000!, or even 10,000! (getting a 35,000 digit result in less than a second), in the closing years of the millennium it's still quite remarkable that you can do something like 1,000,000! and get an answer in a couple of minutes (5.5 million digits). These calculations are possible largely because *Mathematica* now uses the most sophisticated available Fast Fourier Transform (FFT)-based multiplication algorithms, combined with Karatsuba and ordinary schoolbook arithmetic, to do large integer and large floating point multiplications with state-of-the-art speed. (In addition, factorial is computed with a clever algorithm that maximizes the efficiency of the order in which the multiplications are done.)

For your amusement, here are the factorials of the first six powers of ten (10! through 1,000,000!) along with the time to compute each one (on a 266MHz PowerPC laptop). For those tempted to go for 10,000,000!, be warned that the arithmetic gets pretty extreme out there.

```
Table[Prepend[Timing[N[10ⁿ !]], HoldForm[10ⁿⁿ !] /. nn → n],
     {n, 1, 6}] // TableForm
```

10^1 !	0. Second	3.6288×10^6
10^2 !	0. Second	9.33262×10^{157}
10^3 !	0. Second	$4.023872600770938 \times 10^{2567}$
10^4 !	0.233333 Second	$2.846259680917055 \times 10^{35659}$
10^5 !	5.16667 Second	$2.824229407960348 \times 10^{456573}$
10^6 !	164.567 Second	$8.263931688331240 \times 10^{5565708}$

See Chapter 25 for more examples of high-powered numerical calculations.

Chapter **11**

How do I use my old notebooks in V4?

Notebooks created by Version 3 of *Mathematica* can be opened in Version 4 without difficulty. They will simply open and work normally. However, notebooks created with older versions (V2.2 and earlier) require a conversion before they can be opened.

When you attempt to open such an older notebook, the front end will offer to convert it for you. If you agree to do the conversion, a new V4 notebook will be created alongside your older notebook. Typically it will have the same name except now ending in ".nb" instead of ".ma".

There are several options that affect the conversion. Here is the dialog box you will see when you open an old notebook, listing these options:

The notebook you asked to open is in an old format and needs to be converted. The new file will have a name ending in ".nb".

You may choose to automatically convert all input and/or output cells to StandardForm, the editable 2D form used by default in Version 3.

☐ Convert Input cells to StandardForm
☐ Convert Output cells to StandardForm

Version 3 supports a more sophisticated style sheet. Check the option below only if you have changed the style definitions in this notebook.

☐ Preserve customized style sheet

Bitmap caches for PostScript cells cannot be converted. Check the option below to regenerate them automatically (can be very slow).

☐ Generate bitmap caches for all graphics cells

☐ Convert all notebooks in this folder
☐ Convert all sub-folders

If new file already exists: ● Ask for new name ○ Overwrite ○ Skip

[Help] [Cancel] [**Convert**]

▪ Convert Input/Output cells to StandardForm

The first two options allow you to automatically take advantage of the new typeset notations available since V3, converting all the input and/or output cells in your notebook into 2-D typeset notation. For example, `x^y` will become x^y, and `Integrate[1/(1-x^3), x]` will turn into $\int \frac{1}{1-x^3} \, dx$.

In order to do this, the front end must start a kernel, and send all the input/output expressions to this kernel for conversion. This process can be fairly slow for large notebooks with many input/output cells. If the notebook contains particularly large and complex expressions, they can also use a lot of memory.

For many kinds of notebooks, you will want these two options turned on. However, there are some cases in which they would not be a good idea. If your notebook contains fairly large program-like input cells (e.g., a package with large `Block` or `Module` statements) you may prefer to leave these in text form rather than convert to typeset notation.

The conversion process also strips out any `(* comments *)` in Input cells, so if you use many such comments, you will probably not want to do the automatic conversion.

If you don't like the results of an automatic conversion, just re-open the old notebook. This time, when *Mathematica* asks to do the conversion again, un-check those two options.

You can always convert individual cells using commands in the **Convert To** submenu of the **Cell** menu.

▪ Preserve custom style sheet

This option allows you to preserve all the settings from the style sheet of an old notebook. It will cause the notebook to look as similar as possible to what it looked like in the old version. However, almost always it would look *better* if you allowed *Mathematica* to use the new default style sheet. Style sheets since V3 are much more sophisticated than they were in older versions; preserving the settings from the old style sheet results in a somewhat inadequate style sheet.

▪ Generate bitmap caches for all graphics cells

When PostScript graphics cells are converted, the bitmap image cache normally stored as part of the notebook is lost. If this option is checked, all the graphics cells will be re-rendered and new bitmap image caches will be stored.

For a notebook containing large complex graphics, this rendering process can take a very long time: Check this option only if you want to avoid the wait for rendering when you open the notebook later, and you're willing to wait for it now.

■ **Convert all notebooks in this folder**

If this option is checked, all other old notebooks in the folder containing the file you opened will also be converted.

■ **Convert all sub-folders**

If this option is checked, all other old notebooks in all the folders and sub-folders in the folder containing the file you opened will also be converted. This option allows you to convert entire folder trees full of old notebooks at once.

■ **If new file already exists:**

These options determine what happens if there is already a file with the same name as the proposed newly converted file. If you are repeatedly converting whole folders full of files, you may want to choose Overwrite to automatically replace the previously converted files; or Skip, to pick up where you left off during an interrupted conversion.

Chapter **12**

I really liked *<insert your favorite feature>* in V2! How do I get it in V4?

(If you are not a frequent user of Version 2, you should skip this chapter.)

Several features of earlier versions of *Mathematica* (V2.2 and earlier) seem to be missing in V4. In some cases, they really don't exist. In most cases they are still there, just not in quite the same form.

We tried to retain features that were important to many users. However, in a (somewhat futile) effort to simplify the front end, some features were removed, relocated, or redesigned. While these features may not be *widely* used, there will always be some users for whom they were important.

■ Balance command

The keyboard shortcut for Balance has been changed from lower-case b to capital B (Command-Shift-B). This change made the front end more compatible with standards that dictate Command-b to set Boldface.

■ Convert clipboard

In versions before V4, when you switched out of *Mathematica* after copying a graphic, you would get a dialog box asking you to choose the format you wanted the graphic exported in. You could also do this conversion manually using the Convert Clipboard dialog box, which also allowed you to save the clipboard contents into a file.

In V4, this dialog has been replaced by the **Copy As** and **Save Selection As** submenus of the **Edit** menu: These let you directly specify the format when you do the copy.

If you use the ordinary **Copy** command rather than a specific **Copy As** format, a default will be used. The default may be different on different platforms, and it can be set using the **Preferences...** command in the **Edit** menu. Open the Global Options category and the Data Export Options subcategory: You will find a long list of subcategories that determine the default export format for different types of objects on the clipboard.

▪ Page break above/below menu commands

These settings are now available only in the Option inspector. Select the cell(s) you want to adjust, choose **Option Inspector** from the **Format** menu. In the Cell Options category, Page Breaking subcategory, you will find four options. Each option can be set to True, False, or Automatic. Automatic always means put a page break there if that's where it falls, but don't take any special action.

PageBreakAbove → True	Force page break above cell
PageBreakAbove → False	Prevent page break above cell
PageBreakBelow → True	Force page break below cell
PageBreakBelow → False	Prevent page break below cell
PageBreakWithin → True or Automatic	Allow page breaks inside this cell
PageBreakWithin → False	Keep this cell on one page
GroupPageBreakAbove → True or Automatic	Allow page break in this group
GroupPageBreakAbove → False	Keep this group on one page

▪ Show Lines, Show Filled Areas, Draw Lines Thin, Dithering

In *very* old versions of *Mathematica* there were several small "tabs" that hung off the left edge of the resize box when a graphic was selected. Clicking in these tabs toggled settings for options that determined whether lines were always drawn one pixel thick, whether they were drawn at all, and whether filled areas were drawn.

Later these tabs were replaced with menu commands.

In V4, these options have been buried even deeper, in the Option Inspector. To set one, choose Option Inspector... from the Format menu, open the Graphics Options category and the RenderingOptions subcategory. The options are:

```
RenderLines
RenderThickness
RenderFilledAreas
ObjectDithering
RasterDithering
```

Why have these options gotten harder and harder to find? Because they don't work very well.

■ Custom 1-5 styles

In versions of *Mathematica* before V4, the Style submenu listed five custom styles that you could redefine for your own uses. These are not present in V4.

Instead, you can now define your own new styles, and give them whatever names you like. Since you can add your own, there is no longer a need to have pre-defined custom ones. For information on how to define your own styles, see Chapter 54.

■ Closed group size bar

In earlier versions of *Mathematica*, when you had a closed group of cells, there was a small rectangle to the left of the cell bracket, under the text of the head cell. The width of this box represented the number of hidden cells in the group.

In V4, this box is not shown by default, on the grounds that it was a bit silly in the first place. It causes ranges of closed cell groups to be double-spaced, and the information it provides is often of limited value.

However, it is possible to get the box back. Choose **Preferences...** from the **Edit** menu. Open the Cell Options category, and the Display Options subcategory. Click on the check box at the far right for the option ShowClosedCellArea, which sets it to True.

Chapter 13

Can I use *Mathematica* without learning any new notation?

No—unless you are using *Mathematica* as part of a package designed for a limited audience. If you use *Mathematica's* palettes, however, you can come pretty close.

Mathematica supports three types of input, each with its own strengths:

- **InputForm** is an unambiguous plain-text-only notation. It can be used on text-only terminals, and was the only form available in versions of *Mathematica* before V3.

- **StandardForm** is an unambiguous 2-D typeset notation that has all the advantages of the original *Mathematica* syntax while taking advantage of the compactness of traditional notations like $\sqrt{x}$ and x^2.

- **TraditionalForm** is a notation that comes as close as possible to looking like the notation widely used for mathematics.

Using **TraditionalForm** to enter expressions, you can carry out the full range of calculations possible in *Mathematica* using familiar symbols and notations. Using palettes, you can enter the symbols needed by clicking on a picture of what you want. For functions that do not have any traditional symbol (e.g, **Factor**, **Expand**, etc.), the *Mathematica* name must be used.

The following table shows the three different ways of representing expressions in *Mathematica*. (Note that this table doesn't tell you how to enter these notations, just what they look like. Input methods are discussed in the next two chapters.)

Traditional Notation (TraditionalForm)	New Recommended Notation (StandardForm)	Old *Mathematica* Notation (InputForm)	Meaning
$\frac{a}{b}$	$\frac{a}{b}$	a/b	Division
$\frac{\frac{a}{b}}{\frac{c}{d}}$ or $\frac{a/b}{c/d}$	$\frac{\frac{a}{b}}{\frac{c}{d}}$ or $\frac{a/b}{c/d}$	(a/b)/(c/d)	Fraction divided by fraction
a^b	a^b	a^b	Power
ab	a b	a b	Multiplication
$\sqrt{a}$	$\sqrt{a}$	Sqrt[a]	Square root
$\int f(x)\,dx$	$\int f[x]\,dx$	Integrate[f[x], x]	Indefinite Integral
$\int_a^b f(x)\,dx$	$\int_a^b f[x]\,dx$	Integrate[f[x], {x, a, b}]	Definite Integral
$\frac{\partial y}{\partial x}$ or $\frac{dy}{dx}$ or $\partial_x y$	$\partial_x y$	D[y, x]	Derivative
$\begin{pmatrix} a & b \\ c & d \end{pmatrix}$	$\begin{pmatrix} a & b \\ c & d \end{pmatrix}$	{{a, b}, {c, d}}	Matrix
f (x)	f[x]	f[x]	Function application
$\Gamma(x)$	Gamma[x]	Gamma[x]	Euler Γ function
π	π	Pi	π
e	e	E	Base of the natural log
i or j	i	I	$\sqrt{-1}$
$|x|$	Abs[x]	Abs[x]	Absolute value

Below are some examples of complete expressions, showing the differences among the three forms (again, these are for your viewing pleasure only; the next three chapters discuss how to enter such expressions).

Traditional Notation (TraditionalForm)	New Recommended Notation (StandardForm)	Old *Mathematica* Notation (InputForm)
$\int (\sin(x) + \sqrt{x})\,dx$	$\int (Sin[x] + \sqrt{x})\,dx$	Integrate[Sin[x] + Sqrt[x], x]
$\frac{1}{3}(2\,x^{3/2} - 3\cos(x))$	$\frac{1}{3}(2\,x^{3/2} - 3\,Cos[x])$	1/3 (2 x^(3/2) − 3 Cos[x])
$\sqrt[3]{\frac{2}{27+3\sqrt{69}}}$	$\left(\frac{2}{27+3\sqrt{69}}\right)^{1/3}$	(2/(27 + 3 * Sqrt[69]))^ (1/3)
$\sum_{k=-\infty}^{\infty} 2\,k^2 + k$	$\sum_{k=-\infty}^{\infty} 2\,k^2 + k$	Sum[x^(2*k^2 + k), {k, −Infinity, Infinity}]
$(-i\,x)^{-p-1}\,x^{p+1}$ $\Gamma(p+1, -i\,x)$	$(-I\,x)^{-1-p}\,x^{1+p}$ Gamma[1 + p, −I x]	(−I*x)^(−1 − p) * x^(1 + p) * Gamma[1 + p, −I*x]

As you can see, the *Mathematica* **TraditionalForm** notation is very close to what people have been using for several centuries.

Chapter **14**

What do characters like ^, (, [, {, *, %, etc., mean in *Mathematica*?

Some people have trouble getting started with *Mathematica* because of small, distracting, but important details. We don't want this to happen to you, so here are all those details. (Don't look for a plot in this chapter; it's more like a dictionary.)

In ordinary *Mathematica* input, the following meanings apply:

> ^ indicates exponentiation: **2^3** is two to the third power. (See <u>Chapter</u> 17 for how to enter 2^3.)

> / means division: **34/89** is **34** over **89**. (See <u>Chapter</u> 17 for how to enter $\frac{34}{89}$.)

> * means multiplication: **34*89** is **34** times **89**. Or you can use ⎡ESC⎤*⎡ESC⎤ to enter the attractive × symbol, as in **34×89**.

> Space can be used to indicate multiplication: **34 89** is the same as **34*89**. However, spaces often mean nothing at all; **Sin[x]** and **Sin [x]** are the same as **Sin[x]**.

> () (round parentheses) are to be used only to indicate order of evaluation: **(x+3)/x** is the quantity **x+3** divided by **x**. Don't use square brackets or curly brackets to indicate order of evaluation; only parentheses work.

> [] (square brackets) are used with functions and commands: **Sin[x]** is the sine of **x**. **Sin(x)** does *not* work.

> {} (curly brackets) indicate lists: **{1,3,5,7}** is a list of four numbers.

% represents the result of the last calculation. For example:

3 7

21

%²

441

! means factorial: **5!** is **5** factorial.

= means assignment: **a = 5** means set **a** to **5**.

:= also means assignment (see <u>Chapter</u> 56 to find out what the difference is).

== means equality test: **a == 5** returns **True** if **a** is equal to **5**.

!= means is not equal to: **a != 5** means return **True** if **a** is not equal to **5**. (Note that leaving out spaces in such expressions can result in confusion: **a!=5** might mean **a** factorial equals **5**. In fact, *Mathematica* interprets the unspaced form as **a** is not equal to **5**; don't take chances—just put the spaces in. Another way to avoid ambiguity is to use the ≠ symbol, which you create by typing ESC**!=**ESC.

<, **<=**, **>**, and **>=** mean what you expect. You can create the symbols ≤ and ≥ by typing ESC**<=**ESC and ESC**>=**ESC. These symbols work anywhere **<=** and **>=** work.

Chapter 15

What are some widely used forms in *Mathematica*?

■ Iterator/interval specifications

Some structures keep showing up over and over again in *Mathematica*. For example, here is how you make a table of squares:

Table[x², {x, 1, 10}]

{1, 4, 9, 16, 25, 36, 49, 64, 81, 100}

The second argument to **Table** is a list of three elements—a variable, its minimum, and its maximum. This list-of-three structure is used in many different commands, and once you learn it you can usually guess where it will be used. Here are some examples:

Plot[x², {x, 1, 10}];

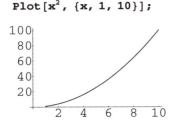

ParametricPlot[{x², x}, {x, -10, 10}];

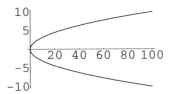

Some commands have more than one triple-list. In the next example, two variable interval specifications are required:

```
Plot3D[Sin[x y], {x, 0, 3}, {y, 0, 3}];
```

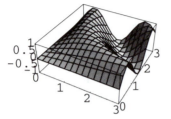

```
ContourPlot[Sin[x y], {x, 0, 3}, {y, 0, 3}];
```

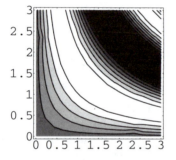

```
DensityPlot[Sin[x y], {x, 0, 3}, {y, 0, 3}];
```

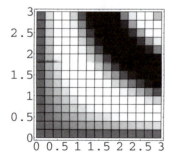

Similarly, **Table** can be used to general multi-dimensional arrays, if it is given more than one range specification:

Table[i + j, {i, 1, 10}, {j, 1, 10}] // MatrixForm

$$
\begin{pmatrix}
2 & 3 & 4 & 5 & 6 & 7 & 8 & 9 & 10 & 11 \\
3 & 4 & 5 & 6 & 7 & 8 & 9 & 10 & 11 & 12 \\
4 & 5 & 6 & 7 & 8 & 9 & 10 & 11 & 12 & 13 \\
5 & 6 & 7 & 8 & 9 & 10 & 11 & 12 & 13 & 14 \\
6 & 7 & 8 & 9 & 10 & 11 & 12 & 13 & 14 & 15 \\
7 & 8 & 9 & 10 & 11 & 12 & 13 & 14 & 15 & 16 \\
8 & 9 & 10 & 11 & 12 & 13 & 14 & 15 & 16 & 17 \\
9 & 10 & 11 & 12 & 13 & 14 & 15 & 16 & 17 & 18 \\
10 & 11 & 12 & 13 & 14 & 15 & 16 & 17 & 18 & 19 \\
11 & 12 & 13 & 14 & 15 & 16 & 17 & 18 & 19 & 20
\end{pmatrix}
$$

You can also use a fourth element to specify a step size:

Table[i, {i, 1, 10, 0.5}]

```
{1, 1.5, 2., 2.5, 3., 3.5, 4., 4.5, 5.,
  5.5, 6., 6.5, 7., 7.5, 8., 8.5, 9., 9.5, 10.}
```

■ Function Names

If you know what you want to do but you don't know the name of the *Mathematica* function to use, some rules can help you guess. (Of course, you could always look it up in the Help Browser, but who wants to read documentation when you can guess instead?)

- All function names start with capital letters, and multi-word names use internal capitalization (the way German should but doesn't).

- Nothing is ever abbr. (except **N** and **D**). Integer is Integer not Int. Integrate is Integrate, not Int.

- Functions named after a person are the person's name plus the commonly used symbol. Examples:
    BesselJ
    AiryAi
    GegenbauerC
  Exception:
    Zeta (should have been **RiemannZ**)

- When in doubt, think long. Examples:
    FactorInteger
    PolynomialGCD
    MathieuCharacteristicExponent

Chapter 16

How do I enter $\int_0^\pi \dfrac{1}{\sqrt{1-m\sin^2(\Theta)}}\,d\Theta$ without using the keyboard?

Here is a step-by-step procedure for using only the mouse to enter this integral.

1) Choose the **File** menu, **Palettes** submenu, **BasicInput** command, to open the Basic Input palette.

2) Place the insertion point in an empty spot in your notebook.

3) Click the ⌠ ⌡ d□ button. You will see:

$$\int_{\square}^{\square} \square\, d\square$$

4) OK, we lied. None of the standard palettes have ordinary letters or numbers on them, so we'll have to use the keyboard. (It would be easy to make such palettes, but they would be pretty useless for most people.)

$$\int_{\square}^{\square} \square\, d\square \quad \xrightarrow{\;0\;} \quad \int_{0}^{\square} \square\, d\square$$

5) Click on the empty box in the upper limit position, and use the $\boxed{\pi}$ button:

$$\int_{0}^{\square} \square\, d\square \quad \xrightarrow{\;\pi\;} \quad \int_{0}^{\pi} \square\, d\square$$

6) Click on the empty box in the middle and use the ▤ button, then type 1:

$$\int_0^\pi \Box\; d\Box \quad \xrightarrow{\;\;\Box\Box\;\;}\quad \int_0^\pi \frac{\Box}{\Box}\; d\Box \quad \xrightarrow{\;\;1\;\;}\quad \int_0^\pi \frac{1}{\Box}\; d\Box$$

7) Click on the empty box in the denominator and use the $\sqrt{\blacksquare}$ button, then type 1 - m:

$$\int_0^\pi \frac{1}{\Box}\; d\Box \quad \xrightarrow{\;\;\sqrt{\blacksquare}\;\;}\quad \int_0^\pi \frac{1}{\sqrt{\Box}}\; d\Box \quad \xrightarrow{\;\;1-m\;\;}\quad \int_0^\pi \frac{1}{\sqrt{1-m}}\; d\Box$$

8) Choose the **File** menu, **Palettes** submenu, **BasicCalculations** command, to open the Basic Calculations palette. Click the triangle to the left of "Trigonometric and Exponential Functions" to open that section, then click the triangle to the left of "Trigonometric". You may want to rearrange the positions of the two palettes to make both of them visible, but not covering your working window. Click on your input window to bring it back to the front.

9) Type a space after the **m**, then click the **Sin[■]** button:

$$\int_0^\pi \frac{1}{\sqrt{1-m}}\; d\Box \quad \xrightarrow{\;\;\text{space, }\; \mathbf{Sin}\left[\blacksquare\right]\;\;}\quad \int_0^\pi \frac{1}{\sqrt{1-m\,\mathbf{Sin}[\Box]}}\; d\Box$$

10) Click the Θ button in the Basic Input palette (the smaller one):

$$\int_0^\pi \frac{1}{\sqrt{1-m\,\mathbf{Sin}[\Box]}}\; d\Box \quad \xrightarrow{\;\;\Theta\;\;}\quad \int_0^\pi \frac{1}{\sqrt{1-m\,\mathbf{Sin}[\theta]}}\; d\Box$$

11) Select the expression **Sin[θ]** by dragging over it, then click the ■□ button in the Basic Input palette:

$$\int_0^\pi \frac{1}{\sqrt{1-m\,\mathbf{Sin}[\theta]}}\; d\Box \quad \xrightarrow{\;\;\blacksquare^\Box\;\;}\quad \int_0^\pi \frac{1}{\sqrt{1-m\,\mathbf{Sin}[\theta]^\Box}}\; d\Box$$

12) Type 2:

$$\int_0^\pi \frac{1}{\sqrt{1-m\,\mathbf{Sin}[\theta]^\Box}}\; d\Box \quad \xrightarrow{\;\;2\;\;}\quad \int_0^\pi \frac{1}{\sqrt{1-m\,\mathbf{Sin}[\theta]^2}}\; d\Box$$

13) Click on the empty box at the very end of the expression and use the $\ominus$ button in the Basic Input palette:

$$\int_0^\pi \frac{1}{\sqrt{1-\mathrm{m\,Sin}[\Theta]^2}}\,\mathrm{d}\Box \quad \xrightarrow{\;\ominus\;} \quad \int_0^\pi \frac{1}{\sqrt{1-\mathrm{m\,Sin}[\Theta]^2}}\,\mathrm{d}\Theta$$

14) You have now entered the integral. It is displayed in **StandardForm**. To make it look exactly like the example in the title, you need to click on the cell bracket containing the integral and choose **TraditionalForm** from the **Cell** menu, **Convert To** submenu. The final result is:

$$\int_0^\pi \frac{1}{\sqrt{1-m\sin^2(\Theta)}}\,d\Theta$$

```
2 EllipticK[m]
```

Several of the steps above are quite clumsy; the expression could be entered quite a bit more quickly using a few keyboard shortcuts. In the next chapter we will show you how to enter this expression using a few keystrokes that can save a lot of time.

Chapter **17**

What is the best way to enter

$$\int_0^\pi \frac{1}{\sqrt{1-m\,\sin^2(\Theta)}}\,d\Theta ?$$

In the last <u>chapter</u> we showed you how to enter this expression using only *Mathematica's* palettes. It was fairly clumsy. By learning a small number of keyboard shortcuts, you can dramatically speed up entry of 2-D typeset expressions of this sort. (Doing it using *only* the keyboard requires memorizing quite a number of control keys and character names, but learning just a few of these keystrokes can make entry much more efficient.)

Here is a list of the keyboard shortcuts everyone should learn:

Operation	Keystroke	Rationalization
Move to the next empty box	Tab	similar to spreadsheet programs
Make a fraction	CTRL − /	slash for division
Make a superscript	CTRL − ^ or CTRL − 6	^ commonly used for power
Make a square root	CTRL − 2	square made us think of 2
Move right one step	CTRL − space	like spacing to the right
Enter π	ESC p ESC or Option − p	p for pi. Option − p is system standard
Enter d	ESC dd ESC	<u>d</u>ifferential d
Enter i	ESC ii ESC	<u>i</u>maginary i
Enter e	ESC ee ESC	<u>e</u>xponential e
Enter ∂	ESC pd ESC	partial <u>d</u>erivative

Using these keystrokes, here is a quicker way to enter the example from the title:

1) Choose the **File** menu, **Palettes** submenu, **BasicInput** command, to open the Basic Input palette.

2) Place the insertion point in an empty spot in your notebook.

3) Click the $\int_\square^\square \blacksquare\, d\square$ button. You will see:

$$\int_\square^\square \square\, d\square$$

4) Type 0, then Tab, then $\boxed{\text{ESC}}\text{p}\boxed{\text{ESC}}$:

$$\int_\square^\square \square\, d\square \xrightarrow{\quad 0 \quad} \int_0^\square \square\, d\square \xrightarrow{\quad \text{Tab} \quad} \int_0^\square \square\, d\square \xrightarrow{\quad \boxed{\text{ESC}}\text{p}\boxed{\text{ESC}} \quad} \int_0^\pi \square\, d\square$$

5) Type Tab to move to the integrand slot, type $\boxed{\text{CTRL}}$-/, then type 1.

$$\int_0^\pi \square\, d\square \xrightarrow{\quad \boxed{\text{CTRL}}-/ \quad} \int_0^\pi \frac{\square}{\square}\, d\square \xrightarrow{\quad 1 \quad} \int_0^\pi \frac{1}{\square}\, d\square$$

6) Type Tab to move to the denominator slot, type $\boxed{\text{CTRL}}$-2, then type 1-m.

$$\int_0^\pi \frac{1}{\square}\, d\square \xrightarrow{\quad \boxed{\text{CTRL}}-2 \quad} \int_0^\pi \frac{1}{\sqrt{\square}}\, d\square \xrightarrow{\quad 1-m \quad} \int_0^\pi \frac{1}{\sqrt{1-m}}\, d\square$$

7) Type space, then Sin[, then use the $\boxed{\Theta}$ button, then type]:

$$\int_0^\pi \frac{1}{\sqrt{1-m}}\, d\square \xrightarrow{\quad \text{Sin}[\quad} \int_0^\pi \frac{1}{\sqrt{1-m\,\text{Sin}[}}\, d\square \xrightarrow{\quad \Theta \quad}$$

$$\int_0^\pi \frac{1}{\sqrt{1-m\,\text{Sin}[\theta}}\, d\square \xrightarrow{\quad] \quad} \int_0^\pi \frac{1}{\sqrt{1-m\,\text{Sin}[\theta]}}\, d\square$$

8) Use $\boxed{\text{CTRL}}$-6, to create the superscript, then type 2:

$$\int_0^\pi \frac{1}{\sqrt{1-m\,\text{Sin}[\theta]}}\, d\square \xrightarrow{\quad \boxed{\text{CTRL}}-6 \quad}$$

$$\int_0^\pi \frac{1}{\sqrt{1-m\,\text{Sin}[\theta]^\square}}\, d\square \xrightarrow{\quad 2 \quad} \int_0^\pi \frac{1}{\sqrt{1-m\,\text{Sin}[\theta]^2}}\, d\square$$

9) Use Tab to move to the last empty box, then use the ⊖ button:

$$\int_0^\pi \frac{1}{\sqrt{1-m\,\text{Sin}[\theta]}^2}\, d\square \quad \overset{\phi}{\longrightarrow} \quad \int_0^\pi \frac{1}{\sqrt{1-m\,\text{Sin}[\theta]}^2}\, d\theta$$

10) You now have the integral entered. It is displayed in **StandardForm**, so to make it look exactly like the example in the title, you need to click on the cell bracket containing the integral, and choose the **Cell** menu, **Convert To** submenu, **TraditionalForm** command. The final result is:

$$\int_0^\pi \frac{1}{\sqrt{1-m\sin^2(\Theta)}}\, d\,\Theta$$

`2 EllipticK[m]`

If you have a copy of *Mathematica*, try it yourself. With a little practice, you will learn to enter complex typeset expressions very quickly.

In the next chapter, we will show you how to go even further, and enter this expression using only the keyboard. For experienced heavy-duty users, *Mathematica* can be the fastest system on earth for entering typeset mathematics.

Chapter 18

How do I enter $\displaystyle\int_0^\pi \frac{1}{\sqrt{1-m\sin^2(\Theta)}} d\,\Theta$ as quickly as possible?

By learning a number of keyboard shortcuts, you will be able to enter any typeset expression into *Mathematica* purely from the keyboard. For the user who enters a lot of expressions, the investment in learning these shortcuts will be paid back rapidly. You will learn to enter complex expressions with fewer keystrokes—and faster—than you could in any other system. (Even text-based systems like T$_E$X or K2 typically require significantly more keystrokes than *Mathematica* does to enter a given expression.)

After learning the shortcuts described in the previous chapter, the next thing to learn is how to enter special characters (mathematical symbols, Greek letters, etc.) from the keyboard. There are three separate ways of entering these symbols from the keyboard, each with its own advantages.

▪ Option/Alt keys

First, on Macintosh and Windows platforms a small number of symbols and Greek letters are available as Option or Alt keys. These are defined by the standard fonts available on these systems. For example, on the Macintosh you can enter π by typing Option-p.

We won't list these, because they depend on what platform you're using and what language your computer is running in. You can find out which ones are available using the Key Caps desk accessory (Macintosh) or Character Map Accessory (Windows).

▪ Long names

The second method for entering special characters from the keyboard is to use the character's "long name". Every character supported by *Mathematica* has been given a unique, usually fairly lengthy and descriptive, name. The conventions for these names are similar to the conventions used to name built-in functions in *Mathematica*: no abbreviations, and initial capitals. The names are enclosed in brackets, as in \[...].

For example the long name for α is \[Alpha], while the long name for $\wp$ is \[Weier strassP]. When you type a long name, it is automatically turned into the character in question as soon as you type the closing bracket.

The experienced *Mathematica* user can often guess the long name for a character without looking it up. For example, once you know $\rightarrow$ is \[RightArrow], it's not too hard to guess \[LongRightArrow], \[LeftArrow], \[DoubleLongLeftArrow], etc. Because there are many hundreds of these characters, we won't list them all. They are documented in the reference guide in The *Mathematica* Book. Click here to see the listing in the Help Browser.

In Version 3.1 or later you can use the command completion feature (Command-K) to finish a partially typed long name. Type the \[and the first few letters of the name, then type Command-K. You will get a menu of possible completions or, if there is only one, you will get that one right away.

▪ Short names

The third method for entering special characters from the keyboard is to use "short names". These are typically one- or two-character abbreviations. You enter them by typing the Escape key ([ESC]), then the short name, then [ESC] again.

For example, the short name for α is [ESC]a[ESC]. When you type [ESC], the symbol ⁝ is inserted, so what you will see while typing is ⁝a⁝, except that as soon as you type the second [ESC] it instantly turns into α.

Unlike long names, which all follow the *Mathematica* conventions for naming functions, short names come from several different directions, as a service to users familiar with other systems. Users of T_EX, SGML, and HTML will find all the character names they are familiar with available as *Mathematica* short names.

Mathematica's T_EX names start with \, as they do in T_EX itself. For example, the experienced T_EX user will know ⁝\alpha⁝ as α. *Mathematica's* SGML/HTML names start with &, as they do in SGML/HTML. For example, ⁝&alpha⁝ is α.

In addition to these compatibility names, there are hundreds of "phonetic", or "pictographic" short names. For example, the Greek letters are all represented by the analogous Roman letters—a for α, b for β, etc. (Again, we can't list all of them! Click here for a complete listing in the Help Browser.)

Here are some examples of pictographic short names:

Short name	Character
->	$\rightarrow$
-->	$\longrightarrow$
<=>	$\Leftrightarrow$
<==>	$\Longleftrightarrow$

In Version 3.1 or later you can use the command completion feature (Command-K) to finish a partially typed short name. Type ESC and the first few letters of the name, then type Command-K. As with long names, you will get a menu of possible completions, or a character right away if there is only one possibility.

There is an interesting analogy between short name input of mathematical symbols and phonetic input of pictographic characters. In both cases, one is faced with the problem of how to enter symbols from an alphabet that is far larger than the number of available keys. In the case of Kanji, the most common solution is to use existing keyboards to enter a phonetic representation of the desired character. Sophisticated software then picks the correct Kanji character, or offers a menu of choices if there is more than one.

Likewise, the _Mathematica_ short names can be thought of as "phonetic" spellings for mathematical symbols, and the Escape-key method of input is analogous to the various input methods provided for entry of Kanji characters.

In fact it is possible, on computers with Kanji input software, to use the Kanji input method to enter mathematical symbols (because the standard Shift-JIS character-encoding used for Kanji also includes a large number of mathematical symbols, Greek letters, etc.). Such input software is a greatly expanded variation of using standard Option/Alt keys to enter the limited number of symbols available on Western keyboards.

Chapter **19**

What is the correct philosophy of notation?

Note: You can skip this chapter if you just want to know how to use *Mathematica*. This chapter will help you understand why things are the way they are, but isn't going to teach you anything concrete (sort of like a liberal arts education).

For about 300 years mathematics has been written using a fairly standard notation. People often wonder why computer systems that do math can't simply *use* this notation and save everyone the trouble of learning a new syntax.

There are several reasons, both practical and theoretical. The core of the problem is that, like other human languages, traditional mathematical notation is beautiful but internally inconsistent and imprecise, and subject to different interpretations in different contexts. While a certain level of "fuzziness" in the exact meaning of notations may be fine when the reader is a human, it is hard for a computer to carry out a calculation unless it knows precisely what calculation it is supposed to do.

Here are two examples of expressions in traditional mathematical notation:

$$f(x) + a\,(b + c)$$

$$\int a\,x^4 + b\,x^3 + c\,x^2 + d\,x + e \; dx$$

Consider the first example. Most people would read this as the function *f* applied to *x* plus *a* times the quantity *b* plus *c*. However, how is the computer supposed to know that *f* is a function while *a* is not? This may be true in certain specific situations, but certainly not in all. For a general purpose system, it would have to be specified in advance that *f* is a function while *a* is a variable. While this is certainly possible, it would introduce a considerable degree of inconvenience, and would mean that expressions must always be accompanied by a list of type declarations; on their own they would be meaningless.

In the second example, there are two uses of the symbol *d*, first as a parameter and second as the differential operator. While a human might be able to figure this out, it is not reasonable for a computer to do so (and even a human might look at this and read it wrong the first time).

The second example also brings up the problem of using symbols like $\int$ in expressions. Because this symbol is not available in typical computer fonts, there are practical difficulties in displaying the symbol, and in representing it in a way that can be understood by all computer systems.

In earlier versions of *Mathematica*, we chose to solve these problems by using a linear text syntax that avoids these ambiguous situations. For example, we used square brackets for functions, and round parentheses only for grouping. The first example was written as:

```
f[x] + a (b + c)
```

To represent integrals, sums, square roots, etc., function names were used. The second example was written as:

```
Integrate[a x^4 + b x^3 + c x^2 + d x + e, x]
```

This notation had the advantage of working on all possible computer systems, because it used only the ordinary characters available in the 7-bit ASCII standard. This is an important consideration for a program that runs on over 20 diverse types of computer. But over the years, as computers become more powerful, it became clear that it was possible to get closer to traditional mathematical notation.

In order to make notations such as summation and integral available in *Mathematica*, we first had to develop the technology to deliver these symbols on screen on all computer systems. We developed an entirely new mathematical symbols font, containing over 600 mathematical and special characters. Only by developing our own font were we able to represent, uniformly across all platforms, the full range of mathematical functions available in *Mathematica*.

Next we developed a method for representing these characters in notebook files that would allow the files to be transported between all the types of computer that *Mathematica* runs on. We chose to adopt the Unicode character-encoding standard because it was the only existing encoding that included most of the mathematical characters we needed.

Only after these problems were solved could we design a system for displaying and entering traditional mathematical notations. The system, developed by Neil Soiffer, allows for almost any 2-dimensional syntax to be defined, including ones that look identical to the old Input Form notation, and ones that look virtually identical to traditional mathematical notations (of which there are of course many variations for different fields and specialties).

Given the freedom to design any syntax we liked, including free use of 2-dimensional structures and mathematical symbols, it became clear that even though it was possible, traditional mathematical notation was probably not the best choice for the serious computer-mathematics user (because of the inherent ambiguities discussed above). The two main advantages of traditional notation are compactness and familiarity. It evolved when people had to write expressions down by hand, often over and over again as they worked through a problem on paper (horrors!). While ease of writing by hand is not such a factor anymore, the generally compact form of traditional notation helps you see more of a large expression at once. And of course, traditional notation is familiar to anyone who has taken math in school, so nothing new needs to be learned.

We set out to see if we could retain these positive features of traditional notation, while removing the problems of ambiguity and inconsistency. It turned out that with fairly minimal modifications, which do not affect the compactness or readability of the notation, it was possible to come up with an unambiguous, self-consistent notation, which we call, with some arrogance, **StandardForm**. We like to think that this notation has all the advantages of traditional notations, with none of the disadvantages. (Of course, there are a *few* ways in which it differs from traditional notation, that do need to be learned, but the differences are quite minor. **StandardForm** is the notation you will see used throughout this book. To see a table comparing the different forms, see <u>Chapter</u> 13.)

For users who can't or won't see the advantages of **StandardForm**, **TraditionalForm** is an extremely close match to traditional notations. However, the user must be aware of the possibility of different interpretations, and take measures to make sure the computer is doing what is wanted. Using palettes can help you make sure that the notations entered are unambiguous. However, one important property of traditional notation is that it can be used to represent things that have no clear computational interpretation. The system will not prevent you from entering such expressions that are meaningless to the computer.

Chapter **20**

What are lists? What can I do with them?

Lists in *Mathematica* are elements enclosed in curly brackets:

> **{10, 20, 30, 40}**
>
> {10, 20, 30, 40}

Many built-in *Mathematica* commands use or return lists. Here are a few examples (these commands are described in more detail in other chapters):

> **Table[x², {x, 1, 10}]**
>
> {1, 4, 9, 16, 25, 36, 49, 64, 81, 100}

> **Solve[x² - 4 == 0, x]**
>
> {{x → 2}, {x → -2}}

> **Plot[{x, x², x³}, {x, -2, 2}];**

Because lists are used in so many ways in *Mathematica*, it is important to know how to manipulate them. The following examples illustrate basic things we can do with lists:

We can add a number to each element in a list:

> **5 + {10, 20, 30, 40}**
>
> {15, 25, 35, 45}

We can multiply each element by a number:

5 {10, 20, 30, 40}

{50, 100, 150, 200}

We can square each element:

{10, 20, 30, 40}^{2}

{100, 400, 900, 1600}

We can join together two lists:

Join[{10, 20, 30, 40}, {40, 50, 60, 70}]

{10, 20, 30, 40, 40, 50, 60, 70}

We can join two lists, removing duplicate elements:

Union[{10, 20, 30, 40}, {40, 50, 60, 70}]

{10, 20, 30, 40, 50, 60, 70}

Union also removes duplicates from a single list, and sorts the entries:

Union[{5, 2, 3, 6, 4, 1, 3, 4, 5, 2, 4, 3, 2, 4}]

{1, 2, 3, 4, 5, 6}

We can get an element from a list:

{10, 20, 30, 40}⟦3⟧

30

The double-square bracket notation means "element of". You can either use two ordinary square brackets, or type [ESC][[ESC] and [ESC]]][ESC] to get the elegant double-struck bracket characters.

We can add two lists element-by-element (note that the lists must have the same number of elements for this to work):

{10, 20, 30, 40} + {100, 200, 300, 400}

{110, 220, 330, 440}

We can multiply two lists element-by-element:

{10, 20, 30, 40} {100, 200, 300, 400}

{1000, 4000, 9000, 16000}

Note that this multiplication is *not* the dot product of two vectors. (Lists as vectors will be explained in <u>Chapter</u> 22.)

Lists can be rearranged:

Reverse[{10, 20, 30, 40}]

{40, 30, 20, 10}

Sort[{4, 2, 3, 1}]

{1, 2, 3, 4}

Reverse[Sort[{4, 2, 3, 1}]]

{4, 3, 2, 1}

The elements of lists don't have to be numbers:

{x, x^2, x^3, x^4, Sin[x]}

{x, x^2, x^3, x^4, Sin[x]}

If the elements are numbers, we can plot them:

ListPlot[{4, 2, 3, 1, 5, 2, 5, 8, 4, 2, 4, 4, 2}];

It is possible to have lists of lists, called nested lists. A common case is a list of pairs of numbers:

{{1, 5}, {4, 2}, {1, 3}, {3, 3}, {7, 1}, {5, 5}, {3, 3}, {2, 5}}

{{1, 5}, {4, 2}, {1, 3}, {3, 3}, {7, 1}, {5, 5}, {3, 3}, {2, 5}}

A list like this can be thought of as a list of x, y points, and **ListPlot** will plot it as such:

ListPlot[
    {{1, 5}, {4, 2}, {1, 3}, {3, 3}, {7, 1}, {5, 5}, {3, 3}, {2, 5}}];

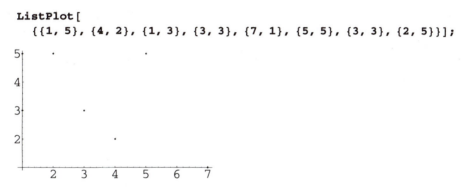

Any arbitrary nesting of lists is possible:

{{a, {b, c}, {{d, e, f}}, {g}}}

{{a, {b, c}, {{d, e, f}}, {g}}}

Lists are sometimes used in special ways. For example, the **Plot** command has a list as its second argument:

Plot[Sin[x], {x, 0, 2 π}];

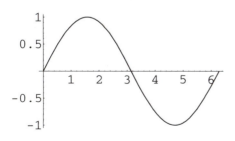

Lists can be displayed as tables using TableForm:

TableForm[{{1, 2, 3}, {4, 5, 6}}]

1	2	3
4	5	6

Chapter 22 discusses how to input lists using 2-D notations.

Mathematica has many other commands for dealing with lists. We won't go into any more of them. If you are reading this in *Mathematica,* click on any of the following command names to read the online help: First, Last, Rest, Part, Take, Drop, Prepend, Append, Insert, Delete, ReplacePart, Union, Intersection, Complement, Transpose, RotateLeft, RotateRight, Partition.

Chapter **21**

How do I make a table of values?

One of the most useful applications of *Mathematica's* list capability is constructing tables of values. Here is a table of squares:

Table[n², {n, 1, 10}]

{1, 4, 9, 16, 25, 36, 49, 64, 81, 100}

• The first argument is the expression that forms each element of the list.
• The second argument is a "<u>range specification</u>"; in this case it means **n** running from 1 to 10 in steps of 1.

We can change the step size by adding a fourth element to the iterator:

$$\textbf{Table}\left[\textbf{n}^2\textbf{, }\left\{\textbf{n, 1, 10, }\frac{\textbf{1}}{\textbf{2}}\right\}\right]$$

$$\left\{1, \frac{9}{4}, 4, \frac{25}{4}, 9, \frac{49}{4}, 16, \frac{81}{4}, 25, \frac{121}{4},\right.$$
$$\left.36, \frac{169}{4}, 49, \frac{225}{4}, 64, \frac{289}{4}, 81, \frac{361}{4}, 100\right\}$$

The elements can be symbolic expressions as well:

Table[Expand[(1 + x)ⁿ], {n, 1, 5}]

$\{1 + x, \ 1 + 2 x + x^2, \ 1 + 3 x + 3 x^2 + x^3,$
$1 + 4 x + 6 x^2 + 4 x^3 + x^4, \ 1 + 5 x + 10 x^2 + 10 x^3 + 5 x^4 + x^5\}$

(**Expand** is explained in <u>Chapter</u> 26.)

We can make lists of lists:

Table[{n, n², n³, n⁴}, {n, 1, 10}]

{{1, 1, 1, 1}, {2, 4, 8, 16}, {3, 9, 27, 81}, {4, 16, 64, 256},
{5, 25, 125, 625}, {6, 36, 216, 1296}, {7, 49, 343, 2401},
{8, 64, 512, 4096}, {9, 81, 729, 6561}, {10, 100, 1000, 10000}}

In this example we made a list whose elements are also lists.

In the next example we make the same list, but using a second iterator:

Table[n^a, {n, 1, 10}, {a, 1, 4}]

{{1, 1, 1, 1}, {2, 4, 8, 16}, {3, 9, 27, 81}, {4, 16, 64, 256},
{5, 25, 125, 625}, {6, 36, 216, 1296}, {7, 49, 343, 2401},
{8, 64, 512, 4096}, {9, 81, 729, 6561}, {10, 100, 1000, 10000}}

- The first argument is the expression that forms each element of the list.
- The second argument is the "slow" iterator (the one that changes when you go from one inner list to the next).
- The third argument is the "fast" iterator (the one that changes from one element to the next inside each of the inner lists).

It is frequently useful to add **//TableForm** or **//MatrixForm** to the end of commands described in this chapter. They display lists, and lists of lists, in a two-dimensional layout:

{{a, b}, {c, d}} // TableForm

a   b
c   d

{{a, b}, {c, d}} // MatrixForm

$$\begin{pmatrix} a & b \\ c & d \end{pmatrix}$$

As you can see from the two examples, the outputs differ only cosmetically. Both objects are still the same: lists of lists.

Table[n^a, {n, 1, 10}, {a, 1, 4}] // TableForm

1	1	1	1
2	4	8	16
3	9	27	81
4	16	64	256
5	25	125	625
6	36	216	1296
7	49	343	2401
8	64	512	4096
9	81	729	6561
10	100	1000	10000

Chapter **22**

How do I manipulate vectors and matrices?

■ Entering and Editing Matrices

Matrices in *Mathematica* are lists of lists. We will first show the several ways of entering and editing matrices in *Mathematica*, then move on to mathematical operations.

Matrices can be entered using the curly bracket list notation:

> **{{a, b}, {c, d}}**

> {{a, b}, {c, d}}

Matrices can also be entered using the Basic Input palette. (If you don't have this palette open, use the **File** menu, **Palettes** submenu, **BasicInput** command to open it.) Clicking on the indicated button will place a 2 by 2 matrix at the current insertion point.

An arbitrary-size matrix can be created using the **Input** menu, **Create Table/Matrix/Palette...** menu command. For example, here is a 5 by 5 matrix created with this menu command:

$$\begin{pmatrix} \square & \square & \square & \square & \square \\ \square & \square & \square & \square & \square \\ \square & \square & \square & \square & \square \\ \square & \square & \square & \square & \square \\ \square & \square & \square & \square & \square \end{pmatrix}$$

Once you have an empty matrix like this, you can start filling in values. Click on an empty box, then type. To move to the next empty box, use the Tab key.

Pretty soon you will want to add or remove a row or column. To remove a row or column, select it by dragging over all the entries, then type the delete key. You can delete multiple rows or columns at the same time by selecting larger blocks of the matrix. If you select a block of the matrix that is not a full row or column, the contents of each element are deleted, but the rows/columns remain.

Adding rows and columns is done with two control keys, CTRL-RET to add a row and CTRL-comma to add a column.

For example, to add a new row below the second row, click anywhere in the second row and type CTRL-RET:

$$\begin{pmatrix} a & b \\ c & d \\ e & f \end{pmatrix} \xrightarrow{\text{CTRL} - \text{RET}} \begin{pmatrix} a & b \\ c & d \\ \square & \square \\ e & f \end{pmatrix}$$

To add a new column after the first column, click anywhere in the first column and type CTRL-comma:

$$\begin{pmatrix} a & b \\ c & d \\ e & f \end{pmatrix} \xrightarrow{\text{CTRL} - \text{comma}} \begin{pmatrix} a & \square & b \\ c & \square & d \\ e & \square & f \end{pmatrix}$$

If you want to add a new row above the first one, or a new column to the left of the first one, put the insertion point at the very beginning of the first row/column and use the same control keys.

To help you remember these two control keys, consider that Return normally makes a new blank line, so CTRL-RET makes a new row, while comma normally separates items in a list, so CTRL-comma makes a new column.

To rearrange rows or columns in a matrix, first create empty slots where you want to insert material, then cut/paste. For example, to interchange the last two columns in this matrix:

$$\begin{pmatrix} a & b & c \\ d & e & f \\ g & h & i \end{pmatrix}$$

first put the insertion point anywhere in the first column, and type CTRL-comma:

$$\begin{pmatrix} a & b & c \\ d & e & f \\ g & h & i \end{pmatrix} \xrightarrow{\boxed{\text{CTRL}}-comma} \begin{pmatrix} a & \square & b & c \\ d & \square & e & f \\ g & \square & h & i \end{pmatrix}$$

then select the last column and choose **Cut** from the **Edit** menu:

$$\begin{pmatrix} a & \square & b & c \\ d & \square & e & f \\ g & \square & h & i \end{pmatrix} \xrightarrow{Cut} \begin{pmatrix} a & \square & b \\ d & \square & e \\ g & \square & h \end{pmatrix}$$

Select the column of empty boxes, and choose **Paste** from the **Edit** menu:

$$\begin{pmatrix} a & \square & b \\ d & \square & e \\ g & \square & h \end{pmatrix} \xrightarrow{Paste} \begin{pmatrix} a & c & b \\ d & f & e \\ g & i & h \end{pmatrix}$$

■ Getting Matrices as Output

Output from calculations can be displayed as a list of lists (using curly brackets) or as a 2-D matrix.

The default is to output matrices as lists of lists, regardless of what the input format is:

{{a, b}, {c, d}}

{{a, b}, {c, d}}

$$\begin{pmatrix} a & b \\ c & d \end{pmatrix}$$

{{a, b}, {c, d}}

To see matrices in 2-D form, one way is to use **//TraditionalForm** in each of your input commands:

>   **{{a, b}, {c, d}} // TraditionalForm**

$$\begin{pmatrix} a & b \\ c & d \end{pmatrix}$$

$$\begin{pmatrix} a & b \\ c & d \end{pmatrix} \text{ // TraditionalForm}$$

$$\begin{pmatrix} a & b \\ c & d \end{pmatrix}$$

If you are doing a lot of calculations with matrices as output, you may want to set **Tradition-alForm** as the default: Use the **TraditionalForm** command in the **Cell** menu, **Default Output FormatType** submenu.

You can also use **MatrixForm** to do more or less the same thing:

>   **{{a, b}, {c, d}} // MatrixForm**

$$\begin{pmatrix} a & b \\ c & d \end{pmatrix}$$

The difference is that **MatrixForm** assumes that the result is a single matrix, while **Traditional-Form** will work even if the result contains matrices inside an algebraic expression. On the other hand, **TraditionalForm** also causes *Mathematica* to typeset functions quite differently from the normal *Mathematica* syntax. Compare these examples.

>   **f[{{a, b}, {c, d}}, {{1, 2}, {3, 4}}] // TraditionalForm**

$$f\!\left(\begin{pmatrix} a & b \\ c & d \end{pmatrix}, \begin{pmatrix} 1 & 2 \\ 3 & 4 \end{pmatrix}\right)$$

>   **f[{{a, b}, {c, d}}, {{1, 2}, {3, 4}}] // MatrixForm**

>   f[{{a, b}, {c, d}}, {{1, 2}, {3, 4}}]

Finally, if the result is a single matrix, you can use **TableForm** to display it as a matrix, but with wider default column spacing and without parentheses (as the name implies, this makes it look more like a table of values than like a matrix):

>   **{{a, b}, {c, d}} // TableForm**

>   a   b
>   c   d

■ Mathematical Operations on Matrices

Chapter 20 and Chapter 21 describe many functions you can use with lists. Most of these functions can be useful when dealing with vectors and matrices as well, since vectors, matrices, and lists are all very much the same thing in *Mathematica*.

We can take the dot product of vectors and/or matrices using the "." operator (an ordinary period character):

$$\begin{pmatrix} a & b \\ c & d \end{pmatrix} . \{x, \, y\}$$

$\{a\,x + b\,y, \ c\,x + d\,y\}$

$$\{x, \, y\} . \begin{pmatrix} a & b \\ c & d \end{pmatrix}$$

$\{a\,x + c\,y, \ b\,x + d\,y\}$

In the first case {**x**, **y**} is acting as a column vector, while in the second case it is acting as a row vector. It can act as both at the same time:

$$\{x, \, y\} . \{x, \, y\}$$

$x^2 + y^2$

Note that if you "multiply" two matrices together, you do *not* get matrix multiplication as you might expect; instead, each pair of corresponding elements is multiplied:

$$\begin{pmatrix} a & b \\ c & d \end{pmatrix} \begin{pmatrix} x & y \\ z & q \end{pmatrix} \ // \ \textbf{TraditionalForm}$$

$$\begin{pmatrix} a\,x & b\,y \\ c\,z & d\,q \end{pmatrix}$$

To get matrix multiplication, you have to use the dot product:

$$\begin{pmatrix} a & b \\ c & d \end{pmatrix} . \begin{pmatrix} x & y \\ z & q \end{pmatrix} \ // \ \textbf{TraditionalForm}$$

$$\begin{pmatrix} a\,x + b\,z & b\,q + a\,y \\ c\,x + d\,z & d\,q + c\,y \end{pmatrix}$$

Likewise if you raise a matrix to a power, each element is raised to that power, rather than the expected matrix multiplication:

$$\begin{pmatrix} a & b \\ c & d \end{pmatrix}^3 \text{ // TraditionalForm}$$

$$\begin{pmatrix} a^3 & b^3 \\ c^3 & d^3 \end{pmatrix}$$

To properly raise the matrix to a power, you have to use the **MatrixPower** function:

$$\text{MatrixPower}\left[\begin{pmatrix} a & b \\ c & d \end{pmatrix}, 3\right] \text{ // TraditionalForm}$$

$$\begin{pmatrix} a\,(a^2 + b\,c) + b\,(a\,c + d\,c) & a\,(a\,b + d\,b) + b\,(d^2 + b\,c) \\ c\,(a^2 + b\,c) + d\,(a\,c + d\,c) & c\,(a\,b + d\,b) + d\,(d^2 + b\,c) \end{pmatrix}$$

The cross product can be entered using the function **Cross[]**, or the × symbol, which is entered as \ [Cross]:

Cross[{a, b, c}, {x, y, z}]

{-c y + b z, c x - a z, -b x + a y}

{a, b, c} × {x, y, z}

{- (c y) + b z, c x - a z, - (b x) + a y}

The following are some of *Mathematica's* built-in vector and matrix manipulation functions. All of these functions work on both numerical and symbolic matrices. We'll demonstrate them on simple symbolic matrices so you can see the results:

$$\text{Det}\left[\begin{pmatrix} a & b \\ c & d \end{pmatrix}\right]$$

-b c + a d

$$\text{Transpose}\left[\begin{pmatrix} a & b \\ c & d \end{pmatrix}\right] \text{ // TraditionalForm}$$

$$\begin{pmatrix} a & c \\ b & d \end{pmatrix}$$

$$\text{Inverse}\left[\begin{pmatrix} a & b \\ c & d \end{pmatrix}\right] \text{ // TraditionalForm}$$

$$\begin{pmatrix} \frac{d}{a\,d - b\,c} & -\frac{b}{a\,d - b\,c} \\ -\frac{c}{a\,d - b\,c} & \frac{a}{a\,d - b\,c} \end{pmatrix}$$

To check the inverse, take the dot product with the original matrix:

$$\begin{pmatrix} a & b \\ c & d \end{pmatrix}.\texttt{Inverse}\left[\begin{pmatrix} a & b \\ c & d \end{pmatrix}\right] \texttt{ // TraditionalForm}$$

$$\begin{pmatrix} \frac{ad}{ad-bc} - \frac{bc}{ad-bc} & 0 \\ 0 & \frac{ad}{ad-bc} - \frac{bc}{ad-bc} \end{pmatrix}$$

Readers will no doubt observe that this is just a more complicated form of the result you can get using the **Simplify** command:

$$\begin{pmatrix} a & b \\ c & d \end{pmatrix}.\texttt{Inverse}\left[\begin{pmatrix} a & b \\ c & d \end{pmatrix}\right] \texttt{ // Simplify // TraditionalForm}$$

$$\begin{pmatrix} 1 & 0 \\ 0 & 1 \end{pmatrix}$$

IdentityMatrix[3] // TraditionalForm

$$\begin{pmatrix} 1 & 0 & 0 \\ 0 & 1 & 0 \\ 0 & 0 & 1 \end{pmatrix}$$

DiagonalMatrix[{a, b, c}] // TraditionalForm

$$\begin{pmatrix} a & 0 & 0 \\ 0 & b & 0 \\ 0 & 0 & c \end{pmatrix}$$

Array[a, {3, 3}] // TraditionalForm

$$\begin{pmatrix} a(1,1) & a(1,2) & a(1,3) \\ a(2,1) & a(2,2) & a(2,3) \\ a(3,1) & a(3,2) & a(3,3) \end{pmatrix}$$

$$\texttt{Dimensions}\left[\begin{pmatrix} a & b & c \\ d & e & f \end{pmatrix}\right]$$

$\{2, 3\}$

$$\texttt{Eigenvalues}\left[\begin{pmatrix} a & b \\ c & d \end{pmatrix}\right]$$

$$\left\{\tfrac{1}{2}\left(a + d - \sqrt{a^2 + 4bc - 2ad + d^2}\right), \tfrac{1}{2}\left(a + d + \sqrt{a^2 + 4bc - 2ad + d^2}\right)\right\}$$

$$\texttt{Eigenvectors}\left[\begin{pmatrix} a & b \\ c & d \end{pmatrix}\right]$$

$$\left\{\left\{-\frac{-a+d+\sqrt{a^2+4\,b\,c-2\,a\,d+d^2}}{2\,c}, 1\right\},\right.$$
$$\left.\left\{-\frac{-a+d-\sqrt{a^2+4\,b\,c-2\,a\,d+d^2}}{2\,c}, 1\right\}\right\}$$

Symbolic matrices larger than about 3 by 3 often produce eigenvalues and eigenvectors that are *HUGE* expressions, and take a long time to compute and print out.

Eigensystem is a combination of **Eigenvalues** and **Eigenvectors**: it returns a list whose first element is a list of eigenvalues and whose second element is a list of eigenvectors. (If you want both, it is faster to use **EigenSystem** instead of both **Eigenvalues** and **Eigenvectors**.)

$$\texttt{Eigensystem}\left[\begin{pmatrix} a & b \\ c & d \end{pmatrix}\right]$$

$$\left\{\left\{\frac{1}{2}\left(a+d-\sqrt{a^2+4\,b\,c-2\,a\,d+d^2}\right), \frac{1}{2}\left(a+d+\sqrt{a^2+4\,b\,c-2\,a\,d+d^2}\right)\right\},\right.$$
$$\left\{\left\{-\frac{-a+d+\sqrt{a^2+4\,b\,c-2\,a\,d+d^2}}{2\,c}, 1\right\},\right.$$
$$\left.\left.\left\{-\frac{-a+d-\sqrt{a^2+4\,b\,c-2\,a\,d+d^2}}{2\,c}, 1\right\}\right\}\right\}$$

CharacteristicPolynomial returns a polynomial whose roots are the eigenvalues of the matrix, written in terms of the variable given in its second argument.

$$\texttt{CharacteristicPolynomial}\left[\begin{pmatrix} a & b \\ c & d \end{pmatrix}, x\right]$$

$$-b\,c+a\,d-a\,x-d\,x+x^2$$

We can demonstrate that this is the case by solving the polynomial:

$$\texttt{Solve}\left[\texttt{CharacteristicPolynomial}\left[\begin{pmatrix} a & b \\ c & d \end{pmatrix}, x\right] == 0, x\right]$$

$$\left\{\left\{x \to \frac{1}{2}\left(a+d-\sqrt{a^2+4\,b\,c-2\,a\,d+d^2}\right)\right\},\right.$$
$$\left.\left\{x \to \frac{1}{2}\left(a+d+\sqrt{a^2+4\,b\,c-2\,a\,d+d^2}\right)\right\}\right\}$$

Many other vector and matrix manipulation functions are available in *Mathematica*, but to use them we have to execute the following command first:

Needs["LinearAlgebra`Master`"];

(Note that the two single quotes used here are "back quotes" usually found on the same key with ~. They are *not* the single quotes found on the double-quote key.) The command loads a set of standard packages (included in all copies of *Mathematica*).

We won't go into any more detail about most of these functions. They are described in the Guide to Standard Packages that comes with each copy of *Mathematica*, and in the on-line help under AddOns/Standard Packages/Linear Algebra.

Chapter **23**

How do I pick out rows, columns, and submatrices?

In several previous chapters we have used the double-square-bracket notation for picking out elements of lists. For example, we can extract the third element of a list:

```
mylist = {a, b, c, d, e, f};

mylist[[3]]
```

    c

It turns out that what seems like a very limited notation for picking elements from lists is, in V4, in fact a very powerful and flexible method for picking rows, columns, and sub-matrices from matrices.

We'll use this sample matrix for the examples that follow:

$$mydata = \begin{pmatrix} 1. & 4.2 & 10.3 \\ 2. & 5.6 & 13.4 \\ 3. & 6.9 & 59.2 \\ 4. & 4.8 & 30.9 \\ 5. & 3.9 & 24.1 \\ 6. & 2.4 & 19.2 \end{pmatrix};$$

The simplest case is picking an individual row (the third one in this example):

```
mydata[[3]]
```

    {3., 6.9, 59.2}

To get a particular element from a particular row, you can add a second index:

```
mydata[[3, 2]]
```

    6.9

Think of the first number as the row index and the second number as the column index, so in this case you're getting the element from the third row, second column location.

So, how do you pick out a column instead of a row? In the past this was rather tricky, but in V4 a clever notation has been introduced to make it easy. The idea is to use the token **All** to represent *all* the elements at a particular level. The following command picks the second column:

mydata[[All, 2]]

{4.2, 5.6, 6.9, 4.8, 3.9, 2.4}

If you think of **mydata[[3, 2]]** as "give me the second column element from the third row" you can think of **mydata[[All, 2]]** as "give me the second column elements from all the rows", in other words, the whole second column.

If this is a bit confusing, it might help to think of the row-picking command given previously as having an implied **All** as the second index. In fact **All** can be included explicitly in the row-picking command, if you like:

mydata[[3, All]]

{3., 6.9, 59.2}

The last two commands are symmetrical, one picking a row and the other picking a column.

You can use lists of numbers as indices, to pick more than one row or column at a time. For example, this command picks the first and last rows:

mydata[[{1, 6}]] // MatrixForm

$$\begin{pmatrix} 1. & 4.2 & 10.3 \\ 6. & 2.4 & 19.2 \end{pmatrix}$$

To pick sub-matrices, you can use the **Range** command to generate the index ranges. **Range** simply returns a list of integers in a specified interval, as in this example:

Range[3, 9]

{3, 4, 5, 6, 7, 8, 9}

To see how this fits in with the double-square-bracket notation, consider the following some-what more complex example. It picks a 2-column, 4-row submatrix from the data (rows 1 through 4 and columns 2 through 3):

mydata[[Range[1, 4], Range[2, 3]]] // MatrixForm

$$\begin{pmatrix} 4.2 & 10.3 \\ 5.6 & 13.4 \\ 6.9 & 59.2 \\ 4.8 & 30.9 \end{pmatrix}$$

Chapter **24**

What's the difference between 2 and 2.0?

In *Mathematica*, **2** is the notation for the exact integer 2, while **2.0** (or even just **2.**) is the notation for a floating point number that has approximately the same magnitude as 2. This difference affects many aspects of how calculations are carried out.

Mathematica generally does not make approximations unless asked to do so. When we take the square root of the integer 2, *Mathematica* returns the expression unchanged:

$\sqrt{2}$

$\sqrt{2}$

There is no better way to write this without making an approximation.

On the other hand, if we take the square root of a decimal number like **2.5**, *Mathematica* will compute the approximate square root automatically, because it assumes that **2.5** is already approximate:

$\sqrt{2.5}$

1.581138830084189

Just adding a decimal point to an integer is enough to let *Mathematica* know that we mean an approximate number, not an exact integer:

$\sqrt{2.}$

1.414213562373095

It may seem somewhat strange, but **2** and **2.0** are different: The first is an exact integer, while the second is an approximate decimal number. Another way to think of it is that **2.0** represents a *range* of possible values centered around the integer 2.

We can convert an exact integer into an approximate number using the **N** function:

N[2]

2.

Notice that the result has a decimal point in it.

The **N** function can be applied to entire expressions:

$$\mathbf{N}\left[\sqrt{2}\right]$$

1.414213562373095

Unlike simpler programs that handle floating point numbers using only a relatively small, fixed number of digits, *Mathematica* can do calculations to arbitrary precision. The second argument to **N** can be used to specify the number of decimal places of precision we want to work with:

$$\mathbf{N}\left[\sqrt{2}, 40\right]$$

1.414213562373095048801688724209698078570

Look what happens when we repeat this command using **2.** instead of **2**:

$$\mathbf{N}\left[\sqrt{2.}, 40\right]$$

1.414213562373095

This is *Mathematica* being careful: It has assumed that **2.** is an approximate number of, by default, about 18 digits of precision ("machine precision"). Since the starting point of the calculation was taken to be accurate to only 18 places, asking for 40 places was not appropriate.

If we want high-precision answers, we have to start either with exact integers (whose infinite precision *Mathematica* honors), or with approximate numbers with enough places of precision:

$$\mathbf{N}\left[\sqrt{2.000000000000000000000000000000000000000}, 40\right]$$

1.414213562373095048801688724209698078570

Mathematica automatically propagates the appropriate precision in calculations, so we don't really need the **N** in the example above:

$$\sqrt{2.000000000000000000000000000000000000000}$$

1.4142135623730950488016887242209698078570

Note that precision can change in a calculation:

$$\mathbf{N}\left[10^{20} + \sqrt{2}, 40\right]$$

1.000000000000000000001414213562373095048810^{20}

This result has 40 digits of precision. But if we do a further calculation, we get a result with only 20 digits of precision, even though the only new number is a perfect integer (**%** means the last result):

$$\mathbf{\% - 10^{20}}$$

1.4142135623730950488

We have asked for the difference between two 40-digit numbers that differ only in the last 20 digits, so 20 digits worth of precision is lost.

When you use **N** and specify a certain number of digits, you are specifying the number of digits at the *start* of the calculation. If precision changes during a calculation, the answer may contain fewer (or in some cases more) digits. Since it's not in general possible to predict how much precision will be lost (or gained) in the course of a calculation, there is no way to ask for a specific number of digits in the *output*.

Here is a calculation that results in *no* significant digits:

$$\mathbf{N\left[10^{50} + \sqrt{2}, 40\right] - 10^{50}}$$

0. $\times 10^{10}$

10^{50} accurate to 40 decimal places means $10^{50} \pm 10^{10}$. Adding 1.414 to a number like this has no effect; the added value is far smaller than the resolution of the original number. When we then remove the 10^{50}, the result is a number somewhere in the range $\pm 10^{10}$, which *Mathematica* indicates with the somewhat peculiar notation you see. The **0.** portion of the result is telling you that the result can't be distinguished from zero, while the $\times \mathbf{10^{10}}$ portion indicates the magnitude of the uncertainty.

See the next Chapter for more on how precision of numbers is propagated through calculations.

■ Machine Precision vs. High Precision Numbers

In the examples above, we were using numbers with 40 or so digits of accuracy—more digits than any computer's floating point unit is able to compute directly. Therefore *Mathematica* had to use its own high-precision floating point routines (which are able to do calculations on numbers with practically unlimited precision). These high-precision routines also keep track of accuracy, which computers' floating point units do not.

Now, a fact of modern computing is that all PC microprocessors contain very-high-speed floating point processing units, which are typically able to do computations with 16 to 18 digits of precision (depending on the processor). These floating point processors do not keep track of accuracy the way *Mathematica*'s routines do, but they are a *lot* faster.

In order to take advantage of the far higher speeds possible using the available floating point hardware, *Mathematica* switches to what is referred to as "machine precision" arithmetic if the precision you request is less than or equal to the machine precision of the platform you are running on. This allows lower-precision calculations to run much faster than would be possible if *Mathematica* were carefully keeping track of errors.

See the next <u>Chapter</u> for more about dealing with precision in numerical calculations.

Chapter **24.0**

How does *Mathematica* handle roundoff error?

Numerical roundoff and its propagation through calculations, a topic closely tied to practical, technological considerations, has been very well-studied since long before the advent of computers. Before computers, people wanted to know how *few* digits they could get away with carrying through a given calculation without compromising the result. (For you kids out there, they cared because they had to personally write down and work out each and every digit by hand. You do *not* want to know what they had to do for square roots.)

Then computers started doing calculations, but always with a fixed number of digits. So people developed an elaborate theory of fixed precision floating point calculation, with ways of minimizing the accumulation of roundoff error. For some reason the computer science community seemed to decide that tracking the number of accurate digits was not important; the goal was to get as many digits as possible to be accurate and hope for the best. The unfortunate result is that you are never quite sure in the end how many digits are still valid.

But computers can also do calculations with arbitrary numbers of digits. While some programs continue to use the fixed-precision, no-tracking-of-significant-digits model even for high-precision calculations, *Mathematica* takes the point of view that it's fine to minimize the number of digits lost, but it's even more important not to overstate the precision of a particular result. Therefore *Mathematica* shows only as many digits as are valid in each result.

Roundoff issues can be divided into two cases, those arising in pure calculations and those arising in calculations that use real-world measurements.

■ Pure Calculations

By pure calculations, we mean calculations in which the inputs are assumed to be perfect, exact numbers that are converted to approximate, floating point form only to allow the calculation to proceed in the desired way. For example, suppose you want to find the sine of a 15° angle. The value is the following exact number:

    `Sin[15 Degree]`

$$\frac{-1 + \sqrt{3}}{2\sqrt{2}}$$

But, *quick* how big is this number? Is it bigger or smaller than one? Sometimes an approximate result is exactly what you want:

N[Sin[15 Degree]]

0.258819

Cos[15 Degree]

$$\frac{1 + \sqrt{3}}{2\sqrt{2}}$$

When you work with exact representations of numbers, things easily get out of hand. Consider a result like the following, which can only be described as obnoxious:

Solve[Sin[15 Degree] x^2 - Cos[60 Degree] == 0, x]

$$\left\{ \left\{ x \to -\frac{1}{\sqrt{2 \left(\frac{\sqrt{\frac{3}{2}}}{2} - \frac{1}{2\sqrt{2}} \right)}} \right\}, \left\{ x \to \frac{1}{\sqrt{2 \left(\frac{\sqrt{\frac{3}{2}}}{2} - \frac{1}{2\sqrt{2}} \right)}} \right\} \right\}$$

Come on, just tell me what x is, please?

N[%]

$\{\{x \to -1.38991\}, \{x \to 1.38991\}\}$

Often when you are doing a series of calculations involving exact numbers, you end up with hugely complex representations of what are really just numbers, and the only practical way to proceed is to reduce them to simple, but approximate, floating point form. But doing so runs the risk of introducing roundoff error, which may accumulate if you do a lot of subsequent operations on your approximate numbers.

Matrix operations are an example. Say you have a matrix containing exact numerical quantities like those above, and you want to find its inverse, determinant, or eigenvalues. *Mathematica* is happy to do such calculations for you, but if the matrix is anything but toy-sized, the results are absolutely horrendous. Calculation quickly becomes impractical. On the other hand, these operations are classic examples in which numerical roundoff error can accumulate, resulting in completely meaningless results if one isn't careful.

In programs that don't support arbitrary precision arithmetic (or exact arithmetic for that matter), roundoff can be devastating, which is why so much effort has been put into studying the problem. But frankly, it rarely need be an issue in *Mathematica*. If you find yourself in a situation where roundoff might be a problem, you have the option of simply increasing the precision with which the calculations are done. Add an extra hundred or so digits of precision, and your roundoff errors are likely to go away. While this might make the calculation run a bit slower, these days there are fewer and fewer problems for which the loss of speed will be a problem: Computers are just very fast, and we should get used to it.

Let's look at a specific problem, finding the determinant of a matrix known for its sensitivity to roundoff error. This is the form of the matrices we'll be looking at:

```
Table[ 1/(i + j) , {i, 1, 3}, {j, 1, 3}] // MatrixForm
```

$$\begin{pmatrix} \frac{1}{2} & \frac{1}{3} & \frac{1}{4} \\ \frac{1}{3} & \frac{1}{4} & \frac{1}{5} \\ \frac{1}{4} & \frac{1}{5} & \frac{1}{6} \end{pmatrix}$$

The absolute reference for calculating the determinant is to do it using exact arithmetic. Here's the answer for a 50 by 50 matrix of this form (along with the time it took to do the calculation):

```
Det[Table[ 1/(i + j) , {i, 1, 50}, {j, 1, 50}]] // Timing
```

{8.03333 Second, 1 /
724473765740752913329701935392042066972600589050564568034461024741982685826506236675187483098
058061147621080075173357206076241660540417975007607038690173982970304352704621350069272335 60
988170563616210912433329757863841955071725149788670139225228899223516481475665598215942628 62
416574663180216071294691149002973851365869101800063115719840236978448567350563057926745232 58
734454338077142061402117279235660751764029430505029980342441949441488461246767658559905374 20
739484967701458920799712282449803281552777199073651638312748388705009067232205184155328243 07
557926424613840153096569513871477045814537991689884036947342227148249585233066762270036765 81
020698317997313959459482524703478001950141601346446083053831236710601900959253304045108565 89
595915386651424876493349991850483968579335016367320293844380913010273267057620162588740958 62
092934389435894107309570311803138854054957099574266946907903060421959547442824693533656776 19
191158090764707720385843331242519864327252292880398864451462770227983231793450177843410129 00
256966300247577220231288861894900669606228104939758205791391427079667780903354796440935540 80
987921837311105660788272851541631202591051359586799904112607978790670876538950142027754447 3
479072581096025055639657529624412241351610079135367955034989257281482778313566355589742005 82
822227645832801773127203896309730814265239091635501512924043194713065955619202909326616904 82
751377946705920000000000000000000000000000000000000000000000000000000000000000000000000000000
0000000000000000000000 }

We can convert this to decimal form to see its magnitude. Since we're converting the perfect, absolutely correct result directly into decimal form, there is no danger of roundoff error being introduced, and we can consider this result definitive for comparison with results we get later:

```
N[%[[2]], 50]
```

$1.3803122311510199316468844508892747093109864058912 \times 10^{-1495}$

Suppose we instead convert all the exact fractions in the matrix into approximate numbers first, then calculate the determinant:

$$\text{Det}\Big[\text{Table}\Big[\text{N}\Big[\frac{1}{i+j}\Big],\ \{i,\ 1,\ 50\},\ \{j,\ 1,\ 50\}\Big]\Big]\ \text{// Timing}$$

{0.0166667 Second, $2.487613107955268 \times 10^{-688}$}

We got the answer in no time flat, but it's, well, *wrong*.

Letting *Mathematica* use fixed, machine precision arithmetic (the kind used, for example, in virtually all statistics programs and spreadsheets) for this particular problem was an exceptionally bad idea. Not only did we get garbage, the output gave us no indication whatsoever that it can't be trusted. If we didn't have the exact answer available for comparison, we might never know that our answer is off by *eight hundred and seven orders of magnitude*. We might continue in blissful ignorance of how wrong we really are (say, as a Republican politician might). (See Chapter 25 for an explanation of why one might actually want to have such a seemingly dangerous mode of computation available. We have no chapter on why one might want to have a Republican politician available.)

The alert user might feel uncomfortable getting an output so astonishingly close to zero, having started with numbers ranging from 1/2 to 1/100. But this hint of a problem is of little help if the options available to follow it up are limited. Do we have a way to test whether there actually is a difficulty? If there seems to be one, do we have a way to deal with it?

With programs that limit us to machine precision, our only option is to try rearranging the order in which the operations are carried out (indeed, a lot of work has been done in this area). We might get a result that is different from the one above, confirming that there is a difficulty. But to what degree could we trust our new result? There is a limit to what can be done without high-precision calculation.

With *Mathematica*, we have many options. For example, we can ask that all the numbers be converted to 50-digit approximate floating point numbers before the determinant is calculated. Because we're starting with high-precision numbers, *Mathematica* will track the accumulation of error for us, and show only the number of digits that are accurate in the end:

$$\text{Det}\Big[\text{Table}\Big[\text{N}\Big[\frac{1}{i+j},\ 50\Big],\ \{i,\ 1,\ 50\},\ \{j,\ 1,\ 50\}\Big]\Big]\ \text{// Timing}$$

{2.51667 Second, $0. \times 10^{-844}$}

Well, we have just been politely informed that there weren't any accurate digits in the end. Apparently, 50-digit precision in the input values is not enough to give us even a single digit of precision in the output.

Of course we're not limited to 50 digits, and since *Mathematica* has alerted us to the problem, we can simply increase the number of digits we start with:

$$\text{Det}\left[\text{Table}\left[\text{N}\left[\frac{1}{i + j}, 100\right], \{i, 1, 50\}, \{j, 1, 50\}\right]\right] \text{ // Timing}$$

{2. Second, 1.38031223115101993164688 × 10^{-1495}}

This time Mathematica gives us a 25-digit result. Moreover, all 25 digits are accurate (as we can see by comparing them with first 25 digits of the exact result). Having found that even with 100-digit input precision we still have only 25 useful digits in our output, we are now in a position to understand why machine precision of about 18 digits failed so abjectly with this particular problem. Pity the person without access to high precision or exact arithmetic!

Note that the high-precision calculation was quite a lot slower than the machine-precision version, but not as slow as the exact version. As you make the example larger, the exact calculation will start to get exponentially slower, while the high-precision numerical version will grow at a more reasonable rate.

Now, just how much should we pity a person without access to high precision arithmetic? In a recent comparison of popular math/statistics packages using a series of standardized reference problems (designed to test the accuracy of results) provided by the National Institute for Standards and Testing (NIST), *Mathematica* was the *only* package that got every single result accurate to the full number of digits provided by NIST as the certified correct result. For the mortification of the competition, here is the table of results from the NIST testing, (using the best solutions available from each package). Out of a total of 58 reference problems:

Package	Able to Solve at All	Perfect Solutions
SAS 6.12	47	1
SPSS 7.5	48	3
S - Plus 4.0	57	1
Excel 97	41	1
Stata 6.0	50	5
Mathematica 4.0	58	58

Ooh, that must sting. All of the big names in statistics completely failed to solve a significant number of the problems; none of them got more than 8% of the problems completely right. *Mathematica* was perfect across the board! *Mathematica*'s use of high precision calculation is largely responsible for its success. (As this book goes to press these results have not yet been officially published, so we can't provide a reference, but by the time you read it they will have been. Check http://www.wolfram.com which will surely provide a reference, as *Mathematica* is justifiably proud of this performance.)

Other statistics programs attempt to deal with roundoff error in the traditional way, using fixed precision arithmetic. There are times when it doesn't work very well. *Mathematica* deals with it by letting you do the calculation with as many digits as necessary, and keeping track so you know when you need more. It's fairly clear which approach works better.

■ Measurements

At some point in virtually any scientific experiment or engineering project, there will be measurements (temperature, pressure, approval rating, etc.), and there will be calculations done with the numbers from those measurements. It's important when doing these calculations that one track the accumulation of roundoff error, to determine how much accuracy one may claim in the final result. In fields like chemistry and physics, this tracking of significant digits is a rigorous discipline with well understood rules. (In the social and political sciences, where practitioners have been less familiar with mathematics and truthfulness, significant digits, not to mention significance in general, are still often ignored.)

With measurements, you start your calculations with numbers that have a finite, usually fairly well quantified, amount of error in them. Say you measure the weight of something as 2.5421 grams on an accurate laboratory balance. This number has 5 significant digits, and there's really nothing you can do to increase it, short of buying a better balance.

So unlike in the section above, you don't have the option of just increasing the number of digits of precision in your calculation; instead you have to track the significant figures through the calculation, and accept what you get in the end. If you end up with no significant digits, as in the examples above, that means one of two things. Either your measurements are simply inadequate to support any conclusion about the quantity you are trying to compute, or you have done the calculation in a way that causes it to lose more precision than necessary, or both. In the former case, you're going to have to buy more expensive instruments, while in the latter case you may be able to do the calculations in a different order to avoid loss of precision. (For example, when computing the value of a polynomial, it makes a difference whether you calculate it in factored or expanded form: Even though they are mathematically equivalent, the amount of roundoff error introduced is different.)

To track errors through a series of calculations in *Mathematica* you have three methods available. We'll describe them in order of increasing neurosis. For each of these methods we'll use the task of determining the elevation of the tip of a pole from measurements of its length and the angle it is leaning at.

■ Traditional Significant Figures Analysis

Say we measure the length of the pole as 200.00 cm, and 45.0° as the angle it makes to the gym floor it is resting on. We might at first think to enter these as follows (**Degree** has the value $\frac{\pi}{180}$ and is used to convert the angle to radians):

```
length = 200.00;
angle = 45.0 Degree;
```

But, as we have seen above, when we enter numbers like these with decimal points, *Mathematica* treats them, by default, as machine precision numbers with about 18 digits of precision, and does not track precision through the calculation. In order to make *Mathematica* track the number of significant figures, we have to tell it explicitly how many digits in each number are accurate:

```
length = SetPrecision[200.00, 5];
angle = SetPrecision[45.0 Degree, 3];
```

To calculate the height, we will multiple the length by the sine of the angle. But, let's pause to look just at the sine:

```
Sin[angle]
```

```
0.707
```

We started with three digits in the angle, and we still have three digits after applying the sine function. Now we multiply by the length:

```
length × Sin[angle]
```

```
141.
```

The number of significant figures in the result was limited by the less-precise of the two quantities.

OK, what happens if the angle is 90.0°?

```
angle = SetPrecision[90.0 Degree, 3];
```

```
Sin[angle]
```

```
1.0000
```

Notice that we got five digits of precision in this result, even though angle measurement was still only accurate to three places. This apparent gain in precision has occurred because the **Sin** function is very flat around 90°; a small variation in the angle translates into a much smaller variation in the sine. (This seems intuitive when you consider that a pole standing on end doesn't change its height very much as its angle changes slightly around the vertical, while the elevation of a pole at a 45° angle depends much more strongly on the exact value of the angle.)

```
length × Sin[angle]
```

```
200.00
```

Again we get five digits in the result. It was a good thing that *Mathematica* carried through enough digits from the sine function, because we needed them in the next stage of the calculation.

As we see from the example above, *Mathematica* can do automatically what generations of chemistry students have done by hand. It uses pretty much the same rules, except that *Mathe-*

matica uses the correct mathematical rules, rather than approximate rules of thumb derived from them (and, to be perfectly honest, *Mathematica* does the calculations internally with considerably more digits than it shows you, to be sure the ones displayed are accurate). The ability of *Mathematica* to track significant figures combined with its ability to carry units through calculations makes it the ideal tool for working scientists. For examples using units, see Chapter 73 and Chapter 67.

But in actuality, significant figures are a fairly crude way of representing error in measurements. It's fine if you have five or six figures to work with, but by the time you're down to two or so digits, it's just too fuzzy a measure. Some systems of significant figures actually go so far as to work with *partial* digits, written in a smaller typeface at the end of the number. Yuck. In the next section, we'll show how to make this concept more precise.

▪ Confidence Intervals

In the real world, perfection is impossible. The quantity you are trying to measure has a true value, but your measurements will always deviate from it by some random amount. But you know the measurement value, not the true value, so a more useful way of saying the same thing is that the true value will always deviate from your measured value by the same random amount.

Or, to put it still another way, you can expect the true value to lie within some interval around the value your measurement yielded. But how big an interval? That depends on the nature and magnitude of the errors inherent in your measuring equipment, and on your tolerance for risk. Typically one picks an interval such that there is, say, a 95% chance that the true value will lie within the stated interval. The size of the interval is determined by repeatedly measuring a known reference standard, by making assumptions based on the physical characteristics of the device, or by guessing.

(Significant figures as we saw them above are really just a shorthand for indicating, crudely, the size of this interval. Generally speaking, unless the error is stated more explicitly, it is assumed that the interval is ±1 in the last digit (unless it's written small, in which case it's ±5, except on alternate Tuesdays when it's ±3).)

Mathematica allows you to work with such intervals explicitly: Virtually all mathematical functions will accept an **Interval** object and return another **Interval** as their result. Let's return to our pole measuring task, this time assuming that the angle measurement is accurate to ±0.5° and the length to ±0.01cm:

```
length = Interval[{200.00 - 0.01, 200.00 + 0.01}];
angle = Interval[{ (45.0 - 0.5) Degree, (45.0 + 0.5) Degree}];

Sin[angle]

Interval[{0.700909, 0.71325}]

length × Sin[angle]

Interval[{140.175, 142.657}]
```

Now we have a very explicit result showing the range of heights that are consistent with the original measurements.

Near 90° the resulting interval is much smaller (confirming the correctness of the result above, in which we got more significant figures at 90° than at 45°):

```
angle = Interval[{(90.0 - 0.5) Degree, (90.0 + 0.5) Degree}];
```

```
length × Sin[angle]
```

```
Interval[{199.982, 200.01}]
```

This is nice, but the notation is a bit ugly, to say the least. The form we'd really like to see is **200.00±0.01** instead of **Interval[{200.00-0.01, 200.00+0.01}]**. Fortunately *Mathematica* allows us the freedom to define new notations like ±, for both input and output.

The following somewhat cryptic set of commands defines ± as a notation for **Interval**. It displays an interval using two significant figures for the error, and a corresponding value (with two uncertain digits) for the center of the interval. Some people might prefer only a single uncertain digit: You can change this by replacing the **2** on the third line with a **1**. (*Please* don't try to understand this code! It is highly specialized and needs to be understood only if you want to define your own new notations, a topic beyond the scope of this book. There is no need to understand the code if you just want to use the interval notation: Close your eyes, evaluate the code, and everything will be fine. Be sure to evaluate the cell only once per session.)

```
Unprotect[Interval];
Interval /: Format[Interval[{l_, u_}]] :=
  Module[{mean, error, digitsInError},
    digitsInError = 2;
    mean = (u + l) / 2;
    error = (u - l) / 2;
    NumberForm[mean,
      {Infinity, digitsInError - 1 - Ceiling[-Log[10, error]]},
      NumberPadding → {"", "0"}] ±
    NumberForm[error, digitsInError, NumberPadding → {"", "0"}]
  ];
Protect[Interval];
MakeExpression[RowBox[{m_, "±", e_}], form_] :=
  MakeExpression[RowBox[
    {"Interval", "[", RowBox[{"{", RowBox[{RowBox[{m, "-", e}],
        ",", RowBox[{m, "+", e}]}], "}"}], "]"}]]
```

To enter the **±** character, type ⎋+- ⎋ where ⎋ represents the escape key and **+-** represent the ordinary plus and minus (dash) keys. After you've typed the first three keys of the sequence you'll see ⦂+- (the ⦂ character represents the escape key you typed). When you type the fourth key in the sequence (escape), the ⦂+- will automatically be replaced by a **±** character.

After evaluating these commands, we can repeat our calculations in *much* more compact form:

(200.00 ± 0.01) × Sin[(45.0 ± 0.5) Degree]

141.4 ± 1.2

(200.00 ± 0.01) × Sin[(90.0 ± 0.5) Degree]

199.996 ± 0.014

(The parentheses are needed to avoid confusion: without them the expression might be interpreted as the quantity is **200.00** with an error of **0.01×Sin[(45.0±0.5)Degree]**.)

This form of interval notation is very nice. The following could have been taken straight out of any chemistry textbook:

$$\frac{\textbf{(27.4 ± 0.5) × (306.7 ± 0.2)}}{\textbf{(62.428 ± 0.002)}}$$

134.6 ± 2.5

But unlike the textbook, *Mathematica* computes the answer for you, and determines exactly the interval to give in the output.

Of course, these intervals aren't absolutes; they are only as good as our assumptions about the measurements. See the next section for a further discussion about how the intervals may be interpreted.

■ Parallel calculation

If you have a single measurement, you can think of the true value as lying somewhere in a cloud of probability centered around that measured value. If, on the other hand, you have a large number of measurements of the same thing, you can think of them as *being* that cloud. Assuming that the errors in each measurement are random (rather than the result of some systematic defect in your device or in your method of using it), you can expect the errors to tend to cancel each other out. Thus their average should be a better estimate of the true value than any individual measurement in the cloud.

Very often it is quite reasonable to assume that the repeated measurements follow a Gaussian distribution, from which one can conclude that the average (mean) of the points is the best estimate of the true value, and the standard deviation (root-mean-square of the deviations from the mean) is an estimate of the degree of uncertainty that remains in that mean value.

The typical procedure is to make a bunch of measurements; then for each quantity you are measuring, average your individual measurements of it into a single value, whose number of significant figures (or confidence interval), is determined from the standard deviation of the measurements on which that value was based. You then use these mean values and their associated uncertainties in your calculations, the uncertainty in each result being computed and reported either by significant figures or intervals, as above.

Returning to our pole height task, let's say we have the following ten measurements of the length and angle:

```
lengthData = {200.0026, 200.0046, 199.9981, 200.0058, 199.9940,
    200.0067, 199.9932, 200.0048, 200.0056, 200.0083};

angleData = {45.13, 45.26, 44.72, 45.27,
    44.26, 45.42, 44.94, 45.15, 45.33, 44.82} Degree;
```

(The astute reader may wonder what kind of ruler could possibly be read to seven significant figures. Our editor insisted that we make the error range in this example consistent with the examples above, so just pretend we're using a laser rangefinding ruler with a seven-digit display.)

Now let's define a utility function that takes a list of datapoints and returns a confidence interval based on the mean and standard deviation of the data. We will arbitrarily choose an interval of ± two standard deviations, corresponding to 95% confidence. (To define the **Mean** and **StandardDeviation** functions we need to load the standard statistics package first.)

```
Needs["Statistics`Master`"]

IntervalFromMeasurements[measurements_] :=
  Module[{mean, stdev},
    mean = Mean[measurements];
    stdev = StandardDeviation[measurements];
    Interval[{mean - 2 stdev, mean + 2 stdev}]
  ];
```

Evaluate the two input cells (above), and the cells (previous section) that define the ± notation.

Now we can convert our raw data into intervals:

```
length = IntervalFromMeasurements[lengthData]
```

200.002 ± 0.011

```
angle = IntervalFromMeasurements[angleData]
```

0.786 ± 0.012

And, as above, *Mathematica* will carry our intervals through the elevation calculation:

```
length × Sin[angle]
```

```
141.5 ± 1.7
```

But there is another way. Instead of getting the mean values first, then doing the calculation, we could instead do the calculation for each and every measurement, then take the mean of the list of results. Because arithmetic functions in *Mathematica* generally work on lists as well as on numbers and intervals, we can calculate all 10 individual elevation results very simply:

```
result = lengthData × Sin[angleData]
```

```
{141.744, 142.065, 140.727, 142.09, 139.579,
  142.459, 141.268, 141.795, 142.238, 140.982}
```

Using our utility function from above, we can determine a confidence interval:

```
IntervalFromMeasurements[result]
```

```
141.5 ± 1.7
```

Of course this only worked because there were the same number of measurements of each quantity, and it was a bit arbitrary to pair them up one-to-one. A more general method is to compute the result for all possible combinations of the measured values (100 in this case):

```
result = Flatten[Table[lengthData[[i]] × Sin[angleData[[j]]],
    {i, 1, Length[lengthData]}, {j, 1, Length[angleData]}]];
```

```
IntervalFromMeasurements[result]
```

```
141.5 ± 1.7
```

This method is, of course, incredibly wasteful of computer time, but *who cares*? Computer time is like air, ubiquitous and virtually unlimited, so you may as well use it.

Chapter **25**

Can *Mathematica* do industrial-strength numerics?

If you read the promotional materials about *Mathematica* V4.0, you find numerical computation high on the list of things that have been improved and expanded. We interviewed Rob Knapp, a developer at Wolfram who worked on many of these features.

Jerry: So, Knapp, what's all this about numerical computation? I thought *Mathematica* was always supposed to be a good system for—what was that slogan?... "Symbolic, Numerical, and Graphical Computation". What needed so much improvement?

Rob: Well, there's numerics and then there's numerics. *Mathematica* has always been good for doing things like developing numerical algorithms, calculating special functions to high precision, and other such detail-oriented numerical operations. The improvements have come mainly in the area of calculations involving large arrays of numbers. Entirely different factors become important in those kinds of problems.

Theo: One way to look at this is that *Mathematica* has always been good at doing problems involving a smallish number of sophisticated operations. V4.0 is now also good at doing problems that involve a largish number of simple operations. (Problems that require a large number of complex operations are, of course, also possible, but by definition they are going to involve more time and memory.)

Jerry: Can you put some numbers on "smallish" and "largish"?

Theo: There's no one answer. It depends very much on the size and speed of your computer. Let's just say that if you have a few thousand numbers and need to do something with them, V3.0 is fine. If you have a few million, you will see significant improvements in V4.0.

Rob: Right. The improvements focus primarily on problems that involve large arrays that contain machine-precision floating point numbers and *only* machine precision floating point numbers. If you have such a simple array (as opposed to an array containing a mixture of floating point numbers, large integers, and symbolic expressions), you can use much more efficient algorithms to operate on them, and you can store them much more efficiently.

Jerry: Now we know what kinds of problems will run better. How do we *see* this benefit? What does it take to get *Mathematica* to do this wonderful new thing?

Theo: It's quite automatic. If the calculation you carry out is one that meets the necessary conditions, it will automatically be done using the new more efficient internal code. For example, let's generate a matrix containing random numbers everywhere except a single symbolic entry at the (1, 1) position:

```
m1 = Table[If[(i == 1) && (j == 1), a, Random[]],
    {i, 1, 500}, {j, 1, 500}];
```

ByteCount tells us how many bytes of memory the matrix is using:

```
ByteCount[m1]
```

```
5012004
```

This is 20 bytes per number plus 12004 bytes of header. Now let's generate a large matrix that contains *only* floating point numbers:

```
m2 = Table[Random[], {i, 1, 500}, {j, 1, 500}];
```

```
ByteCount[m2]
```

```
2000056
```

That's quite a bit smaller! Not counting the insignificant 56 bytes of header, it's 8 bytes per floating point number, the size of a machine-precision floating point number on this particular computer. (Some are 8, some are 10, some are 12, it all depends on the architecture of the processor, which is why they are called *machine*-precision.)

Let's time how long it takes to calculate the sines of all the elements of each of these two arrays:

```
Timing[Sin[m1];]
```

```
{0.7 Second, Null}
```

```
Timing[Sin[m2];]
```

```
{0.1 Second, Null}
```

The only difference between these two arrays is that one of them meets the criteria for the new high speed numerics features; that one uses less than half as much memory and runs seven times faster.

Jerry: I notice that you used the same two commands, **Table** and **Sin**, to do both calculations. That seems convenient on the one hand, since you don't have to learn new commands, but troublesome on the other hand, since you might not know whether you're getting the benefits of the new feature or not.

Theo: Yes, it's a trade-off. An important principle in *Mathematica* has always been not to have a lot of complicated restrictions on what functions can operate on what kinds of data. For example, the function **Det** calculates the determinant of a numerical matrix:

$$\text{Det}\left[\begin{pmatrix} 1 & 2 \\ 3 & 4 \end{pmatrix}\right]$$

-2

Exactly the same function also works if you replace one or more of the entries with symbolic expressions:

$$\text{Det}\left[\begin{pmatrix} 1 & \sqrt{a-b} \\ x & 4 \end{pmatrix}\right]$$

$4 - \sqrt{a-b}\ x$

In many other systems, there would either be no way to do the second example or it would be done with a completely different function. In some systems, you even have to use different functions depending on whether you have integers or floating point numbers!

But *Mathematica*'s generality comes with a price: Because it has to be ready to handle any possible expression at any position in the matrix, it has to keep checking for possible complications, and it has to use very general-purpose datastructures to represent the output.

Rob: It's exactly this generality that made efficiency difficult. In V4.0, a new concept, packed arrays, has been introduced to improve things. A packed array is simply an array (of any dimension) of machine precision floating point numbers or integers (but not both in the same array). When a function like **Det** is given a packed array as input, it knows in advance that there ain't going to be nothin' but numbers in the input, so it can use the fastest numerical algorithm available, without having to keep checking for complications.

Packed arrays have been designed to be a purely *internal* concept, not something users have to explicitly ask for or worry about most of the time. Many functions automatically either create a packed array if they can, or convert a regular list into a packed array. This happens automatically without the user necessarily even knowing it's happening.

Theo: In fact, if this weren't a new thing in V4.0, but had always been part of *Mathematica*, it wouldn't even be a topic of discussion. It would just be a fact about the internal workings of *Mathematica* that was of little concern to the typical user. But, because it's new and because it significantly changes the scale of problems that can be done with *Mathematica*, it's worth talking about in more detail.

Jerry: How internal and automatic is it? Don't I have to do *something* special to get the benefits of this new feature?

Rob: Considerable effort has gone into making the speedups automatic. Here are some rules of thumb about when packed arrays will be used automatically:

> **Table**, **NestList**, and other similar functions that produce lists as output, produce packed arrays automatically if the function generating the entries is a purely numerical function that can be compiled, and if the result is longer than an internal threshold (100 elements).

> **Map** returns a packed array if it can compile its first argument, and if its input is either a packed array or a list of numbers.

> **Fourier** and numerical linear algebra functions which internally use array structures return packed arrays.

Jerry: What's this about functions being compiled? Is this something I have to ask for explicitly?

Theo: No, compiling happens automatically if the functions you are using contain purely numerical operations. It's another internal, automatic optimization you should not have to worry about. See The *Mathematica* Book for more details on exactly what kinds of functions can be compiled.

Rob: In addition to the broad improvements brought by packed arrays, there are quite a few specific improvements to particular functions and packages. For example, the nonlinear fit in Statistics`NonlinearFit` is now orders of magnitude faster. And **Fourier** is much faster for non-power-of-two cases; in particular, prime lengths are now $n \log(n)$, not n^2. So you don't have to worry much about the length of your dataset anymore.

Theo: A detailed description of all the improvements is beyond the scope of this book, so we won't go any further here. To see one of the dramatic benefits of the new speed, look at <u>Chapter</u> 45 which shows how to do image processing in *Mathematica*.

Chapter **26**

How do I manipulate polynomials?

Factoring and expanding are a good place to start. For now we're going to type these functions in manually. Later in this chapter we'll see how to use palettes to do the same things.

> `Factor[a² + 2 a b + b²]`
>
> $(a + b)^2$
>
> `Expand[(1 + x)⁵]`
>
> $1 + 5\,x + 10\,x^2 + 10\,x^3 + 5\,x^4 + x^5$

Notice that *Mathematica* displays polynomials in the sensible increasing-powers order. Some people prefer the other order, which is available by adding `//TraditionalForm` to the end of your command:

> `Expand[(1 + x)⁵] // TraditionalForm`
>
> $x^5 + 5\,x^4 + 10\,x^3 + 10\,x^2 + 5\,x + 1$

By default, *Mathematica* factors over the integers, so the following example doesn't factor:

> `Factor[9 + x²]`
>
> $9 + x^2$

If we want to allow complex numbers, we can use a variation:

> `Factor[9 + x², GaussianIntegers → True]`
>
> $(-3\,I + x)\,(3\,I + x)$

`GaussianIntegers → True` is what's called an option. Don't worry about what `Gaussian‑Integers` means; it's a somewhat pretentious term for "I want to allow complex numbers (with integer coefficients) in the answer". The arrow (→) used in this option can be typed as ⎋->⎋, or you can use the plain form `->` instead.

Mathematica does not "factor over the radicals":

Factor[x² - 3]

$-3 + x^2$

Factoring over the radicals is not factoring in the usual sense of the word; it is more like finding the roots of the expression, which can be done with the **Solve** command:

Solve[x² - 3 == 0, x]

$\{\{x \to \sqrt{3}\}, \{x \to -\sqrt{3}\}\}$

This somewhat strange-looking result means that the two roots are the square root of three, and the negative of that. (See Chapter 27 for more information about the **Solve** command and an explanation of its result format.)

If you factor a polynomial involving fractions, *Mathematica* puts everything over a common denominator:

$$\textbf{Factor}\left[\textbf{x}^2 - \frac{\textbf{4}}{\textbf{9}}\right]$$

$\frac{1}{9} (-2 + 3 x) (2 + 3 x)$

Mathematica can factor expressions involving functions as well as simple variables:

Factor[Sin[x]² - Cos[x]²]

$(-\text{Cos}[x] + \text{Sin}[x]) (\text{Cos}[x] + \text{Sin}[x])$

Factor[Sin[x]² - E²ˣ]

$(-E^x + \text{Sin}[x]) (E^x + \text{Sin}[x])$

There are several commands for carrying out structural rearrangements of expressions:

Combining terms over a common denominator:

$$\textbf{Together}\left[\frac{\textbf{a}}{\textbf{b}} + \frac{\textbf{c}}{\textbf{d}}\right]$$

$\frac{b c + a d}{b d}$

Splitting fractions apart:

$$\mathbf{Apart}\left[\frac{b\,c+a\,d}{b\,d}\right]$$

$$\frac{a}{b}+\frac{c}{d}$$

Collecting coefficients of equal powers of the variable specified by the second argument:

$$\mathbf{Collect}[a\,x+b\,x+c\,y+d\,y,\ x]$$

$$(a+b)\,x+c\,y+d\,y$$

Simplifying:

$$\mathbf{Simplify}\left[\frac{x^2+2\,x\,y+y^2}{x+y}\right]$$

$$x+y$$

Simplify is a very complex command. It tries to find the "simplest" form of the expression. It is often not clear which of several possible forms is the simplest; different people may consider different forms to be simpler. The goal of **Simplify** is to reduce the expression to as few elements as possible (minimal leaf count).

In some cases, you may be dissatisfied with **Simplify**'s output. Try **FullSimplify**. It will work longer and harder to find a simplification—in some cases for a *very* long time.

■ Using Palettes

There are two palettes that can help you manipulate polynomials. To open a palette, choose it from the **Palettes** submenu in the **File** menu.

The Basic Calculations palette has a section with most of the functions described in this chapter. To open a section in this palette (which contains many other functions as well), click on the triangle next to the name of the section. Select the expression you want to operate on, then click the button with the function you want. The function will be pasted around your expression, and you can then use Shift-Return to evaluate the expression. Or you can use the button first and then type your expression into the space provided.

The Algebraic Manipulation palette has a similar list of functions, but it *automatically* evaluates the expression after pasting the function, and replaces the input with the result of the evaluation. In other words, it does the manipulation in place, automatically destroying the original expression in the process.

Which palette you use depends on what you are trying to do. If you want to carry out a series of calculations, occasionally backtracking, and want to leave a record of what you did, use Basic Calculations. If you have a complicated expression and want explore it interactively by applying manipulations to subparts, use Algebraic Manipulation.

Chapter **27**

How do I solve equations?

The **Solve** command can be used to solve equations:

$$\texttt{Solve[x}^2 \texttt{ - 2 x == 0, x]}$$

$$\{\{x \rightarrow 2\}, \{x \rightarrow 0\}\}$$

- The first argument is the equation to be solved.
- The second argument is the variable for which we're solving.

(In *Mathematica*, **==** means equality. Single **=** means assignment.)

The result is given in the form of a list of replacement rules (→). See Chapter 58 for a discussion of what → really means. In this case the solution shown is **x** equals **2** or **0**. (The astute reader may notice that the result is actually a list of *lists of* replacement rules. We can ignore this for now and look just at the expressions to the right of the arrows.)

If your equation involves other variables, they will be treated as constants:

$$\texttt{Solve[x}^2 \texttt{ - 5 x y + 4 y}^2 \texttt{ == 0, x]}$$

$$\{\{x \rightarrow 4\,y\}, \{x \rightarrow y\}\}$$

You can solve systems of equations involving more than one variable by using lists for both the first and second arguments to **Solve**:

$$\texttt{Solve[\{2 x + 3 y == 7, 3 x - 2 y == 11\}, \{x, y\}]}$$

$$\left\{\left\{x \rightarrow \frac{47}{13}, \; y \rightarrow -\frac{1}{13}\right\}\right\}$$

- The first argument is a list of the equations to be solved.
- The second argument is a list of the variables to be solved for.

The system above had one solution. If there is more than one solution, you will get a list of lists of values:

$$\texttt{Solve[\{x}^2\texttt{ +y}^2\texttt{ == 16, x}^2\texttt{ - 4 == y\}, \{x, y\}]}$$

$$\{\{y \to 3, x \to \sqrt{7}\}, \{y \to 3, x \to -\sqrt{7}\}, \{y \to -4, x \to 0\}, \{y \to -4, x \to 0\}\}$$

The first element of the result, $\{y \to 3, x \to \sqrt{7}\}$, is the first solution, and so on.

Adding the useful command **//TableForm** to such a **Solve** command causes the output to be formatted more readably:

$$\texttt{Solve[\{x}^2\texttt{ +y}^2\texttt{ == 16, x}^2\texttt{ - 4 == y\}, \{x, y\}] // TableForm}$$

$y \to -4$ $x \to 0$
$y \to -4$ $x \to 0$
$y \to 3$ $x \to -\sqrt{7}$
$y \to 3$ $x \to \sqrt{7}$

Each row represents one solution. (Notice the double root.)

If there is no solution, an empty list is returned:

$$\texttt{Solve[\{x}^2\texttt{ == 3, x}^2\texttt{ == 4\}, x]}$$

$$\{\}$$

Solve returns a list of replacement rules because this is a versatile form for the results. The results are fairly clear, and can be used to calculate the value of expressions involving the variables.

To explain replacement rules, some examples follow (see Chapter 58 for a more detailed explanation):

$$\texttt{x}^2\texttt{ /. x} \to \texttt{5}$$

$$25$$

This means replace **x** with **5** in the expression **x²**. The **/.** operator should be read "replace" and → should be read "with". The whole expression is "in **x²** replace **x** with **5**".

You can use a list of rules to replace more than one variable at a time:

$$\texttt{x}^2\texttt{ +y}^2\texttt{ /. \{x} \to \texttt{5, y} \to \texttt{10\}}$$

$$125$$

When we use a list of lists of replacement rules, we get a list of results:

$$x^2 \; / . \; \{\{x \rightarrow 5\}, \; \{x \rightarrow 6\}\}$$

{25, 36}

$$x^2 + y^2 \; / . \; \{\{x \rightarrow 5, \; y \rightarrow 10\}, \; \{x \rightarrow 6, \; y \rightarrow 10\}\}$$

{125, 136}

Returning to the first example in this chapter:

$$\texttt{solution = Solve}[x^2 - 2\,x == 0, \; x]$$

{{x → 2}, {x → 0}}

This is a list of lists of replacement rules, and we can use it to replace values in any expression we like. For example, we can check that the answer is correct by substituting the solution into the original expression:

$$x^2 - 2\,x \; / . \; \texttt{solution}$$

{0, 0}

The list of two zeros indicates that both solutions give a value of zero when substituted into the original expression.

We can use the **Solve** command directly in the replace expression:

$$x^2 \; / . \; \texttt{Solve}[x^2 == 4, \; x]$$

{4, 4}

These two **4**'s are the result of substituting the two solutions in the expression **x^2**.

To get a simple list of the values of the solution, use the following form:

$$x \; / . \; \texttt{Solve}[x^2 == 4, \; x]$$

{2, -2}

For more information about how lists and replacement rules interact, see The *Mathematica* Book.

Some equations (for example, some polynomials of fifth degree and higher) can't be solved in explicit form:

```
Solve[x⁶ + x⁵ + x² + 1 == 0, x]
```

$$\{\{x \to \text{Root}[1 + \#1^2 + \#1^5 + \#1^6 \&, 1]\},$$
$$\{x \to \text{Root}[1 + \#1^2 + \#1^5 + \#1^6 \&, 2]\},$$
$$\{x \to \text{Root}[1 + \#1^2 + \#1^5 + \#1^6 \&, 3]\},$$
$$\{x \to \text{Root}[1 + \#1^2 + \#1^5 + \#1^6 \&, 4]\},$$
$$\{x \to \text{Root}[1 + \#1^2 + \#1^5 + \#1^6 \&, 5]\},$$
$$\{x \to \text{Root}[1 + \#1^2 + \#1^5 + \#1^6 \&, 6]\}\}$$

(Ignore the result; it's confusing.) Using the **N** function you can get a numerical approximation to the solution:

```
N[Solve[x⁶ + x⁵ + x² + 1 == 0, x]] // TableForm
```

$$x \to -1.15408 - 0.613723\,\text{I}$$
$$x \to -1.15408 + 0.613723\,\text{I}$$
$$x \to -0.08275 - 0.795302\,\text{I}$$
$$x \to -0.08275 + 0.795302\,\text{I}$$
$$x \to 0.736832 - 0.610339\,\text{I}$$
$$x \to 0.736832 + 0.610339\,\text{I}$$

The imaginary constant (square root of -1) is represented by **I**, which is consistent with *Mathematica's* rule that all built-in functions, constants, and variables start with capital letters. You can also use the new double-struck *i* symbol for input: Enter it by typing [ESC]**ii**[ESC].

If you want higher precision, you can add a second argument to the **N** function, specifying the number of digits you want to work with:

```
N[Solve[x⁶ + x⁵ + x² + 1 == 0, x], 20] // TableForm
```

$$x \to -1.1540824762585313148 - 0.6137229683549870418 3\,\text{I}$$
$$x \to -1.1540824762585313148 + 0.6137229683549878428 3\,\text{I}$$
$$x \to -0.08275000929153482285 3 - 0.7953024282282060341 9\,\text{I}$$
$$x \to -0.08275000929153482285 3 + 0.7953024282282060341 9\,\text{I}$$
$$x \to 0.7368324855500661376 6 - 0.6103394166974002668 3\,\text{I}$$
$$x \to 0.7368324855500661376 6 + 0.6103394166974002668 3\,\text{I}$$

Solve can also solve non-polynomial equations:

```
Solve[Sin[x²] == a, x]
```

```
Solve::ifun : Inverse functions are being
    used by Solve, so some solutions may not be found.
```

$$\{\{x \to -\sqrt{\text{ArcSin}[a]}\}, \{x \to \sqrt{\text{ArcSin}[a]}\}\}$$

The error message indicates that this is an equation for which *Mathematica* cannot guarantee that it has found all the solutions.

Many non-polynomial equations cannot be solved at all by **Solve**:

$$\texttt{Solve}\left[\texttt{Sin[x]} \; \texttt{==} \; \frac{\texttt{x}}{\texttt{2}}, \; \texttt{x}\right]$$

Solve::tdep :
   The equations appear to involve transcendental functions of
     the variables in an essentially non-algebraic way.

$$\texttt{Solve}\left[\texttt{Sin[x]} \; \texttt{==} \; \frac{\texttt{x}}{\texttt{2}}, \; \texttt{x}\right]$$

Evaluating this numerically has no effect:

$$\texttt{N}\left[\texttt{Solve}\left[\texttt{Sin[x]} \; \texttt{==} \; \frac{\texttt{x}}{\texttt{2}}, \; \texttt{x}\right]\right]$$

Solve::tdep :
   The equations appear to involve transcendental functions of
     the variables in an essentially non-algebraic way.

Solve::tdep :
   The equations appear to involve transcendental functions of
     the variables in an essentially non-algebraic way.

Solve[Sin[x] == 0.5 x, x]

To get an answer to this problem it is necessary to use **FindRoot**, which uses purely numerical techniques to locate solutions. You have to give **FindRoot** a suggested starting point; the solution you get will depend on the starting point you give it, and you can never be quite sure that you have found all the solutions (unless you can figure this out independently).

$$\texttt{FindRoot}\left[\texttt{Sin[x]} \; \texttt{==} \; \frac{\texttt{x}}{\texttt{2}}, \; \texttt{\{x, 1.5\}}\right]$$

$\{x \rightarrow 1.89549\}$

$$\texttt{FindRoot}\left[\texttt{Sin[x]} \; \texttt{==} \; \frac{\texttt{x}}{\texttt{2}}, \; \texttt{\{x, -0.5\}}\right]$$

$\{x \rightarrow 3.9465 \times 10^{-10}\}$

$$\texttt{FindRoot}\left[\texttt{Sin[x]} \; \texttt{==} \; \frac{\texttt{x}}{\texttt{2}}, \; \texttt{\{x, -1.5\}}\right]$$

$\{x \rightarrow -1.89549\}$

A quick plot will verify that these are the only solutions:

$$\texttt{Plot}\left[\left\{\texttt{Sin[x]},\ \frac{\texttt{x}}{\texttt{2}}\right\},\ \{\texttt{x},\ -5,\ 5\}\right];$$

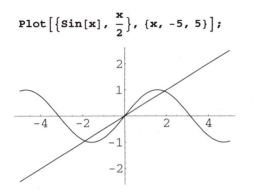

It's sometimes interesting to watch how **FindRoot** approaches the solution. A trick you can use here and in many other situations is to include a **Print** statement in your function. Consider this example:

```
Print["Hello"]; goodbye
```

```
Hello
```

```
goodbye
```

This is a *compound expression* containing two separate expressions separated by a semicolon. The return value of the compound expression is the value of the last element, **goodbye**, while the first element has the side effect of printing **Hello**.

Here is what happens if we make the first argument to **FindRoot** a compound expression that prints the value of **x** each time it is evaluated:

$$\texttt{FindRoot}\left[\texttt{Print[x]};\ \texttt{Sin[x]}\ ==\ \frac{\texttt{x}}{\texttt{2}},\ \{\texttt{x},\ 10\}\right]$$

```
x
```

```
10.
```

```
5.8598
```

```
13.9742
```

```
9.91702
```

```
7.88841
```

```
2.37818
```

```
1.97106
```

```
1.89848
```

```
1.8955
```

```
1.89549
```

```
{x → 1.89549}
```

Apparently, the expression was evaluated once with no numerical value for **x**, then *Mathematica* took ten iterations to arrive at its final value of the root.

A variant of this is to collect the values into a list:

```
myList = {};
```

$$\texttt{FindRoot}\left[\texttt{AppendTo[myList, x]; Sin[x]} == \frac{\texttt{x}}{\texttt{2}}, \texttt{\{x, 10\}}\right]$$

$\{x \to 1.89549\}$

```
myList
```

$\{10., 10., 5.8598, 13.9742, 9.91702, 7.88841,$
$2.37818, 1.97106, 1.89848, 1.8955, 1.89549\}$

This allows us to plot the values, together with the two functions:

$$\texttt{Plot}\left[\left\{\texttt{Sin[x]}, \frac{\texttt{x}}{\texttt{2}}\right\}, \texttt{\{x, 0, 14\}}, \texttt{Epilog} \to\right.$$

$$\left.\texttt{Map}\left[\texttt{Line}\left[\left\{\texttt{\{\#, Sin[\#]\}}, \left\{\texttt{\#}, \frac{\texttt{\#}}{\texttt{2}}\right\}\right\}\right] \texttt{ \&, myList}\right], \texttt{PlotRange} \to \texttt{All}\right];$$

Here is a function that puts this all together:

```
ApproachPlot[f1_ == f2_, {x_, xmin_, xmax_}, xinit_] :=
Module[{myList, returnValue},
myList = {};
returnValue =
    FindRoot[AppendTo[myList, x]; f1 == f2, {x, xinit}];
Plot[{f1, f2}, {x, xmin, xmax},
    Epilog → Map[Line[{{x, f1}, {x, f2}} /. x → #] &, myList],
    PlotRange -> All];
returnValue
]
```

The first argument is the equation to solve, the second argument is the variable and range to plot over, and the third argument is the starting point for **FindRoot**. The following command reproduces the example above:

ApproachPlot $\left[\text{Sin}[y] == \dfrac{y}{2}, \{y, 0, 14\}, 10\right]$

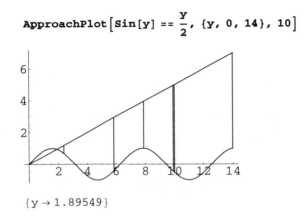

{y → 1.89549}

Here is a nasty example that confuses the numerical method used by **FindRoot**:

ApproachPlot [Sin[y] == Cos[y] + y - 5, {y, 0, 14}, 10]

```
FindRoot::cvnwt : Newton's method failed to
    converge to the prescribed accuracy after 15 iterations.
```

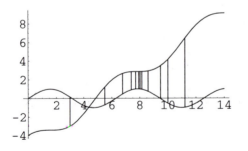

{y → -15.3593}

FindRoot has been trapped by a local minimum. Picking a different starting point allows it to converge easily:

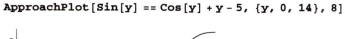

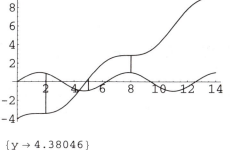

$\{y \to 4.38046\}$

If you have *Mathematica* and the electronic edition of this book, evaluate the function definition above, and try your own examples! Consider using the trick of putting a **Print** statement into functions in other places, too. You can use it almost anywhere you are passing an expression to a built-in function whose internal workings you want to probe.

Chapter **28**

What is a package? How do I load one?

Many commands are built into *Mathematica*, but many more specialized ones are defined in "packages". Packages are files that contain definitions of *Mathematica* functions. To use a package, you need to "load" it into *Mathematica*.

To load a package, you need to know its name and the directory (folder) in which it is located. All the packages that come with *Mathematica* are in several subdirectories inside a directory called StandardPackages, which is inside the AddOns directory. For example, the package FilledPlot.m is inside the directory Graphics, inside of StandardPackages.

To load FilledPlot.m, you can evaluate the following command:

> **<< Graphics`FilledPlot`**

The two single-quotes used here are "back-quotes" usually found on the same key with ~. They are *not* the single quotes found on the double-quote key. The back-quote character is used to separate the package name from the directory name, and at the end in place of .m. The reasons for this are somewhat complex and are explained in detail here and in The *Mathematica* Book.

In the command above, it was not necessary to specify the directory StandardPackages, because it is one of the directories that *Mathematica* automatically looks in (it is on the search path). Which directories are on this list depends on the version of *Mathematica* you are using and how it has been installed. With few exceptions, the StandardPackages directory will be on the list. (If you write your own packages and want to load them in, you should read the appropriate sections in The *Mathematica* Book to learn about how to load packages in directories that are not on the list, or how to change the list itself.)

The << command always loads the named package. A more reliable command to use is **Needs**. It loads the specified package only if it has not already been loaded in the same session (loading the same package twice may cause problems). Here is an example:

> **Needs["Graphics`FilledPlot`"]**

Don't use any commands defined in a package before you load the package. Doing so will cause problems, as described in Chapter 29.

Chapter **29**

The package didn't load! Why?

Suppose you want to plot the area between two curves. Let's pretend you've read <u>Chapter</u> 35, "How do I show the area between curves?", so you know to use the **FilledPlot** command. You might try this example:

FilledPlot[{x^2, Sin[x]}, {x, -5, 5}]

FilledPlot[{x^2, Sin[x]}, {x, -5, 5}]

Having this input repeated back to you is not what you wanted!

The problem is that **FilledPlot** is not a built-in function; it doesn't work until you load the package FilledPlot.m. So you reread the chapter and find out that you need to type in and execute the following expression:

Needs["Graphics`FilledPlot`"]

FilledPlot::shdw : Symbol FilledPlot appears in multiple contexts
    {Graphics`FilledPlot`, Global`}; definitions in context
    Graphics`FilledPlot` may shadow or be shadowed by other definitions.

Confused by this unexpected message, you ignore it and just try your command again:

FilledPlot[{x^2, Sin[x]}, {x, -5, 5}]

FilledPlot[{x^2, Sin[x]}, {x, -5, 5}]

Loading the package seems to have had no effect! The command still doesn't work. Looking more closely at the message, you realize that this "shadow other definitions" may indicate a problem.

Here is what has happened. By using **FilledPlot** *before* loading the package, you made *Mathematica* create an instance of the symbol **FilledPlot** (sort of an empty definition). This definition was entered in the **Global`** <u>context</u>.  When you loaded FilledPlot.m, you created a new definition for **FilledPlot**, this time in a special context called **Graphics`** ⁚ **FilledPlot`**.  Unfortunately, when looking for a definition, *Mathematica* starts in the **Global`** context and looks in other contexts only if it doesn't find a definition there. By using the function once before loading the package, you unwittingly created a definition in **Global`**.

Fortunately, we can escape this mess easily. Evaluate the following command:

Remove[FilledPlot]

This removes the (empty) definition from the **Global** context, allowing the real definition to be seen. Now you can make plots:

FilledPlot[{x², Sin[x]}, {x, -5, 5}]

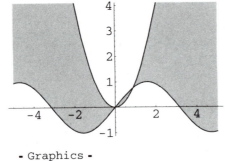

- Graphics -

As a general rule, any time you see a message about "shadowing" when you load a file, it's something to worry about. Using **Remove** on the function(s) named in the message(s) will usually get you out of trouble.

Chapter **30**

What packages are available?

Many packages are available for *Mathematica*, covering a bewildering range of topics.

- Standard packages come as part of *Mathematica*. Different versions of *Mathematica* may include different sets of standard packages. Click here for a listing of your built-in packages.

- Free packages are available from many sources, for example the *MathSource* web site at http://www.wolfram.com/mathsource/.

- Packages are for sale by Wolfram Research and others. http://www.wolfram.com/applications/index.html provides a current listing of packages for sale.

You can look at http://www.wolfram.com/community/links/ for an extensive listing of *Mathematica* related links, many of which offer *Mathematica* packages.

■ Examples of packages

To whet your appetite, below are some screen shots from a few of the packages available at the sites above. Note that the specific web addresses given below are more likely to change than are the general ones given above. If a website below doesn't work, the package may still be available; try the main site and you may be able to find the desired package in a slightly different location.

The Optica package, developed by Donald Barnhart, is available at http://www.wolfram.com/applications/optica/index.html. This package allows you to design and simulate a great variety of optical systems.

Optica.ma 1

7.4 Modeling a Cassegrain Telescope

In this section, we model a Cassegrain telescope with *Optica* including the primary and secondary mirror objectives. For this example, we combine several component functions into a special function that we call CassegrainTelescope. As inputs to CassegrainTelescope, we use the f/number of the system, the diameter of the primary mirror, the diameter of the secondary mirror, and the desired position in space of the eyepiece focal point.

We use DrawSystem to trace a circle of rays through CassegrainTelescope.

```
DrawSystem[
Move[ {Move[CircleOfRays[15 inch],{15 inch,0,180}],
   CassegrainTelescope[2.5,20 inch,4 inch,10 inch,
   OpenSide->{-.25 Pi,1.3 Pi},GraphicDesign->Solid]},
   {0,0,90}],Boxed->False];
```

100%

The Mechanical Systems pack by Robert Beretta allows you to simulate a variety of mechanical systems. It is available at http://www.wolfram.com/applications/mechsystems/index.html:

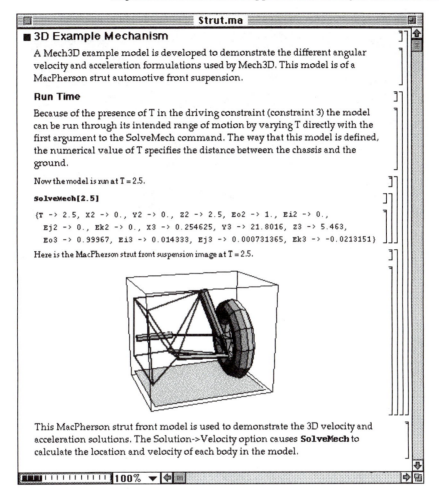

Stewart Dickson has produced many 2-D and 3-D (by which we mean actual 3-D objects) *Mathematica* graphics. Here is a small example, a stereogram, from his site at http://www.wolfram.com/~mathart/:

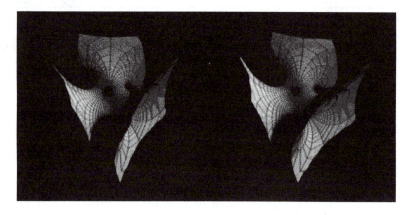

Chapter 31

How do I plot a function in two dimensions?

There are many plotting commands in *Mathematica*, but to plot functions in two dimensions you need only **Plot**:

```
Plot[x², {x, -1, 1}];
```

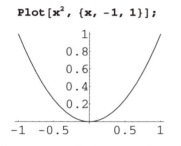

- The first argument is the expression to be plotted.
- The second argument tells *Mathematica* to use the variable **x** and let it run from **-1** to **1**.

Mathematica automatically chooses the vertical axis range and enough sample points to make the curve smooth. You can adjust or override the choices using options (click <u>here</u> or see The *Mathematica* Book for information).

If you plot a function with extreme values, such as the trig function **Tan[x]**, *Mathematica* tries to pick a reasonable vertical range:

```
Plot[Tan[x], {x, -2, 2}];
```

If you don't like the range it picks, you can adjust it with the **PlotRange** option:

$$\text{Plot}[\text{Tan}[x], \{x, -2, 2\}, \text{PlotRange} \rightarrow \{-10, 10\}];$$

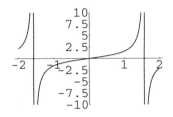

You can plot two or more functions on the same set of axes by using a list as the first argument to the **Plot** command:

$$\text{Plot}\left[\left\{\text{Sin}[x], x - \frac{x^3}{6} + \frac{x^5}{120}\right\}, \{x, -7, 7\}\right];$$

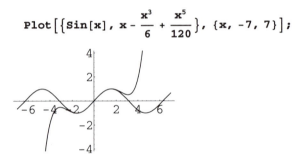

You can change the color and/or dashing pattern of the curve using the **PlotStyle** option. The following curve will be blue on a color computer:

$$\text{Plot}\left[\text{Sin}[x], \{x, -7, 7\}, \text{PlotStyle} \rightarrow \text{Hue}\left[\frac{2}{3}\right]\right];$$

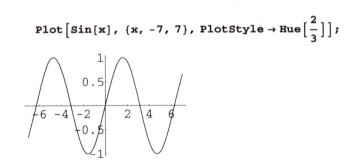

See the electronic edition of this book for a color version.

The following curve has a regular dashing pattern. Its dashes and spaces are equal in length to 0.05 times the width of the plot:

Plot[Sin[x], {x, -7, 7}, PlotStyle → Dashing[{0.05}]];

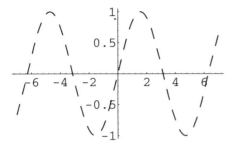

If you have several curves on the same axes, you can distinguish them using color and/or dashing patterns. In the following example the first element of the **PlotStyle** list applies to the first expression in the **Plot** command, etc.:

$$\text{Plot}\left[\left\{\text{Sin}[x],\ x - \frac{x^3}{6} + \frac{x^5}{120}\right\},\right.$$

$$\left.\{x, -7, 7\},\ \text{PlotStyle} \rightarrow \left\{\text{Hue}\left[\frac{2}{3}\right],\ \text{Hue}\left[\frac{1}{3}\right]\right\}\right];$$

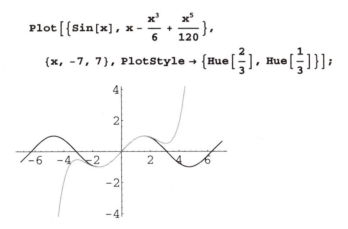

See the electronic edition of this book for a color version.

You can label the plot using the **PlotLabel** option:

Plot[Sin[x], {x, 0, 2 π}, PlotLabel → "The Sine Function"];

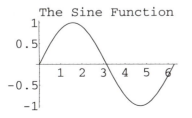

You can label the axes using the **AxesLabel** option:

```
Plot[Sin[x], {x, 0, 2 π}, AxesLabel → {"x", "Sin[x]"}];
```

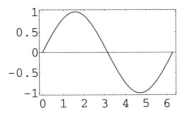

You can put a frame around the whole plot:

```
Plot[Sin[x], {x, 0, 2 π}, Frame → True];
```

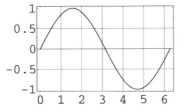

You can superimpose grid lines (by default, blue):

```
Plot[Sin[x], {x, 0, 2 π}, Frame → True, GridLines → Automatic];
```

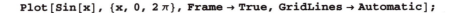

You can change the fonts used in the plot. Fonts are specified as a list; the first element is the font name, and the second element is the point size. In the next example we specify a font to use for all text in the plot:

```
Plot[Sin[x], {x, 0, 2 π}, DefaultFont → {"Helvetica", 18}];
```

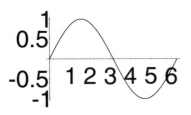

The naming of fonts is a very delicate issue. *Mathematica* uses PostScript to generate all its graphics, so fonts must be named in the PostScript way. This is not always the same way fonts are named in other programs on your computer. For example to get an *Italic Times* font, you need to use "Times-Italic", but to get an *Italic Helvetica* you have to use "Helvetica-Oblique". In general it is impossible to predict how any given font will handle style variations; you have to look up each one in an Adobe font catalog.

To change the font of an individual text element (label, tick mark, etc.), use the **FontForm** command. **FontForm** takes two arguments—the text or expression to be displayed, and a font specification.

```
Plot[Sin[x], {x, 0, 2 π}, PlotLabel →
    FontForm["The Sine Function", {"Times-BoldItalic", 16}]];
```

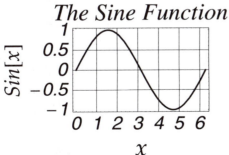

Of course, these options can be combined in the same plot. (Some options don't go well together. For example, **AxesLabel** is not useful combined with **Frame->True**, because there are no axes when there is a frame. Use **FrameLabel** instead.)

```
Plot[Sin[x], {x, 0, 2 π}, PlotStyle → Thickness[0.01],
    Frame → True, GridLines → Automatic, PlotLabel →
     FontForm["The Sine Function", {"Times-Italic", 18}],
     FrameLabel → {FontForm["x", {"Palatino-Italic", 18}],
      FontForm["Sin[x]", {"Palatino-Italic", 16}]},
    DefaultFont → {"Helvetica-Oblique", 14}];
```

Mathematica normally displays all plots with an aspect ratio (ratio of height/width) of about $\frac{1}{1.6}$ ($\frac{1}{\text{Golden Ratio}}$). Sometimes you may want to override this, which you can do using the **AspectRatio** option. For example, the following plot looks crowded:

Plot[Sin[x], {x, 0, 40 π}];

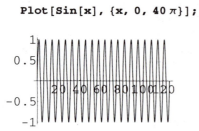

It would look better wider (that is, with a smaller aspect ratio):

Plot[Sin[x], {x, 0, 40 π}, AspectRatio → 0.2];

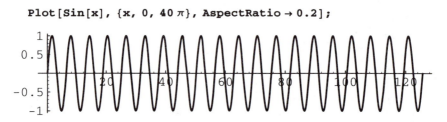

In the following example, the physical slope of the line is different from what we might expect from the equation:

Plot[2 x, {x, 0, 5}];

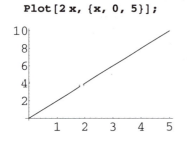

This happened because the default aspect ratio gives us different scales in the horizontal and vertical directions. The setting **AspectRatio→Automatic** tells *Mathematica* to use the same scale for both axes:

Plot[2 x, {x, 0, 5}, AspectRatio → Automatic];

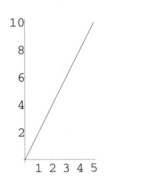

■ Discussion

Jerry: Many graphing programs have a Zoom feature that allows you to magnify a plot around some chosen point. How do we do this in *Mathematica*?

Theo: By changing the numbers in the **Plot** command. Start with this plot:

Plot[{Sin[x], Cos[x]}, {x, 0, 2 π}];

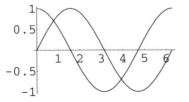

You might like to look closely at a point where the lines cross, so you change the **x** range:

Plot[{Sin[x], Cos[x]}, {x, 0.7, 0.9}];

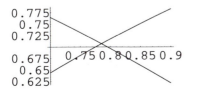

Jerry: How did you choose those two values, `0.7` and `0.9`?

Theo: I used the coordinate display feature in the front end. To use this feature, click on a graph. A bounding box will appear around the graph. Hold down the Command key (Macintosh or NeXT) or the Alt key (Windows) and move the mouse over the graph. You will see the mouse-pointer coordinates at the bottom of the window.

Jerry: That's nice. I suppose you could use the same feature to see where the curves cross.

I like using the option `AspectRatio→Automatic` because circles look like circles, not ovals. The slopes of straight lines also look correct. Why isn't this option set by default?

Theo: Try plotting `8x`. *Most* plots are likely to be much too tall or much too wide with an automatic aspect ratio.

Chapter **32**

How do I plot a parametric equation in two dimensions?

The **ParametricPlot** command is much like the **Plot** command:

ParametricPlot[{t², t}, {t, -2, 2}];

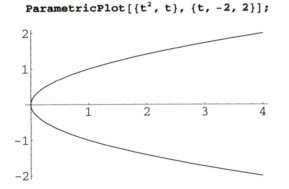

• The first argument is a list of two functions that specify the *x* and *y* coordinates as a function of the single parameter, **t**. Here *x* is **t²** and *y* is **t**.
• The second argument specifies the range of the parameter. Here **t** goes from **-2** to **2**.

If you want to plot more than one parametric equation on the same set of axes, you can give **ParametricPlot** a list of two lists of functions. For example:

ParametricPlot[{{t³, t²}, {t², t³}, {Cos[t], Sin[t]}}, {t, -π, π}];

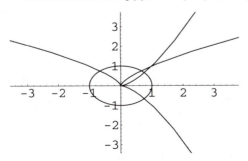

Most of the options that can be used with **Plot** (explained in <u>Chapter</u> 31) can also be used with **ParametricPlot**. For example, the option **AspectRatio→Automatic** can be used to force the horizontal and vertical directions to be scaled uniformly:

```
ParametricPlot[{{t³, t²}, {t², t³}, {Cos[t], Sin[t]}},
    {t, -π, π}, AspectRatio → Automatic];
```

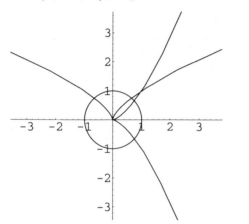

The option **PlotStyle** can be used, for example, to draw one of the curves dashed:

```
ParametricPlot[{{t³, t²}, {t², t³}}, {t, -2, 2},
    AspectRatio → Automatic, PlotStyle → {{}, Dashing[{0.02}]}];
```

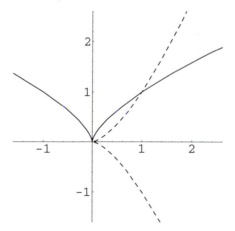

Many people use parametric plots when they want to plot non-functions (such as the first example in this chapter, which is not a function because a vertical line at any positive value of *x* will intersect two branches). An alternative approach is to use implicit plot, described in <u>Chapter</u> 34.

See The *Mathematica* Book or <u>Chapter</u> 31 for more information about plotting options.

Chapter **33**

How do I plot in polar coordinates?

To make a polar plot, you first need to execute the following command:

Needs["Graphics`Graphics`"];

(Note that the two single quotes used here are "back quotes" usually found on the same key with ~. They are *not* the single quotes found on the double-quote key.)

The **Needs** command loads the standard package Graphics.m, which is included in all copies of *Mathematica*. The package defines a variety of useful graphics functions, including **PolarPlot**.

PolarPlot is similar to **Plot**:

PolarPlot[t, {t, 0, 2 π}];

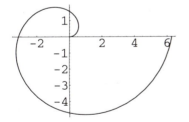

- The first argument is the radial function.
- The second argument specifies the range of the angular variable **t**, in this case from **0** to **2Pi**.

If you want to plot more than one function on the same set of axes, you can give **PolarPlot** a list of functions as its first argument:

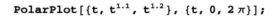

PolarPlot[{t, t$^{1.1}$, t$^{1.2}$}, {t, 0, 2 π}];

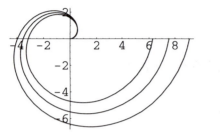

PolarPlot automatically makes the horizontal and vertical scales equal, so that a circle looks like a circle, not an oval:

PolarPlot[1, {t, 0, 2 π}];

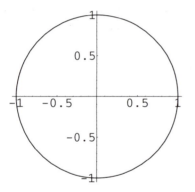

PolarPlot can take most of the same options as **Plot**. See The *Mathematica* Book or Chapter 31 for more information about plotting options.

The coordinate display feature described in Chapter 31 also works for plots generated by **PolarPlot**, but the points will be displayed in Cartesian coordinates instead of polar.

Chapter 34

How do I plot implicitly-defined functions?

To make plots of implicitly-defined functions, you first need to execute the following command:

```
Needs["Graphics`ImplicitPlot`"];
```

(Note that the two single quotes used here are "back quotes" usually found on the same key with ~. They are *not* the single quotes found on the double-quote key.)

The **Needs** command loads the standard package ImplicitPlot.m, which is included in all copies of *Mathematica*. This package defines the function **ImplicitPlot** (written by the late Jerry Keiper and based on an idea by Dan Grayson).

ImplicitPlot is similar to **Plot** except that, instead of an expression involving only one variable, you give it an equation involving two variables (conventionally, **x** and **y**). Here is an example:

```
ImplicitPlot[x² + y² == 16, {x, -5, 5}];
```

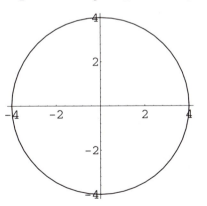

- The first argument is the equation to be plotted. Note that in *Mathematica* equality is denoted by a double-equal symbol (**==**).
- The second argument gives the range of the horizontal variable. *Mathematica* automatically chooses a suitable range for the other variable.

Here are a few more examples that can be made with this command.

The ellipse:

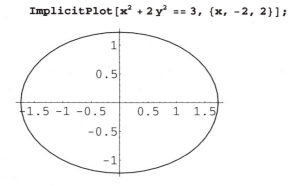

The lemniscate:

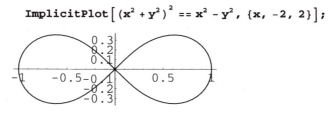

The folium of Descartes:

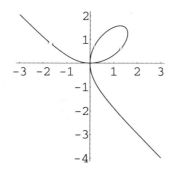

You can plot two equations on the same set of axes by giving **ImplicitPlot** a list of two equations as its first argument:

$$\texttt{ImplicitPlot}\left[\left\{(x^2+y^2)^2 == x^2-y^2,\ (x^2+y^2)^2 == 2\,x\,y\right\},\ \{x,\ -2,\ 2\}\right];$$

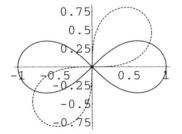

The **PlotStyle** option can be used to distinguish the curves from each other. **PlotStyle** is explained in Chapter 31.

$$\texttt{ImplicitPlot}\left[\left\{(x^2+y^2)^2 == x^2-y^2,\ (x^2+y^2)^2 == 2\,x\,y\right\},\right.$$
$$\left.\{x,\ -2,\ 2\},\ \texttt{PlotStyle} \rightarrow \{\texttt{Dashing}[\{\}],\ \texttt{Dashing}[\{.01\}]\}\right];$$

When used in the form described so far, **ImplicitPlot** must be able to solve the equations for one or the other variable. In certain cases this is not possible. For example:

```
ImplicitPlot[x^y == y^x, {x, 0, 5}]
```

Solve::dinv : The expression x^{1-y} involves unknowns in more
    than one argument, so inverse functions cannot be used.

ImplicitPlot::epfail :
  Equation $x^y == y^x$ could not be solved for points to plot.

```
ImplicitPlot[x^y == y^x, {x, 0, 5}]
```

In cases such as this, you can make **ImplicitPlot** use a completely different technique by giving it a third argument that specifies the range for the second variable. For example:

ImplicitPlot[x^y == y^x, {x, 0, 5}, {y, 0, 5}];

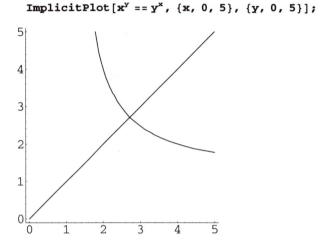

When used in this form, **ImplicitPlot** does not try to solve the equations. Instead it evaluates both sides on a regular grid across the *x-y* plane, and draws lines along where the difference between the two sides changes sign. (It uses the built-in function **ContourPlot** to do this. The interested reader should consult The *Mathematica* Book for more information about **ContourPlot**. Options added to **ImplicitPlot** will be passed on to **ContourPlot**.)

Generally, the three-argument form of **ImplicitPlot** is quite slow and produces plots with non-smooth curves. On the other hand, the three-argument form is able to plot just about any equation, including many that the two-argument form can't. So it is often sensible to try the two-argument form first; if it doesn't work, switch to the slower three-argument form.

Chapter **35**

How do I show the area between curves?

To show the area between two curves (or the area between one curve and the x-axis), you first need to execute the following command:

Needs["Graphics`FilledPlot`"];

(Note that the two single quotes used here are "back quotes" usually found on the same key with ~. They are *not* the single quotes found on the double-quote key.)

The **Needs** command loads the standard package FilledPlot.m, which is included in all copies of *Mathematica* Version 4. The package defines **FilledPlot** (written by John M. Novak).

FilledPlot is similar to **Plot**. The following command plots the area between x^2 and the x axis:

FilledPlot[x², {x, -2, 2}];

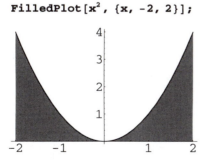

- The first argument is the expression to be plotted.
- The second argument tells *Mathematica* to use the variable **x** and let it run from **-2** to **2**.

If we give **FilledPlot** a list of two elements as its first argument, the resulting plot shows the area between these two curves:

FilledPlot[{x, x^2}, {x, -1, 2}];

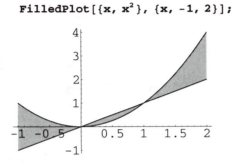

Note that both positive and negative areas are shown.

Here are some more examples:

FilledPlot[{Abs[x], Sin[x]}, {x, -2, 2}];

FilledPlot$\left[\left\{\dfrac{x^2 - 4}{x - 2}, \text{Sin[x]}\right\}, \{x, -5, 2\}\right]$;

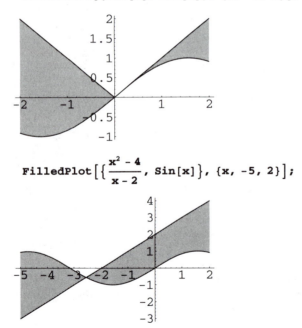

You can give **FilledPlot** a list of more than two functions, and the areas between successive functions will be colored automatically.

FilledPlot[{x, x^2, x^3, x^4}, {x, -1, 2}];

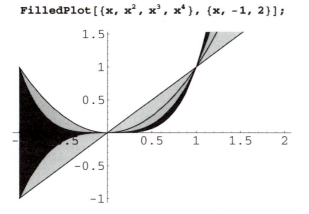

FilledPlot can take most of the same options that **Plot** can: See <u>Chapter</u> 31 or The *Mathematica* Book for more information. Several options are unique to **FilledPlot**; see the standard package documentation that comes with each copy of *Mathematica*, or click here for more information.

Chapter **36**

How do I plot complex numbers?

It is conventional to plot complex numbers as points in the *x-y* plane, with the real component along the x-axis and the imaginary component along the y-axis. There are no built-in plotting functions to do this in *Mathematica*, but we've written some for you.

In this chapter, we'll define three functions—one to plot lists of complex numbers, one to plot a complex-valued function, and one to plot the roots of a polynomial.

■ ComplexListPlot

This function plots a list of complex numbers as points in the *x-y* plane. It accepts all the same options as **ListPlot**.

```
ComplexListPlot[points_, options___] :=
 ListPlot[Map[{Re[#1], Im[#1]} &, points],
  options, AxesLabel → {"Re", "Im"}]
```

Here is an example:

```
ComplexListPlot[{-1 + I, 2 + I, 1 - 2 I}];
```

Since few of us can see these points on our computer screens, a good idea is to make our points bigger:

```
ComplexListPlot[
   {-1 + I, 2 + I, 1 - 2 I}, PlotStyle → PointSize[0.02]];
```

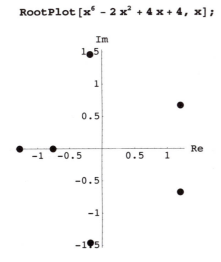

▪ RootPlot

This function plots the roots of a polynomial as points in the *x-y* plane. It uses the definition of `ComplexListPlot` above, so be sure to evaluate it first.

```
RootPlot[expr_, x_] :=
  ComplexListPlot[x /. N[Solve[expr == 0, x]],
     AspectRatio → Automatic, PlotStyle -> PointSize[0.04]]
```

Here is an example of a polynomial:

```
RootPlot[x^6 - 2 x^2 + 4 x + 4, x];
```

Amusing circles can be made by plotting the roots of unity:

```
RootPlot[x^20 - 1, x];
```

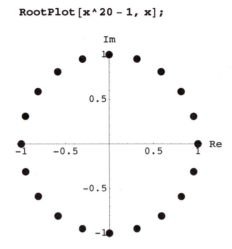

This last section shows clearly the advantage of the electronic version of this book. If you have *Mathematica* and the electronic version, you can run thousands of experiments on different polynomials. With the paper book, you can read our two miserable examples. You choose.

■ ComplexPlot3D

This function plots complex-valued functions in three dimensions. The x and y axes represent the real and imaginary components of the input. The z axis represents the magnitude (absolute value) of the output, and the color represents the complex phase angle of the output. (As usual, you don't have to *understand* this function in order to *use* it. Just evaluate the two cells and be on your way.)

```
complexToHeightandColor[z_] := Block[{nz, az},
    nz = N[z]; az = Abs[nz];
    {az, Hue[(π + If[nz == 0, 0, Arg[nz/az]]) / (2 π)]}]

ComplexPlot3D[f_, {z_, zmin_, zmax_}, options___] :=
  Plot3D[complexToHeightandColor[f /. z -> (x + y I)],
    {x, Re[zmin], Re[zmax]}, {y, Im[zmin], Im[zmax]}, options]
```

The range is specified as two complex numbers, representing the lower left and upper right corners of the complex plane. The following example plots a function over the region -1 to 1 and -*i* to *i*:

ComplexPlot3D[z³, {z, -1 - I, 1 + I}];

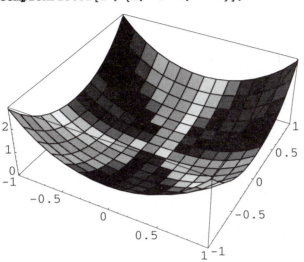

Chapter **37**

How do I plot a function in three dimensions?

Plotting in three dimensions is one of the great pleasures of *Mathematica*. The command you need to know in order to plot functions of two variables in three dimensions is **Plot3D**:

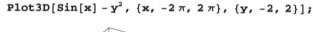

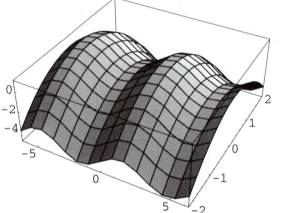

(In the electronic edition of this book, this and all subsequent plots are in color.)

• The first argument is the expression to be plotted. You can think of it as the right hand side of $z = f(x, y)$.
• The second argument says use **x** as one variable, going from **-2π** to **2π**.
• The third argument says use **y** as the other variable, going from **-2** to **2**.

By default the function is plotted on a 15 by 15 grid, and each patch is colored (shaded in the print version) according to a simple reflected-light model (more details in the <u>Coloring</u> section later in this chapter).

Mathematica puts 3-D plots in a box. The orientation of this box is determined by the viewpoint from which it is being observed. With the default viewpoint, the orientation has the following features:

- the *x* scale is roughly horizontal in the front left, with *x* values increasing to the right
- the *y* scale runs roughly front to back on the right, with *y* values increasing to the back
- the *z* scale runs vertically on the left, with *z* values increasing upward.

This means that the *x-y* plane in the plot is seen about the same way as a piece of *x-y* graph paper lying on a table in front of you, with the *y* axis increasing away from you and the *x* axis increasing to the right. (Some programs that make 3-D plots choose a default viewpoint such that the *x* axis increases from the back to the front left, and the *y* axis increases from the back to the front right.) With *Mathematica*'s default viewpoint, it is easy to go from a 2-D plot to a 3-D plot to see how they relate to each other.

If you look at the front vertical face of the plot, you'll see something that looks like a sine wave. On this plane the horizontal axis is *x* and the vertical axis is *z*. It makes sense that you would see a sine wave, since the function at that plane is `z = Sin[x] - 2`^{2}.

All the features described above can be changed using options for the `Plot3D` command. The most useful of these options are described below; the rest are described in The *Mathematica* Book.

▪ Real-time 3-D rotation

One of the most exciting new features in *Mathematica* V4.0 is the ability to rotate 3-D graphics in real time. Before we show you how, a note about how graphics are handled in *Mathematica*: By default, all graphics output is generated as PostScript text, which is then rendered in the front end to display the image. PostScript is a graphics language used in many printers; its main purpose is to allow very high quality display and printing of images on any sort of output device (be it screen, printer, phototypesetter, etc.).

By using PostScript to represent graphics, *Mathematica* ensures that you can print your notebook on any sort of printer and get a very high quality result for 3-D graphics. Unfortunately, it also ensures that you can't rotate the graphic except by regenerating the entire PostScript representation from scratch, which is very slow.

To get around this limitation, in V4.0 we introduce a new method for generating 3-D graphics. It sacrifices the resolution-independent high quality representation for one that can be rotated in real time. To get a rotatable 3-D graph, you need to execute the following command, which puts you in real-time mode:

```
<< RealTime3D`
```

From now on, any 3-D graphics you generate will come out in rotatable mode. For example:

```
Plot3D[Sin[x] - y², {x, -2 π, 2 π}, {y, -2, 2}];
```

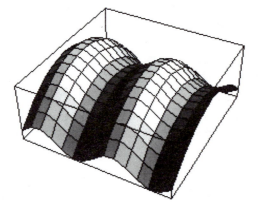

Note that the graph looks quite similar to the one above, except that the axis labels are missing, and in the printed version it looks blocky. Both of these are limitations that will be removed in future versions (in fact, if you're reading this in the electronic edition of this book, and you have a version of *Mathematica* newer than that of the authors, you might be seeing axis labels and wondering what we are talking about.)

To rotate the graph, click on it and drag the mouse in whatever direction you want to rotate. There's really no way we can show this in a printed book, so you'll have to take our word for it.

If you do require high quality printing of a graphic, you can switch back to PostScript output with the following command:

```
<< Default3D`
```

In the sections below we'll discuss various options that control 3-D plotting. In general these options apply to both kinds of 3-D output unless otherwise noted. For the purposes of printing this book, we're going to use the PostScript mode, since it looks better on paper.

■ Fineness of the grid

Here is an example of a plot that does not come out very well with the default settings:

```
Plot3D[Sin[x Sin[x y]], {x, 0, 4}, {y, 0, 3}];
```

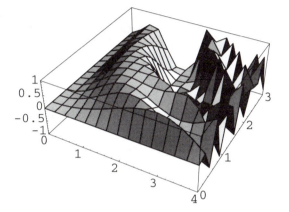

The left side is reasonable, but it's hard to tell what's happening on the right side. We can use the **PlotPoints** option to help resolve the shape:

```
Plot3D[Sin[x Sin[x y]], {x, 0, 4}, {y, 0, 3}, PlotPoints → 50];
```

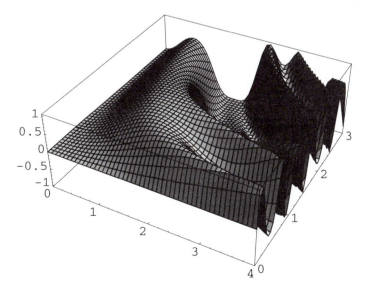

The grid has been increased to 50 by 50 from the default 15 by 15.

At this point we should warn you that making 3-D plots with a large number of plot points can require a large amount of memory. This has become less a problem in recent years as memory prices have come down, and most computers today should have no problem making plots of at least 100 by 100. However, the memory required goes up as the square of the number of plot points, so you'll reach a limit sooner or later. Try making a variety of different 3-D plots to learn how large a plot you can make with your particular computer. Try a simple plot first, then increase the plot points until things stop working well.

When using real-time rotation mode, the more plot points you specify the slower the plot will rotate for you. Again, try some experiments to see what is practical with your computer.

■ Viewpoint

The following plot is a little hard to decipher (**zeta** means the Riemann ζ function):

Plot3D[Abs[Zeta[y + x I]], {x, 1, 60}, {y, -1, 1}, PlotPoints → 40];

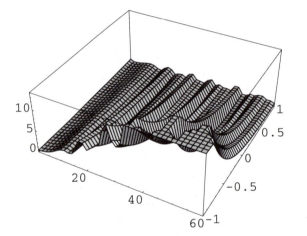

Changing to a different viewpoint can help us to see it better. This is a good place to use the real-time rotation mode:

```
<< RealTime3D`

Plot3D[Abs[Zeta[y + x I]], {x, 1, 60}, {y, -1, 1}, PlotPoints → 40];
```

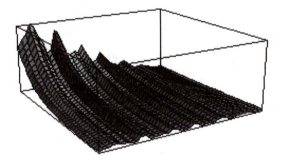

Here we've used the mouse to rotate the plot to an angle that seems pleasing.

If you want to generate a PostScript version of a 3-D plot, you can use the **ViewPoint** option to specify the (x, y, z) coordinates of the point from which the plot should be viewed:

```
<< Default3D`

Plot3D[Abs[Zeta[y + x I]], {x, 1, 60}, {y, -1, 1},
    PlotPoints → 40, ViewPoint → {2.005, 2.664, 0.580}];
```

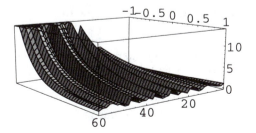

You can type in a **ViewPoint** option manually, but it's a lot easier to use the automatic 3-D viewpoint selector. The 3-D **ViewPoint Selector** command in the **Input** menu brings up a panel that lets you choose a viewpoint by moving a cube with the mouse. Here is what the panel looks like on a Macintosh:

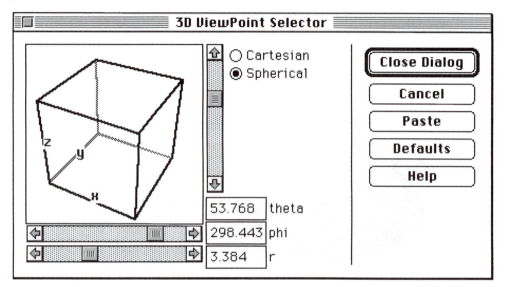

Its appearance is similar on other types of computers.

To use this panel, first type out your **Plot3D** command. For example:

$$\texttt{Plot3D[x}^2 - \texttt{y}^2, \texttt{ \{x, -5, 5\}, \{y, -5, 5\}];}$$

Add a comma just before the closing square bracket:

$$\texttt{Plot3D[x}^2 - \texttt{y}^2, \texttt{ \{x, -5, 5\}, \{y, -5, 5\},];}$$

Leave the text insertion point (flashing vertical bar) where it is, just before the square bracket, and then open the 3-D viewpoint selector (either with the menu or by using its command-key equivalent, Command-Shift-V).

Click on the cube and hold down the mouse button while moving the mouse around. The cube will rotate in response to your movements. Once you have gotten to a good viewpoint, release the mouse button. Then click the Paste button. The dialog box will be hidden, and an appropriate **ViewPoint** option will be inserted into your **Plot3D** command. It should look like this (with different numbers, depending on the viewpoint you selected):

$$\texttt{Plot3D[x}^2 - \texttt{y}^2, \texttt{ \{x, -5, 5\},}$$
$$\texttt{\{y, -5, 5\}, ViewPoint} \rightarrow \texttt{\{1.300, -2.400, 2.000\}];}$$

Now you can evaluate this expression in the normal way.

You can use the **ViewPoint** option in both PostScript and real-time rotatable graphics modes. In the case of real-time rotatable output, the **ViewPoint** option determines the initial view-point, and you are free to rotate the graphic after it has been generated.

▪ Coloring

By default, *Mathematica* colors plots according to a simple lighting model. There are, also by default, three colored lights (red, green, and blue) at three locations. The color of each patch on the surface is determined by the light it reflects to the viewer from each light source. This means that the color depends mainly on the orientation of the patch relative to the lights.

This lighting model sometimes results in poorly colored plots. For example, the first plot in this chapter has a fairly uniform color across the whole surface (visible in the printed version of this book as a uniform shade of gray). If we add the option **Lighting→False** to the **Plot3D** command, *Mathematica* will color the plot with shades of gray increasing in bright-ness as the *z* value increases:

Plot3D[Sin[x] - y², {x, -2 π, 2 π}, {y, -2, 2}, Lighting → False];

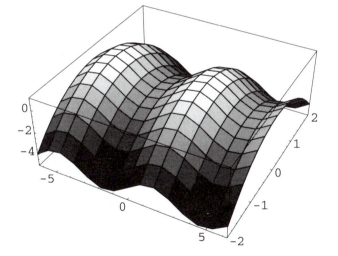

We can also specify the coloring manually for each point on the surface. If the first argument to the **Plot3D** command is a list of two elements, then the first element will be taken as the *z*-value, and the second element will be taken as a color specification. There are many different ways of specifying colors, including **GrayLevel**, **RGBColor**, and **Hue**; they are explained in detail in The *Mathematica* Book. It can be tricky to get a good-looking manual color specification. Here is one:

$$\texttt{Plot3D}\Big[\Big\{\texttt{Sin[x] - y}^2\texttt{, Hue}\Big[\frac{\texttt{Sin[x] - y}^2}{\texttt{6}}\Big]\Big\}\texttt{, \{x, -2}\,\pi\texttt{, 2}\,\pi\}\texttt{, \{y, -2, 2\}}\Big]\texttt{;}$$

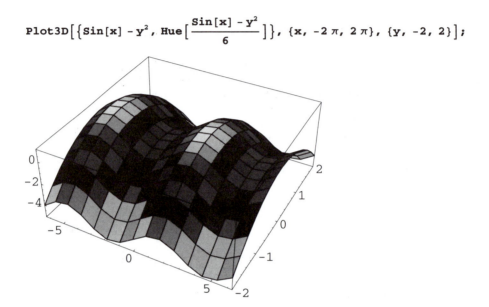

Note that coloring a surface this way does not work in real-time rotation mode.

Chapter **38**

How do I plot a parametric equation in three dimensions?

There are two forms of **ParametricPlot3D**. Which form to use depends on whether you want space curves or surfaces. To make a space curve, use the following form:

```
ParametricPlot3D[{t, t³, t²}, {t, -1, 1}];
```

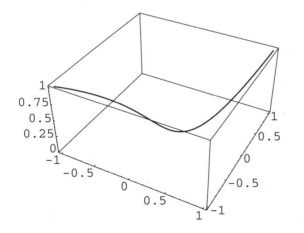

- The first argument is a list of three functions that specify the x, y, and z coordinates as a function of the single parameter, **t**. In this case x is **t**, y is **t³**, and z is **t²**.
- The second argument specifies the range of the parameter. In this case **t** goes from **-1** to **1**.

As with 3-D surfaces, you can use the new real-time rotation mode in V4.0 to view parametric functions (see <u>Chapter</u> 37 for more information about real-time rotation mode).

```
<< RealTime3D`
```

```
ParametricPlot3D[{t, t³, t²}, {t, -1, 1}];
```

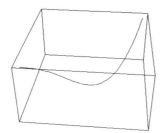

We'll continue using PostScript graphics mode in this chapter, because it looks better in printed form.

```
<< Default3D`
```

To make a surface, use the following form, with two range specifications:

```
ParametricPlot3D[{u² , v, u v}, {u, -1, 1}, {v, -1, 1}];
```

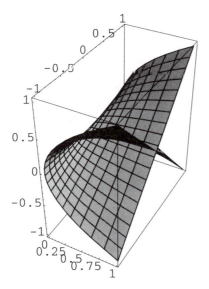

• The first argument is a list of three functions that specify the *x*, *y*, and *z* coordinates as a function of the two parameters **u** and **v**. In this case *x* is **u²**, *y* is **v**, and *z* is **uv**.
• The second argument specifies the range of the first parameter. In this case **u** goes from -1 to 1.
• The third argument specifies the range of the second parameter. In this case **v** goes from -1 to 1.

If you want to plot more than one parametric equation on the same set of axes, you can give **ParametricPlot3D** a list of two lists of functions. For example:

ParametricPlot3D[{{t, t³, t²}, {t², t, t³}}, {t, -1, 1}];

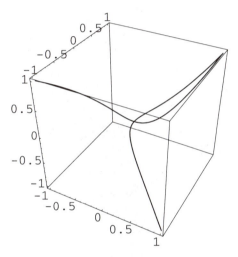

ParametricPlot3D[
   {{u, -v², v}, {u, v, u² v²}}, {u, -1, 1}, {v, -1, 1}];

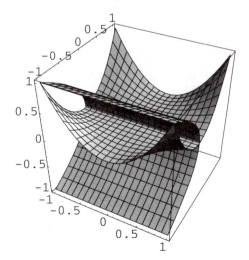

Most of the options that can be used with **Plot3D** (which are explained in <u>Chapter</u> 37) can also be used with **ParametricPlot3D**. For example, the following options remove the bounding box and axes:

```
ParametricPlot3D[{{u, -v², v}, {u, v, u² v²}},
    {u, -1, 1}, {v, -1, 1}, Boxed → False, Axes → None];
```

It is OK to have surfaces that intersect themselves. For example:

$$\texttt{ParametricPlot3D}\Big[\Big\{\texttt{u\,Cos[v], -v\,Sin[u], } \frac{\texttt{u\,v}}{\texttt{4}}\Big\}\texttt{, \{u, -2\,}\pi\texttt{, 2\,}\pi\texttt{\},}$$

$$\texttt{\{v, -2\,}\pi\texttt{, 2\,}\pi\texttt{\}, Boxed} \rightarrow \texttt{False, Axes} \rightarrow \texttt{None, PlotPoints} \rightarrow \texttt{\{80, 40\}}\Big]\texttt{;}$$

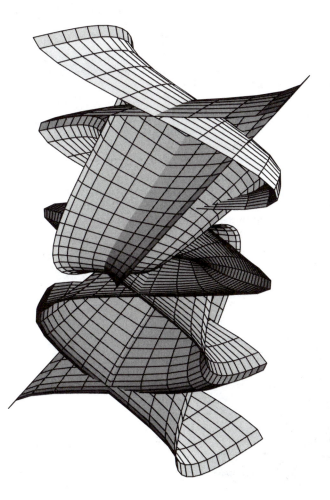

Surfaces that intersect themselves many times can take a very long time to render. This is a good surface to try in real-time rotation mode (see Chapter 37 for more information about real-time rotation mode).

Chapter **39**

How do I plot 3-D implicitly-defined functions?

There is no built-in function for plotting implicitly-defined functions, but it's quite easy to create such plots using the 3-D contour plotting function. First, you need to load the appropriate package by evaluating the following command:

Needs["Graphics`ContourPlot3D`"]

(Note that the two single quotes used here are "back quotes" usually found on the same key with ~. They are *not* the single quotes found on the double-quote key.)

This package defines **ContourPlot3D**, which is able to plot multiple contours of a function of three parameters. To plot the value where $f = g$, you can equivalently plot the contour where $f - g = 0$. Since the default for **ContourPlot3D** is to plot a single contour at zero, there is no need to specify which contours you want. Here we plot the sphere $x^2 + y^2 + z^2 = 1$:

ContourPlot3D[x^2 + y^2 + z^2 - 1, {x, -1, 1}, {y, -1, 1}, {z, -1, 1}];

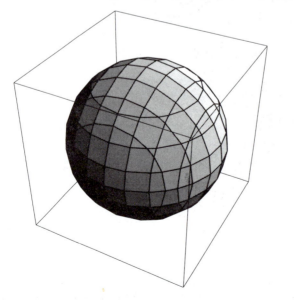

The following function allows us to use the *f* = *g* notation explicitly:

```
ImplicitPlot3D[f_ == g_, args___] := ContourPlot3D[f - g, args];
```

Here are a set of examples you can try. Use real-time rotation mode if you want to be able to spin them around (see Chapter 37 for more information about real-time rotation mode):

```
<< RealTime3D`
```

```
ImplicitPlot3D[Abs[x y z] == 0.1,
  {x, -1, 1}, {y, -1, 1}, {z, -1, 1}];
```

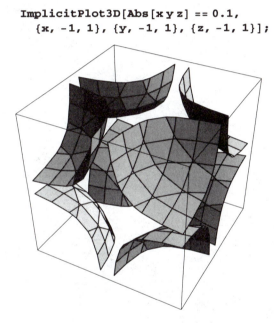

```
ImplicitPlot3D[Sin[x y] == z^2, {x, -π, π},
  {y, -π, π}, {z, -1, 1}, PlotPoints -> {5, 7}];
```

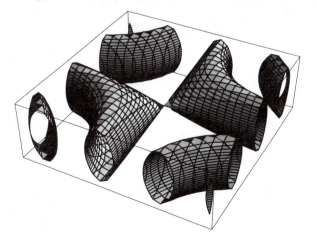

```
ImplicitPlot3D[Sin[x] + Sin[y] == Sin[z], {x, -6.3, 6.3},
   {y, -6.3, 6.3}, {z, -6.3, 6.3}, PlotPoints -> {5, 7}];
```

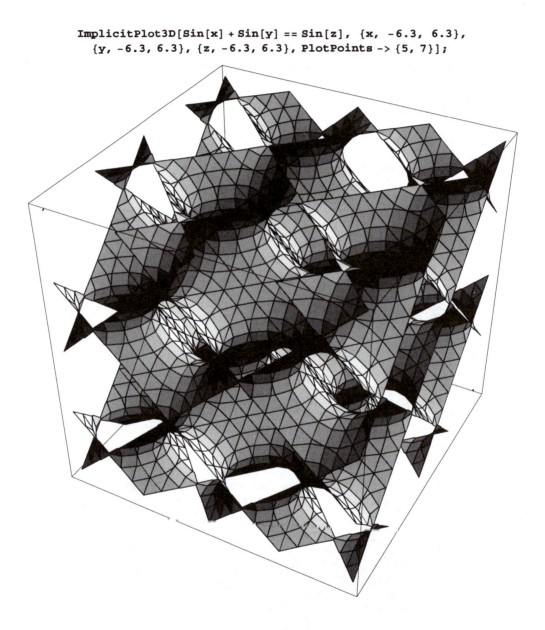

Chapter **40**

How do I plot in cylindrical and spherical coordinates?

To make a cylindrical or spherical coordinate plot, you first need to execute the following command:

Needs["Graphics`ParametricPlot3D`"];

(Note that the two single quotes used here are "back quotes" usually found on the same key with ~. They are *not* the single quotes found on the double-quote key.)

This command loads the standard package `ParametricPlot3D.m`, which is included in all copies of *Mathematica*. The package contains definitions for a variety of useful graphics functions, including **CylindricalPlot3D** and **SphericalPlot3D**.

CylindricalPlot3D is similar to **Plot3D**:

$$\textbf{CylindricalPlot3D}\left[\frac{1}{2}\, \textbf{r}^2\, \textbf{Sin[2 t]},\ \{\textbf{r, 0, 1}\},\ \{\textbf{t, 0, 2}\,\pi\}\right];$$

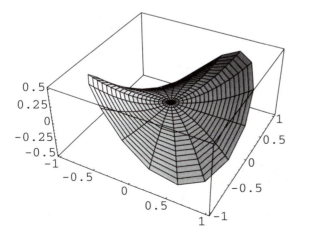

- The first argument gives *z* as a function of radius and angle from *x* axis.
- The second argument gives the radius parameter **r**, going from **0** to **1**.
- The third argument gives the angle parameter **t**, going from **0** to **2π**.

You can change the ranges to plot only part of the surface:

$$\texttt{CylindricalPlot3D}\left[\frac{1}{2}\,\mathbf{r}^2\,\texttt{Sin[2 t]},\;\{\mathbf{r},\;.5,\;1\},\;\left\{\mathbf{t},\;0,\;\frac{3\,\pi}{2}\right\}\right];$$

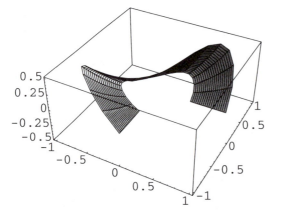

SphericalPlot3D is also similar to **Plot3D**:

$$\texttt{SphericalPlot3D[2 + Sin[3 t] Sin[3 p], \{t, 0, }\pi\texttt{\}, \{p, 0, 2 }\pi\texttt{\}];}$$

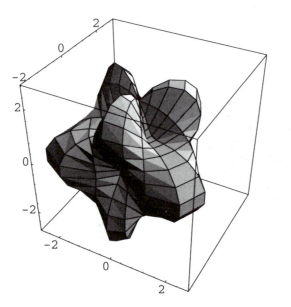

- The first argument gives the radius as a function of theta (**t**) and phi (**p**).
- The second argument gives the range for **t**, the angle from the *z* axis.
- The third argument gives the range for **p**, the angle from the *x* axis in the *x-y* plane.

You can specify only a portion of the full surface:

$$\texttt{SphericalPlot3D}\left[\texttt{2 + Sin[3 t] Sin[3 p]},\ \left\{\texttt{t},\ \frac{\pi}{2},\ \pi\right\},\ \left\{\texttt{p},\ 0,\ \frac{3\pi}{2}\right\}\right];$$

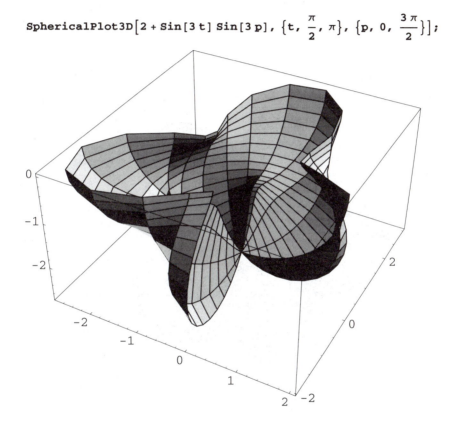

Both **SphericalPlot3D** and **CylindricalPlot3D** can take most of the same options as **Plot3D**, described in <u>Chapter</u> 37. For example, you can change the number of grid points using the **PlotPoints** option:

```
SphericalPlot3D[2 + Sin[3 t] Sin[3 p],
    {t, 0, π}, {p, 0, 2 π}, PlotPoints → {40, 60}];
```

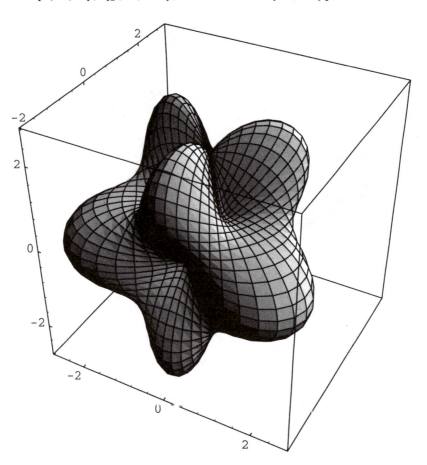

These are all good examples of plots to view in real-time rotation mode. Evaluate the following command to go into real-time mode, then re-evaluate the examples:

```
<< RealTime3D`
```

(See <u>Chapter</u> 37 for more information about real-time rotation mode.)

Chapter **41**

How do I make contour and density plots?

The functions **Plot3D**, **ContourPlot**, and **DensityPlot** can be used almost interchangeably. Here is the same function plotted with each of these three functions:

Plot3D[Sin[x y], {x, 0, 3}, {y, 0, 3}];

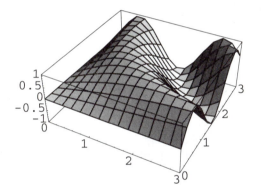

ContourPlot[Sin[x y], {x, 0, 3}, {y, 0, 3}];

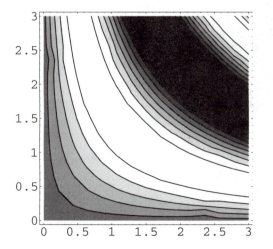

DensityPlot[Sin[x y], {x, 0, 3}, {y, 0, 3}];

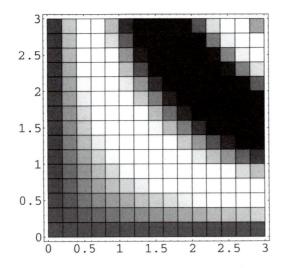

In each case:
- the first argument gives *z* as a function of *x* and *y*
- the second argument gives the *x* range; in this case from 0 to 3
- the third argument gives the *y* range; in this case from 0 to 3.

ContourPlot and **DensityPlot** can take most of the same options as **Plot3D**, which are described in <u>Chapter</u> 37. For example, the **PlotPoints** option can be used to increase the resolution of the plots:

ContourPlot[Sin[x y], {x, 0, 3}, {y, 0, 3}, PlotPoints → 30];

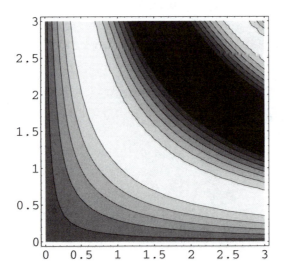

DensityPlot[Sin[x y], {x, 0, 3}, {y, 0, 3}, PlotPoints → 30];

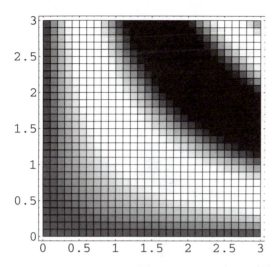

Particularly in the case of **ContourPlot** it is often necessary to adjust several options to get a good-looking plot.

One of the most useful options to use with **DensityPlot** is **Mesh → False**. This allows us to make much higher resolution plots. Consider this example:

DensityPlot$\left[\text{Sin}\left[\frac{x}{y}\right], \{x, -10, 10\}, \{y, -5, 5\}, \text{PlotPoints} \to 500\right]$;

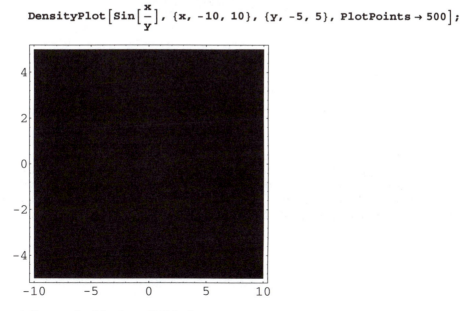

The mesh lines make this plot solid black.

Adding **Mesh→False** allows us to see the plot:

$$\texttt{DensityPlot}\left[\texttt{Sin}\left[\frac{\texttt{x}}{\texttt{y}}\right],\ \{\texttt{x, -10, 10}\},\right.$$

$$\left.\{\texttt{y, -5, 5}\},\ \texttt{PlotPoints} \rightarrow \texttt{500, Mesh} \rightarrow \texttt{False}\right];$$

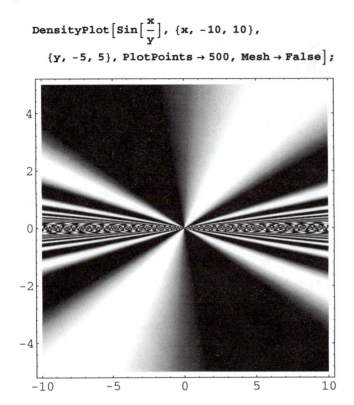

■ Discussion

Jerry: How would you decide which to choose: **Plot3D**, **ContourPlot**, or **DensityPlot**?

Theo: Your choice depends mostly on the function you are plotting. **Plot3D** is usually the first one I try. It gives the most easily interpreted picture. **ContourPlot** allows you to see the shapes of peaks and valleys more accurately. The main advantage of **DensityPlot**, in most cases, is that it is the fastest and most efficient of the three. The example of a 500 by 500 grid we did above would not be practical as a **Plot3D** or a **ContourPlot** on all but the largest computers. But as a **DensityPlot** it is quite practical.

Chapter **42**

How do I plot a list of values?

The **ListPlot** command allows us to plot a list of values in two dimensions:

```
ListPlot[{3, 1, 4, 6, 3, 5, 3, 3, 4, 6, 2, 6, 3}];
```

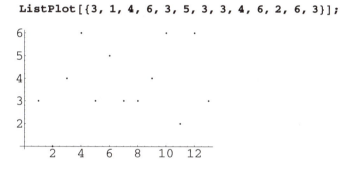

The dots used by **ListPlot** are sometimes too small. They can be increased using the **PlotStyle** option:

```
ListPlot[{3, 1, 4, 6, 3, 5, 3, 3, 4, 6, 2, 6, 3},
   PlotStyle → PointSize[0.02]];
```

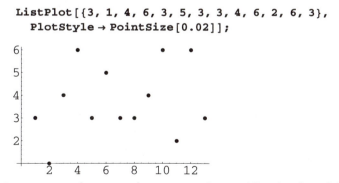

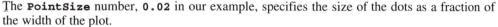

The **PointSize** number, **0.02** in our example, specifies the size of the dots as a fraction of the width of the plot.

The option **PlotJoined→True** draws a line connecting the points:

ListPlot[{3, 1, 4, 6, 3, 5, 3, 3, 4, 6, 2, 6, 3}, PlotJoined → True];

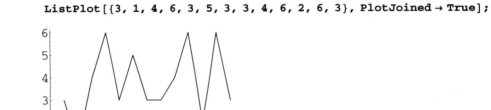

In all these cases the points were drawn with even horizontal spacing.

If you want to specify both *x* and *y* values for the points, you can give **ListPlot** a list of pairs of numbers:

**ListPlot[{{2, 5}, {1, 7}, {2, 9}, {3, 8},
     {4, 9}, {3, 6}, {4, 5}, {0, 0}}, PlotJoined → True];**

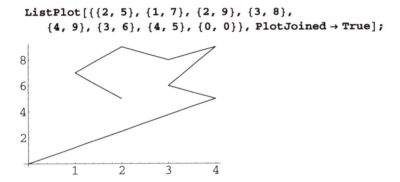

There are, as usual, many options and additional features associated with **ListPlot**. See The *Mathematica* Book or click <u>here</u> for more details.

It is frequently convenient to use the **Table** command together with **ListPlot**. Here is an example:

ListPlot[Table[k², {k, 1, 10}]];

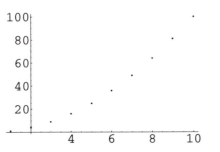

The command **ListPlot3D** works a little differently from **ListPlot**. It takes a matrix (list of lists) of *z* values:

ListPlot3D[{{1, 3, 5}, {4, 3, 2}, {2, 3, 4}}];

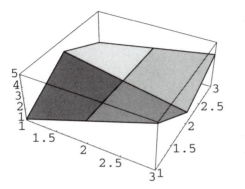

This is analogous to the form of **ListPlot** in which you don't specify *x* values. The matrix of *z* values is drawn with regularly spaced *x* and *y* values. (There is no way to specify *x* and *y* values manually; you must have a regular grid. There is also no way to plot points instead of a surface. Both of these things can be done using more complicated *Mathematica* commands, but that is beyond the scope of this book.)

Here is an example made with **Table**:

ListPlot3D[Table[Mod[i, j], {i, 1, 20}, {j, 1, 20}]];

The commands **ListContourPlot** and **ListDensityPlot** work the same way:

ListContourPlot[Table[Mod[i, j], {i, 1, 20}, {j, 1, 20}]];

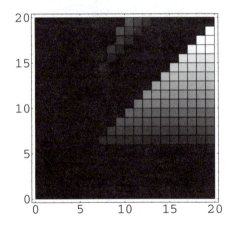

ListDensityPlot[Table[Mod[i, j], {i, 1, 20}, {j, 1, 20}]];

We can define a function to allow us to plot (x, y, z) points in 3-D. (You don't need to understand how this function works to use it; type in the definition below, evaluate it, and use it.)

```
pointListPlot3D[list_, options___] :=
    Show[Graphics3D[Point /@ list], options, Axes → Automatic]
```

Here is an example using this function:

```
pointListPlot3D[{{1, 2, 2}, {3, 2, 1}, {2, 1, 1}, {3, 1, 2}}];
```

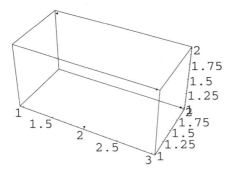

You probably can't see these points, because they are small and there are not very many of them. The next example uses **Table** to generate a much larger number of points:

```
pointListPlot3D[
    Table[{n Cos[n], n Cos[n] Sin[n], n Sin[n]}, {n, 0, 100, 0.1}]];
```

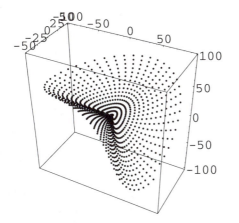

You can use options with this command, just as with built-in plotting commands. For example, you can change the viewpoint:

```
pointListPlot3D[
    Table[{n Cos[n], n Cos[n] Sin[n], n Sin[n]}, {n, 0, 100, 0.1}],
    ViewPoint → {3.0, 0.0, 0.0}];
```

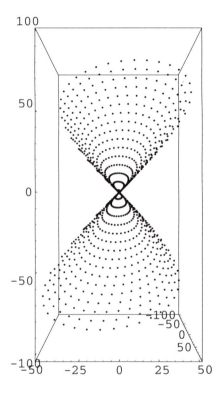

This viewpoint could have been generated with the graphical 3-D viewpoint selector, or you could view this using the real-time 3-D rotation mode, both described in Chapter 37.

Chapter **43**

How do I make sounds?

The **Play** command works very much like the **Plot** command. Here is a one-second burst of middle C:

```
Play[Sin[263 2Pi t], {t, 0, 1}];
```

- The first argument is a function that specifies the amplitude waveform, in this case a sine wave that oscillates 263 times per second.
- The second argument is a standard iterator specification, in this case saying that **t** should run from **0** to **1**. (The variable range is always in units of seconds; in this example, we have specified a one-second sound.)

The output shown above is a rough plot of the waveform. (Don't try to read too much into the pictures associated with sounds; they are mostly placeholders.)

The sound will be played once automatically when the command is executed. The sound can be replayed at any time by double-clicking on the small speaker-like icon at the top of the cell bracket of the output cell (the cell bracket is the tall, thin bracket on the right edge of the window).

In *Mathematica*, sounds are represented as amplitude waveforms. You can think of an amplitude waveform as a specification of how the speaker cone should move back and forth in time. A sine function oscillating between about 20 and 20,000 times per second will produce a pure tone that most of us or our dogs have a chance of hearing.

The relationship between a function and what it sounds like is delightful and often surprising. Experimentation is rewarding. The following books may be helpful to people interested in learning more about computer-generated sounds and music:

• The beginning chapters of *The Technology of Computer Music* by Max V. Matthews contain a good introduction to waveforms, samples, and sound.
• *The Technology of Electronic Music* by Thomas H. Wells, has a good description of the mathematics of sound production. It is written for musicians.
• *Horns, Strings, and Harmony* by Arthur Benade is a good general introduction to acoustics.

Let's generate a few more examples of sounds. We'll begin with a tone that rises in volume:

```
Play[t Sin[263 2Pi t], {t, 0, 2}];
```

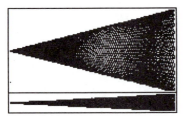

This one falls in volume:

```
Play[(2-t) Sin[263 2Pi t], {t, 0, 2}];
```

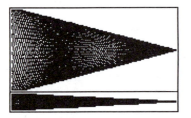

Here is a tone that changes in frequency over time:

```
Play[Sin[263 2Pi t + 2 Sin[5 2Pi t]], {t, 0, 1}];
```

And finally, here is a quite strange sound:

```
Play[Sin[263 2Pi t Sin[5 2Pi t]], {t, 0, 4}];
```

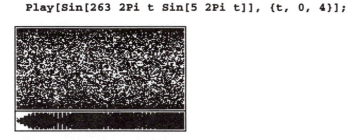

If you want to generate a stereo sound, you can give **Play** a list of two functions as its first argument. This example generates a sound that oscillates from left to right:

```
Play[
    {Sin[2 2Pi t] Sin[263 2Pi t],
     Cos[2 2Pi t] Sin[263 2Pi t]},
    {t, 0, 4}];
```

Just as **Play** is analogous to **Plot**, the function **ListPlay** is analogous to **ListPlot**. It takes a list of amplitude values as its first argument. In order to get an audible sound, you need at least several hundred elements in the list.

We can use a **Table** command to generate a list of 10000 random numbers:

```
theList = Table[Random[], {10000}];
```

Now we can play the list. It sounds like noise:

```
ListPlay[theList];
```

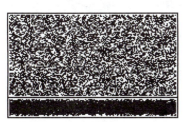

The preceding samples are assumed to be spaced regularly in time, at a sample rate that depends on the type of computer you are using. You can find the sample rate of your computer by executing the following command:

```
Options[ListPlay]
```

{Epilog → {}, PlayRange → Automatic, Prolog → {}, SampleDepth → 8, SampleRate → 8192, DisplayFunction :→ $SoundDisplayFunction}

This indicates that the default sample rate on our computer is 8192 samples per second.

We have seen how to generate sounds. *Why* we generate them is a little harder to answer. Sound is a bit like graphics. If you go to your tight-fisted boss and ask for an expensive new graphics computer so you can look at pretty pictures of your data, she might well say: "Why do you need an expensive new graphics computer? Can't you just look at tables of numbers? There's nothing in the graph that isn't in the table of numbers, too!"

Your boss is right, of course: A graph is just a different way of presenting a table of numbers. But consider the following table of numbers:

```
theList = {0.319715, 0.485847, 0.0923159, 0.0098825, 0.385929, 0.178038, 0.341105, 0.0715364,
    0.324725, 0.311999, 0.388032, 0.263058, 0.11791, 0.320445, 0.343071, 0.0754845, 0.130683,
    0.424873, 0.279234, 0.037206, 0.07216, 0.112803, 0.374125, 0.327434, 0.216648, 0.0244873,
    0.238622, 0.206607, 0.437618, 0.379319, 0.415, 0.392528, 0.194673, 0.251138, 0.262301,
    0.28169, 0.425391, 0.0162718, 0.0444506, 0.185095, 0.114933, 0.378389, 0.171372, 0.45134,
    0.395277, 0.339315, 0.0261299, 0.141234, 0.291518, 0.0446079, 0.0847202, 0.152716, 0.0554939,
    0.323003, 0.439467, 0.356329, 0.205486, 0.310317, 0.304329, 0.314771, 0.431105, 0.3075,
    0.226201, 0.45382, 0.21717, 0.0663305, 0.107625, 0.286818, 0.326595, 0.252058, 0.493203,
    0.0588209, 0.421135, 0.310719, 0.149446, 0.316892, 0.370461, 0.424399, 0.31233, 0.437353,
    0.262912, 0.355528, 0.133567, 0.105028, 0.226203, 0.539964, 0.316752, 0.351406, 0.140764,
    0.472047, 0.50166, 0.350244, 0.445996, 0.421884, 0.418805, 0.533522, 0.749913, 0.721833,
    0.563492, 0.857063, 0.925731, 0.692484, 0.928162, 0.786661, 0.466355, 0.796613, 0.828478,
    0.699389, 0.692961, 0.531652, 0.2786, 0.247609, 0.575035, 0.185248, 0.287415, 0.329739,
    0.428317, 0.27165, 0.0751154, 0.288455, 0.433856, 0.211975, 0.362165, 0.0665307, 0.240438,
    0.0322182, 0.0630494, 0.373264, 0.450873, 0.397439, 0.0888916, 0.051499, 0.270546, 0.351316,
    0.102244, 0.448887, 0.196265, 0.176743, 0.00485408, 0.0265342, 0.405754, 0.407488, 0.140808,
    0.450605, 0.255624, 0.470927, 0.0312255, 0.204807, 0.486395, 0.466302, 0.393382, 0.406347,
    0.0162974, 0.498776, 0.48806, 0.237831, 0.465167, 0.14923, 0.229618, 0.0469642, 0.0742334,
    0.218713, 0.319047, 0.0478268, 0.326195, 0.105225, 0.0610618, 0.432484, 0.211114, 0.333835,
    0.205898, 0.1406, 0.0290034, 0.490678, 0.0952388, 0.000152, 0.0834089, 0.296256, 0.0182374,
    0.122067, 0.392832, 0.198725, 0.462634, 0.0451753, 0.0203656, 0.1584, 0.263841, 0.242207,
    0.0865999, 0.318615, 0.46402, 0.0559252, 0.314072, 0.155495, 0.179808, 0.0758203, 0.271105,
    0.216623, 0.203976, 0.298223, 0.414241, 0.0561329, 0.43637, 0.0667133, 0.454853, 0.485276,
    0.259964, 0.0832396, 0.246328, 0.137695, 0.232986, 0.486746, 0.220911, 0.47477, 0.454641,
    0.21976, 0.259378, 0.366005, 0.1741, 0.299719, 0.271224, 0.239087, 0.260021, 0.359904,
    0.0967571, 0.0157834, 0.494801, 0.281239, 0.167156, 0.0995831, 0.327325, 0.284685, 0.493202,
    0.433524, 0.319655, 0.331418, 0.432356, 0.105132, 0.118675, 0.00205324, 0.447886, 0.226593,
    0.453255, 0.167673, 0.404586, 0.0286443, 0.39542, 0.147305, 0.244961, 0.277885, 0.451088};
```

Not very enlightening. We would have to stare at this list for quite a long time to see what we can see easily in this plot of the same list:

ListPlot[theList];

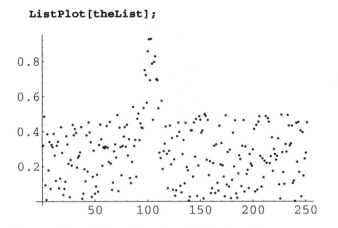

Likewise, consider this list of numbers (abbreviated for space reasons):

```
theList = {
0.00781,  0.00000, -0.01562, -0.01562, -0.03125, -0.00781,  0.03125,  0.05469,
0.03906, -0.03906, -0.08594, -0.10156, -0.10156, -0.05469, -0.01562,  0.00781,
0.03906,  0.03125,  0.03906,  0.06250,  0.08594,  0.08594,  0.02344, -0.00781,
-0.00781, -0.04688, -0.05469, -0.03906, -0.03906, -0.03906, -0.07031, -0.04688,
0.02344,  0.03125,  0.00781, -0.04688, -0.08594, -0.08594, -0.10156, -0.08594,
-0.03125, -0.00781,  0.01562,  0.03125,  0.04688,  0.08594,  0.06250,  0.02344,
0.00781,  0.00781, -0.00781, -0.06250, -0.09375, -0.06250, -0.05469, -0.03906,
-0.01562, -0.00781,  0.02344, -0.00781, -0.03125, -0.00781,  0.00781, -0.01562,
-0.07031, -0.08594, -0.04688, -0.02344,  0.00000,  0.04688,  0.07031,  0.09375,
0.10938,  0.14062,  0.14844,  0.14062,  0.11719,  0.01562, -0.07031, -0.08594,
-0.10156, -0.09375, -0.03125, -0.00781,  0.00000,  0.00781,  0.03906,  0.05469,
0.01562, -0.03906, -0.09375, -0.16406, -0.10156, -0.04688,  0.01562,
0.01562, -0.00781,  0.01562,  0.05469,  0.11719,  0.09375,  0.00000, -0.03906,
-0.11719, -0.15625, -0.11719, -0.09375, -0.03906, -0.03906, -0.02344,  0.07812,
0.10156,  0.10156,  0.07812, -0.04688, -0.12500, -0.17188, -0.21094, -0.16406,
-0.07031,  0.01562,  0.01562,  0.00781,  0.10938,  0.15625,  0.16406,  0.16406,
0.13281,  0.03906, -0.08594, -0.14062, -0.09375, -0.03906,  0.02344,  0.07812,
0.07812,  0.07812,  0.08594,  0.03125, -0.06250, -0.10156, -0.08594, -0.12500,
-0.10938, -0.01562,  0.00000, -0.00781,  0.02344,  0.03125,  0.06250,  0.08594,
0.10156,  0.09375,  0.01562,  0.00781,  0.00781, -0.08594, -0.07812, -0.05469,
-0.13281, -0.13281, -0.08594, -0.05469, -0.03906,  0.01562,  0.10156,  0.09375,
```

Also not very enlightening. Let's use **ListPlay** on the complete list:

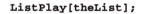

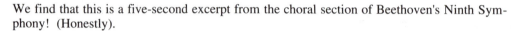

We find that this is a five-second excerpt from the choral section of Beethoven's Ninth Symphony! (Honestly).

It's rare for a *Mathematica* command to produce sounds as beautiful as these of the immortal Ninth, but listening to any function may give you new insights into its mathematical properties. It's also a lot of fun.

Chapter **44**

How do I make animations?

Many a pleasant Sunday afternoon can be spent in front of the screen making *Mathematica* animations.

Mathematica animation is much like Hollywood animation: An animation is a sequence of pictures that, when displayed in rapid succession, appear to move. (If you aren't familiar with the graphics commands in *Mathematica*, you might want to read some of the chapters on 2-D and 3-D plotting in this book before reading this chapter.)

In *Mathematica,* any sequence of graphics cells can be animated using the Animate Selected Graphics command in the Graph menu. For example, the following command will generate a sequence of six graphics, each slightly different from the others:

```
Do[Plot[Sin[n x], {x, 0, 2 π}], {n, 1, 2, 0.2}];
```

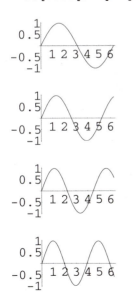

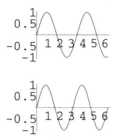

(**Do** is a general-purpose iteration command: This example says to repeat the **Plot** command six times, with values of **n** ranging from **1** to **2** in steps of **0.2**.)

To see these graphics animated, double-click on one of the pictures (any one will do). The cell group containing the pictures will be selected and the animation started, automatically.

From now on we'll show the frames of the animations in a two-dimensional layout, to save space. When you make these animations in your own copy of *Mathematica*, they will not be displayed in this form.

There are a number of issues that we did not need to deal with in our first, fairly simple animation. The most important is the plot range. Consider this slight variation:

Do[Plot[Sin[n x], {x, 0, 2 π}], {n, 0, 1, 0.2}];

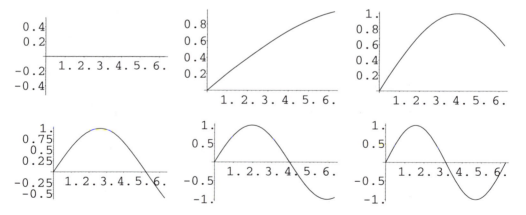

In this example, *Mathematica* automatically chose a different *y* range for each of the first few plots. This makes the axes jump around. When making animations it is almost always necessary to specify a fixed plot range. The **PlotRange** option allows us to do so:

```
Do[Plot[Sin[n x], {x, 0, 2 π}, PlotRange → {-1, 1}], {n, 0, 1, 0.2}];
```

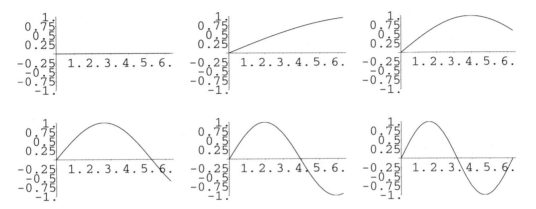

For more details of how to specify plot ranges, see Chapter 31.

Below are some edifying animations. They show how to use the animation parameter to move a parabola around in different ways:

```
Do[Plot[a x², {x, -3, 3}, PlotRange → {{-3, 3}, {-25, 25}}],
  {a, -4, 4, 0.25}];

Do[Plot[x² + a, {x, -3, 3}, PlotRange → {{-3, 3}, {-25, 25}}],
  {a, -4, 4, 0.25}];

Do[Plot[(x - a)², {x, -12, 12}, PlotRange → {{-3, 3}, {0, 64}}],
  {a, -4, 4, 0.25}];
```

We can make 3-D animations in the same way, using **Plot3D** instead of **Plot**. (Warning: 3-D animations can take a long time to generate, and they use a *lot* of memory!)

```
Do[Plot3D[Sin[n x] Sin[n y], {x, 0, 2 π},
   {y, 0, 2 π}, PlotRange → {-1, 1}], {n, 1, 2, 0.1}];
```

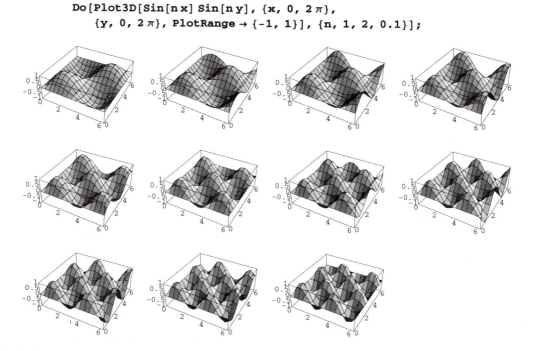

In fact, we can make animations with any *Mathematica* graphics command. For example, the following are contour and density plot animations you can try. (It is just as easy to make animations using the various other graphics commands.)

```
Do[ContourPlot[Sin[x² + y²] Cos[(x - n)² + y²], {x, -2, 2},
   {y, -2, 2}, PlotRange → {-1, 1}], {n, -2, 2, 0.2}];
```

```
Do[DensityPlot[Sin[x² + y²] Cos[(x - n)² + y²], {x, -2, 2},
   {y, -2, 2}, PlotRange → {-1, 1}], {n, -2, 2, 0.2}];
```

We can also make animations in which we change options of the plotting commands instead of changing the function being plotted. For example, in this animation we change the range over which the function is plotted:

```
Do[Plot3D[Sin[x y], {x, -n, n}, {y, -n, n}], {n, 1, 3, 0.2}];
```

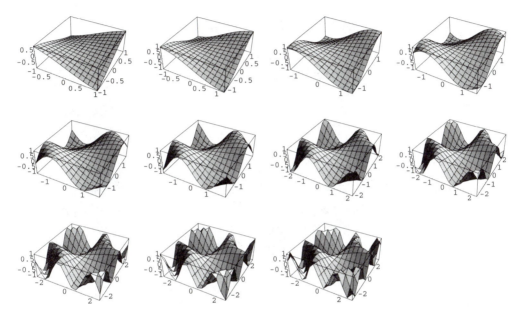

A particularly common variation of this is to change the viewpoint, so that the surface appears to rotate. Although you could do this using **Do** and the **ViewPoint** option, there is a special function, **SpinShow** that does it for you.

To use **SpinShow** you have to load the package Animation.m using the following command:

```
Needs["Graphics`Animation`"];
```

(Note that the two single quotes used here are "back quotes" usually found on the same key with ~. They are not the single quotes found on the double-quote key.)

First generate the surface you want to rotate. (It's important to use the option **Axes→None**; if there are any axes in the plot, the animation will not come out right.)

```
Plot3D[Sin[x y], {x, 0, 3}, {y, 0, 3}, Axes → None];
```

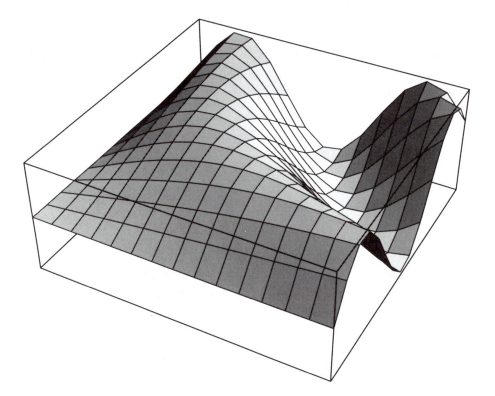

Then use **SpinShow** on the result (**%** means the result of the last evaluation):

```
SpinShow[%];
```

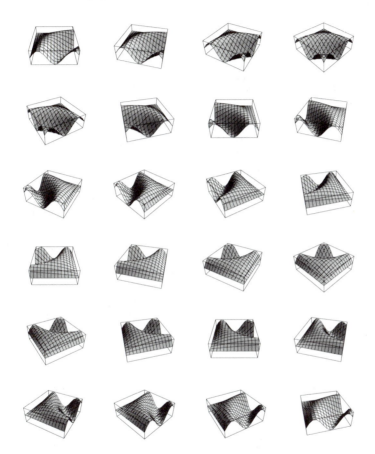

Several options to **SpinShow** specify how many steps to generate, over what range to rotate the surface, etc. They are described in the `package documentation` that came with your copy of *Mathematica*.

For further examples of peculiar animations, see our earlier book, *Exploring Mathematics with Mathematica*.

Chapter **45**

How do I do image manipulation in *Mathematica*?

While it has always been possible to do image manipulation in *Mathematica*, several new features in V4.0 make it quick, easy, and fun.

First you need to import an image. Fortunately, V4.0 includes a powerful `Import` command that is able to handle a wide range of image formats automatically. In general, you just give it the name of the file you want to import and it figures out the format automatically:

```
myimage = Import["MyImage.JPG"];
```

Given just the file name, *Mathematica* looks in several directories (the one containing *Mathematica* itself, your home directory, etc.). If the file is not located in one of these standard locations, you may need to include the full path name to locate the file. For example, owners of the electronic edition of this book can use the following command to load a picture of a very cute puppy (used throughout this chapter):

```
puppyImage =
   Import[ToFileName[{$TopDirectory, "AddOns", "Autoload",
      "Beginner's Guide 4.0 Source", "Documentation",
      "English"}, "Puppy.JPG"]];
```

(If you don't have the electronic edition, you will have to substitute a picture of your own puppy. If you don't have a puppy, go to your local animal shelter and get one.)

Or, the following command can be used to import any file on your disk (you will get an open-file dialog box in which you can choose the file to import):

```
myimage = Import[Experimental`FileBrowse[False]];
```

The `Import` command returns an ordinary *Mathematica* expression containing a representation of the data in the file. The exact format of the expression of course depends on the type of data in the file. In the case of an image, the expression is a bit too long to print out, but it has the overall structure:

```
Graphics[
 Raster[data, pixelrange, valuerange,
   ColorFunction → RGBColor],
 AspectRatio → Automatic]
```

where **data** is a 2-dimensional list of triplets (red, green, blue), **pixelrange** represents the dimensions of the image, and **valuerange** represents the minimum and maximum values of the numbers in the data. This expression is intentionally constructed in such a way that the standard **Show** function will reproduce the image, as seen here:

```
Show[puppyImage];
```

(Readers of the paper edition, please imagine this image in color, as it is in the electronic edition.)

Import is a very powerful command explained in more detail in Chapter 79. When **Import** is used to import image files, the structure will always be similar to what is described above, but some details may vary depending on the image format. For example, if the image is a grayscale image the **ColorFunction** option will be set to **GrayLevel**. If the image is an index color image, the **ColorFunction** will be a large expression containing the color lookup table for the image.

In this chapter, we're going to assume you're using an RGB color image such as a JPEG.

■ Discrete grayscale image manipulations

While you can manipulate color images, for purposes of illustration it's much easier to work with grayscale images. They can be represented as simple rectangular matrices of numbers, which can be manipulated as mathematical objects. (Color images must be represented as matrices of red, green, blue triplets, which are more complicated to deal with.) So, we'll start our manipulations by extracting the image data from the expression, scaling it so the values run between 0 and 1, and adding up a weighted average of the red, green, and blue components of each pixel (the weights are based on the sensitivity of the eye to each color).

$$\texttt{grayscalePuppy = Map}\left[\frac{\texttt{0.3 \#[[1]] + 0.59 \#[[2]] + 0.11 \#[[3]]}}{255}\ \&,\right.$$
$$\left.\texttt{N[puppyImage[[1, 1]]], \{2\}}\right];$$

We can use the **Dimensions** function to see how many rows and columns are in our image:

```
Dimensions[grayscalePuppy]
```

{238, 200}

Let's look at one line of this dataset (row number 119 is about half way down the image):

```
grayscalePuppy[[119]]
```

{0.152235, 0.0617647, 0.0616078, 0.0673333, 0.0747451, 0.0661569, 0.0735294, 0.0661569, 0.0700392,
0.0619608, 0.0658824, 0.0600392, 0.0709412, 0.0830196, 0.0947843, 0.107255, 0.102196, 0.098549,
0.098549, 0.0994118, 0.0971765, 0.0983137, 0.0943922, 0.0818039, 0.0748235, 0.0546667,
0.0557647, 0.0545882, 0.0576078, 0.0509804, 0.0557647, 0.0476471, 0.0473725, 0.0518431,
0.0431373, 0.0743529, 0.0585882, 0.0622353, 0.0943529, 0.109412, 0.156235, 0.145098, 0.160627,
0.154039, 0.117647, 0.0826275, 0.117137, 0.121529, 0.088, 0.0466275, 0.0785882, 0.140471,
0.162078, 0.154314, 0.181765, 0.22451, 0.271176, 0.278902, 0.310196, 0.356196, 0.377804,
0.388353, 0.368, 0.254275, 0.13451, 0.145961, 0.152941, 0.187608, 0.223137, 0.188471, 0.231294,
0.255098, 0.24349, 0.148627, 0.144549, 0.191333, 0.188549, 0.19698, 0.23251, 0.275922, 0.369176,
0.64051, 0.92898, 0.953294, 0.949725, 0.795137, 0.505529, 0.547294, 0.532784, 0.45898,
0.278353, 0.239137, 0.254706, 0.238431, 0.263843, 0.278667, 0.368863, 0.36051, 0.351529,
0.360118, 0.326745, 0.318667, 0.376902, 0.377216, 0.440039, 0.452078, 0.443373, 0.521647,
0.563765, 0.608118, 0.623255, 0.617608, 0.561059, 0.559471, 0.544627, 0.455725, 0.448235,
0.376118, 0.319176, 0.290784, 0.279569, 0.265804, 0.334039, 0.350431, 0.382314, 0.416863,
0.478745, 0.505961, 0.529804, 0.546745, 0.572745, 0.588314, 0.596588, 0.596431, 0.620784,
0.631686, 0.630824, 0.664549, 0.698667, 0.687216, 0.668471, 0.644588, 0.616549, 0.596353,
0.552745, 0.551255, 0.557098, 0.552235, 0.556863, 0.572549, 0.569529, 0.558039, 0.554902,
0.564, 0.567922, 0.588235, 0.583765, 0.580353, 0.56902, 0.578, 0.570431, 0.568471, 0.560745,
0.565647, 0.566235, 0.584039, 0.574, 0.570706, 0.534706, 0.497765, 0.459686, 0.439373,
0.346157, 0.267922, 0.192157, 0.137216, 0.132863, 0.120431, 0.129647, 0.121804, 0.121804,
0.118353, 0.110314, 0.111529, 0.106588, 0.11298, 0.11702, 0.117608, 0.11702, 0.118157, 0.126314,
0.12498, 0.124863, 0.134196, 0.134157, 0.13298, 0.140549, 0.134706, 0.137765, 0.136902}

Values near 0 are dark, and values near 1 are light. As you can see from just one line, there are a lot of numbers in this image (47600 to be exact).

We can see the graylevel image using a **Show** command:

```
Show[Graphics[Raster[grayscalePuppy]], AspectRatio -> Automatic];
```

Now that we have the dataset as a simple 2-dimensional matrix of numbers, it's easy to do all sorts of things to it. For example, if we subtract each element in it from 1, we will get an effect like a photographic negative (remember the dataset is scaled to have values between 0 and 1). Note that we are making use of the fact that in *Mathematica* you can perform mathematical operations on nested lists and the operations will automatically be applied to each element. So in this example, we are in fact subtracting each element of the matrix from 1, individually.

```
Show[
    Graphics[Raster[1 - grayscalePuppy], AspectRatio -> Automatic]];
```

Simple operations like changing the brightness and contrast of the image are easily done by multiplying and adding scalar quantities to the matrix. For example, the following command greatly increases the contrast of the image:

```
Show[Graphics[
    Raster[grayscalePuppy * 2 - 0.5], AspectRatio → Automatic]];
```

A common artistic effect, called "posterization", involves reducing the number of distinct shades of gray in the image. In the following command we multiply the image by 5, round to the nearest integer, then divide by 5. This has the effect of leaving the overall range of values between 0 and 1, but restricted to only six different values.

```
Show[Graphics[Raster[Round[5 * grayscalePuppy] / 5],
    AspectRatio → Automatic]];
```

Jerry: OK, I think I'm going to have to step in here and put a stop to this nonsense. We all know Theo likes to go off and do all sorts of things that have no practical use in the real world, but this is going a bit far. Surely, this sort of thing could be done much more easily in a program like Adobe Photoshop, or KidPix for that matter. Why on earth would anyone go to the trouble of importing an image into *Mathematica* and turning it into a matrix, just to apply trivial operations that any paint program could do 8,000 times faster?

Theo: You're absolutely right that a paint program, especially a heavy-duty one like Photo-Shop, can do a lot of image processing of this sort. If what you want to do is one of the things that PhotoShop can do, you would be nuts to use *Mathematica* instead. But suppose it's not? Or, suppose you're trying to develop a totally new image processing algorithm that's never been done before. PhotoShop isn't going to do you a bit of good: You need a flexible, program-mable system that allows you to play with the mathematics of your algorithm in a mathematics-friendly environment. *Mathematica* is a great system for developing algorithms you might want to turn into PhotoShop plug-ins, or for doing image manipulations and analyses beyond what fixed systems are capable of.

Jerry: What about all the programs designed for image analysis? Aren't some of them better for this sort of thing than *Mathematica*?

Theo: I repeat: If there's a special purpose package that does what you want, it may be a better choice, if only because it's likely to be faster. But there is no "image analysis" software that has anything close to the flexibility of *Mathematica* in terms of the numerical, symbolic, and graphic tools you can bring to bear on an image analysis problem. This flexibility means you are not restricted to the same old stuff everyone else does; you can do things that have never been done before.

It's also interesting to use *Mathematica* to understand what's going on inside programs like PhotoShop. Understanding the mathematics behind visual manipulations can help you appreci-ate them and use them better.

Jerry: Now *that* sounds interesting.

Theo: Let's start with convolution. Many common image processing operations, like blurring, sharpening, or edge highlighting, can be described mathematically as convolutions.

To do a convolution, you start with a *kernel*, which is usually a fairly small matrix whose elements add up to a total of one (they don't have to, but this usually works best, and we'll see why in a minute).

Let's use the example of the matrix $\begin{pmatrix} 1/9 & 1/9 & 1/9 \\ 1/9 & 1/9 & 1/9 \\ 1/9 & 1/9 & 1/9 \end{pmatrix}$ as our kernel.

Think of the original image as a matrix of numbers, like this small sub-section taken around the area of the left eye:

```
(eye = Take[grayscalePuppy, {157, 167}, {70, 80}]) // MatrixForm
```

```
0.267059  0.392902  0.420588  0.309137  0.251843  0.168863  0.177333   0.140549  0.132902  0.203725  0.364431
0.340824  0.507176  0.431529  0.236863  0.179922  0.314667  0.361961   0.287412  0.242392  0.179922  0.204784
0.454784  0.591294  0.269529  0.184549  0.401216  0.456118  0.431961   0.418275  0.412431  0.376667  0.255255
0.539961  0.411608  0.180235  0.378196  0.452471  0.357137  0.337843   0.400157  0.452     0.474627  0.432235
0.551882  0.298549  0.246314  0.458824  0.368078  0.259961  0.168275   0.173098  0.251216  0.40102   0.497569
0.363647  0.160431  0.308941  0.409451  0.282784  0.152353  0.0946667  0.0673333 0.196314  0.265843  0.419608
0.234588  0.101098  0.273765  0.428078  0.302392  0.145686  0.118039   0.0853725 0.615098  0.399451  0.328824
0.173529  0.149098  0.161725  0.384706  0.384118  0.215961  0.152235   0.0892549 0.157255  0.352196  0.32498
0.187569  0.188627  0.145843  0.15749   0.282902  0.274549  0.22298    0.200588  0.196235  0.185137  0.198941
0.298941  0.217569  0.224     0.175961  0.146314  0.137882  0.140627   0.156039  0.137333  0.184196  0.379569
0.514667  0.408667  0.365373  0.305647  0.263843  0.259451  0.250275   0.272118  0.367569  0.451373  0.439843
```

The nine numbers in the top left corner form a 3 by 3 sub-matrix, which we can multiply (element by element) with the kernel, then add up the resulting numbers to give a single result:

```
Apply[Plus,

     Apply[Plus, ⎛ 0.267059  0.392902  0.420588 ⎞ ⎛ 1/9  1/9  1/9 ⎞ ]]
                 ⎜ 0.340824  0.507176  0.431529 ⎟ ⎜ 1/9  1/9  1/9 ⎟
                 ⎝ 0.454784  0.591294  0.269529 ⎠ ⎝ 1/9  1/9  1/9 ⎠

0.40841
```

This result will become one pixel in the output image. To get the next pixel, we slide over by one and multiply/add the kernel with the next sub-matrix (the one starting at the first row, second column in the image):

```
Apply[Plus,

     Apply[Plus, ⎛ 0.392902  0.420588  0.309137 ⎞ ⎛ 1/9  1/9  1/9 ⎞ ]]
                 ⎜ 0.507176  0.431529  0.236863 ⎟ ⎜ 1/9  1/9  1/9 ⎟
                 ⎝ 0.591294  0.269529  0.184549 ⎠ ⎝ 1/9  1/9  1/9 ⎠

0.371508
```

Repeating this process of multiply/adding the kernel with every possible 3 by 3 sub-matrix in the original image, we can build up a new matrix in which each number is the result of a single operation like the two above. Here is what we get:

```
ListConvolve[ ⎛ 1/9  1/9  1/9 ⎞ , eye] // MatrixForm
              ⎜ 1/9  1/9  1/9 ⎟
              ⎝ 1/9  1/9  1/9 ⎠
```

```
0.40841   0.371508  0.298353  0.278131  0.304876  0.306349  0.289468  0.266031  0.263612
0.414105  0.354553  0.301612  0.329015  0.365922  0.373948  0.371603  0.360431  0.336702
0.393795  0.335455  0.326601  0.368505  0.359229  0.333647  0.338362  0.373277  0.39478
0.340174  0.31695   0.34281   0.346584  0.274841  0.223425  0.237878  0.297956  0.376715
0.282135  0.298383  0.34207   0.311956  0.210248  0.140532  0.196601  0.272749  0.374993
0.214092  0.264144  0.326218  0.300614  0.205359  0.124545  0.175063  0.247569  0.339952
0.179538  0.221159  0.280113  0.286209  0.233207  0.167185  0.204118  0.253399  0.306458
0.1941    0.200558  0.229229  0.239987  0.217508  0.17668   0.161394  0.184248  0.235094
0.283473  0.243242  0.229708  0.222671  0.219869  0.212723  0.215974  0.238954  0.282244
```

Notice that the first two numbers in the result are the same two we did individually. Also notice that the result is smaller by two rows and columns than the original. This is because in order to construct a 3 by 3 submatrix around the outermost set of elements, you would have to invent numbers for elements that fall outside the original matrix. (There are optional arguments to **ListConvolve** that allow you to do just that, and get back a result the same size as your original, but that is beyond the scope of this book.)

Let's see what this looks like, applied to the whole original image:

```
Show[Graphics[Raster[
                   ⎛ 1 / 9   1 / 9   1 / 9 ⎞
    ListConvolve[  ⎜ 1 / 9   1 / 9   1 / 9 ⎟ , grayscalePuppy]],
                   ⎝ 1 / 9   1 / 9   1 / 9 ⎠

    AspectRatio → Automatic]];
```

Jerry: Blurry! It seems to me that what you're doing is averaging each group of nine numbers. That is, you're adding them all up and dividing by the count (9), except that you did the division first by having each element of the kernel be $\frac{1}{9}$. So, the resulting image is a sort of 3 by 3 moving average of the original.

Theo: Exactly. That's why having all the elements in the kernel add up to one is useful: It means that the overall scaling (which translates into brightness) of the output image is the same as that of the original. You can blur the image even more by simply increasing the size of the kernel. This results in the moving average being taken over a larger area. For example, we can use the **Table** command to construct a 10 by 10 matrix where each element is $\frac{1}{100}$:

```
averageTenByTen = Table[ 1/10², {10}, {10}];
```

```
Show[Graphics[Raster[
    ListConvolve[averageTenByTen, grayscalePuppy]],
  AspectRatio → Automatic]];
```

Blurrier! Let's try a slightly more interesting kernel:

```
Show[Graphics[Raster[
    ListConvolve[ ( 1   1   1
                    1  -8   1
                    1   1   1 ), grayscalePuppy]],
    AspectRatio → Automatic]];
```

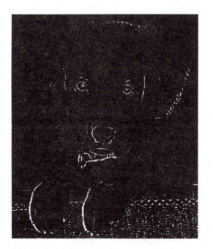

In this case, the elements add up to zero, not one. If the pixel values in the original image are all fairly similar in a given area, the multiply/add operation will add up to zero (black). So, it's only where the pixel values are *changing* that the resulting image has brighter pixels. This gives you a simple sort of edge detection.

Next, how about motion blur? By putting isolated coefficients in a larger kernel, you can effectively overlay shifted copies of the image at different intensities:

```
Show[Graphics[Raster[
```

$$
\text{ListConvolve}\left[
\begin{pmatrix}
0 & 0 & 0 & 0 & 0 & 0 & 0.8 \\
0 & 0 & 0 & 0 & 0 & 0 & 0 \\
0 & 0 & 0 & 0 & 0 & 0 & 0 \\
0 & 0 & 0 & 0 & 0 & 0 & 0 \\
0 & 0 & 0 & 0 & 0 & 0 & 0 \\
0 & 0 & 0 & 0 & 0 & 0 & 0 \\
0.5 & 0 & 0 & 0 & 0 & 0 & 0
\end{pmatrix}
, \text{grayscalePuppy}\right]\right],
$$

```
AspectRatio → Automatic]];
```

Jerry: I have to say, these images are popping out very quickly. How is it possible to do so many matrix operations in a fraction of a second? After all, our computer must be performing 47600 matrix multiply/add operations, one for each pixel, and each matrix operation involves dozens of multiplications and additions. That's a lot of multiplying and adding....

Theo: What makes you think it's multiplying and adding? This is sort of like the discussion in Chapter 69 (Can *Mathematica* Show Me the Steps?). When you start to talk about what *Mathematica* is actually doing, you often find that it's nothing like what you expect. Let's do a little test:

```
dataset = Table[Random[], {500}, {500}];
```

$$\text{kernel} = \text{Table}\left[\frac{1.}{100^2}, \{100\}, \{100\}\right];$$

```
Timing[ListConvolve[kernel, dataset];]
```

{2.15 Second, Null}

We took a matrix with 250,000 elements and convolved it with a matrix with 10,000 elements. If we count each multiplication and each addition as one operation, then it should take 20,000 operations to calculate each output pixel (10,000 multiplications and 10,000 additions). The total number of operations thus would be:

400 * 400 * 20000 Operations

3200000000 Operations

(Note that the output image is only 400 by 400 pixels, as discussed above.) Divide the number of operations by the time it took, and we get:

$$\frac{3200000000 \text{ Operations}}{2.15 \text{ Second}}$$

$$\frac{1.48837 \times 10^9 \text{ Operations}}{\text{Second}}$$

The computer this test was done on operates at a speed of 266MHz. If this is what happened, how good is our computer at packing operations into clock cycles?

$$\frac{1.48837 \times 10^9 \frac{\text{Operations}}{\text{Second}}}{266 \times 10^6 \frac{\text{Cycle}}{\text{Second}}}$$

$$\frac{5.59538 \text{ Operations}}{\text{Cycle}}$$

Wait a minute, it appears to be doing more than five floating point operations *per clock cycle*. How can that be? Is this a vector processing supercomputer with six or more parallel floating point units? Well, no. It can't even do one whole floating point operation per cycle; and if it could, it wouldn't be able to get the data in and out of memory fast enough to keep up the pace. There must be something else going on.

In fact, *Mathematica* is using a very clever FFT algorithm. By taking the discrete Fourier transform of both the data and the kernel, messing with them, and then taking the inverse transform, it is possible to get the answer using many fewer operations. This is a good example of how a better algorithm can be far more valuable than a better implementation of a naive algorithm. Say someone had spent a year writing the most efficient possible assembly language version of the multiply/add algorithm: It would still be probably 10 to 15 times slower than even a sloppy implementation of the FFT algorithm.

So, does PhotoShop use an FFT algorithm when it applies filters that use convolution? Probably not. And, truth be told, it probably wouldn't benefit that much anyway. The FFT algorithm's benefits are mainly visible when the kernel is very large, and PhotoShop's kernels are typically small. But it's something they might want to think about.

■ Continuous function image manipulation

Convolution is a very powerful image manipulation tool, but it is possible to go much further with *Mathematica*. We are now going to see how to use the unique combination of symbolic and numerical capabilities of *Mathematica* to manipulate images in ways impossible in any other system.

The key idea is to transform the image from a discrete matrix of values into a continuous mathematical function, which can then be manipulated mathematically.

Mathematica includes a tremendously clever and powerful feature for doing this. **InterpolatingFunction** objects, introduced originally to represent the solutions to differential equations, are objects that act just like ordinary functions, but are based on tables of values. The function **ListInterpolation** takes a list or matrix of numbers, and returns an **InterpolatingFunction** that can be used to get interpolated values out of the array.

```
puppyFunction = ListInterpolation[Transpose[grayscalePuppy]]
```

```
InterpolatingFunction[{{1., 200.}, {1., 238.}}, <>]
```

(A small annoyance: The **Transpose** function (which interchanges rows with columns in the matrix) is necessary because, without it, the *x* and *y* dimensions of the resulting function would be interchanged, which is inconvenient.)

Let's see how this function works. Say you want to find out the value of a pixel in the image. You could pick out a particular element from the original data using [[ ]] notation. For example, here is the pixel from the 130th row, 40th column:

```
grayscalePuppy[[130, 40]]
```

```
0.329765
```

Using the **InterpolatingFunction**, we can get the same value by giving the "function" these same two values as arguments:

```
puppyFunction[40, 130]
```

```
0.329765
```

So far, nothing remarkable. But the powerful thing about **InterpolatingFunction**s is that they work even when the arguments are *not* integers. Using [[ ]] to extract pixels, you can only pick existing pixels. With **InterpolatingFunction**s, you can also pick pseudo pixel values from anywhere in between. For example:

```
puppyFunction[40, 130]
```

```
0.329765
```

```
puppyFunction[40.5, 130]
```

```
0.315517
```

```
puppyFunction[41, 130]
```

```
0.297804
```

Instead of thinking in terms of arrays of pixels, we can now think in terms of a mathematical function (of two variables) that happens to have *z*-values that correspond to the brightness of patches of our image. So, let's start thinking mathematically. What's the first thing you do with a function of two variables? Why, plot it of course:

```
Plot3D[puppyFunction[x, y],
    {x, 1, 200}, {y, 1, 238}, PlotPoints → 50];
```

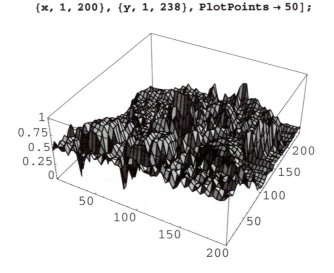

Note that the *x* and *y* plot ranges correspond to the number of pixels in the original image. This is merely the default used by **ListInterpolate**. Later we'll see how to re-scale the image to more generic ranges of values. For now, we are still recovering from the disappointment caused by this plot. It certainly doesn't look much like a puppy. But, it turns out this is mainly a matter of the viewpoint. Let's try a slightly different one:

```
Plot3D[puppyFunction[x, y], {x, 1, 200}, {y, 1, 238},
    PlotPoints → 50, ViewPoint → {0.0, -0.1, 2}];
```

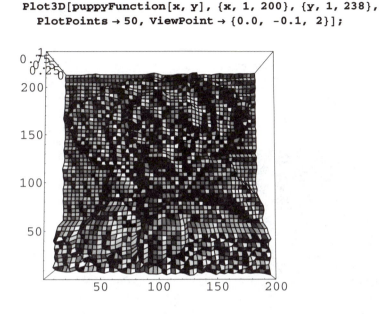

Ah, there's the puppy.

Going one step further, we can turn off the lighting model. With the option **Lighting→**
False, *Mathematica* uses whiter shades of gray for high values and darker shades of gray for
low values.

```
Plot3D[puppyFunction[x, y], {x, 1, 200}, {y, 1, 238},
    PlotPoints → 50, ViewPoint → {0.0, -0.1, 2}, Lighting → False];
```

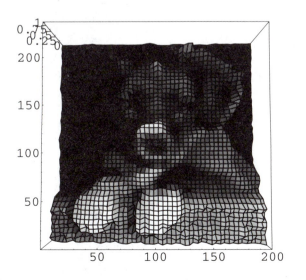

Remove the mesh, increase the number of plot points, and you have something pretty familiar looking:

```
Plot3D[puppyFunction[x, y],
   {x, 1, 200}, {y, 1, 238}, PlotPoints → 100,
   ViewPoint → {0.0, -0.1, 2}, Lighting → False, Mesh → False];
```

Here is a case where the new real-time 3-D rotation available in V4.0 is great fun. See Chapter 37 for more information about this feature. The short instructions are: evaluate the following command, then re-evaluate the plot command above. The resulting image can be rotated in real time by clicking and dragging it. Highly recommended.

```
<< RealTime3D`
```

Now, while making 3-D plots of puppies is fun, it's really not the most useful thing you can do. **DensityPlot** and **ContourPlot** are really much more effective. In fact, the limiting case of a 3-D plot viewed from directly above, with no perspective, is a **DensityPlot**, as you can see by comparing the plot above with the one below:

```
DensityPlot[puppyFunction[x, y], {x, 1, 200}, {y, 1, 238},
    PlotPoints → 200, Mesh → False,
    AspectRatio → Automatic, Frame → None];
```

Because **puppyFunction** is a mathematical function, we are not restricted to plotting it with the same number of sample points as it started with. For example, let's zoom in on the left eye. We select a 20 by 20 pixel area in the original image and plot it with 20 plot points, so we are seeing what amount to the original pixels:

```
DensityPlot[puppyFunction[x, y], {x, 65, 85}, {y, 150, 170},
    PlotPoints → 20, Mesh → False,
    AspectRatio → Automatic, Frame → None];
```

But we're not limited to the original pixels: Let's plot the same region with 10 times as many sample points in each direction:

```
DensityPlot[puppyFunction[x, y], {x, 65, 85}, {y, 150, 170},
   PlotPoints → 200, Mesh → False,
   AspectRatio → Automatic, Frame → None];
```

Now, it's important to remember that this is *made up* resolution: There is no new information that wasn't in the original image. But you have to admit it's pretty impressive! Note especially how realistic the highlight on the eyeball looks. Is that highlight in the original image or not? You be the judge.

By default, **ListInterpolation** creates an **InterpolationFunction** that uses cubic (third order) interpolation. By changing the order of the interpolation, we can significantly affect the appearance of the interpolated images.

Setting the order to zero results in no interpolation at, so the image with 200 plot points looks quite similar to the image with 20 plot points:

```
puppyFunction0 = ListInterpolation[
   Transpose[grayscalePuppy], InterpolationOrder → 0];

DensityPlot[puppyFunction0[x, y], {x, 65, 85}, {y, 150, 170},
   PlotPoints → 200, Mesh → False,
   AspectRatio → Automatic, Frame → None];
```

First order (linear) interpolation results in obvious horizontal and vertical artifacts (notice for example the stairstep effect in the first dark band down and to the left of the eyeball):

```
puppyFunction1 = ListInterpolation[
    Transpose[grayscalePuppy], InterpolationOrder → 1];

DensityPlot[puppyFunction1[x, y], {x, 65, 85}, {y, 150, 170},
    PlotPoints → 200, Mesh → False,
    AspectRatio → Automatic, Frame → None];
```

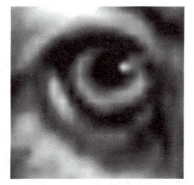

Increasing the interpolation order beyond three has little effect: As you can see in the next image, 10th order interpolation is not significantly different from third order. So it's no surprise that the default in, for example, Adobe Photoshop is third order interpolation when increasing the resolution of images. (Note that 10th order does provide *some* improvement: Look again at the first dark band below and to the left of the eyeball. It is smoother than in the third order interpolation.)

```
puppyFunction10 = ListInterpolation[
    Transpose[grayscalePuppy], InterpolationOrder → 10];

DensityPlot[puppyFunction10[x, y], {x, 65, 85}, {y, 150, 170},
    PlotPoints → 200, Mesh → False,
    AspectRatio → Automatic, Frame → None];
```

Another approach to images is to plot contours. This is in effect a type of interpolation as well. However, instead of discrete pixels, we now have discrete grayscale thresholds (by default, 10 levels of gray):

```
ContourPlot[puppyFunction[x, y], {x, 1, 200}, {y, 1, 238},
    PlotPoints → 50, AspectRatio → Automatic, Frame → None];
```

```
ContourPlot[puppyFunction[x, y], {x, 1, 200}, {y, 1, 238},
    PlotPoints → 50, AspectRatio → Automatic,
    Frame → None, ContourShading → False];
```

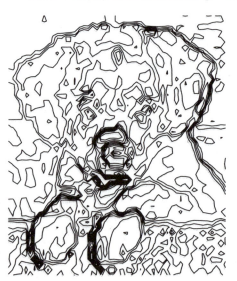

Jerry: I think I am starting to realize what it means for this puppy to be a mathematical function, rather than an image. Extracting these contours is clearly something you would do to a smooth, mathematical function, not a collection of pixel values.

Theo: Absolutely. Of course any of these things can be done to discrete images as well, but it's just a whole lot more *natural* to think of doing them to continuous functions. It's also dramatically easier to use *Mathematica*'s library of functions than it is to write routines for dealing with discrete data.

Removing the contour lines and increasing the resolution of the grid from which the contours are computed allows us to see the image more clearly (as before, the limit of such a process is the original image):

```
ContourPlot[puppyFunction[x, y], {x, 1, 200}, {y, 1, 238},
    PlotPoints → 200, ContourLines → False,
    AspectRatio → Automatic, Frame → None];
```

Let's zoom in on the eye again:

```
ContourPlot[puppyFunction[x, y], {x, 65, 85}, {y, 150, 170},
    PlotPoints → 100, AspectRatio → Automatic, Frame → None];
```

By removing the lines and increasing the number of contour levels, we see a different interpretation of a higher resolution version. Note that this version has some artifacts that the **Density-Plot** version doesn't, but is also better in other ways. It's interesting to have both available for comparison.

```
ContourPlot[puppyFunction[x, y], {x, 65, 85}, {y, 150, 170},
    PlotPoints → 70, ContourLines → False,
    Contours → 200, AspectRatio → Automatic, Frame → None];
```

Theo: OK, enough serious stuff, it's time for some warped puppies.

We'll go back to using **DensityPlot**, because it is the fastest function for generating images of this sort.

What happens if we apply a function to the x and y variables before passing them to **puppy‑Function**? This has the effect of changing the spacing at which the original image is sampled, as a function of the x and y coordinates. Perhaps an example will make this clear:

```
DensityPlot[puppyFunction[x², y²], {x, 1, √200 }, {y, 1, √238 },
   PlotPoints → 200, Mesh → False,
   AspectRatio → Automatic, Frame → None];
```

Jerry: Whoa, someone throw that puppy a line before he blows away in the wind! You said an example might make things clear, but I'm afraid it's only served to make me feel windswept.

Theo: OK, maybe this clever diagram will help:

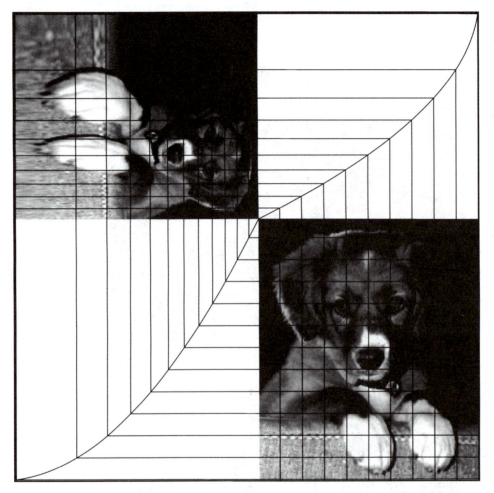

The parabolas represents the x^2 and y^2 functions we are using to distort the image. Towards the bottom of the image where the slope is shallow, a small portion of the original image is stretched to fill a large portion of the output image. Near the top where the slope is steep, the image is instead compressed. The same thing holds in the left/right direction.

For example, look at the square at the lower right of the original image. Follow the lines, and you'll see that it turns into a much bigger square in the output image. Conversely, the upper left square, which starts out the same size, turns into a smaller square in the output image. The lower left square turns into a wide rectangle, while the upper right square turns into a tall rectangle.

Jerry: This diagram is nice because it allows us to focus on corresponding areas between the original and the distorted images. It reminds me a little of the diagrams in D'Arcy Thompson's *On Growth and Form* (1917). He typically shows the output images (fish rather than dogs) with the distorted grid superimposed. You're supposed to assume that the grid started out rectangular, as in our case.

Theo: By the way, this diagram was generated with a *Mathematica* command, but the code is sort of big and ugly, too big to include in the book. (Readers of the electronic edition can click here to open a notebook showing the commands used to create the diagram.)

Before we continue, let's redo the **puppyFunction** so that its *x* and *y* values run over more mathematically sensible ranges (namely, -1 to 1 in the horizontal direction, and the appropriate range in the y direction to keep the coordinate system square):

```
puppyFunction2 = ListInterpolation[
   Transpose[grayscalePuppy], {{-1, 1}, {-1.19, 1.19}}];
```

```
DensityPlot[puppyFunction2[Sign[x] x², Sign[y] y²],
   {x, -1, 1}, {y, -√1.19 , √1.19 },
   PlotPoints → 200, Mesh → False,
   AspectRatio → Automatic, Frame → None];
```

Here are a few animations based on this theme:

```
Do[DensityPlot[puppyFunction2[Sign[x] Abs[x]ⁿ, Sign[y] Abs[y]ⁿ],
   {x, -1, 1}, {y, -ⁿ√1.19 , ⁿ√1.19 },
   PlotPoints → 200, Mesh → False,
   AspectRatio → 1.19, Frame → None],
   {n, 0.1, 2, .1}];
```

$$Do\big[DensityPlot[puppyFunction2[Sign[x]\, Abs[x]^n,\; Sign[y]\, Abs[y]^n],$$
$$\{x,\,-1,\,1\},\; \{y,\,-\sqrt[n]{1.19}\,,\; \sqrt[n]{1.19}\,\},$$
$$PlotPoints \to 200,\; Mesh \to False,$$
$$AspectRatio \to 1.19,\; Frame \to None\big],$$
$$\{n,\,0.1,\,2,\,.1\}\big];$$

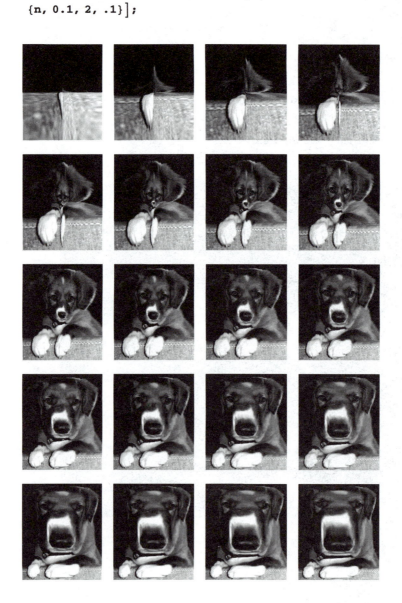

```
Do[DensityPlot[Apply[puppyFunction2, {x, y} * (x² + y²)^((n-1)/2)],
   {x, -1, 1}, {y, -1.19, 1.19},
   PlotPoints → 200, Mesh → False, AspectRatio → Automatic,
   Frame → None, PlotRange → {0, 1}],
   {n, .1, 2, .1}];
```

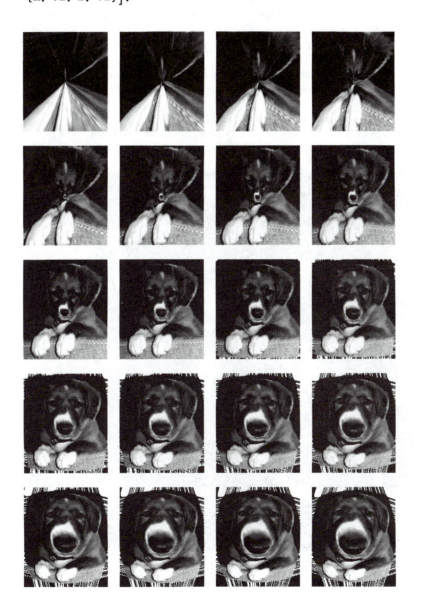

While there are many discrete-pixel based edge detection algorithms, perhaps the most fundamental way to define an edge in an image is as a point where the gradient (rate of change) of the brightness is high. This can be plotted easily using the fact that **Interpolat〈 ingFunctions** objects (such as our **puppyFunction2**) can be differentiated efficiently:

```
derivativePuppyFunctionX = Derivative[1, 0][puppyFunction2];
derivativePuppyFunctionY = Derivative[0, 1][puppyFunction2];
derivativePuppyFunctionXY[x_, y_] :=
   derivativePuppyFunctionX[x, y] + derivativePuppyFunctionY[x, y];

gradPuppyFunction[x_, y_] := √ (derivativePuppyFunctionX[x, y]² +
      derivativePuppyFunctionY[x, y]²);

DensityPlot[gradPuppyFunction[x, y],
   {x, -1, 1}, {y, -1.19, 1.19}, PlotPoints → {200, 238},
   Mesh → False, AspectRatio → Automatic, Frame → None];
```

It's also amusing to plot the rate of change of the image brightness in just the *x* or *y* direction independently, or the sum of the two. This gives a pleasing embossed look:

```
Show[GraphicsArray[{
    DensityPlot[derivativePuppyFunctionX[x, y],
      {x, -1, 1}, {y, -1.19, 1.19}, PlotPoints → {200, 238},
      Mesh → False, AspectRatio → Automatic,
      Frame → None, DisplayFunction → Identity],
    DensityPlot[derivativePuppyFunctionY[x, y],
      {x, -1, 1}, {y, -1.19, 1.19}, PlotPoints → {200, 238},
      Mesh → False, AspectRatio → Automatic,
      Frame → None, DisplayFunction → Identity],
    DensityPlot[derivativePuppyFunctionXY[x, y],
      {x, -1, 1}, {y, -1.19, 1.19}, PlotPoints → {200, 238},
      Mesh → False, AspectRatio → Automatic,
      Frame → None, DisplayFunction → Identity]}]];
```

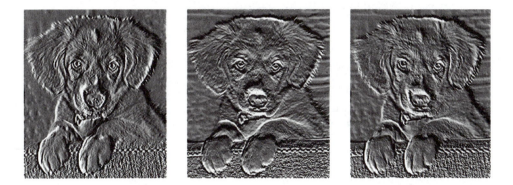

■ Image manipulation in color

Color image manipulation is just like grayscale image manipulation times three. Unfortunately, it uses at least three times as much time and memory, and because color involves triplets of numbers (red, green, blue) rather than a single grayscale value, it's harder to treat the image as a mathematical object. Be warned! The examples below, when applied to the 200x238 pixel image we're using as an example, use a *very large amount* of memory in the kernel. You'll need at least 60MB for the kernel to do even a few examples like these.

Of course, you can always treat a color image as three separate grayscale images, one for each color channel. Fortunately it's possible to be a bit more clever. The **ListInterpolation** function we used for grayscale images is able to handle not just two-dimensional data, but n-dimensional. You can think of a color image as a three-dimensional dataset, two physical dimensions plus a color dimension (which happens to have only three sample points). The following command constructs an **InterpolatingFunction** where the third argument to the function specifies which color component you want (1 for red, 2 for green, and 3 for blue).

The option **InterpolationOrder** tells it to use cubic interpolation in the x and y dimensions (this is the default used for grayscale images as well). Zero-order interpolation is adequate in the third (color) dimension, since we're not going to ask for values other than at exactly the sample points.

We should emphasize that using the third argument (the third dimension) to represent the color is purely a trick with no mathematical significance. You *could* specify values other than 1, 2, or 3 for the third argument, but the resulting images would be uninteresting. If you don't believe us, try it yourself.

```
colorPuppyFunction3D =
  ListInterpolation[Transpose[puppyImage[[1, 1]]] / 256.,
    {{-1, 1}, {-1.19, 1.19}, {1, 3}},
    InterpolationOrder → {3, 3, 0}];
```

For example, to get the red color component at **{0.2, 0.3}**:

```
colorPuppyFunction3D[0.2, 0.3, 1]
```

```
0.313843
```

We can make a function that returns all three components at once, by generating a three-element table:

```
colorPuppyFunction[x_, y_] =
  Table[colorPuppyFunction3D[x, y, c], {c, 1, 3}];
```

Here is the same point as in the example above, but this time we get all three colors:

```
colorPuppyFunction[0.2, 0.3]
```

```
{0.313843, 0.313843, 0.204156}
```

Now we are ready to begin plotting this image. Unfortunately, we can't use **DensityPlot**, because **DensityPlot** requires that the return value of the function being plotted be a single number. Fortunately, the way we are using **DensityPlot**, it's really just a simple wrapper for creating a **Raster** object, which we can do manually.

To simplify further examples, we'll use the following utility function to encapsulate the necessary steps:

```
Options[PlotColorImage] = {PlotPoints -> 20};
Attributes[PlotColorImage] = {HoldFirst};
PlotColorImage[func_, {x_, xmin_, xmax_}, {y_, ymin_, ymax_}, opts___] :=
 Module[{plotPoints},

  plotPoints = PlotPoints /. {opts} /. Options[PlotColorImage];
  If[Head[plotPoints] =!= List,
   plotPoints = {plotPoints, plotPoints}];

  Show[Graphics[Raster[Table[func,
     {y, ymin, ymax, (ymax - ymin)/plotPoints[[2]]}, {x, xmin, xmax, (xmax - xmin)/plotPoints[[1]]}],
    {{xmin, ymin}, {xmax, ymax}}, ColorFunction -> RGBColor],
    AspectRatio -> Automatic, PlotRange -> {{xmin, xmax}, {ymin, ymax}}]];
 ]
```

Here is an example using this utility function (note that the arguments are pretty much the same as they were for the grayscale examples done using **DensityPlot**).

```
Off[InterpolatingFunction::dmval]
```

```
PlotColorImage[colorPuppyFunction[x, y + Sin[30 x] / 20],
  {x, -1, 1}, {y, -1.19, 1.19}, PlotPoints -> 200];
```

You can combine both coordinate distortions and manipulations of the color values. For example, the following function will convert any color near white into red:

```
highlightBlaze[{r_, g_, b_}] :=
 If[r > 0.8 && g > 0.8 && b > 0.8, {1, 0, 0}, {r, g, b}]
```

Applied to the image, it highlights in red anything that is close enough to white in the original image (we are also reflecting and distorting the image):

```
PlotColorImage[highlightBlaze[colorPuppyFunction[x², y]],
 {x, -1, 1}, {y, -1.19, 1.19}, PlotPoints → 200];
```

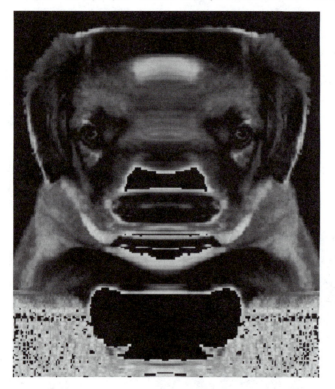

What about rotation? To simplify the syntax, we can define a variation of **colorPuppyFunc-** **tion** that accepts a list (vector) of two values as a single argument, rather than two separate arguments. This allows us to use matrix manipulations to transform the coordinates:

```
colorPuppyFunction[{x_, y_}] := colorPuppyFunction[x, y]
```

Here is a simple rotation of the image (done by multiplying the (x, y) coordinate vector by a standard rotation matrix). In this case we are rotating by one radian (about 57 degrees):

```
PlotColorImage[
    colorPuppyFunction[θ = 1.0; ( Cos[θ]   Sin[θ] ) . {x, y}],
                                 (-Sin[θ]   Cos[θ] )
    {x, -1, 1}, {y, -1.19, 1.19}, PlotPoints → 200];
```

Theo: Oh! I'm dazzled by colored stripes! (And you are too if you are reading the electronic edition of this book.)

Jerry: Calmly, can you explain why there are stripes in the picture?

Theo: It all goes back to Plato. For millennia, philosophers have wondered what lies beyond our limited perceptions: What is *outside the canvas*. Now, just in time for the latest millennium, *Mathematica* has answered this question. We created an interpolating function that represents the image, and then we asked it to *extrapolate*, to give us values outside the range for which we specified sample points. Notice how the boundary between the image and the wild colored stripes is not sharp. The extrapolation works for a short while, before bursting into exuberant color.

Let's try some examples where the angle of rotation depends on the distance from the center of the image. First, linearly proportional to the distance:

```
PlotColorImage[
  colorPuppyFunction[θ = √(x² + y²) ; ( Cos[θ]   Sin[θ] ) . {x, y}],
                                       ( -Sin[θ]  Cos[θ] )
  {x, -1, 1}, {y, -1.19, 1.19}, PlotPoints → 200];
```

Next, proportional to the square of the distance, which turns out to give a more pleasing result, probably because it keeps the face intact while providing more twist farther out:

```
PlotColorImage[
  colorPuppyFunction[θ = x² + y²; ( Cos[θ]   Sin[θ]  ) . {x, y}],
                                   ( -Sin[θ]  Cos[θ] )
  {x, -1, 1}, {y, -1.19, 1.19}, PlotPoints → 400];
```

Ah, what more could anyone ask for!

Chapter **46**

How do I integrate and differentiate?

To do an integral in *Mathematica*, use the Basic Input palette. (If this palette isn't open, use the **BasicInput** command found in the **File** menu, **Palettes** submenu.) The four buttons of interest are in the top half of the palette, and look like this:

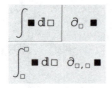

With a fresh input notebook open, click the top left button to get this input template:

$$\int \square \, \mathbf{d}\square$$

Fill in the integrand, then use the Tab key to skip to the variable of integration. For example:

$$\int \mathbf{x^2} \, \mathbf{d}\mathbf{x}$$

$$\frac{x^3}{3}$$

(You can also use the linear notation **Integrate[x^2, x]** or **Integrate[x², x]**, or enter the 2-D notation from the keyboard. To enter the integral sign from the keyboard, type ⎡ESC⎤**int**⎡ESC⎤. To enter the **d** symbol, type ⎡ESC⎤**dd**⎡ESC⎤. Note that **d** is *not* the ordinary letter "d".)

You can integrate expressions containing more than one variable; the other variables are treated as constants:

$$\int \mathbf{a} \, \mathbf{x^2} \, \mathbf{d}\mathbf{x}$$

$$\frac{a \, x^3}{3}$$

$$\int x^2 \, y^3 \, dx$$

$$\frac{x^3 \, y^3}{3}$$

$$\int x^2 \, y^3 \, dy$$

$$\frac{x^2 \, y^4}{4}$$

We can do double integrals (the inner variable is integrated first):

$$\int \int x^2 \, y^3 \, dy \, dx$$

$$\frac{x^3 \, y^4}{12}$$

Differentiation is done with the ∂ operator. Use the Basic Input palette to create a differentiation template:

$$\partial_\Box \, \Box$$

Type the variable first, then use Tab to move to the second position and type the function to be differentiated.

$$\partial_x \, x^2$$

2 x

$$\partial_x \, (a \, x^2)$$

2 a x

$$\partial_x \, (x^2 \, y^3)$$

$2 \, x \, y^3$

$$\partial_y \, (x^2 \, y^3)$$

$3 \, x^2 \, y^2$

You can use the linear notation **D[f,x]** to do the same thing, or enter the 2-D structure from the keyboard. To enter the ∂ symbol, type [ESC]**pd**[ESC], then use Control-dash to enter the subscript position, type the variable, type Control-space to move back to the baseline, then type the function to be differentiated.

Derivatives with respect to several variables can be done as follows:

$\partial_{\mathbf{x},\mathbf{y}}\,(\mathbf{x^2\ y^3}\,)$

$6\,\mathrm{x}\,\mathrm{y}^2$

$\partial_{x,y}$ uses a comma-separated list. Such a list can have as many variables as you like; the differentiation is done in the order the variables appear in the list.

Multiple derivatives with respect to the same variable can be done as follows:

$\partial_{\{\mathbf{x},5\}}\,(\mathbf{x^{10}}\,)$

$30240\,\mathrm{x}^5$

To do a definite integral, create the appropriate template using the Basic Input palette:

$$\int_{\square}^{\square}\square\,\mathbf{d}\square$$

Type in the lower limit, upper limit, integrand, and variable, using the Tab key to move to the next position. For example, this command gives the integral of $\mathbf{x^2}$ from $\mathbf{0}$ to $\mathbf{1}$:

$$\int_0^1\mathbf{x^2}\ \mathbf{d\,x}$$

$\dfrac{1}{3}$

You can do derivatives involving undefined functions of the variable. For example, the chain rule:

$\partial_{\mathbf{x}}\,\mathbf{u\,[v\,[x]\,]}$

$\mathrm{u}'\,[\mathrm{v}\,[\mathrm{x}]\,]\ \mathrm{v}'\,[\mathrm{x}]$

The notation $\mathbf{v'\,[x]}$ means the first derivative of $\mathbf{v}$ with respect to $\mathbf{x}$. Since we haven't defined $\mathbf{v}$ to be any specific function, its derivative can't be evaluated further.

Here is an example of the product rule with three functions:

$\partial_{\mathbf{x}}\,(\mathbf{u\,[x]\ v\,[x]\ w\,[x]}\,)$

$\mathrm{v}\,[\mathrm{x}]\ \mathrm{w}\,[\mathrm{x}]\ \mathrm{u}'\,[\mathrm{x}]\ +\mathrm{u}\,[\mathrm{x}]\ \mathrm{w}\,[\mathrm{x}]\ \mathrm{v}'\,[\mathrm{x}]\ +\mathrm{u}\,[\mathrm{x}]\ \mathrm{v}\,[\mathrm{x}]\ \mathrm{w}'\,[\mathrm{x}]$

There are various ways to specify which elements of the expression should be treated as constants and which should be assumed to depend on the variable. See The *Mathematica* Book, or click here, for more information.

Although it is easy to differentiate any function using only a few simple rules, most integrals are very hard or impossible to solve exactly. *Mathematica* has a very good integrator. (See The *Mathematica Book*, or click here, for more details about what kinds of functions can and can't be integrated). If you want to try out what integrals *Mathematica* can do, but don't have a copy of *Mathematica*, you can visit the Wolfram Research sponsored site for doing integrals on the web, at http://integrals.com.

Mathematica can integrate rational functions (that is, quotients of two polynomials):

$$\int \frac{x^5}{x^3 + 3 x^2 + 7 x} \, dx$$

$$2 x - \frac{3 x^2}{2} + \frac{x^3}{3} - \frac{73 \, \text{ArcTan}\left[\frac{3+2 x}{\sqrt{19}}\right]}{\sqrt{19}} + \frac{15}{2} \, \text{Log}[7 + 3 x + x^2]$$

It can integrate many other kinds of functions:

$$\int \text{Sin}[x]^2 \, dx$$

$$\frac{x}{2} - \frac{1}{4} \, \text{Sin}[2 x]$$

It recognizes many integrals that can be defined in terms of special functions:

$$\int a \, b^{-x^2} \, dx$$

$$\frac{a \sqrt{\pi} \, \text{Erf}[x \sqrt{\text{Log}[b]}]}{2 \sqrt{\text{Log}[b]}}$$

$$\int \text{Sin}[x^2]^2 \, dx$$

$$\frac{1}{4} \left(2 x - \sqrt{\pi} \, \text{FresnelC}\left[\frac{2 x}{\sqrt{\pi}}\right]\right)$$

$$\int \frac{\text{Sin}[x^2]}{x^5} \, dx$$

$$-\frac{\text{Cos}[x^2]}{4 x^2} - \frac{\text{Sin}[x^2]}{4 x^4} - \frac{\text{SinIntegral}[x^2]}{4}$$

Note: Doing complex integrals like the ones above will cause *Mathematica* to load packages before the integral is done. This loading is automatic, and the only thing you will notice is an additional delay the first time an integral of this type is done. Be warned, however, that loading the packages can take a lot of memory.

When *Mathematica* can't do an integral symbolically, it returns the command unevaluated:

$$\int \text{Cos}[\text{Cos}[\text{x}]] \, d\text{x}$$

$$\int \text{Cos}[\text{Cos}[\text{x}]] \, d\text{x}$$

Mathematica can also do definite integration:

$$\int_0^1 \text{x}^3 \, d\text{x}$$

$$\frac{1}{4}$$

and improper definite integrals:

$$\int_0^\infty \text{a} \, \text{b}^{-\text{x}^2} \, d\text{x}$$

$$\frac{\text{a} \, \sqrt{\pi}}{2 \, \sqrt{\text{Log}[\text{b}]}}$$

As with indefinite integrals, when *Mathematica* can't do a definite integral, it returns the command unevaluated:

$$\int_0^1 \text{Cos}[\text{Cos}[\text{x}]] \, d\text{x}$$

$$\int_0^1 \text{Cos}[\text{Cos}[\text{x}]] \, d\text{x}$$

You can use **N** to compute the integral numerically:

$$\text{N}\left[\int_0^1 \text{Cos}[\text{Cos}[\text{x}]] \, d\text{x}\right]$$

0.659781053601222

If you know you want to do the integration numerically, you can use **NIntegrate**. This prevents *Mathematica* from *trying* to do the integration symbolically first:

```
NIntegrate[Cos[Cos[x]], {x, 0, 1}]

0.659781053601222
```

You might think that indefinite integrals can't be computed numerically, because the answer is a function, not a number. But just as you can have a numerical approximation of a number, in *Mathematica* you can also have a numerical approximation of a function (called an **InterpolatingFunction**).

To compute an indefinite integral numerically, you must use **NDSolve**, not **NIntegrate**. The following example computes and then plots the indefinite numerical integral of **Cos[** **Cos[x]]**, over a range from **-10** to **10**.

```
NDSolve[{y'[x] == Cos[Cos[x]], y[0] == 0}, y[x], {x, -10, 10}]

{{y[x] -> InterpolatingFunction[{-10., 10.}, <>][x]}}

Plot[y[x] /. %, {x, -10, 10}];
```

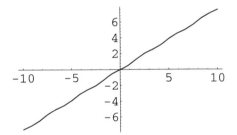

You can use this example as a template. Replace **Cos[Cos[x]]** with your function, and **-10, 10** with the range over which you want the result to be valid. If you want to know more about how **NDSolve** works, see <u>Chapter</u> 48.

■ Example

Jerry: Most calculus textbooks have a section in which they plot a function, then plot its derivative, then its second derivative, etc. Can we do this?

Theo: The following commands will make such plots. (2-D Plotting is explained in more detail in <u>Chapter</u> 31.) We use the notation **D[f, {x, 2}]**, which means differentiate with respect to **x** twice. (Don't worry about what **Evaluate** means; for now just type it in and use it.)

We're going to look at x^3 (to make plots of your own favorite function, change the definition in the first line):

```
f = x³;
Plot[f, {x, -3, 3}];
Plot[Evaluate[∂ₓ f], {x, -3, 3}];
Plot[Evaluate[∂₍ₓ,₂₎ f], {x, -3, 3}];
```

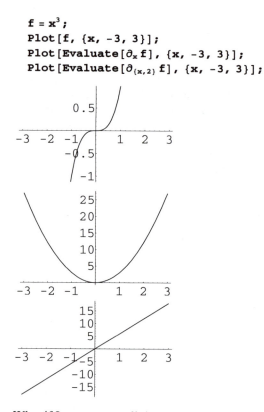

Jerry: What if I want to see all three on the same set of axes?

Theo: Use the following command:

```
f = x³;
Plot[Evaluate[{f, ∂ₓ f, ∂₍ₓ,₂₎ f}], {x, -3, 3}];
```

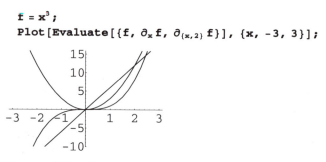

Jerry: How would I make a table of derivatives of a function?

Theo: Here's a nice little command that makes a formatted table of derivatives (again, change the definition of **f** to whatever function you like):

```
f = x⁶ + Sin[x];
Do[Print[n, Switch[n,
0, "th",
1, "st",
2, "nd",
3, "rd",
_, "th"], " Derivative = ", ∂{x,n} f], {n, 0, 10}]
```

0th Derivative = $x^6 + Sin[x]$

1st Derivative = $6 x^5 + Cos[x]$

2nd Derivative = $30 x^4 - Sin[x]$

3rd Derivative = $120 x^3 - Cos[x]$

4th Derivative = $360 x^2 + Sin[x]$

5th Derivative = $720 x + Cos[x]$

6th Derivative = $720 - Sin[x]$

7th Derivative = $-Cos[x]$

8th Derivative = $Sin[x]$

9th Derivative = $Cos[x]$

10th Derivative = $-Sin[x]$

You can ignore the tricky **Switch** command; it just makes the output look pretty.

Jerry: The product rule is usually seen with two functions:

$$\partial_x (u[x] \, v[x])$$

$$v[x] \, u'[x] + u[x] \, v'[x]$$

My interest increases if there are three or more functions involved:

$$\partial_x (u[x] \, v[x] \, w[x])$$

$$v[x] \, w[x] \, u'[x] + u[x] \, w[x] \, v'[x] + u[x] \, v[x] \, w'[x]$$

$$\partial_x (u[x] \, v[x] \, w[x] \, y[x])$$

$$v[x] \, w[x] \, y[x] \, u'[x] + u[x] \, w[x] \, y[x] \, v'[x] + \\ u[x] \, v[x] \, y[x] \, w'[x] + u[x] \, v[x] \, w[x] \, y'[x]$$

From this we can see that there is a fairly simple general pattern.

Chapter **47**

How do I find limits?

To calculate the limit of a function, use the **Limit** command. For example:

$$\text{Limit}\left[\frac{\text{Sin}[x]}{x}, x \to 0\right]$$

1

- The first argument is the function.
- The second argument specifies the variable to use and the value to approach. The notation **x→0** should be read as "**x** goes to **0**".

In some cases, when you approach a limit from different directions, you get different limiting values. You can specify a direction using the **Direction** option. The following command calculates the limit approaching from the left (that is, traveling towards the right, or in a positive direction):

$$\text{Limit}\left[\text{Tan}[x], x \to \frac{\pi}{2}, \text{Direction} \to 1\right]$$

∞

The next example approaches from the right. Note that the value you give **Direction** indicates what direction you want to travel in, not where you are coming from. Thus a negative value means traveling in the negative direction, or from the right. Only the sign is important, not the magnitude (the number can be complex, in which case only the phase is important).

$$\text{Limit}\left[\text{Tan}[x], x \to \frac{\pi}{2}, \text{Direction} \to -1\right]$$

$-\infty$

You can use **Limit** to calculate derivatives, just as people did before television was invented:

$$g[x\_] := x^2 ;$$
$$\text{Limit}\left[\frac{g[x + dx] - g[x]}{dx}, dx \to 0\right]$$

$$2 x$$

To try this with your own function, change the definition of **g[x_]** in the command above.

■ Discussion

Jerry: I've heard from many people who say they have gotten wrong answers from various different mathematics programs. Although I'm sure these programs will all be perfect in future versions, how much can we trust them now?

Theo: You should never *really* trust the result of any single calculation, whether done by a computer program or by a human. If you're going to build a bridge, check your work at least twice before you let the mayor cut the ribbon, or you may end up the laughing stock of future bridge-building classes.

Jerry: So, for example, if we have any doubts about a symbolic limit, it's always a good idea to try making some plots and calculating a few numerical values around the limit. That way we can see if the claimed limit makes any sense. Let's try an example:

$$\text{Limit}\left[\frac{1 - \text{Cos}[x^2]}{x^4}, x \to 0\right]$$

$$\frac{1}{2}$$

Does this make sense? Let's make a plot:

$$\text{Plot}\left[\frac{1 - \text{Cos}[x^2]}{x^4}, \{x, -5, 5\}\right];$$

From the plot it's certainly reasonable to think that the limit might be 1/2. Let's try substituting a few values near zero:

$$\frac{1 - \text{Cos}[x^2]}{x^4} \; / . \; x \to 0.1$$

0.4999958333472195046

$$\frac{1 - \text{Cos}[x^2]}{x^4} \; / . \; x \to 0.01$$

0.4999999995741917501

$$\frac{1 - \text{Cos}[x^2]}{x^4} \; / . \; x \to 0.0001$$

0.4998172015158175441

$$\frac{1 - \text{Cos}[x^2]}{x^4} \; / . \; x \to 0.000001$$

0.

This looks strange. The limit seems to be close to $\frac{1}{2}$, but then it suddenly becomes zero.

Theo: That zero is probably caused by numerical round-off. Let's try the same expression but with more decimal places. (*Mathematica* notices how many decimal places you start with and preserves accuracy in the course of the calculation.)

$$\frac{1 - \text{Cos}[x^2]}{x^4} \; / . \; x \to 0.0000010000000000000000000000000000000000000000$$

0.4999999999999999999999999958333333

Jerry: So, it looks as if in this case *Mathematica* probably did get the correct exact answer, since the numerical values do seem to approach 1/2.

Theo: Naturally this is not a proof of anything, but this sort of sanity check is a good idea if the result really matters. See <u>Chapter</u> 24.0 for more about using high precision arithmatic.

Chapter **48**

How do I solve differential equations?

The function **DSolve** solves symbolic differential equations in much the same way that **Solve** solves algebraic equations. The function **NDSolve**, described later in this chapter, solves differential equations numerically.

Here is an example of **DSolve**:

$$\texttt{DSolve[y'[x] == x^2, y[x], x]}$$

$$\left\{\left\{ y[x] \to \frac{x^3}{3} + C[1] \right\}\right\}$$

• The first argument is the equation to be solved, written in terms of a function (**y[x]**) and its derivatives (**y'[x]**, **y''[x]**, etc.).
• The second argument is the function to be solved for.
• The third argument is the independent variable.

The result is given as a list of replacement rules. **C[1]** represents an arbitrary constant of integration. See <u>Chapter</u> 27 for more information about how to read and use results in this form.

You can give **DSolve** a list of equations as its first argument and it will solve them simultaneously. This is useful for specifying initial conditions and/or boundary conditions:

$$\texttt{DSolve[\{y'[x] == x^2, y[0] == 1\}, y[x], x]}$$

$$\left\{\left\{ y[x] \to 1 + \frac{x^3}{3} \right\}\right\}$$

DSolve can solve a wide variety of differential equations. Here are a few examples:

$$\texttt{DSolve[y''[x] + y[x] == 0, y[x], x]}$$

$$\{\{y[x] \to C[2] \, Cos[x] - C[1] \, Sin[x]\}\}$$

$$\texttt{DSolve[\{y''[x] + y[x] == 0, y''[0] == 0\}, y[x], x]}$$

$$\{\{y[x] \to - (C[1] \, Sin[x])\}\}$$

$$\text{DSolve}\left[\left\{\mathbf{y''[x]} + \mathbf{y[x]} == 0, \; \mathbf{y''[0]} == 0, \; \mathbf{y}\left[\frac{\pi}{2}\right] == 1\right\}, \; \mathbf{y[x]}, \; \mathbf{x}\right]$$

$$\{\{y[x] \to \text{Sin}[x]\}\}$$

$$\text{DSolve}[\{\mathbf{x}\,\mathbf{y'[x]} == 3\,\mathbf{y[x]} + \mathbf{x^4}\,\text{Cos}[\mathbf{x}], \; \mathbf{y[2\pi]} == 0\}, \; \mathbf{y[x]}, \; \mathbf{x}]$$

$$\{\{y[x] \to x^3\,\text{Sin}[x]\}\}$$

$$\text{DSolve}[\{\mathbf{y'[x]} + \mathbf{y[x]} == \mathbf{E^x}, \; \mathbf{y[0]} == 1\}, \; \mathbf{y[x]}, \; \mathbf{x}]$$

$$\left\{\left\{y[x] \to \frac{1}{2\,E^x} + \frac{E^x}{2}\right\}\right\}$$

DSolve can also solve systems of equations involving more than one function. In such cases you give **DSolve** a list of functions as its second argument instead of a single function:

$$\text{DSolve}[\{\mathbf{u'[x]} == \mathbf{v[x]}, \; \mathbf{v'[x]} == \mathbf{u[x]}\}, \; \{\mathbf{u[x]}, \; \mathbf{v[x]}\}, \; \mathbf{x}]$$

$$\left\{\left\{u[x] \to \frac{C[1] + E^{2x}\,C[1] - C[2] + E^{2x}\,C[2]}{2\,E^x}, \right.\right.$$
$$\left.\left. v[x] \to \frac{-C[1] + E^{2x}\,C[1] + C[2] + E^{2x}\,C[2]}{2\,E^x}\right\}\right\}$$

DSolve has a number of additional features and capabilities; anyone using it extensively should read about them in The *Mathematica* Book, or click <u>here</u>.

NDSolve allows you to solve differential equations numerically. This function takes the same arguments as **DSolve**, with a few extra restrictions. You must specify enough initial conditions to give completely determined solutions, and all the conditions must be specified at the same value of the independent variable. You must also specify a numerical range for the independent variable (this is the range over which the solution will be valid). Here is an example:

$$\text{NDSolve}[\{\mathbf{y'[x]} == \mathbf{x^2}, \; \mathbf{y[0]} == 1\}, \; \mathbf{y[x]}, \; \{\mathbf{x}, \; -1, \; 1\}]$$

$$\{\{y[x] \to \text{InterpolatingFunction}[\{\{-1., \; 1.\}\}, \; <>][x]\}\}$$

- The first argument is the system of equations to be solved.
- The second argument is the function to solve for.
- The third argument is a standard range specification list, indicating that the independent variable, **x**, should run, in this example, from **-1** to **1**.

The result is given in the same format as for **Solve** or **DSolve**, except that the solution is an **InterpolatingFunction** object. An **InterpolatingFunction** is like a black box; given an input value it produces an output, but you can't see anything of its internal structure. Usually the best thing to do with an **InterpolatingFunction** is to plot it.

The first step in plotting the solution is to extract the **InterpolatingFunction**s from the result of the **NDSolve** command. This is done in much the same way as one extracts results from a **Solve** command (see Chapter 27 for more information):

```
solutions =
  y[x] /. NDSolve[{y'[x] == x², y[0] == 1}, y[x], {x, -1, 1}]

{InterpolatingFunction[{{-1., 1.}}, <>][x]}
```

Now we can plot the solution (but only over the range that was originally specified for the solution):

```
Plot[solutions, {x, -1, 1}];
```

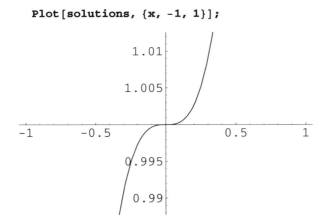

In this case we could have solved the equation symbolically using **DSolve**, but there are many differential equations that can be solved only numerically. As with **DSolve**, there are many more features and capabilities of **NDSolve**. The interested reader should consult The *Mathematica* Book or click here.

Chapter 49

How do I use *Mathematica* as a word processor?

Just start typing.

The *Mathematica* notebook interface is, in many ways, a word processor with a few extra features. When you open a new *Mathematica* notebook window, you see an empty space with a horizontal line near the top (this line is called the *cell insertion point*). Here is what an empty window looks like on a Macintosh:

Except for the items in the window frame, everything would look almost identical on any other brand of computer.

As soon as you start typing, a new "cell" is created to hold what you type. The cell is shown by a bracket on the right side of the window. If you type several lines (using the Return key to begin new lines) the cell bracket will grow to enclose everything you type. Here is what a two-line cell looks like:

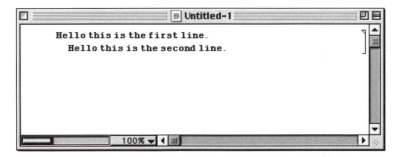

Hello this is the first line.
     Hello this is the second line.

The text in a cell can be manipulated in much the same way as you manipulate text in any other word processor. You can use the mouse and the Cut, Copy, Paste, and Delete (or Clear) commands in the normal way. (The versions of *Mathematica* for Macintosh, NeXT, and MS Windows each conform to the local customs and traditions of their respective hosts.)

If you click the mouse just below the bottom of your cell, you will get a horizontal line across the width of the window. This is the cell insertion point again:

If you start typing, a new cell will be created below the first one. You can tell the difference between one large cell and two smaller cells by the brackets on the right hand side:

You can select and manipulate cells in much the same way as you select and manipulate characters in text:

- To select a cell, click on its cell bracket.

- To place the cell insertion point, click between two cells, or above the first cell or below the last cell.

- To select more than one cell, click on one cell bracket and then drag over the others holding down the mouse button.

- To cut, copy, or delete cells, select them and then use the appropriate menu command.

- To insert cells you have copied, place the cell insertion point and then use the Paste command.

Every cell has a *cell style* that determines the default attributes of that cell. When you create a new cell by typing, it is, by default, in the Input cell style, which is normally Courier font, boldface, 12-point type.

When you evaluate an input cell, the output is placed in a new cell in Output cell style. This style is similar to Input, except that it is not boldface. The combination of these two styles gives the typical bold/nonbold look of a calculation session:

If you use *Mathematica* only as a calculator, these are the only two styles you will typically see in the notebooks that you create. By using a few other styles, though, you can turn your notebooks into complete documents.

You may notice that our example now has two cell brackets and a third larger one that encloses them. This enclosing bracket is called a *group bracket* and is discussed in Chapter 50, "How do I use *Mathematica* as an outliner?".

There are several ways to change the cell style of a cell. The easiest is to choose the Show Toolbar command in the Format menu. This will put a toolbar at the top of the window:

Click above the first cell to place the cell insertion point, and then choose Text from the cell style pop-up menu:

Now start typing:

The new cell is in the Text style. (Choosing a cell style while the selection is a cell insertion point is like choosing a font while the selection is a text insertion point–it affects the style of the next cell created there.)

This style has a nicer-looking (proportionally spaced) font, is aligned to the left of input and output, and is set up so lines longer than one page width are automatically wrapped.

Each cell style is a collection of many individual settings (called *options*). See Chapter 64 for more information about options. Cell styles in turn are collected together in a *style sheet*, which determines the overall look of the notebook. See Chapter 52 and Chapter 54 for more information about style sheets.

We might want to make the first cell in this example into a section heading. To do this, we first select the cell by clicking on its cell bracket:

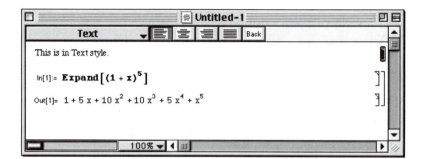

Then we choose the Section style from the cell style pop-up menu:

Of course, the text "This is in the Text style." no longer describes itself accurately!

The Section style includes larger, bold text and a square dingbat.

A very useful shortcut to know is that each style has a command-key equivalent. Following are the command keys (Alt keys on Windows) for the most useful predefined styles:

Command-1: **Title style**

Command-2: Subtitle style

Command-3: *Subsubtitle style*

■ Command-4: **Section style**

■ Command-5: **Subsection style**

■ Command-6: **Subsubsection style**

Command-7: Text style

Command-8: Small Text style

Command-9: `Input style`

The toolbar can be used to change some of the attributes of cells. We've already seen how to use the cell style pop-up menu to change the style of cells. The three buttons to the right of the pop-up menu are used to change the alignment of the text in the selected cells. For example, to center-align the Section heading in the last example, select the first cell and click the center button:

To change the left or right indentation of the cell, choose **Show Ruler** from the **Format** menu to get a margins ruler:

The two small markers in the ruler section can be used to change the left and right cell margins.

The left and right page margins can't be adjusted using this ruler (they can be changed only by using the Printing Options dialog box, from the **Printing Settings** submenu of the **File** menu).

To change a margin setting, select the cells you want to affect and then click and drag one of the margin indicators. For example, we could crunch the section heading into a narrow band:

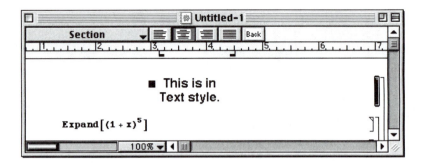

■ Worked Example

Let us imagine that we want to write a book about *Mathematica* called *The Beginner's Guide to Mathematica.* We want to do it entirely in *Mathematica,* of course. We'll do a short chapter on factoring and expanding polynomials.

First we need to think of a few good examples of factoring and expanding. We can quickly type these in, using *Mathematica* like a calculator:

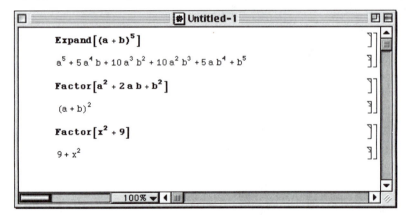

Let's add a title.

We move the mouse to the space between the top of the first cell and the top of the window (the pointer will change into a horizontal bar when we are in the right place), and then click. A horizontal bar (the cell insertion point) appears across the whole width of the window. We type Command-1 (one), or Alt-1 on a Windows computer, to choose the Title style. Then we type in our title. A new cell in the Title style will be created when we type the first character.

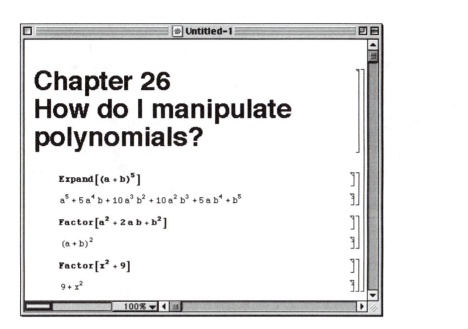

Ignore for now the growing number of large, enclosing brackets on the right side. They are described in Chapter 50, "How do I use *Mathematica* as an outliner?".

Since the Title cell style specifies bold text, the title is bold. We want only the "Chapter 26" to be bold, so we select the rest of the title with the mouse and choose **Bold** from the **Face** submenu of the **Format** menu:

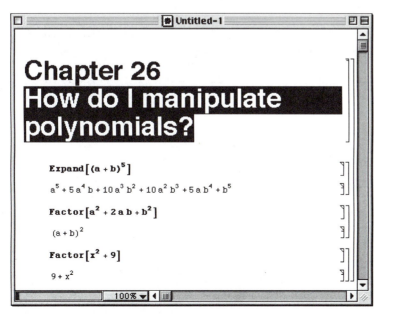

Next we click between the bottom of the Title cell and the top of the first example cell, to get another cell insertion point. This time we use Command-7 to get the Text style, and then type some text. We can add more Text cells in the same way, giving this result:

Chapter 26
How do I manipulate polynomials?

The commands to know are:

Expand$\left[(a+b)^5\right]$

$a^5 + 5\,a^4\,b + 10\,a^3\,b^2 + 10\,a^2\,b^3 + 5\,a\,b^4 + b^5$

Factor$\left[a^2 + 2\,a\,b + b^2\right]$

$(a+b)^2$

By default, *Mathematica* factors over the integers:

Factor$\left[x^2 + 9\right]$

$9 + x^2$

The word *Mathematica* is put in italics automatically whenever it is typed.

Now we have the beginnings of a chapter. If you want to see the rest, turn to Chapter 26, "How do I manipulate polynomials?", in this book.

Yes, this whole book was printed directly from *Mathematica*. The words you are reading right now are in a text cell created in exactly the way described here.

Chapter **50**

How do I use *Mathematica* as an outliner?

Before reading this chapter, you should read **Chapter** 49, "How do I use *Mathematica* as a word processor?", which describes cells and cell styles. You need to understand cells before reading this chapter.

In **Chapter** 49 we mentioned the large, enclosing brackets (called group brackets) that appear in some of the examples, such as this one:

These group brackets are the heart of the *Mathematica* outlining system. If you double-click a group bracket, all the cells in the group are collapsed, leaving only the first cell (called the *head cell*) visible. For example, if you double-click the group bracket enclosing the bottom two cells, the result looks like this:

If you double-click the outermost (right-most) group bracket, the result looks like this:

Double-clicking the closed group bracket opens it up again:

Notice that the inner group is still closed: Each group remains open or closed individually, regardless of groups enclosing it.

To see the usefulness of groups, consider the following notebook (you can use the techniques discussed in **Chapter** 49, "How do I use *Mathematica* as a word processor?", to create this notebook):

Some Commands

■ Expand Section

Here is an expand command:

In[2]:= $\mathbf{Expand}\left[(1 + x)^5\right]$

Out[2]= $1 + 5\,x + 10\,x^2 + 10\,x^3 + 5\,x^4 + x^5$

■ Factor Section

Here is a factor command:

In[3]:= $\mathbf{Factor}\left[x^9 - 1\right]$

Out[3]= $(-1 + x)\,(1 + x + x^2)\,(1 + x^3 + x^6)$

■ Integrate Section

Here is an integrate command:

In[4]:= $\int \dfrac{1}{1 - x^2}\, dx$

Out[4]= $-\dfrac{1}{2}\,\mathrm{Log}\,[-1 + x] + \dfrac{1}{2}\,\mathrm{Log}\,[1 + x]$

As long as all the cells are in the appropriate cell styles (title in the Title style, section headings in the Section style, commentary cells in the Text style, etc.), the cells will automatically be grouped as shown.

Now if we double-click each of the group brackets that enclose a section, we get this:

Some Commands

■ Expand Section
■ Factor Section
■ Integrate Section

(The window doesn't actually get smaller, we're just showing it that way to save space.)

If these sections were longer than in this example, this form would allow you to see much more of the notebook at once. For example, if you wanted to see what was in the Factor Section, you could double-click the closed group bracket for that section and see this:

By adding more sections, or subsections within sections (using the Subsection or Subsubsection cell styles), you can create a whole structured document and get to anywhere in it quickly.

Cell groupings are ordinarily created automatically, based on the cell styles of the cells in the notebook. For example, Section headings begin a group that encloses everything up to the next Section. Subsection headings enclose everything up to the next Section or Subsection, etc. Titles enclose everything up to the next Title.

Sometimes you might want to override the default groups and make your own, which you can do by turning off automatic grouping. Choose the **Manual Grouping** command in the **Cell Grouping** submenu of the **Cell** menu. Automatic grouping is now disabled for the current notebook (other notebooks are not affected, because this setting is set individually for each notebook).

Any existing groups will remain in the notebook, but if you add new cells they will not be grouped in with existing ones. You can use the **Group Cells** and **Ungroup Cells** commands in the **Cell Grouping** submenu of the **Cell** menu to add and remove groups manually.

To remove a group, select the whole group by clicking on the group bracket that encloses it and then choose Ungroup Cells. To group a range of cells together, select all of them and then choose Group Cells. To add a cell to the bottom of a group, select the last cell in the group and the cell you want to add and then choose Group Cells.

Chapter **51**

I never learned to spell. Can you help me?

One of the most glaring omissions in *Mathematica*, before V4.0, was its lack of a spell checker. This problem has been resolved in V4.0 with the inclusion of a high quality spelling system from Proximity Linguistic Systems.

It has all the standard word processor features, such as suggesting alternatives generated by clever phonetic algorithms, spell checking large documents rapidly, etc. But we've also tried to extend it to work particularly well with the kind of text *Mathematica* users typically include in their notebooks.

We have added a large number of scientific and technical words not usually found in non-scientific word processors. We include both Proximity's math and scientific dictionary and a further list of words gathered from actual user notebooks (double checked, of course). And naturally we include in our dictionary all the *Mathematica* function names, including those from standard add-on packages.

The next customization takes into account certain common conventions used in programmer-speak. For example, it is quite common in *Mathematica* (and other computer languages) to build up compound words using internal capitalization. So for example, you might make up a variable called `RateOfChange`. In a typical word processor, this would be flagged as a spelling mistake, with some ridiculous alternative suggestions. But in *Mathematica*, it is recognized as three separate words, each of which is spell checked individually. If you genuinely misspell it as `RateOfChaange`, it will catch the misspelling in the last sub-word and make a reasonable suggestion for correcting it. (And if you don't see a misspelling in this example, it probably means our proofreader caught and incorrectly corrected it.)

Besides splitting words at internal capitalizations, the spell checker treats words containing hyphens or underscores as compound words that should be checked element by element. So `rate_of_change` and `change-rate` will both be checked as you would probably want.

Of course, there are options available to override the spell checker's automatic splitting of compound words (you can either have it spell check them as a whole, or have it flag any word containing internal capitalization as an error).

Mathematica notebooks typically contain both human-language text (typically in Text, Title, or Section heading cells) and input/output expressions (typically in Input and Output style cells). Recognizing this, the spelling system checks the human text using its human text spell checker, and automatically skips the input/output expressions (which would miserably fail human language spelling tests!). In the future, we expect to add new spell check features that will be able to intelligently "program check" *Mathematica* input/output expressions.

And finally, recognizing that scientific documents often contain a mix of languages (for example, the body might be in German, with some paragraphs quoted from another work in English), you can specify the language to be used individually for each cell. Dictionaries are available (for a fee) for quite a few languages.

■ Using the Spelling Dialog Box

To spell check a notebook, start by placing the insertion point at the very beginning (scroll to the top and click). Then choose **Check Spelling...** from the **Edit** menu. You'll get a dialog box something like this:

At the top it tells you that the reason it stopped on "Chaange" is that it's not in the dictionary (which makes one suspect that it might be misspelled). Other reasons might include that it's an uncapitalized word at the start of a sentence, that it's a repeated word, etc. (see the section on spelling options below for a complete list).

If you agree that it's incorect, and if you agree with the primary suggested correction (in the Replace field), click the **Replace** button (or just type Return). It will do the replacement and automatically go on to the next apparently incorrrect word.

If you want to use one of the alternative replacements, double click on the one you want. It will do the replacement and move on to the next misspelling.

If you think the word is spelled correctly, you have several choices. If you just want to move on, click **Skip** and it will go on to the next apparent misspelling. If you're sure the word is spelled correctly, and you want to add it to the dictionary so it will be found in future, click the **Add Word** button. The word will be remembered permanently, and will be available in all notebooks in the future. In some situations, you may want to have the word be remembered only for the individual notebook you're working on (for example if it's a specialized term that applies only to one document). To store the word as part of the notebook's private dictionary, choose "this notebook" from the popup menu in the lower right corner of the dialog box. You can also choose to store the word in a private dictionary just for the cell containing it, or just for this session (until you quit *Mathematica*).

If the spell checker stops for a reason other than a misspelled word (for example a repeated word), you'll see something like this:

Notice that the dialog tells you why it stopped at the top (alternatives are still provided, just in case you're interested). Clicking **Replace** will replace the repeated word with a single copy.

If you don't like the spell checker stopping for the particular reason it's giving, you can click the **Skip These** button and that reason will be removed as a condition for stopping (for example, in the case above it would no longer stop for repeated words). As with the **Add Word** button, the popup menu determines whether this change is remembered permanently for all notebooks, or just for the particular notebook or cell you're working on at the moment.

When the spell checker has gone through the whole notebook and reached the end, it will scroll you back to the top of the document and present the following reason for stopping:

This indicates that no more questionable spellings were found.

You can start spell checking anywhere in the middle of a document by placing the insertion point where you want to start. If you started in the middle, then the above dialog doesn't necessarily indicate that there are no mistakes in the document, only that you reached the end. (**Warning:** When the spell checker reaches the end, the document is scrolled back to the *top*, not to the point where you started the spell check operation. Some improvements can be expected in this behavior in future versions of *Mathematica*.)

■ Setting Spell Checking Options

As with everything else in *Mathematica*, the behavior of the spell checking system is controlled by a set of options. They determine what conditions will trigger the spell checker to stop or not stop on a word and how words are broken into sub-words; they also hold lists of user-added words. The spelling dialog's **Add Word** and **Skip These** buttons automatically set or modify these option values. These options are included to let you fine-tune the behavior of the system for unusual situations; normal use of the spell checker should not require you to modify or even know about them.

To see the options related to spell checking, open the spelling dialog, then click the **Options...** button. This will open the Option Inspector and automatically focus it on the spelling options. (See **Chapter** 55 for more information about using the Option Inspector.)

■ SpellingOptions/AlwaysStop → {...}
SpellingOptions/AlwaysSkip → {...}

These options specify a list of conditions that will cause the spell checker to stop at a word, or to *not* stop at a word. A word being misspelled will of course cause it to stop, but the following conditions are also supported:

```
"UncapitalizedStartOfSentence"
"RepeatedWords"
"SingleCharacterWords"
"Numbers"
"WordsWithNumbers"
"WordsInAllCaps"
"RomanNumerals"
"AlternateSpellings"
"CaseDifferences"
"EncliticForms"
"HyphenatedWords"
"WordsWithUnderscores"
"WordsWithInternalCapitals"
```

The **AlwaysStop** and **AlwaysSkip** options both consist of a list of zero or more of these conditions (it's not sensible to include the same condition in both lists at the same time, but no one will stop you if you do). In the option inspector, choosing a condition from the pop-up menu to the right of the option value field will toggle whether it is included in the list or not.

For example, take the **"WordsWithNumbers"** condition. If it's included in the **AlwaysStop** list, then any word containing a digit (e.g. "foo1") will cause the spell checker to stop. If it's included in the **AlwaysSkip** list, then all such words will be ignored (skipped over). If it's not included in either list, then words with numbers will be treated just like normal words (which means it will attempt to look them up in the dictionary and stop only if it can't find them).

When you click the **Skip These** button in the spelling dialog, the values of these two options are modified, for the duration you have chosen from the pop-up menu.

■ SpellingOptions/WordSplitting → {...}

This option lists the point(s) at which compound words will be split before sub-units are separately spell checked. The choices are:

> "Hyphen"
> "Underscore"
> "InternalCapitals"

■ SpellingDictionaries/CorrectWords
SpellingDictionaries/IncorrectWords
SpellingDictionaries/Suggestions

These options can be used to add/remove words to/from the spelling dictionary. When you click the **Add Word** button in the spelling dialog the word is added to the **CorrectWords** option. If you add a word to the **IncorrectWords** option, it is effectively removed from the main spelling dictionary. The **Suggestions** option can be used to specify what should be used as the primary suggested correction if a given word is encountered. It consists of a list of pairs of words, **{"incorrectword", "alternative"}**.

■ LanguageCategory → *languagetype*
DefaultNaturalLanguage → *language*

We should warn you ahead of time that these two options are a bit tricky in the way they interact with each other. Fortunately, it works out in the end that everything is pretty much automatic and unless you're writing a custom style sheet, you shouldn't have to set either of these options yourself.

LanguageCategory is typically used only in style sheets, though it can be set for an individual cell if necessary to handle an unusual situation. It tells *Mathematica* what *type* of text is in the cell, allowing it to pick the right class of spell checker to use. The possible values are:

"NaturalLanguage"	A human language like English or German
"Formula"	A math formula
"Mathematica"	*Mathematica* program text
"None"	No spell checking desired

The default style sheet sets this option appropriately for different styles. So, for example, Input and Output style cells are **"Mathematica"**, graphics cells are **"None"**, while Text, Title, etc., cells are **"NaturalLanguage"**.

If the value of **LanguageCategory** is **"NaturalLanguage"**, then it uses the value of the **DefaultNaturalLanguage** option to determine what specific language is intended (English, German, etc.). Now, the default setting is **DefaultNaturalLanguage → Language**, which means to use the value of the **Language** option (the option used to control the language in which menus and dialog boxes are displayed). So, by default, text is spell checked in the language chosen for your menus and dialog boxes.

If you have purchased a language kit to localize *Mathematica* to a language other than English, you will find a submenu in the Edit menu that allows you to choose the default spell checking language separately from the language used to display menus and dialog boxes. Since people who speak English are rarely inclined to use other languages, this menu is not included in the English version of *Mathematica*.

■ Adding your own dictionaries

The **SpellingDictionaries** option described above allows you to add a relatively modest number (a few hundred) words. If you want to include thousands or tens of thousands of new words (such as replacing the entire main English dictionary or adding many terms from a specific technical field), you can do this far more efficiently by installing new dictionary files.

Mathematica supports three file formats for user-added dictionary files. It supports Proximity-format compressed dictionaries (available from Wolfram Research, Inc. for a number of languages). And it supports two plain-text formats that you can create yourself or bring over from other spell checkers you may have.

The simplest format is a file consisting of one word per line (separated by carriage return or newline characters). This allows you to use dictionaries from the Unix "spell" utility, for example, or any other source of words you may have access to. Files in this format must end in **".tr"**.

The second format is a *Mathematica*-style list of quoted strings, separated by commas and with curly braces around it. In this form, you can include both correct and incorrect words, with a suggested correction for each incorrect word. Files in this format must end in " .m". For example:

```
{
  "Bob",
  "Betty",
  "Sally",
  {"Silly", "Sally"},
  "Joe"
}
```

This dictionary adds four names to the list of correct words, and it tells the spell checker that if it encounters "Silly" it should stop and suggest "Sally" as a replacement.

Once you've collected your words in a dictionary, you need to decide where to put it. There are several locations that *Mathematica* searches for dictionary files: After you put your file in one of these locations, it will be located and used automatically (when you restart the front end).

The standard dictionary files that come with *Mathematica* are located in the SpellingDictionaries subdirectory of the SystemFiles directory (located in the main *Mathematica* installation location, which varies depending on your installation). You should usually not add your own dictionaries here, because they will might get overwritten the next time you update your copy of *Mathematica*.

The best place to add your own is in the SpellingDictionaries subdirectory of the Configuration directory. (You may have to create the SpellingDictionaries directory if it doesn't exist already).

When you place a dictionary directly in Configuration/SpellingDictionaries, it is used regardless of what current language is selected as your spell checking language (see above). This is appropriate if the dictionary contains, for example, function names from a particular package, or scientific terms that are never translated. But if your dictionary contains words in a particular language, you may want to have it used only when that language is selected. You can do this by placing it in a subdirectory named after the language in question. So for example, a dictionary located in Configuration/SpellingDictionaries/German will be used only when spell checking in German.

Chapter **52**

How do I use style sheets to see my notebooks in new ways?

Theo: *Mathematica* comes with a wide selection of style sheets. (You can also write your own; see Chapter 54 for information on creating a style sheet.) Once you've written a note-book containing a mixture of cell types (Title, Section, Text, Input, Output, etc.), you can view it under the control of different style sheets to see completely different presentations.

To use a new style sheet for a notebook, choose an item from the **Style Sheet** submenu of the **Format** menu. For those of you reading the electronic edition of this book, by far the best way to experiment is to open one of the other chapters (one that has some Input/Output cells) or your own notebook. Choose style sheets one after the other and enjoy the show.

You will see your background colors change, font sizes change, boxes appear around inputs, etc., all without modifying the contents of the notebook itself. Because almost all the attributes that control the display of text are controlled by the style sheet, it is possible to reformat a notebook simply by changing its style sheet.

Jerry: The above paragraphs clearly demonstrate the problem with books like this. Too much talk and not enough examples. Show me what these style sheets do and stop the Professor Gray lecture.

Theo: Fine, let's start with a chapter from this book. Here is what it looks like using the default style sheet:

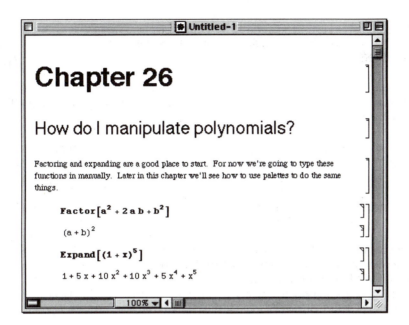

If this looks a bit plain (it is intentionally so), try choosing **DemoText** (one of the default style sheets that come with *Mathematica*) from the **Style Sheet** submenu of the **Format** menu:

Readers of the electronic edition will see this in color, while on paper only shades of gray will be visible.

Jerry: Oh, that's pretty. I guess it was worth the lecture. Do you mean that if the reader were to choose this same menu command *right now*, the whole chapter they are reading would change to look like this?

Theo: Yes it would. Of course, if someone is reading this in the paper edition, there would be trouble, but anyone reading the electronic version can make the text on the screen change appearance at will.

Jerry: Not all parts of the chapter will change: The screen shots are fixed bitmaps which, like printed paper, don't respond to changes in the style sheet. But the rest of the text is "live" and reformattable.

Theo: A style sheet defines how everything in a notebook should look, and in fact it defines several variations of each style. These variations are used in different *style environments*. Typically each style sheet defines variations for four style environments, called "Working", "Printout", "Presentation", and "Condensed" (not all style sheets define all these environments). The **Screen Style Environment** and **Printing Style Environment** submenus of the **Format** menu allow you to choose which variation is used for screen display and which is used for printing. (As explained in <u>Chapter</u> 53 there are several good reasons why you wouldn't want the appearance on screen to be identical to the appearance when printing.)

By default, notebooks are displayed in "Working" style environment on screen and printed out in "Printout" style environment. To switch to a different environment, choose an item from the **Screen Style Environment** submenu of the **Format** menu.

Jerry: OK, time's up, let's have an example.

Here's what our sample notebook looks like with the "Demo" style sheet in "Working" style environment:

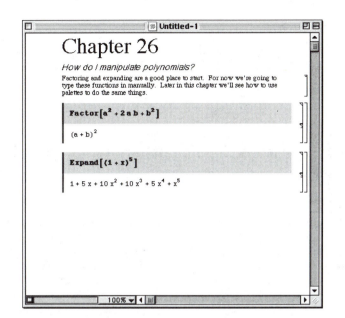

And here's what it looks like in "Presentation" style environment:

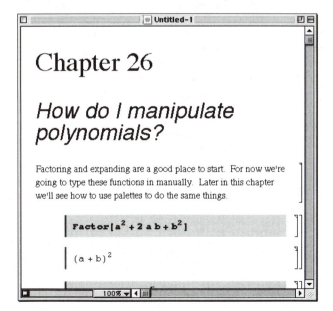

Theo: Notice how everything is bigger, as would be appropriate for giving a presentation using a projector or large screen.

For more information about the difference between screen and printer style environments, see **Chapter** 53.

Chapter **53**

Why does my notebook look different printed than on screen?

When you print a notebook from *Mathematica*, you may notice some differences from what you saw on the screen. For example, the line breaks may be in slightly different places, and some font sizes will be different. Why? Because it's better that way. The doctrine of WYSI-WYG (What You See Is What You Get) that is popular in word processing programs has its limitations, especially when it comes to math typesetting.

In the early days of computing, word processors were extremely non-WYSIWYG; for example, users saw strange control codes on screen instead of bold or italic text. It was a great innovation when word processors were able to display an accurate representation of what the final printed output would look like. During the period in history in which the main purpose of writing on a computer was to produce printed output, the most important factor in WYSI-WYG products was the accuracy of their simulation of the printed output. In more recent times, the printed output has become less and less important (how many web sites have you printed out recently?). Thus, the simulation of printed output has become less important than the quality of the screen display, since the screen display is itself very often the end product.

Mathematica is intended primarily as an interactive working environment; most users will spend much more time working and creating in *Mathematica* than they will printing out their work. Therefore, the choice of fonts, math layout, etc., is optimized to work well on screen.

However, many users will eventually want high quality printout for a scientific paper, book, or other report. Thus, at least at present, *Mathematica* is caught in the transition between the paper and all-electronic worlds, and must do an excellent job in both.

Unfortunately the choices that work well on screen are not ideal for paper output. For example, 12 point type, which is good for text on screen, is slightly larger than most people find ideal for printed output; 11 point is a more natural size. A more dramatic example is nested exponents, such as x^{y^2}. On screen, font sizes smaller than about 9 point are impossible to read, whereas fonts down to 5 point are routinely used in printed math texts.

A solution used by some programs is to make the working environment a magnification of the printed output. The problem is that in order to magnify 5 point exponents to the point of legibility, the base font size must be about 20 point. This very large font size limits the amount of text you can see on screen, resulting in an unsatisfactory working environment.

Other programs have legible display on screen, but use the same font sizes for printing, which results in ugly output.

The solution taken in *Mathematica*, which we feel is superior to *any* other solution, is to have parameters that control the layout of math in sophisticated ways, and to adjust these parameters differently for screen and printout. For example, regardless of the size of the base font, nested exponents are never allowed to get smaller than 9 point on screen. They get progressively smaller, but not indefinitely. This allows both a convenient working font size, and legible exponents. In printed output, however, exponents are allowed to become as small as 5 point.

To see the effect of these choices, consider the following examples:

Printed form: x^{y^2}

Screen form: x^{y^2}

Printed form magnified: x^{y^2}

If you're reading this book in electronic form, you will find the printed form impossible to read, the magnified form too big, and the screen form just right. Conversely, if you're reading this in printed form, you'll find the screen form ugly (exponent too big), the magnified form huge, and the printed form just right.

There are a few other differences between screen and printout. On screen, text is word-wrapped at the width of the window, while on paper it is wrapped at the width of the paper (minus the page margins you have specified). On screen, *Mathematica* uses bitmap integer-width fonts, while on paper it uses high resolution outline fonts. On screen, there is more vertical spacing between elements, to increase readability (screen space is free but paper costs money).

■ I want *real* WYSIWYG! What can I do?

Sometimes you really do want to see exactly what is going to be printed. For example, in the final stages of producing a book or a paper, you may want to check and manually adjust some of the page breaks.

Fortunately, it is easy to do this in *Mathematica*. Choose **Show Page Breaks** from the **Format** menu. Because "pages" is a concept that makes sense only when printing on "paper", *Mathematica* automatically switches to true-WYSIWYG when it is asked to show the page breaks. You will notice a sudden reduction in readability because *Mathematica* switches to outline fonts and fractional-width character positioning. This frequently results in characters on screen running into each other.

All the differences between screen and printout are controlled by *style environments*. There are two settings for style environment, one for screen display and another for printout. If both settings are the same, you will get the same thing on the printer as you see on screen.

In the **Format** menu, you will find two submenus, **Screen Style Environment** and **Printing Style Environment**. Each submenu lists the environments defined by the current style sheet. The choices are usually "Working", "Presentation", "Condensed", and "Printout"; the default is "Working" for the screen and "Printout" for printing.

If you choose "Printout" for your Screen Style Environment, your notebook will be displayed exactly as it would be printed.

Alternately, if you choose "Working" for your Printing Style Environment, your printouts will look just like the screen display. They will be quite ugly in many cases.

The other style environments, "Presentation" and "Condensed" specify different combinations of formatting rules. "Presentation" makes the text big, suitable for projecting to an audience, whereas "Condensed" tries to fit as much text on screen as possible.

To give a presentation electronically, choose "Presentation" from the **Screen Style Environment** menu. To print out overhead transparencies, choose "Presentation" from the **Printing Style Environment** menu. You can, for example, set your screen environment to "Working" but your printing environment to "Presentation": This allows you to work on screen in a reasonably small font size, while automatically printing out in a large size.

Chapter **54**

What *exactly* are styles, style sheets, and style environments?

At first, your primary use of *Mathematica* will probably be to do math. After a while you may progress to writing small notebooks and reports, perhaps using Text, Title, and Section style cells. You can use *Mathematica* this way for years and be completely satisfied.

However, if you're going to use *Mathematica* to write complex documents, such as scientific papers or books, and want to exercise more precise control over the appearance of the text, you need to learn about options, styles, and style sheets.

■ Options

Options are used to control the appearance and behavior of everything in the front end. For example, the option **FontSize** determines the size of characters in text.

Let's start by making a text cell with one enlarged word in it. Open a new Untitled notebook window, go to the **Format** menu, **Style** submenu, and choose **Text**. Type "This is a sentence with one word in a different size" then select the word "word". Go to the **Format** menu, **Size** submenu, and choose **18 Point**. You should see something like this:

This is a sentence with one **word** in a different size.

All words appear in "Text" style's 12 point default size, except the one word we selected.

Now let's change the size of the text in the entire cell. Click on the cell bracket enclosing the sentence, go to the **Size** submenu, and choose **9 Point**. You should see:

Notice that the text as a whole got smaller, but the individual word remained large: This cell now has two separate settings for the `FontSize` option, one for the cell as a whole and another, inside, for the individual word. The inner setting for that one word overrides the outer one for the cell.

We have just demonstrated that options can be set at different *levels*. In the example above, we set the option at two levels, character and cell. Below we learn about other levels at which options can be set.

■ Styles and Style Sheets

At a higher level, we might want to change the size of *all* the ordinary text in an entire document. We could select everything in the notebook and choose the new size from the menu, but we probably don't want titles and section headings to change size. And, what if we added new text? Would it be in the new size?

To make global changes possible, *Mathematica* uses *style sheets*. All the options that control the appearance of text are defined by styles with names like "Text", "Title", "Input", "Output", etc. You can think of a style as a name that refers to a collection of one or more specific option settings.

Many such definitions are collected into a style sheet. Style sheets are actually notebook documents containing special style definition cells. Style sheets can be shared among notebooks (that is, many notebooks can refer to the same style sheet, which is stored in a separate file), or a notebook can have a private collection of style definitions stored within the same file as the rest of the notebook.

Back to our example: We want to redefine "Text" style to change the size of all existing and future ordinary text in our notebook. We go to the **Format** menu and choose **Edit Style Sheet...**, resulting in this dialog box:

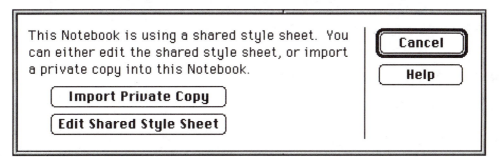

In this case, our notebook uses a style sheet that is also used by other notebooks (indeed, the notebooks that make up this very book all refer to a style sheet that we named `Book Styles.nb`). When you create a new Untitled notebook it will use a style sheet named `Default.nb` (which is included in *Mathematica* in `SystemFiles/FrontEnd/Style Sheets`), until you choose or create a different style sheet. See <u>Chapter</u> 52 to learn how to switch between different built-in style sheets.

While we're experimenting, we don't want to damage the shared style sheet accidentally, so we will click **Import Private Copy**.

We now see the notebook containing all the style definitions for our Untitled notebook:

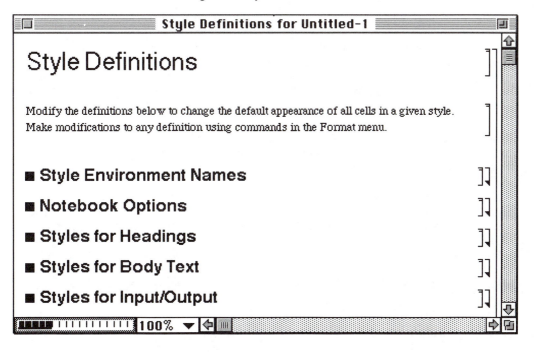

The style definitions are organized into groups. We double-click the group bracket for the "Styles for Body Text" section to open that section:

```
▤▤        Style Definitions for Untitled-1        ▤▤

   Make modifications to any definition using commands in the Format menu.        ⌉


 ■ Style Environment Names                                                        ⌉⌋

 ■ Notebook Options                                                               ⌉⌋

 ■ Styles for Headings                                                            ⌉⌋

 ■ Styles for Body Text                                                           ⌉

   ─────────────────────────────────────────────────────────────
   Prototype for style: "Text":                                                   ▌
   Text
   ─────────────────────────────────────────────────────────────
   Prototype for style: "SmallText":                                              ⌉⌋
   SmallText
 ■ Styles for Input/Output                                                        ⌉⌋

 ▮▮▮▮▮▮ | | | | | | | | | | 100% ▼ ⇦ ▥                                            ⇨
```

(Ignore for the moment the fact that there is another level of closed groups inside this one.)

We click on the innermost cell bracket for "Text" style to make the selection look like the picture above. Now we go to the **Format** menu, **Size** submenu, and choose a new size.

We have just redefined the "Text" style: If we have any "Text" style cells in the notebook this style sheet is associated with, they will *all* change size.

Well, almost all…. Just as with the individual word that did not change size in the example above, if you have a "Text" style cell that has an individually set font size, it will not follow the redefinition of the style.

It should now be clear that making such local settings for individual cells may not always be a good idea. To decide whether to make a change locally or in the style definition, think about why you are making the change. If you're making it because this word or cell is somehow unique, different from any of the others in your notebook, then making a local change is usually the right thing. If you're making the change because you just don't like the way something looks, you may want to change the style definition; after all, if you create another object in the same style, you're probably not going to like what that looks like, either.

If you make too many local settings, you will end up with an inflexible notebook. By using the style sheet to make changes, you will end up with a notebook that can be more easily adjusted as a whole.

For example, say you decide that you'd like all your section headings to be green. You could set each individual section heading cell to green by going to the **Format** menu, **Text Color** submenu, and choosing **Green** . But, what if you came to your senses and realized that green is a horrible color for section headings? You would have to fix each individual heading manually.

If instead you redefined the "Section" style in the style sheet, you could fix your lapse of judgment in one central place, and all the individual section headings would change to mauve automatically.

While you can use menus and the Option Inspector to see and change the option settings defined by a style, it is often a lot quicker and less confusing to view the `Cell[]` expression for the style in question. (See Chapter 62 for an extensive discussion of the symbolic expressions that represent cells in the front end.) First select the "Text" style definition cell, then go to the **Format** menu and choose **Show Expression**:

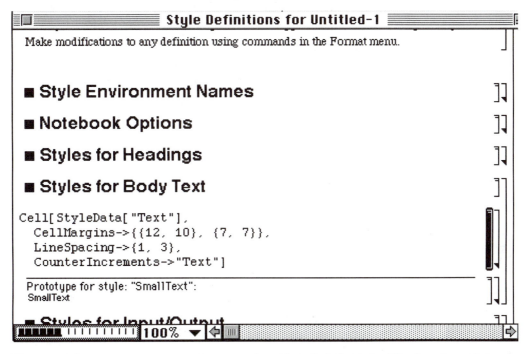

The expression `StyleData["Text"]` says that this cell defines the "Text" style; and the remaining three options constitute the definition of "Text" style. You can edit this expression directly, adding or removing options or even renaming the style itself.

For example, click just to the left of the final close-bracket character, type a comma, then type `TextAlignment→Center` and choose **Show Expression** to re-format the cell, activating the new definition of the style. The result will be that all your text cells are now center-aligned.

■ Style Environments

Take a deep breath. It's going to get thick for a while.

In Chapter 53 we discussed the fact that *Mathematica's* printed output is not exactly the same as what you see on screen. If you haven't already, you may want to read that chapter now to understand the importance (and desirability) of what follows.

The difference between what you see on screen and what you get on paper is implemented by different definitions of the styles. For example, "Text" style is normally defined to set **Font Size→12** on screen but **FontSize→11** on paper.

In designing this system, we considered two approaches. One was to have two separate definitions for each style. The other was to have a single main definition, plus sub-styles to define modifications applied to the main style for screen display and for printing.

We chose the second approach because we found it was often the case that a given style would define many options (as many as a dozen) but typically only one or two options would be set differently between screen and paper. Rather than duplicate all the common settings, it seemed more natural to have a single definition plus a (usually short) list of variations. This approach makes it easier to edit the style definition, since a change made to the primary definition is automatically used both on screen and on paper, unless it is specifically overridden by one of the variations.

After implementing this system, we realized that it could be used for more than just screen and printing—any number of useful variations could be defined. In the default style sheet, for example, there are four variations, called *style environments*:

Style Environment	Main uses
Working	Normal editing
Printout	Printing
Presentation	Overhead presentations (large fonts)
Condensed	Seeing as much on one screen as possible (small fonts, little space between cells)

Variations for a style environment are defined at two levels: A variation that applies to all styles when displayed in that environment, and variations specific to a particular style.

Open the first section in the style sheet, "Style Environment Names" to see the variations applied to all styles:

```
▤▢ ▤▤▤▤▤▤ Style Definitions for Untitled-1 ▤▤▤▤▤▤ ▤◪
Modify the definitions below to change the default appearance of all cells in a given style.
Make modifications to any definition using commands in the Format menu.

■ Style Environment Names

Modification for all styles in style environment "Working":
Working

Modification for all styles in style environment "Presentation":
Presentation

Modification for all styles in style environment "Condensed":
Condensed

Modification for all styles in style environment "Printout":
Printout

▤▤▤▤▤ ‖‖‖‖‖ 100% ▼ ⇦▥
```

The easiest way to understand these variations is to use **Show Expression** in the **Format** menu to see the underlying `Cell` expressions:

```
▤▢ ▤▤▤▤▤▤ Style Definitions for Untitled-1 ▤▤▤▤▤▤ ▤◪
■ Style Environment Names

Cell[StyleData[All, "Working"],
  PageWidth->WindowWidth,
  ScriptMinSize->9]

Cell[StyleData[All, "Presentation"],
  PageWidth->WindowWidth,
  ScriptMinSize->12,
  FontSize->16]

Cell[StyleData[All, "Condensed"],
  PageWidth->WindowWidth,
  CellBracketOptions->{"Margins"->{1, 1},
  "Widths"->{0, 5}},
  ScriptMinSize->8,
  FontSize->11]

Cell[StyleData[All, "Printout"],
  PageWidth->PaperWidth,
  ScriptMinSize->5,
  FontSize->10,
  PrivateFontOptions->{"FontType"->"Outline"}]

▤▤▤▤▤ ‖‖‖‖‖ 100% ▼ ⇦▥
```

If you take the time to study these option settings you will learn a lot about how some of the magic described in Chapter 53 is implemented.

Returning to the definition of "Text" style, you'll notice that the cell defining "Text" style is the head of a closed group. If you open this group, you'll see the definitions of the specific variations for "Text" style in particular style environments:

```
╔══════════════ Style Definitions for Untitled-1 ══════════════╗

■ Styles for Headings                                          ]]

■ Styles for Body Text                                         ]

  ──────────────────────────────────────────────────────────
  Prototype for style: "Text":
  Text


      ──────────────────────────────────────────────────────
      Modification for style "Text" in style environment "Presentation":
      Text/Presentation

  ──────────────────────────────────────────────────────────
  Modification for style "Text" in style environment "Condensed":
  Text/Condensed

──────────────────────────────────────────────────────────────
Modification for style "Text" in style environment "Printout":
Text/Printout

  ──────────────────────────────────────────────────────────
  Prototype for style: "SmallText":
  SmallText
╠═══════════ 100% ▼ ◁ ▥ ══════════════════════════════════ ▷╣
```

(There is typically no modification for the ordinary editing environment "Working", because the main style definitions are correct for that environment.)

Each style cell is drawn using the attributes defined by that style; one thing you'll notice is that each of the "Text" style variations has a different left margin. As before, using **Show Expression (Format** menu) is often the quickest way to see the definitions of these styles. Use it on all four cells to see the whole story on "Text" style:

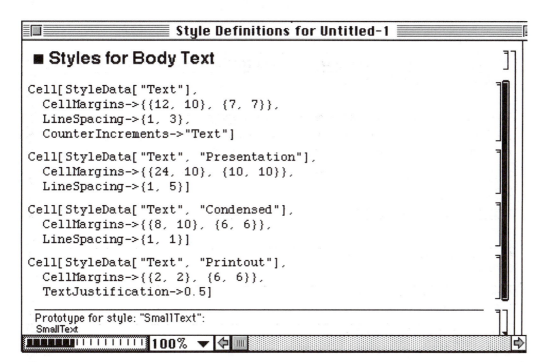

Notice that these variations do not change the **FontSize** attribute: "Text" style uses the default font size defined for each environment. If you were to look at the same set of definitions for "Title" style, you would see individual font size settings for each environment.

■ FormatType styles

Hang in there, we're almost there! There is one more factor that goes into the style mix. Every cell is in a particular **FormatType**, for example **InputForm**, **StandardForm**, etc. There are styles with the same names as each possible format type, and the attributes defined by these styles are mixed in after the main style of the cell.

For example, consider two "Input" style cells, one in **StandardForm** and the other in **Tradi₋ tionalForm**. The **StandardForm** cell will typically be in Courier font, while the **Tradi₋ tionalForm** cell will be in Times font. This difference is created by the "StandardForm" style defining **FontFamily→Courier**.

Here are the typical format type styles:

```
▤ □ ═══════ Style Definitions for Untitled-1 ═══════
■ FormatType Styles

  The cells below define styles that are mixed in with the styles of most cells.  If a cell's For-
  matType matches the name of one of the styles defined below, then that style is applied
  between the cell's style and its own options.
  ─────────────────────────────────────────────────────────────
  Prototype for style: "CellExpression":
  CellExpression
  ─────────────────────────────────────────────────────────────
  Prototype for style: "InputForm":
  InputForm
  ─────────────────────────────────────────────────────────────
  Prototype for style: "OutputForm":
  OutputForm
  ─────────────────────────────────────────────────────────────
  Prototype for style: "StandardForm":
  StandardForm
  ─────────────────────────────────────────────────────────────
  Prototype for style: "TraditionalForm":
  TraditionalForm

   The style defined below is mixed in to any cell that is in an inline cell within another.
  ─────────────────────────────────────────────────────────────
  Prototype for style: "InlineCell":
  InlineCell
  ─────────────────────────────────────────────────────────────
    Prototype for style: "InlineCellEditing":
    InlineCellEditing

  ▦▦▦▦▦▦▦▏ ▏▏▏▏▏▏▏  100%  ▼  ⇦ ▥                              ⇨
```

Chapter **55**

How do I use that darn Option Inspector anyway?

Many programs have dialog boxes in which "options" can be set. These may be user preference settings, or font properties, or whatever is appropriate to the application in question. Most programs also have menus, such as the Font, Face, and Size menus, for setting options.

Mathematica has these same menus and dialog boxes, but in V3 a new, centralized *Option Inspector* was added to provide a uniform way to set any option for any object in the front end.

Most of the old menus and dialog boxes still exist, but many new options can be set only via the Option Inspector. This is a good thing, because there are several hundred new options; it would be impossible to put them all in menus or special-purpose dialog boxes. The Option Inspector is a very compact way to see and change a large number of options.

We will begin by describing how to set font and paragraph attributes for a sample paragraph of text. (Most of these options can be set using submenus in the **Format** menu; we're using them because they have particularly clear, visible effects, not because you would normally use the option inspector to set them.)

Begin by selecting the object (character, cell, graphic, etc.) you want to affect. We will be altering the following paragraph of text:

> This is a book about how to grow mathematicians. Probably you have no intention of trying to grow mathematicians. Even so, I hope you will find something of interest here. I myself have no intention of growing plants.
>
> *W. W. Sawyer, Prelude to Mathematics (Penguin, 1955)*

Click on the cell bracket containing this cell, then open the Option Inspector by choosing **Option Inspector...** from the **Format** menu:

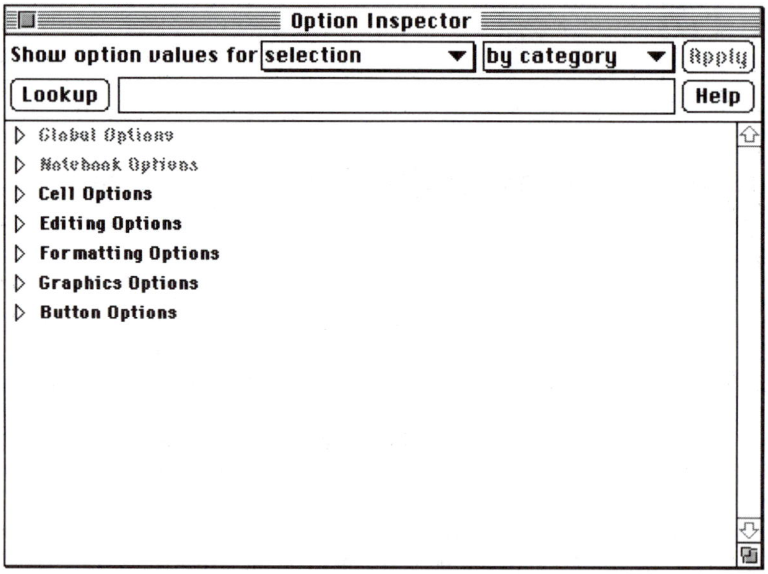

The Option Inspector groups *Mathematica*'s huge number of options into categories and subcategories. In the picture above, you are seeing the highest level of categories. To open a category, click on the small triangle to the left of the category name. (The picture shown is from a Macintosh. On other platforms there are squares or circles instead of triangles, but they work the same.). We'll open the **Formatting Options** category:

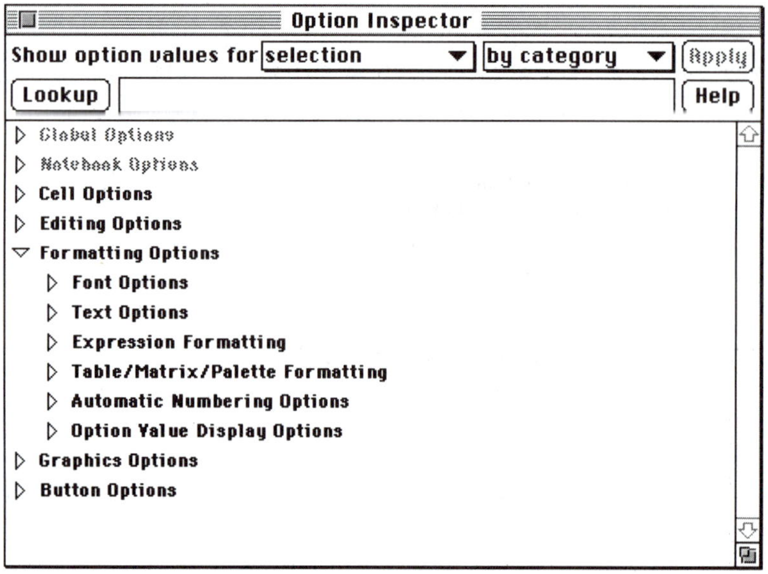

Next we'll open the **Font Options** category:

Here you see collected in one place almost all the options that affect the appearance of individual letters in text (you can see the rest of them by scrolling down a few lines).

You can change the value of an option by clicking on the text to the right of the arrow, or by clicking the icon on the far right. For example, we'll set the font size to 15 point, a size not available in any menu. Highlight the 12 by click and drag:

Type 15, then type Return to enter the new value. The result is:

> This is a book about how to grow mathematicians. Probably you have no intention of trying to grow mathe-maticians. Even so, I hope you will find something of interest here. I myself have no intention of growing plants.
>
> *W. W. Sawyer, Prelude to Mathemat-ics (Penguin, 1955)*

To set the font to a more common size, say 9 point, we click on the icon to the far right to bring up a pop-up menu of common sizes, from which we select 9:

> This is a book about how to grow mathematicians. Probably you have no intention of trying to grow mathematicians. Even so, I hope you will find something of interest here. I myself have no intention of growing plants.
>
> *W. W. Sawyer, Prelude to Mathematics (Penguin, 1955)*

Before we set the **FontSize** option, the text in our example was 12 point. Why? Because it is in a "Text" style cell, and "Text" style sets the value of **FontSize** to 12. The cell was *inheriting* the value of **FontSize** from its style.

Since we adjusted the option in the Option Inspector, this cell now has a size different from the one specified by the style it is in. We have assigned it a *private* value of **FontSize**, overrid-ing the value inherited from the style. Even if the style were redefined to set a different size, this cell would stay the same size.

This property of having a privately defined value is indicated by the + sign to the left of the option. Clicking on the left hand side (the option name) will restore the option to its default value, and of course also remove the + sign.

(To understand the following paragraphs better, you may want to read <u>Chapter</u> 54 first. It explains the style inheritance mechanism in great detail.)

The first popup menu at the top of the Option Inspector allows you to view and set options at any of several different levels. By default, the Option Inspector starts out showing options for whatever is currently selected, such as the cell in the example above.

If you choose Notebook from the popup menu, you can set options for the entire notebook. The Notebook Options category, which had been dimmed, now becomes available. It contains options that can be set only at the notebook or higher level.

Likewise if you choose Global from the popup menu, the Global Options category becomes available. It contains options that correspond to what are normally called user preferences—settings that apply to the whole program, and are saved in a preferences file.

Chapter **56**

How do I program in *Mathematica*?

Programming in *Mathematica* is a deep subject, but you can do a lot of very useful things without having to learn an unreasonable amount of information. This chapter covers traditional procedural programming. Chapter 58 examines pattern-based programming. The advanced reader is advised to consult The *Mathematica* Book or one of the several other books on advanced *Mathematica* programming.

We start with the most basic operation, defining a function using **:=**

$$f[n\_] := Expand[(a + b)^n]$$

Here is what this function does:

f[2]

$a^2 + 2\, a\, b + b^2$

f[3]

$a^3 + 3\, a^2\, b + 3\, a\, b^2 + b^3$

For the purposes of this chapter, we can think of the left hand side of the function definition as an idiomatic form not to be analyzed further. Just think of **f[n_]** as "the function **f** with one argument, named **n**". The definition **f[n_, m_]** is a function of two arguments, named **n** and **m**.

The **:=** means "delayed assignment". The "delayed" part is important here. It means that the right-hand side is not evaluated when we *define* the function, but only when we *use* it. If the right-hand side were evaluated when the function was defined, the **Expand** function would attempt to expand the expression **(a+b)^n**, with **n** not having any specific numerical value. Here is what **Expand** would do:

Expand[(a + b)^n]

$(a + b)^n$

The **Expand** function returned the expression unchanged. So if the function were stored with the right-hand side already evaluated, it would be equivalent to this definition:

```
f[n_] := (a + b)^n
```

This version does not expand anything and is not what we want.

Sometimes you *do* want to evaluate the right-hand side of an expression when you make the definition, not when you use it. Here is an example:

```
nSin = N[Sin[2]];
```

The **=** means "non-delayed assignment". In this case we want to evaluate the right-hand side only once, when the definition is made, so we store the numerical value and can access it rapidly without having to recompute the **Sin** each time.

It's usually the case that if you have an _ on the left-hand side of the definition, then you want to use delayed assignment (**:=**). Otherwise you want to use immediate assignment (**=**). This is not a hard and fast rule, but it is a useful rule of thumb.

You can define many useful functions by combining the technique described above with a few built-in *Mathematica* functions. For example, here is a definition of a function that returns the average of a list of numbers:

$$\texttt{average[list\_] := } \frac{\texttt{Apply[Plus, list]}}{\texttt{Length[list]}}$$

The expression **Apply[Plus, list]** means apply the **Plus** function (addition) to all the elements of the list **list**. This has the effect of adding together all the elements of the list. Dividing by the length of (number of elements in) **list** gives the average. Here's what the function does:

```
average[{1, 5, 2, 3, 4}]
```

3

More-complicated functions may require the use of local variables. To avoid possible name conflicts with global variables, it is best to use the **Module** function. Here is an example, a function that generates a list of a specified number of random numbers, prints some facts about the list, and then returns the list as its value:

```
randomStatistics[n_] := Module[{data},
   data = Table[Random[], {n}]; Print["Maximum = ", Max[data]];
   Print["Minimum = ", Min[data]];
   Print["Average = ", average[data]]; data]
```

- The first argument to **Module**, **{data}**, is a list of local variables to be used inside the **Module**.
- The second argument to **Module** is the body of the function. The value of the last expression in the body (**data**) is returned as the value of the **Module** function, and thus as the value of **randomStatistics**.

Note that there are several statements separated by semicolons. All these statements together constitute a single "compound" statement, which is the (single) second argument to **Module**. Whenever you have a sequence of statements in a function, be *sure* to separate them with semicolons. Otherwise *Mathematica* assumes that you mean to multiply them together (since blank space, including a line break, means multiplication).

Here is an example of what this function does:

```
randomStatistics[10]

Maximum = 0.918463
Minimum = 0.0169047
Average = 0.354447

{0.6169321976041655, 0.2293500894106836,
  0.918463424721488, 0.263260087452812, 0.01802218440966584,
  0.6848865537233423, 0.1588354639686913, 0.1228507409032357,
  0.5149689108970879, 0.01690473152178491}
```

Recursion is allowed in *Mathematica* function definitions. Often it is easiest to do recursion using pattern matching, discussed in Chapter 58.

We have described the fundamental elements needed to do procedural programming in *Mathematica*. Here are some of the most useful *Mathematica* functions for procedural programming:

- **Table[expr, {var, min, max}]** evaluates **expr** repeatedly and saves up the results in a list, which it returns.

- **Map[f, list]** applies the function **f** to each element of **list**.

- **Do[expr, {var, min, max}]** evaluates **expr** repeatedly but does not save up the results. (**Do** is the most useful way of doing simple iteration.)

- **While[test, body]** evaluates **body** repeatedly as long as **test** returns **True** (**test** is checked before **body** is evaluated the first time).

- **If[test, truecase, falsecase]** evaluates **truecase** if **test** returns **True**, and **falsecase** if it returns **False**. If **test** returns anything else, the statement is left unevaluated. If you add a fourth argument to the **If**, that argument is evaluated if **test** returns neither **True** nor **False**.

- **lhs == rhs** returns **True** if the two sides are structurally identical and remains unevaluated otherwise. (The comparison is structural, not mathematical, so **Sin[x]^2 + Cos[x]^2 == 1** is not **True**. On the other hand, **a + b == b + a** is **True**, because the right hand side is automatically sorted before the comparison.)

- **lhs === rhs** returns **True** if the two sides are identical, and **False** otherwise. (The comparison is the same as for **==**, except that **===** returns **False** instead of remaining unevaluated when the two sides are not identical.)

- **lhs != rhs** returns **False** if the two sides are identical, and remains unevaluated otherwise (**!=** means "not equal"). You can also use ≠, which you type as [ESC]!=[ESC].

- **lhs =!= rhs** returns **False** if the two sides are identical, and **True** otherwise.

- **lhs > rhs** returns **True** if **lhs** is numerically greater than **rhs**, and remains unevaluated otherwise.

- **lhs < rhs** returns **True** if **lhs** is numerically less than **rhs**, and remains unevaluated otherwise.

- **lhs >= rhs** returns **True** if **lhs** is numerically greater than or equal to **rhs**, and remains unevaluated otherwise. You can also use ≥, which you type as [ESC]>=[ESC].

- **lhs <= rhs** returns **True** if **lhs** is numerically less than or equal to **rhs**, and remains unevaluated otherwise. You can also use ≤, which you type as [ESC]<=[ESC].

Although the functions **For**, **Goto**, **Return**, **Throw**, and **Catch** exist, their use is not recommended except for certain rare circumstances in which they are genuinely unavoidable.

You can debug *Mathematica* programs in a variety of ways. Since *Mathematica* is an interpreted language, you always have interactive access to your variables and definitions. Tracing the flow of a program is a little harder, though. The most useful functions in this connection are **Print**, **Dialog**, and **Trace**.

Print can be used to print out the values of variables during the execution of a program, so you can see what is happening. For example, here is a program to draw polygons with a given number of sides:

```
drawPoly[n_] := Module[{list},

    list = Table[{Cos[t], Sin[t]}, {t, 0, 2 π, (2 π)/n}];

    Show[Graphics[Polygon[list]], AspectRatio → Automatic];
]
```

```
drawPoly[7]
```

If we wanted to see what the value of **list** was during the execution of this function, we could insert a **Print** statement in the definition, like this:

$$\texttt{drawPoly[n\_] := Module}\Big[\texttt{\{list\}},$$

$$\texttt{list = Table}\Big[\texttt{\{Cos[t], Sin[t]\}, } \{\texttt{t, 0, 2}\,\pi\texttt{, } \frac{2\,\pi}{\texttt{n}}\}\Big];$$

$$\texttt{Print[list];}$$

$$\texttt{Show[Graphics[Polygon[list]], AspectRatio} \rightarrow \texttt{Automatic];}$$

$$\Big]$$

```
drawPoly[7]
```

$$\Big\{\{1, 0\}, \Big\{\text{Cos}\Big[\tfrac{2\,\pi}{7}\Big], \text{Sin}\Big[\tfrac{2\,\pi}{7}\Big]\Big\}, \Big\{\text{Cos}\Big[\tfrac{4\,\pi}{7}\Big], \text{Sin}\Big[\tfrac{4\,\pi}{7}\Big]\Big\},$$

$$\Big\{\text{Cos}\Big[\tfrac{6\,\pi}{7}\Big], \text{Sin}\Big[\tfrac{6\,\pi}{7}\Big]\Big\}, \Big\{\text{Cos}\Big[\tfrac{8\,\pi}{7}\Big], \text{Sin}\Big[\tfrac{8\,\pi}{7}\Big]\Big\},$$

$$\Big\{\text{Cos}\Big[\tfrac{10\,\pi}{7}\Big], \text{Sin}\Big[\tfrac{10\,\pi}{7}\Big]\Big\}, \Big\{\text{Cos}\Big[\tfrac{12\,\pi}{7}\Big], \text{Sin}\Big[\tfrac{12\,\pi}{7}\Big]\Big\}, \{1, 0\}\Big\}$$

Seeing the output might suggest that we insert an **N** function in the **Table** command, to avoid building up a large symbolic table (which is slow):

$$\texttt{drawPoly[n\_] := Module}\Big[\texttt{\{list\}},$$

$$\texttt{list = Table}\Big[\texttt{N[\{Cos[t], Sin[t]\}], } \{\texttt{t, 0, 2}\,\pi\texttt{, } \frac{2\,\pi}{\texttt{n}}\}\Big];$$

$$\texttt{Print[list];}$$

$$\texttt{Show[Graphics[Polygon[list]], AspectRatio} \rightarrow \texttt{Automatic];}$$

$$\Big]$$

```
drawPoly[7]
```

```
{{1., 0}, {0.62349, 0.781831}, {-0.222521, 0.974928},
 {-0.900969, 0.433884}, {-0.900969, -0.433884},
 {-0.222521, -0.974928}, {0.62349, -0.781831}, {1., 0}}
```

When you are satisfied with the definition, remove the **Print** statement.

A different way to get the same information is to insert a **Dialog** command instead of a **Print** command. When execution of the function reaches the **Dialog** command, execution stops. We then enter *subsession mode*. The cell bracket of the cell being evaluated turns gray. (Note that the words Inspector, Subsession, and Dialog are used somewhat interchangeably in *Mathematica* documentation.)

Once we are in subsession mode, we can evaluate any expressions we want (for example, to find out the values of variables). When we exit subsession mode (either by choosing the **Exit Subsession** command from the **Kernel** menu, **Evaluation** submenu, or by evaluating **Return[]**), the main evaluation continues.

There is one slight complication: **Module** avoids name conflicts with local variables by appending a serial number to each name you specify. So, for example, the variable **list** in the definition above will, when it is used, be called something like **list$20**. You will find it tricky to determine the actual name being used. A simple solution is to temporarily remove the names of the local variables from the first argument to **Module**. Here is the modified definition:

```
drawPoly[n_] := Module[{},

    list = Table[N[{Cos[t], Sin[t]}], {t, 0, 2 π, (2 π)/n}];

    Dialog[];
    Show[Graphics[Polygon[list]], AspectRatio → Automatic];
]
```

Now we can try out the function:

```
drawPoly[7]
```

No output is produced; the cell bracket of the cell containing **drawPoly[7]** is in gray, indicating that we are in subsession mode.

We can now ask for the value of **list** by evaluating the following expression:

    list

    {{1., 0}, {0.62349, 0.781831}, {-0.222521, 0.974928},
     {-0.900969, 0.433884}, {-0.900969, -0.433884},
     {-0.222521, -0.974928}, {0.62349, -0.781831}, {1., 0}}

If this were a more complicated function, we could evaluate a variety of different expressions to learn what is going on. We could also change the values of variables, although this can sometimes be quite confusing. When we are done, we choose **Exit Subsession** from the **Kernel** menu, **Evaluation** submenu, to continue with the main evaluation. Now the output is produced:

Normally the output would be placed directly below the cell being evaluated; we've separated it here for clarity.

You can enter subsession mode several ways. We've just seen how to do it by placing a **Dialog** command at a specific location in a function. A second way is to interrupt a running calculation by using the **Interrupt Evaluation...** command in the **Kernel** menu (or by typing Command-comma). This will bring up the Interrupt options panel, one of whose choices is Enter Subsession. Since you can't tell exactly where the interrupt will stop the calculation, this is a somewhat haphazard way of seeing what is happening. On the other hand, if you have a program with one long loop, an interrupt command can be a good way to find out how far it's gotten after you lose patience. A subsession entered this way can be exited the same way as one entered using the **Dialog** command.

A third way to enter a subsession is to use the **Evaluate In Subsession** command in the **Kernel** menu, **Evaluation** submenu. **Evaluate In Subsession**, which can be used only when another calculation is running, automatically interrupts the calculation, enters subsession mode, evaluates the selected cell or cells, and then exits the subsession. This is useful to find out the instantaneous value of an expression without stopping the main calculation any longer than necessary. A shortcut for **Evaluate In Subsession** is Shift-Option-Return.

Trace is perhaps the most powerful debugging tool, but it is so complicated and confusing that even experienced *Mathematica* users find it all but impossible to understand.

Before illustrating **Trace**, we will restore the definition of **drawPoly** to its original form:

```
drawPoly[n_] := Module[{list},
        list = Table[N[{Cos[t], Sin[t]}], {t, 0, 2 π, (2 π)/n}];
        Show[Graphics[Polygon[list]], AspectRatio → Automatic];
]
```

Now we can apply **Trace**:

```
Trace[drawPoly[3], list]
```

```
{{{{{{list$6, {{1., 0},
        {-0.5, 0.866025}, {-0.5, -0.866025}, {1., 0}}}}}}}}}
```

In this form, the first argument is the expression to be evaluated and the second argument is a symbol name. All transformation rules involving the symbol **list** will be accumulated into the output of the **Trace** command. In this case there was only one, the assignment to **list**.

The power of **Trace** lies in its second argument. That argument can be either a symbol name (in which case the output of **Trace** will be a list of all the expressions involving that symbol), or it can be a *Mathematica* pattern (in which case the output will be a list of all the expressions matching the pattern). The latter form allows very selective display of the flow of evaluation.

Advanced readers are advised to read about **Trace** in The *Mathematica* Book.

Chapter **57**

Should anyone *ever* use a `For` loop?

If you go to a fancy research university and take a fancy programming class, they will tell you that commands such as "for", "goto", and "return" are amateurish and old fashioned. They are, surprisingly, right. In a proper modern language, using these commands is never necessary and often a bad idea. There are alternatives that are more efficient, easier to understand, and less likely to cause confusion.

The following example of *Mathematica* code was found in a manuscript from an author who shall remain nameless:

```
list2 = {};
For[i = 1, i ≤ Length[list1], ++i, AppendTo[list2, Sin[list1[[i]]]]]
```

After some consideration, it is possible to determine that this statement builds up a list (**list2**) that contains the sine of each element of **list1**. The following command does *exactly* the same thing:

```
list2 = Sin[list1]
```

The **Sin** function has the attribute **Listable**, which means that, when it's applied to a list, it is automatically applied to each element in the list. Here's a specific example:

```
Sin[{1, 2, 3, 4}]
```

```
{Sin[1], Sin[2], Sin[3], Sin[4]}
```

The **Listable** attribute is one of the features of *Mathematica* in which iteration over elements in a list is done automatically for you, without the need for an explicit loop. Let's explore **Listable** in more detail.

Most built-in functions for which it makes sense have the **Listable** attribute, so it's easy to apply them to lists. The following (rather intimidating) piece of *Mathematica* code generates a list of all the built-in Listable functions (don't worry about understanding the code, we just want to look at the list):

```
Map[First, Select[Map[{#, Attributes[#]} &, Names["*"]],
  ! (FreeQ[#1, Listable]) &]]
```

{Abs, AiryAi, AiryAiPrime, AiryBi, AiryBiPrime, Apart, ArcCos, ArcCosh, ArcCot,
ArcCoth, ArcCsc, ArcCsch, ArcSec, ArcSech, ArcSin, ArcSinh, ArcTan, ArcTanh,
Arg, ArithmeticGeometricMean, Attributes, BernoulliB, BesselI, BesselJ,
BesselK, BesselY, Beta, BetaRegularized, Binomial, Cancel, Ceiling, Characters,
ChebyshevT, ChebyshevU, Coefficient, Conjugate, Cos, Cosh, CoshIntegral,
CosIntegral, Cot, Coth, Csc, Csch, Denominator, Divide, Divisors, DivisorSigma,
EllipticE, EllipticF, EllipticK, EllipticPi, EllipticTheta, EllipticThetaPrime,
Erf, Erfc, Erfi, EulerE, EulerPhi, EvenQ, Exp, ExpIntegralE, ExpIntegralEi,
Exponent, Factor, Factorial, Factorial2, FactorInteger, FactorSquareFree,
Fibonacci, Floor, FractionalPart, FresnelC, FresnelS, Gamma, GammaRegularized,
GCD, GegenbauerC, HermiteH, Hypergeometric0F1, Hypergeometric0F1Regularized,
Hypergeometric1F1, Hypergeometric1F1Regularized, Hypergeometric2F1,
Hypergeometric2F1Regularized, HypergeometricU, Im, In, InString, IntegerDigits,
IntegerPart, IntervalMemberQ, JacobiP, JacobiSymbol, JacobiZeta, LaguerreL,
LCM, LegendreP, LegendreQ, LerchPhi, Limit, Log, LogGamma, LogIntegral,
MantissaExponent, MathieuC, MathieuCharacteristicA, MathieuCharacteristicB,
MathieuCharacteristicExponent, MathieuCPrime, MathieuS, MathieuSPrime,
MessageList, Minus, Mod, MoebiusMu, Multinomial, Negative, NonNegative,
NonPositive, Numerator, OddQ, Out, PartitionsP, PartitionsQ, Plus, Pochhammer,
PolyGamma, PolyLog, PolynomialGCD, PolynomialLCM, Positive, Power, PowerMod,
Prime, PrimePi, PrimeQ, ProductLog, Quotient, Range, Re, RealDigits, Resultant,
RiemannSiegelTheta, RiemannSiegelZ, Round, Sec, Sech, SetAccuracy, SetPrecision,
Sign, Sin, Sinh, SinhIntegral, SinIntegral, SphericalHarmonicY, Sqrt,
StirlingS1, StirlingS2, Subtract, Tan, Tanh, Times, ToExpression, Together,
ToHeldExpression, ToLowerCase, ToUpperCase, TrigFactor, Zeta, $NumberBits}

Listability also works for functions with more than one argument (for example, **Mod**). Here is an example of **Mod** applied to two numbers:

```
Mod[10, 3]
```

1

The result, 1, is 10 modulo 3 (the remainder after dividing 10 by 3). If you have several numbers and you want to see what each of them is, modulo a given number, you can give **Mod** a list as its first argument:

```
Mod[{10, 11, 12, 13, 14}, 3]
```

{1, 2, 0, 1, 2}

Conversely, if you have a number and you want to see what it is modulo several given numbers, you can give **Mod** a list as its second argument:

```
Mod[10, {3, 4, 5, 6, 7}]
```

{1, 2, 0, 4, 3}

If you have several numbers and you want to see each of them modulo its own given number, you can give **Mod** two lists:

```
Mod[{10, 11, 12, 13, 14}, {3, 4, 5, 6, 7}]
```

```
{1, 3, 2, 1, 0}
```

If you are using two lists, as we have just done, they must be the same length; otherwise they can't be matched element by element:

```
Mod[{10, 11, 12, 13, 14}, {3, 4, 5}]
```

```
Thread::tdlen:
    Objects of unequal length in
     Mod[{10, 11, 12, 13, 14}, {3, 4, 5}]
       cannot be combined.
```

```
Mod[{10, 11, 12, 13, 14}, {3, 4, 5}]
```

If you define your own function and then want to apply it to a list, you can either give it the **Listable** attribute or use the **Map** function:

```
Map[f, {1, 2, 3}]
```

```
{f[1], f[2], f[3]}
```

Or:

```
Attributes[f] = {Listable};
```

```
f[{1, 2, 3}]
```

```
{f[1], f[2], f[3]}
```

You can think of the **Listable** attribute as meaning that the function will automatically invoke the **Map** command whenever it is applied to a list. For functions with more than one argument, the corresponding command that is automatically applied is called **Thread**. This command is beyond the scope of this book.

Another instance in which people are tempted to use the **For** command is when they want a table of numbers. For example, the following code will build up a table of squares:

```
list = {};
For[i = 1, i ≤ 10, ++i, AppendTo[list, i²]];
list
```

```
{1, 4, 9, 16, 25, 36, 49, 64, 81, 100}
```

This code is hard to understand and runs quite slowly. The following much simpler command generates the same list:

```
Table[i², {i, 1, 10}]

{1, 4, 9, 16, 25, 36, 49, 64, 81, 100}
```

This **Table** command is easier to understand than the **For** loop, particularly if one is familiar with the iterator form **{variable, start, end}**, which is commonly used in *Mathematica*.

The examples above all involve list manipulation. In *Mathematica* there are many commands for dealing with lists without using explicit loops. <u>Chapter</u> 20 explains some of these functions.

Sometimes you do need an actual loop, but even then **For** is rarely the best choice. The following example prints Hello five times:

```
For[i = 1, i ≤ 5, ++i, Print["Hello"]]

Hello
Hello
Hello
Hello
Hello
```

But consider this command:

```
Do[Print["Hello"], {i, 1, 5}]

Hello
Hello
Hello
Hello
Hello
```

Notice that the syntax of **Do** is very similar, in fact identical, to that of **Table**. This sort of consistency makes it easy to remember how to use *Mathematica* commands. See <u>Chapter</u> 15 for more about consistency in *Mathematica*.

Since we don't use the variable **i** anywhere in the body of this loop, we can actually use an abbreviated form of the **Do** loop:

```
Do[Print["Hello"], {5}]

Hello
Hello
Hello
Hello
Hello
```

In many cases, **Do** provides a very clear and efficient way to do a fixed-length loop. In cases where you need a more complicated stopping condition, the **While** command may be a good choice. See The *Mathematica* Book for more information about these commands.

Chapter **58**

How do I use *Mathematica's* pattern matcher?

Mathematica's pattern matcher is, excepting only the <u>front end</u>, the feature that most distinguishes it from other symbolic mathematics programs. Pattern matching can be used in a startling variety of ways and is fundamental to almost anything you do in *Mathematica*.

Let's start by seeing how patterns can be used to transform expressions. Here is an expression:

a + b

a + b

We can use the substitute operator (**/.**) along with a replacement rule (→) to substitute a new expression for **b**:

a + b /. b → x²

a + x²

The **/.** operator should be read "replace" and → should be read "with". The whole expression should be read as "in **a + b** replace **b** with **x²**".

To create the arrow, you can type **->** (dash greater than), or ⌜ESC⌝**->**⌜ESC⌝, which gives the nice → arrow character. The two forms are equivalent:

a + b /. b -> x²

a + x²

In this example, the **b** in the replacement rule is a pattern. It is a simple pattern, in that it only matches a literal "b". Let's try a more complicated expression:

a + log[Eˣ]

a + log[Eˣ]

We could simplify by canceling the log with the power:

$$\mathtt{a + log[E^x] \; / . \; log[E^x] \to x}$$

```
a + x
```

In this case, $\mathtt{log[E^x]}$ is a somewhat more complicated pattern: *Mathematica* compares it with the expression to find what subpart of the expression matches the pattern.

Both the patterns we've seen are literal patterns. That is, they match one and only one possible expression. For example, the following does not work:

$$\mathtt{a + log[E^y] \; / . \; log[E^x] \to x}$$

```
a + log[E^y]
```

Since the pattern matches only expressions involving $\mathtt{x}$, it does not match $\mathtt{log[E^y]}$. If we want to write a pattern that matches $\mathtt{log[E^{anything}]}$, we use an underscore (_). The pattern $\mathtt{log[E^{n\_}]}$ means "match any expression of this form, regardless of what $\mathtt{n\_}$ is":

$$\mathtt{a + log[E^y] \; / . \; log[E^{n\_}] \to n}$$

```
a + y
```

Here are some more examples of expressions that match this pattern:

$$\mathtt{a + log[E^{x+y}] \; / . \; log[E^{n\_}] \to n}$$

```
a + x + y
```

$$\mathtt{a + log[E^{Sin[x+y]}] \; / . \; log[E^{n\_}] \to n}$$

```
a + Sin[x + y]
```

In each case, *Mathematica* figured out what $\mathtt{n\_}$ needed to be to match the pattern, and used that value as the replacement.

You can write patterns with more than one underscore:

$$\mathtt{x + Sin[a + b] \; / . \; Sin[n\_ + m\_] \to Cos[n] \; Sin[m] + Cos[m] \; Sin[n]}$$

```
x + Cos[b] Sin[a] + Cos[a] Sin[b]
```

Let's consider this more complicated expression:

$$\texttt{Cos[x] + Cos[x]}^2 \texttt{ + Sin[x] + Sin[x]}^2$$

$$\texttt{Cos[x] + Cos[x]}^2 \texttt{ + Sin[x] + Sin[x]}^2$$

It could be simplified using the identity "sine squared plus cosine squared equals one". We could write this using a literal pattern:

$$\texttt{Cos[x] + Cos[x]}^2 \texttt{ + Sin[x] + Sin[x]}^2 \texttt{ /. Sin[x]}^2 \texttt{ + Cos[x]}^2 \rightarrow \texttt{1}$$

$$\texttt{1 + Cos[x] + Sin[x]}$$

(Notice that *Mathematica* was able to make this pattern match even though the structure's two terms were separated. *Mathematica* had to reorder the expression to find the structure hidden in it. Later we'll learn more about what kinds of rearrangements *Mathematica* will do to get a pattern to match.)

A literal pattern, however, is not a very satisfactory way to do this transformation. We want to write a pattern that matches $\texttt{Sin[}\textit{anything}\texttt{]}^2 \texttt{ + Cos[}\textit{anything}\texttt{]}^2$ with the further restriction that both *anythings* must be the same. This can be done by using a pattern with two underscores, both with the same name:

$$\texttt{Cos[x] + Cos[x]}^2 \texttt{ + Sin[x] + Sin[x]}^2 \texttt{ /. Sin[n\_]}^2 \texttt{ + Cos[n\_]}^2 \rightarrow \texttt{1}$$

$$\texttt{1 + Cos[x] + Sin[x]}$$

In the following example, this pattern matches one pair but not the other:

$$\texttt{Cos[a]}^2 \texttt{ + Cos[x]}^2 \texttt{ + Sin[a]}^2 \texttt{ + Sin[y]}^2 \texttt{ /. Sin[n\_]}^2 \texttt{ + Cos[n\_]}^2 \rightarrow \texttt{1}$$

$$\texttt{1 + Cos[x]}^2 \texttt{ + Sin[y]}^2$$

If you are not at least slightly amazed at this example, consider rereading it.

So far we have been applying pattern transformations manually to individual expressions. It is also possible to enter such transformations into the global rule base so they are applied automatically whenever an expression is evaluated. This is called *assignment*.

For example, the following assignment adds a pattern transformation rule to the global rule base:

$$\texttt{h = 5}$$

$$\texttt{5}$$

The pattern in this case is the literal **h**. Now, anytime we evaluate an expression involving **h**, the value **5** will be substituted:

h²

25

Note that this is exactly the same as if we had applied the transformation manually:

h² /. h → 5

25

So we see that assigning a value to a variable is really the same thing as writing a transformation rule and adding it to the global rule base. (Internally, that is how *Mathematica* implements it.)

We can add a more complicated rule such as the one we were looking at earlier:

log[E$^{n\_}$] = n

n

Now we don't have to apply any rules manually:

a + log[E^y]

a + y

a + log[E^{x+y}]

a + x + y

a + log[E$^{Sin[x+y]}$]

a + Sin[x + y]

Just like variable definitions, function definitions are also patterns. For example, here is a pattern rule that implements a function:

square[n_] = n^2

n^2

This patterns says **square[***anything***]** is to be transformed into *anything* squared. This is just what a function should do, and indeed we can use **square** like any other function:

>   **square[5]**

>   25

In fact, *all* functions in *Mathematica* are defined in much this way.

There is one complication. Consider the following example:

>   **expanding[n_] = Expand[(a + b)^n]**

> $(a + b)^n$

Let's use it:

>   **expanding[5]**

> $(a + b)^5$

The problem is that the **Expand** function was evaluated at the time the definition was made, before **n** had any specific numerical value. It returned the expression unexpanded, and this resulting expression became part of the rule. What we want instead is to have the *unevaluated* **Expand** expression become part of the rule. This is done using **:=** instead of **=**.

>   **expanding[n_] := Expand[(a + b)^n]**

Let's use this new version:

>   **expanding[5]**

> $a^5 + 5\,a^4\,b + 10\,a^3\,b^2 + 10\,a^2\,b^3 + 5\,a\,b^4 + b^5$

It's usually the case that if you have an _ on the left-hand side of the definition, then you want to use delayed assignment (**:=**) because _'s on the left-hand side mean that there are variables on the right-hand side that are going to take on different values when the definition is used. If you have only literal expressions on the left hand side, then every time you evaluate the expression, exactly the same thing is going to be evaluated. You may as well do the evaluation once at the time the definition is made, rather than every time it is used. (The exception is when the right hand side contains commands, such as **Print**, that have side effects. But we digress.)

Since function definitions are patterns, we are not restricted to functions that take just one or more arguments. We can define functions that automatically "recognize" patterns and transform them. We can even make multiple definitions for the same function so it can do different things to different patterns.

For example, here is a function that, when applied to a single number, returns its absolute value, but when applied to a list of two numbers (a vector) returns the length of the vector (this is like a generalized speed function that works in both one and two dimensions):

```
speed[n_] := Abs[n]
speed[{x_, y_}] := √(x² + y²)
```

Here is how it works in each case:

```
speed[-3]
```

3

```
speed[{3, 5}]
```

$\sqrt{34}$

The reader may have anticipated a complication: The first definition is for **speed[*anything*]**. When **speed** is applied to a list of two elements, it could match either rule because, after all, a list of two elements is an *anything*. This problem is dealt with in *Mathematica* by automatically arranging the rules in order of increasing generality. Since the second definition is more specific than the first, it is tried first. (This ordering is not always completely determined, nor does it always work as intended. The problem is a deep and subtle one about which tomes are written. *Mathematica*'s solution is expedient, but not perfect.)

Recursion is another example in which having multiple definitions for the same function is useful. Any time you evaluate an expression, *Mathematica* applies every rule it has, once. Then it applies every rule again, and again, and so on until the expression stops changing. So if you have a rule that transforms an expression into another expression to which the same rule can also be applied, it will be applied again and again (potentially forever).

Consider the classic definition of the factorial function:

```
fac[n_] := n fac[n - 1]
```

This says, **fac[*anything*]** is *anything* times **fac** of one less than *anything*. This is fine, except that it is an infinite loop: It will never stop. We need to add a special case that allows the recursion to come to an end. The usual way is to say that **fac[0]** is 1:

```
fac[0] = 1
```

1

Now we can use the definition:

```
fac[10]
```

```
3628800
```

The first rule was used 10 times and the second rule once. Although a factorial function could be written without using patterns in this way, the definition would not be nearly as neat and easy to understand.

We mentioned earlier that *Mathematica* sometimes has to reorder expressions to get a pattern to match. Consider this example:

```
a + b + c + d /. a + d → x
```

```
b + c + x
```

Mathematica had to try several reorderings of the addition before it could notice that **a** and **d** could be brought together, thereby matching the pattern.

On the other hand, consider this example:

```
(a + b) c /. a c → x
```

```
(a + b) c
```

Mathematica did *not* notice that it could rewrite the expression as **a c + b c** and then apply the rule.

When will *Mathematica* reorganize an expression? There are only two specific things *Mathematica* will do to try to match an expression. First, it will change the order of commutative functions (like addition and multiplication). Second, it will try different groupings of associative functions (like addition and multiplication).

It will never try any structural rearrangements (such as expanding, factoring, distributing, etc.). That is, patterns in *Mathematica* are strictly structural, not mathematical or algebraic. Two expressions may be mathematically identical (e.g., **a (b + c)** and **a c + b c**), but they are not structurally identical, and *Mathematica* will not match them as patterns.

There are *Mathematica* objects called **AlgebraicRules** that can be used to carry out true algebraic transformations, but their use is beyond the scope of this book. The reader is advised to consult The *Mathematica* Book for information about **AlgebraicRules** and other features available for structural pattern matching.

■ Example

We'll write a set of rules to expand any trigonometric expression into the lowest possible angle. That is, if we see **Sin[2 a]**, we want to rewrite it in a form involving only **Sin[a]** and **Cos[a]**. (We do this for illustrative purposes only: There are built-in *Mathematica* functions to do this, such as **Factor**, **Expand**, **Apart**, and **Together** with the option **Trig→ ⟩ True**. See The *Mathematica* Book for more information.)

Since we don't want any conflicts with the built-in **Sin** and **Cos** functions, we'll write all our rules in terms of **sin** and **cos** instead. The lowercase first letter will distinguish our functions from the built-in ones.

First we write the formulas for the sum of two angles:

$$\texttt{sin[a\_ + b\_] := cos[a] sin[b] + cos[b] sin[a]}$$

$$\texttt{cos[a\_ + b\_] := cos[a] cos[b] - sin[a] sin[b]}$$

Next we want to write the rule for integer multiples of angles. If we have, for example, **sin[3x]**, we can write this as **sin[x + 2x]** and then use one of the added angle formulas for addition. More generally, **sin[n x]** can be written as **sin[x+(n-1)x]**.

Our first attempt to write the rule might be:

$$\texttt{sin[n\_ a\_] := cos[a] sin[(n - 1) a] + cos[(n - 1) a] sin[a]}$$

This is just like the rule for **sin[a + b]**, with **b** being **(n-1) a**.

Here we run into some complications that will require learning about new types of patterns. This pattern matches **sin[***anything* times *anythingelse***]**. The problem is that we treat the **n** and the **a** differently: **n** must be an integer for the formula to work. When a rule like the one above is applied to, say, **sin[5 x]**, we can't be sure whether it will match **5** with **n** and **x** with **a**, or the reverse (since multiplication is commutative).

We need to tell *Mathematica* that **n** must be an integer for the pattern to match. This is done by using **n_Integer** instead of **n_**. The pattern **n_Integer** matches anything that is an integer. (Technically, it matches any expression whose "Head" is **Integer**. The *Mathematica* Book explains in detail what this means.)

The improved rule is:

$$\texttt{sin[n\_Integer a\_] := cos[a] sin[(n - 1) a] + cos[(n - 1) a] sin[a]}$$

But there is still a problem. If **n** is a negative integer, this rule will go into an infinite loop. We need to add another condition that says this rule applies only if **n** is positive. **Positive** is a function that returns **True** or **False** depending on whether or not its argument is positive.

We can add a condition to any rule by appending a **/;** clause at the end:

```
sin[n_Integer a_] :=
  cos[a] sin[(n - 1) a] + cos[(n - 1) a] sin[a] /; Positive[n]
```

You can add arbitrarily complicated conditions to a rule, as long as they return **True** or **False** in the end.

If your condition is a single function of one argument, you can use a shortcut and write the same rule like this:

```
sin[n_Integer ? Positive a_] :=
  cos[a] sin[(n - 1) a] + cos[(n - 1) a] sin[a]
```

You may wonder why there are two different ways to specify conditions. That is, why does the **Integer** go right after the _, and the **Positive** after a question mark? This is a somewhat complicated issue, and it mainly concerns efficiency. If you like, you can write all the conditions in the **/;** clause like this:

```
sin[n_ a_] := cos[a] sin[(n - 1) a] + cos[(n - 1) a] sin[a] /;
  IntegerQ[n] && Positive[n]
```

The *Mathematica* Book explains these issues in great detail. We'll use the shorter form for now.

Using what we've learned, we can write the multiple angle rules for **sin** and **cos**:

```
sin[n_Integer ? Positive a_] :=
  cos[a] sin[(n - 1) a] + cos[(n - 1) a] sin[a]

cos[n_Integer ? Positive a_] :=
  cos[a] cos[(n - 1) a] - sin[a] sin[(n - 1) a]
```

What about negative integers? We can write two more rules that turn negative integers into positive ones:

```
sin[n_Integer ? Negative a_] := -sin[-n a]

cos[n_Integer ? Negative a_] := cos[-n a]
```

Here, together in one place, are all the rules we've developed. We've added **Expand** to the multiple angle formulas because it makes the answer look nicer.

```
sin[a_ + b_] := cos[a] sin[b] + cos[b] sin[a]
cos[a_ + b_] := cos[a] cos[b] - sin[a] sin[b]
sin[n_Integer? Negative a_] := -sin[-n a]
cos[n_Integer? Negative a_] := cos[-n a]
sin[n_Integer? Positive a_] :=
  Expand[cos[a] sin[(n - 1) a] + cos[(n - 1) a] sin[a]]
cos[n_Integer? Positive a_] :=
  Expand[cos[a] cos[(n - 1) a] - sin[a] sin[(n - 1) a]]
```

Let's try our rules on a few examples:

```
sin[x + y]
```

$\cos[y] \sin[x] + \cos[x] \sin[y]$

```
sin[2 x]
```

$2 \cos[x] \sin[x]$

```
cos[4 x]
```

$\cos[x]^4 - 6 \cos[x]^2 \sin[x]^2 + \sin[x]^4$

```
sin[2 x - 5 y]
```

$2 \cos[x] \sin[x] (\cos[y]^5 - 10 \cos[y]^3 \sin[y]^2 + 5 \cos[y] \sin[y]^4) + (\cos[x]^2 - \sin[x]^2) (-5 \cos[y]^4 \sin[y] + 10 \cos[y]^2 \sin[y]^3 - \sin[y]^5)$

In this last example we can see that the rules all work together, even if they have to be applied several times before the answer is reduced to lowest possible terms.

We might want a function that calculates the distance between two points in two dimensions. We could do this by defining a function with four arguments:

$$\texttt{distance[x1\_, y1\_, x2\_, y2\_]} := \sqrt{(x2 - x1)^2 + (y2 - y1)^2}$$

We can try **distance** on the points (3, 7) and (6, 2):

```
distance[3, 7, 6, 2]
```

$\sqrt{34}$

This was not the best way to define the function we wanted. In *Mathematica*, points are usually represented as lists of two numbers. For example, we might assign the variable **pointA** to hold our first point, and **pointB** to hold our second point:

> **pointA = {3, 7};**
> **pointB = {6, 2};**

We can't use our distance function directly on these two points, because our function takes four arguments, not two. That is, we can't say:

> **distance[pointA, pointB]**

Instead we would have to say (the notation **pointA[[1]]** means the first element of **pointA**):

> **distance[pointA[[1]], pointA[[2]], pointB[[1]], pointB[[2]]]**

> $\sqrt{34}$

This input is very ugly. Better would be to define **distance** in such a way that it takes two lists as arguments:

> **betterDistance[pA_, pB_] :=** $\sqrt{(pB[[1]] - pA[[1]])^2 + (pB[[2]] - pA[[2]])^2}$

Let's apply our improved definition to our point variables:

> **betterDistance[pointA, pointB]**

> $\sqrt{34}$

The definition is still rather ugly. We can use a pattern definition to "pick out" the elements of the lists automatically:

> **evenBetterDistance[{x1_, y1_}, {x2_, y2_}] :=**
> $\sqrt{(x2 - x1)^2 + (y2 - y1)^2}$

This function can be used on our point variables:

> **evenBetterDistance[pointA, pointB]**

> $\sqrt{34}$

Or we can enter the points directly:

> **evenBetterDistance[{3, 7}, {6, 2}]**

> $\sqrt{34}$

Chapter **59**

Is *Mathematica* Year-2000 compatible?

Let us begin by saying that absolutely everything in this chapter is pure speculation, presented without any authority or basis in research or fact, and is not supported, represented as true, endorsed, condoned, or even proofread by the authors, their publishers, Wolfram Research, Inc, nor any of their spouses, kinfolk or dogs. All legal liability as to the contents of this chapter is expressely disclaimed, the contents are presented for amusement purposes only, and are not to be used with life support equipment.

There, now that we've made the lawyers happy, the answer is **yes**, *Mathematica* is fully Year-2000 compatible, complient, and contented. (The biggest Year-2000 problem is, of course, lawyers, and if anything goes wrong with, say, the banking system, it will be because of the unprecedently huge sums of money being transferring into the pockets of Y2K lawyers.)

Why do programs have Year-2000 bugs? There are two main reasons. The most obvious is that some programs store years as two-digit numbers, so 2007 and 1907 are both recorded as 07, and the program has trouble telling the difference.

The second is that, in a perverse coincidence, the year 2000 is an exception to an exception to an exception to the rule that every fourth year is a leap year. Yes, every fourth year is a leap year, except that every 100 years you skip a leap year, *except* that every 400 years you *don't* skip the leap year. 2000 is that 400th year, and some programmers didn't know that fact. Why they knew that every 100th year isn't a leap year, but not the one extra fact about every 400 years, is one of those mysteries to which we may never know the answer. Maybe programmers figured 400 years is such a long time, longer even than 100 years, that surely they didn't have to worry about it.

Why do leap years matter? Because if you are calculating daily compounded interest you need to know how many days fall between two dates; if the interval includes a leap year, you have to take that into account. A program with the Year-2000-is-not-a-leap-year bug will pay one day's worth too little interest, or charge it, as the case may be.

Dates in *Mathematica* are stored as a list of six numbers; year, month, day, hour, minute, second. For example, this command gives the current date:

```
Date[]
```

```
{1999, 7, 21, 23, 47, 31}
```

So now you know one of the moments when we were working on this chapter, exactly. This list means:

{1999, July, 21th, 11PM, 47 minutes, and 31 seconds}

Notice that the year is a four-digit number, which right from the start means that *Mathematica* doesn't have the most obvious sort of Year-2000 bug. But actually, it goes well beyond that: As with any other numbers in *Mathematica*, all the numbers in a *Mathematica* date list can be arbitrary-size integers. For example, you might enter this list

{12345678987654321, 7, 21, 21, 35, 45}

to represent a moment some considerable distance in the future. Put this way, it's almost a silly question whether *Mathematica* has a Year-2000 problem, since a date in *Mathematica* is just a list, and obviously in *Mathematica* there's no reason why the first element of a list should be restricted to two digits, or suddenly fall apart if the number gets bigger than 2000.

Which leaves the second issue, leap years. *Mathematica* gets this issue right, and, as usual, goes well beyond what one might expect. To do calculations involving dates, one needs to load the calendar package:

Needs["Miscellaneous`Calendar`"]

After it is loaded, we can do things like ask what day of the week it is:

DayOfWeek[Date[]]

Wednesday

Or, what day of the week it will be at some point in the future:

DayOfWeek[{12345678987654321, 7, 21, 21, 35, 45}]

Thursday

These calculations are done using the correct official definitions of such things, and are accurate for any date, both in the future and in the past. In the distant past (e.g., before television) some interesting questions come up, like the 12 days missing from 1752, except in Catholic countries where 11 days are missing from 1582, etc. Suffice it to say that the Calendar package implements Julian, Gregorian, and Islamic calendars, and can do various date-related calculations in any of these calendar systems. Each of these calendars has certain ranges of years for which it is not well defined, but within these limitations *Mathematica* will get the correct answers.

Of course, when you're talking about the day of the week in a year well after the heat death of the universe, "correct" is a relative term. And since the rotation of the earth is slowing down at an only partially predictable rate, undoubtedly one of these centuries it will be necessary to introduce a new exception to the tower of leap year exceptions, and *Mathematica* obviously doesn't know about this yet.

▪ Limitations caused by interaction with the operating system

While date calculations within *Mathematica* have absolutely no arbitrary limitations, the same is not true of the operating systems *Mathematica* runs on. In order to find out the current date, *Mathematica* has to ask the operating system, since it has no independent way of knowing the current date and time. Every operating system has its own limitations, but none have a problem with the year 2000: They typically have problems in 2030 or beyond. Of course, these problems will, in about 30 years, cause exactly the same sort of trouble that the Year-2000 bugs are causing now. But, this is a chapter about the Year-2000 bug, so we will, like the rest of the computer industry, pretend that 2030 is so far in the future there's no need to worry about it, especially since only the manufacturers of the operating systems can fix the problem. (After all, if it weren't for this sort of thinking, how could history repeat itself?)

Since the interaction with the operating system is limited to asking for the current date and time, there really isn't any *immediate* problem. Date calculations involving dates beyond the one supported by the operating system can certainly be done (for example, calculating interest due on a loan that will still be outstanding after the operating system you are using has run out of time). Such calculations reley only on *Mathematica*'s internal date representations, which have no arbitrary limitations.

▪ Absolute seconds

Another form of date/time representation used in *Mathematica* is a count of the number of seconds since midnight on the beginning of Jan 1, 1900, counting that time when it would have occurred in your current time zone:

```
AbsoluteTime[]
```

$3.141530097000000 \times 10^9$

Note that this is a floating point number, though on most platforms it has a granularity of one second. There are functions to convert between this absolute number of seconds and the 6-element list described above:

```
ToDate[3141530097]
```

{1999, 7, 21, 7, 14, 57}

```
FromDate[{1999, 7, 21, 7, 2, 32}]
```

3141529352

Having noticed the interesting sequence of digits in this number, we decided to perfect it:

ToDate[N[1000000000 π]]

{1999, 7, 22, 0, 37, 33.5898}

In other words, just a few hours after we finished this section of this chapter, the number of seconds since January 1, 1900 was exactly 1,000,000,000 times π!

Note that the conversion from absolute seconds to dates is far from trivial. It requires knowledge of all the details of leap years.

You might think that this representation, starting as it does at the arbitrary point of January 1, 1900, would have Year-2000 sorts of problems. It doesn't, because numbers in *Mathematica* can be of arbitrary size, and of course they can be negative:

FromDate[{123456789, 7, 21, 21, 35, 45}]

3895860023818545

FromDate[{1066, 10, 14, 13, 32, 15}]

-26293717665

Absolute seconds allow you to easily calculate things involving intervals of time. For example, here are the dates of the next 30 Wednesdays from today:

weekOfSeconds = 7 × 24 × 60 × 60

604800

Table[
 Take[ToDate[AbsoluteTime[] + n weekOfSeconds], 3], {n, 0, 30}]

{{1999, 7, 21}, {1999, 7, 28}, {1999, 8, 4}, {1999, 8, 11},
 {1999, 8, 18}, {1999, 8, 25}, {1999, 9, 1}, {1999, 9, 8},
 {1999, 9, 15}, {1999, 9, 22}, {1999, 9, 29}, {1999, 10, 6},
 {1999, 10, 13}, {1999, 10, 20}, {1999, 10, 27},
 {1999, 11, 3}, {1999, 11, 10}, {1999, 11, 17}, {1999, 11, 24},
 {1999, 12, 1}, {1999, 12, 8}, {1999, 12, 15}, {1999, 12, 22},
 {1999, 12, 29}, {2000, 1, 5}, {2000, 1, 12}, {2000, 1, 19},
 {2000, 1, 26}, {2000, 2, 2}, {2000, 2, 9}, {2000, 2, 16}}

Otherwise known as a month of Wednesdays.

Chapter **60**

The problem Prof. Eugene Nichols goes around showing people

Jerry: Some time ago I ran into my friend Prof. Gene Nichols at a Math Association meeting in sunny San Diego. He took me aside in a conspiratorial way, and asked if I'd seen the following problem:

Take a number—57, for example. Break it into single digits, square them, then add them up. Repeat.

> **5² + 7²**

> 74

So far we have a sequence of two numbers, 57 and 74. Where does it go from here?

Theo: I wonder if we could use a computer to do this?

With a problem like this, a lot of programs might run into trouble breaking the number into digits. Such an operation is not available in, for example, most spreadsheets (yes, of course you could do it, but it would be very clumsy and slow). Fortunately, *Mathematica* has the function **IntegerDigits**:

> **IntegerDigits[57]**

> {5, 7}

> **IntegerDigits[8758976729871029865272375297347]**

> {8, 7, 5, 8, 9, 7, 6, 7, 2, 9, 8, 7, 1, 0, 2,
> 9, 8, 6, 5, 2, 7, 7, 2, 3, 7, 5, 2, 9, 7, 3, 4, 7}

The next step is to square each of these digits. An interesting and useful property of many functions in *Mathematica*, such as multiplication, raising to a power, **Sin**, etc., is that when they are applied to a list they are automatically applied to each of the elements of the list. In our current example:

{5, 7}^{2}

{25, 49}

Now we have to add up these digits. You might think **Sum** would do this, but that's not what **Sum** is for. There is in fact a much more direct way to do it in *Mathematica*, but it requires knowing how addition is represented internally. If you enter the expression

a + b

Mathematica translates it into a function, **Plus**, applied to two arguments. You can see this using **FullForm**:

FullForm[a + b]

Plus[a, b]

FullForm[a + b + c + d]

Plus[a, b, c, d]

So, we need to apply the function **Plus** to the list of squared digits. We can use the function **Apply**, which works as follows:

Apply[Plus, {25, 49}]

74

Jerry: Couldn't you just write **Plus[25,49]** instead of using **Apply**?

Theo: You could if you were doing it manually, but to automate the calculation we have to be able to combine the three steps of splitting, squaring, and summing. The result of squaring is a list of numbers; **Apply** allows us to turn that list into arguments of **Plus**.

We can combine all the steps into a single calculation:

Apply[Plus, IntegerDigits[57]^2]

74

Notice the smooth integration of functional programming and typesetting.

To continue with the problem, we need to be able to repeat this calculation with any starting number, so let's make it into a function:

```
oneStep[s_] := Apply[Plus, IntegerDigits[s]²]

oneStep[57]

74

oneStep[74]

65

oneStep[65]

61
```

Jerry: Enough!

Theo: Clearly we need to automate not only the calculation but also the repeated application. The ideal function at times like this, one that experienced *Mathematica* users usually come to know and love, is **NestList**. It applies a given function to a starting point a specified number of times, and builds up a list of each of the values computed along the way.

```
NestList[oneStep, 57, 20]

{57, 74, 65, 61, 37, 58, 89, 145, 42,
  20, 4, 16, 37, 58, 89, 145, 42, 20, 4, 16, 37}
```

Jerry: Let me see if I understand this. I notice that the first 4 numbers in this list are the same as the four you did manually above: 57, 74, 65, 61. So **NestList** applied **oneStep** starting at 57, got a result, applied **oneStep** to that, got a result, and so on, a total of 20 times (the list contains 21 elements since the starting point is included).

Readers with *Mathematica* may want to experiment with different starting values (the second argument to **NestList**), and different lengths (the third argument).

Do we notice any patterns, so far? Let's have more raw data to study.

Theo: Using **Table** we can make a matrix in which each row begins with a different starting point, and the columns show the steps from that point.

Table[NestList[oneStep, i, 20], {i, 1, 30}] // MatrixForm

1	1	1	1	1	1	1	1	1	1	1	1	1	1	1	1	1	1	1	1	1
2	4	16	37	58	89	145	42	20	4	16	37	58	89	145	42	20	4	16	37	58
3	9	81	65	61	37	58	89	145	42	20	4	16	37	58	89	145	42	20	4	16
4	16	37	58	89	145	42	20	4	16	37	58	89	145	42	20	4	16	37	58	89
5	25	29	85	89	145	42	20	4	16	37	58	89	145	42	20	4	16	37	58	89
6	36	45	41	17	50	25	29	85	89	145	42	20	4	16	37	58	89	145	42	20
7	49	97	130	10	1	1	1	1	1	1	1	1	1	1	1	1	1	1	1	1
8	64	52	29	85	89	145	42	20	4	16	37	58	89	145	42	20	4	16	37	58
9	81	65	61	37	58	89	145	42	20	4	16	37	58	89	145	42	20	4	16	37
10	1	1	1	1	1	1	1	1	1	1	1	1	1	1	1	1	1	1	1	1
11	2	4	16	37	58	89	145	42	20	4	16	37	58	89	145	42	20	4	16	37
12	5	25	29	85	89	145	42	20	4	16	37	58	89	145	42	20	4	16	37	58
13	10	1	1	1	1	1	1	1	1	1	1	1	1	1	1	1	1	1	1	1
14	17	50	25	29	85	89	145	42	20	4	16	37	58	89	145	42	20	4	16	37
15	26	40	16	37	58	89	145	42	20	4	16	37	58	89	145	42	20	4	16	37
16	37	58	89	145	42	20	4	16	37	58	89	145	42	20	4	16	37	58	89	145
17	50	25	29	85	89	145	42	20	4	16	37	58	89	145	42	20	4	16	37	58
18	65	61	37	58	89	145	42	20	4	16	37	58	89	145	42	20	4	16	37	58
19	82	68	100	1	1	1	1	1	1	1	1	1	1	1	1	1	1	1	1	1
20	4	16	37	58	89	145	42	20	4	16	37	58	89	145	42	20	4	16	37	58
21	5	25	29	85	89	145	42	20	4	16	37	58	89	145	42	20	4	16	37	58
22	8	64	52	29	85	89	145	42	20	4	16	37	58	89	145	42	20	4	16	37
23	13	10	1	1	1	1	1	1	1	1	1	1	1	1	1	1	1	1	1	1
24	20	4	16	37	58	89	145	42	20	4	16	37	58	89	145	42	20	4	16	37
25	29	85	89	145	42	20	4	16	37	58	89	145	42	20	4	16	37	58	89	145
26	40	16	37	58	89	145	42	20	4	16	37	58	89	145	42	20	4	16	37	58
27	53	34	25	29	85	89	145	42	20	4	16	37	58	89	145	42	20	4	16	37
28	68	100	1	1	1	1	1	1	1	1	1	1	1	1	1	1	1	1	1	1
29	85	89	145	42	20	4	16	37	58	89	145	42	20	4	16	37	58	89	145	42
30	9	81	65	61	37	58	89	145	42	20	4	16	37	58	89	145	42	20	4	16

If you have *Mathematica*, you can experiment with this command to expand this table to cover any range of numbers you like. Teachers might make copies of these tables for their students to study.

Jerry: It's pretty clear to me that some of these rows contain cycles. For example:

NestList[oneStep, 14, 40]

```
{14, 17, 50, 25, 29, 85, 89, 145, 42, 20, 4, 16, 37,
 58, 89, 145, 42, 20, 4, 16, 37, 58, 89, 145, 42, 20, 4,
 16, 37, 58, 89, 145, 42, 20, 4, 16, 37, 58, 89, 145, 42}
```

This goes through some non-recurring numbers, but ends up in a cycle of eight numbers: 89, 145, 42, 20, 4, 16, 37, 58, 89, ...

Theo: There are many questions. Do all starting numbers eventually enter a cycle? How many different cycles are there? How long are the cycles? What about different exponents?

Jerry: Perhaps we should first explore some more examples. Can we write a program to find cycles?

Theo: Why, sure! Let's start with a program that iterates until it runs into a number it has seen before.

```
findCycle[s_] := Module[
        {l = {}, n = s},
        While[FreeQ[l, n],
                AppendTo[l, n];
                n = oneStep[n]
        ];
        l = AppendTo[l, n];
    Drop[l, Position[l, Last[l]][[1, 1]] - 1]]
```

This program starts with an empty list (**l**), and adds to it, stopping when it finds that the number is already there. It returns the sequence of numbers between the two repeated values.

```
findCycle[57]
```

{37, 58, 89, 145, 42, 20, 4, 16, 37}

Jerry: Can we now find cycles for a list of starting numbers?

Theo: Of course! We can make a table with the starting number in the first column and its cycle in the second column:

```
Table[{i, findCycle[i]}, {i, 1, 20}] // MatrixForm
```

$$\begin{pmatrix}
1 & \{1, 1\} \\
2 & \{4, 16, 37, 58, 89, 145, 42, 20, 4\} \\
3 & \{37, 58, 89, 145, 42, 20, 4, 16, 37\} \\
4 & \{4, 16, 37, 58, 89, 145, 42, 20, 4\} \\
5 & \{89, 145, 42, 20, 4, 16, 37, 58, 89\} \\
6 & \{89, 145, 42, 20, 4, 16, 37, 58, 89\} \\
7 & \{1, 1\} \\
8 & \{89, 145, 42, 20, 4, 16, 37, 58, 89\} \\
9 & \{37, 58, 89, 145, 42, 20, 4, 16, 37\} \\
10 & \{1, 1\} \\
11 & \{4, 16, 37, 58, 89, 145, 42, 20, 4\} \\
12 & \{89, 145, 42, 20, 4, 16, 37, 58, 89\} \\
13 & \{1, 1\} \\
14 & \{89, 145, 42, 20, 4, 16, 37, 58, 89\} \\
15 & \{16, 37, 58, 89, 145, 42, 20, 4, 16\} \\
16 & \{16, 37, 58, 89, 145, 42, 20, 4, 16\} \\
17 & \{89, 145, 42, 20, 4, 16, 37, 58, 89\} \\
18 & \{37, 58, 89, 145, 42, 20, 4, 16, 37\} \\
19 & \{1, 1\} \\
20 & \{20, 4, 16, 37, 58, 89, 145, 42, 20\}
\end{pmatrix}$$

Theo: I notice that all the eight-element cycles are really the same, just entered at a different point. Let's try to make them all print the same. Hmm. We need a way to identify which cycles are really the same. Being clever, we can realize that the *minimum* number present in a cycle is unique to that cycle, regardless of the starting point. We can use that number as the starting point to re-calculate the cycle, giving a canonical form of the cycle:

```
findCanonicalCycle[n_] := findCycle[Min[findCycle[n]]];
```

Rather than repeat the same table, let's look at some larger starting points:

```
Table[{i, findCanonicalCycle[i]}, {i, 123456, 123466}] //
MatrixForm
```

$$\begin{pmatrix} 123456 & \{1, 1\} \\ 123457 & \{4, 16, 37, 58, 89, 145, 42, 20, 4\} \\ 123458 & \{4, 16, 37, 58, 89, 145, 42, 20, 4\} \\ 123459 & \{4, 16, 37, 58, 89, 145, 42, 20, 4\} \\ 123460 & \{4, 16, 37, 58, 89, 145, 42, 20, 4\} \\ 123461 & \{4, 16, 37, 58, 89, 145, 42, 20, 4\} \\ 123462 & \{1, 1\} \\ 123463 & \{4, 16, 37, 58, 89, 145, 42, 20, 4\} \\ 123464 & \{1, 1\} \\ 123465 & \{1, 1\} \\ 123466 & \{4, 16, 37, 58, 89, 145, 42, 20, 4\} \end{pmatrix}$$

Theo: It looks like the same two cycles, even this high up! Being clever and inclined to the abstract, we can realize that the *minimum* from a cycle is all we need to identify the cycle. There is no need to see the whole cycle.

Jerry: What do you mean, no *need*? What if I *want* to see the whole cycle?

Theo. Well, we have a job to do here. We're trying to figure out how many different cycles emerge from Prof. Nichols's algorithm. All we need is a single number that identifies each cycle. For example, let's make a list of the unique identifying numbers for all the cycles we get with starting numbers up to 100:

```
Table[Min[findCycle[i]], {i, 1, 100}]
```

```
{1, 4, 4, 4, 4, 4, 1, 4, 4, 1, 4, 4, 1, 4, 4, 4, 4, 4, 1, 4,
 4, 4, 1, 4, 4, 4, 4, 1, 4, 4, 1, 1, 4, 4, 4, 4, 4, 4, 4, 4,
 4, 4, 4, 1, 4, 4, 4, 4, 1, 4, 4, 4, 4, 4, 4, 4, 4, 4, 4, 4,
 4, 4, 4, 4, 4, 4, 4, 1, 4, 1, 4, 4, 4, 4, 4, 4, 4, 1, 4,
 4, 1, 4, 4, 1, 4, 4, 4, 1, 4, 4, 1, 4, 4, 1, 4, 4, 1}
```

Theo: We can use the **Union** function to make a list of the unique values:

    Union[%]

    {1, 4}

Jerry: I see. You're saying that starting numbers from 1 to 100 result in just two different cycles, one whose minimum value is 1, and another whose minimum value is 4.

Theo: Right. If you wanted to see those cycles, you could do it like this:

    Map[findCycle, %] // MatrixForm

$$\begin{pmatrix} \{1, 1\} \\ \{4, 16, 37, 58, 89, 145, 42, 20, 4\} \end{pmatrix}$$

Jerry: So we've looked from 1 to 100 and found two cycles. I assume two is it, right? I mean, surely testing 100 values is enough!

Theo: I'm sure it is, Jerry, but let's see if we can convince our *readers* that we've found all the cycles. For starts, let's go up to 1000:

    Union[Table[Min[findCycle[i]], {i, 1, 1000}]]

    {1, 4}

Jerry: So far, so good.

Theo: OK, but let's prove it. At first glance, it might seem difficult to prove that, no matter how far we look, we will *never* find a third cycle. Fortunately, we can make an observation: For sufficiently large numbers, the first step in the sequence is *always smaller* than the starting number.

Take for example a five-digit number. The largest possible result of applying our algorithm to a five-digit number would be for the number each of whose five digits is 9:

    oneStep[99999]

    405

Jerry: It makes sense that as our starting numbers get bigger, the **oneStep** of the number should be smaller than the number itself, since we are breaking off digits—the 10^{100}-digit in a number counts for no more than the units digit.

Theo: Yes, it's sort of like taking the log of the number. But back to our clever proof. We have shown that there is no five-digit number that does not become smaller. Same for any 6 or more digit number. In other words, we have established that there is an *upper limit* beyond which the sequence cannot go, and no matter how large a number you start with, it cannot cycle until it has fallen below this limit.

The fact that there is such a limit immediately proves the following facts:

(1) All starting numbers yield a cycle (because there is a finite number of numbers below any limit; and, because the process is not random, numbers must eventually be repeated).
(2) The number of different cycles is finite (see (1)).

Now the question is, what is the smallest number such that no starting point above it gets bigger? For example, starting with the largest two-digit number, we see that it gets bigger:

      oneStep[99]

      162

What happens with the largest three-digit number?

      oneStep[999]

      243

It gets smaller. Does this mean that no three-digit starting number yields a number bigger than itself? No: It means that no three-digit number ever ends up bigger than 243; numbers between 100 and 242 *may* grow, but not bigger than 243.

Let's check four-digit starting points:

      oneStep[9999]

      324

Not only is this number smaller than the starting number, it even has fewer digits! This shows that *no* four-digit number produces a four-digit answer (i.e., *all* four-digit starting numbers yield a smaller result).

Putting this all together, we have *proven* that it is sufficient to test numbers up to 243. Any number larger than that will always be reduced eventually to a number less than 243, and all cycle elements will always stay under 243. (These limits could be reduced by further analysis, but for the purposes of enumerating all possible cycles it's easier just to have the computer test all the cases. That's what computers are for.)

Jerry: So, when I declared 100 cases to be enough I was premature, but 1000 cases really was more than sufficient. We can say without fear of contradiction that there are only two cycles! Can we look at something to see what it means that the numbers always get smaller?

Theo: How about a plot of a number on the x-axis and the next step on the y-axis. In this plot, any point below the line represents a starting value that yields a smaller result, while a point above the line represents a starting value that yields a larger result.

```
ListPlot[Table[{i, oneStep[i]}, {i, 1, 500}],
   AspectRatio -> Automatic, Epilog -> {Line[{{0, 0}, {250, 250}}]},
   PlotStyle -> {AbsolutePointSize[2]}, PlotRange -> {0, 250}];
```

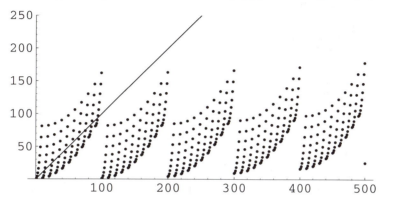

It's very clear that numbers past 100 always get smaller.

Jerry: OK, I think that's enough of the squares. How about cubing the digits instead?

Theo: We can make new versions of our functions that let you specify any exponent you want:

```
oneStep[n_, e_] := Apply[Plus, IntegerDigits[n]^e]

findCycle[s_, e_] := Module[
        {l = {}, n = s},
        While[FreeQ[l, n],
                AppendTo[l, n];
                n = oneStep[n, e]
        ];
        l = AppendTo[l, n];
     Drop[l, Position[l, Last[l]][[1, 1]] - 1]]
```

Let's see what happens to 57, with exponent 3:

```
NestList[oneStep[#, 3] &, 57, 10]
```

```
{57, 468, 792, 1080, 513, 153, 153, 153, 153, 153}
```

Here is a table of raw data, like we had above, but for exponent 3:

```
Table[NestList[oneStep[#, 3] &, i, 20], {i, 1, 30}] // MatrixForm
```

1	1	1	1	1	1	1	1	1	1	1	1	1	1	1	1	1	1	1	1	1
2	8	512	134	92	737	713	371	371	371	371	371	371	371	371	371	371	371	371	371	371
3	27	351	153	153	153	153	153	153	153	153	153	153	153	153	153	153	153	153	153	153
4	64	280	520	133	55	250	133	55	250	133	55	250	133	55	250	133	55	250	133	55
5	125	134	92	737	713	371	371	371	371	371	371	371	371	371	371	371	371	371	371	371
6	216	225	141	66	432	99	1458	702	351	153	153	153	153	153	153	153	153	153	153	153
7	343	118	514	190	730	370	370	370	370	370	370	370	370	370	370	370	370	370	370	370
8	512	134	92	737	713	371	371	371	371	371	371	371	371	371	371	371	371	371	371	371
9	729	1080	513	153	153	153	153	153	153	153	153	153	153	153	153	153	153	153	153	153
10	1	1	1	1	1	1	1	1	1	1	1	1	1	1	1	1	1	1	1	1
11	2	8	512	134	92	737	713	371	371	371	371	371	371	371	371	371	371	371	371	371
12	9	729	1080	513	153	153	153	153	153	153	153	153	153	153	153	153	153	153	153	153
13	28	520	133	55	250	133	55	250	133	55	250	133	55	250	133	55	250	133	55	250
14	65	341	92	737	713	371	371	371	371	371	371	371	371	371	371	371	371	371	371	371
15	126	225	141	66	432	99	1458	702	351	153	153	153	153	153	153	153	153	153	153	153
16	217	352	160	217	352	160	217	352	160	217	352	160	217	352	160	217	352	160	217	352
17	344	155	251	134	92	737	713	371	371	371	371	371	371	371	371	371	371	371	371	371
18	513	153	153	153	153	153	153	153	153	153	153	153	153	153	153	153	153	153	153	153
19	730	370	370	370	370	370	370	370	370	370	370	370	370	370	370	370	370	370	370	370
20	8	512	134	92	737	713	371	371	371	371	371	371	371	371	371	371	371	371	371	371
21	9	729	1080	513	153	153	153	153	153	153	153	153	153	153	153	153	153	153	153	153
22	16	217	352	160	217	352	160	217	352	160	217	352	160	217	352	160	217	352	160	217
23	35	152	134	92	737	713	371	371	371	371	371	371	371	371	371	371	371	371	371	371
24	72	351	153	153	153	153	153	153	153	153	153	153	153	153	153	153	153	153	153	153
25	133	55	250	133	55	250	133	55	250	133	55	250	133	55	250	133	55	250	133	55
26	224	80	512	134	92	737	713	371	371	371	371	371	371	371	371	371	371	371	371	371
27	351	153	153	153	153	153	153	153	153	153	153	153	153	153	153	153	153	153	153	153
28	520	133	55	250	133	55	250	133	55	250	133	55	250	133	55	250	133	55	250	133
29	737	713	371	371	371	371	371	371	371	371	371	371	371	371	371	371	371	371	371	371
30	27	351	153	153	153	153	153	153	153	153	153	153	153	153	153	153	153	153	153	153

Or we can let the computer find the cycles:

```
Table[{i, findCycle[i, 3]}, {i, 10}] // MatrixForm
```

1	{1, 1}
2	{371, 371}
3	{153, 153}
4	{133, 55, 250, 133}
5	{371, 371}
6	{153, 153}
7	{370, 370}
8	{371, 371}
9	{153, 153}
10	{1, 1}

Theo: Let's figure out how high we have to go to be sure we have found all the cycles.

```
oneStep[999, 3]
```

2187

oneStep[9999, 3]

2916

oneStep[99999, 3]

3645

Jerry: Since the result for the largest five-digit number is a four-digit number, we can safely say all five-digit numbers have a next step which is smaller. Also, all four-digit numbers have a next step which is smaller than 2916. As above with exponent 2, this means that no number above 2916 ever gets bigger, so we only have to test for cycles up to 2916.

Theo: So, here is the definitive list of all cycles for exponent 3 (first the minimum number in each cycle, to identify it, then a table of the actual cycles):

Union[Table[Min[findCycle[i, 3]], {i, 1, 2916}]]

{1, 55, 136, 153, 160, 370, 371, 407, 919}

Map[findCycle[#, 3] &, %] // MatrixForm

$$
\begin{pmatrix}
\{1, 1\} \\
\{55, 250, 133, 55\} \\
\{136, 244, 136\} \\
\{153, 153\} \\
\{160, 217, 352, 160\} \\
\{370, 370\} \\
\{371, 371\} \\
\{407, 407\} \\
\{919, 1459, 919\}
\end{pmatrix}
$$

This process could be repeated for any exponent. As the exponents get bigger, the number of starting points you have to check increases, and the calculation takes longer. In the on-line version of this book, you can find an extensive discussion and analysis for larger exponents. Many tricks are possible to speed up the calculation, and reduce the number of starting points that must be checked.

Below is a highlight from this analysis: The length of the cycle as a function of starting point (from 1 to 100) and exponent (from 1 to 30). Each rectangle in the plot is colored according to the length of the cycle reached from that starting point. Lighter gray means longer cycle.

Normalized Cycle Length

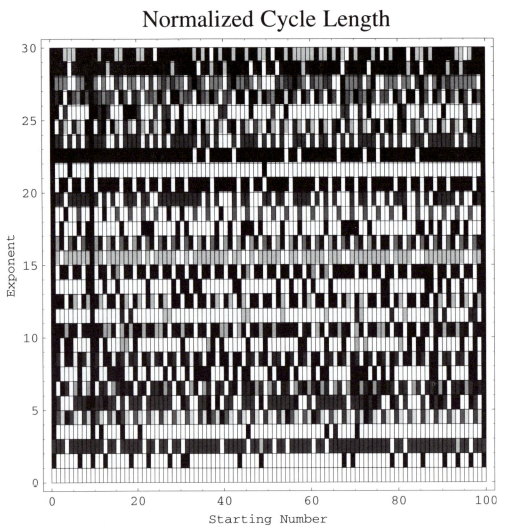

Jerry: My God! Look at exponent 22! Where did *that* come from? It looks dramatically different from the others. What does it mean? Help!

Theo: Well, the graph is telling us that for exponent 22, all the cycles except 1, 5, 10, 50, and 100 are very long. Let's look at these short cycles. We know that 1, 10, and 100 will all give the same result, because zeros don't count:

```
findCycle[1, 22]
```

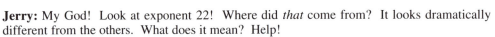

```
{1, 1}
```

Likewise, 5 and 50 will give the same result:

```
findCycle[5, 22]
```

```
{1214480361852785330091, 1210178077470656794979, 3051824271915021666437, 1066777189305871039067, 2137062111559893755189, 3109847459747452925136,
3039967990684150868757, 4172573651902765511356, 996907169024798628807, 5157339785652040982377, 2132896217284574772374, 1152028018745177092803,
1217866080209036534611, 1136783564477987270273, 1156069443936784780269, 3110235225078160618610, 1518834071841429357 70, 1217866115424781294444,
1140430230017058021217, 8160903782494198915 4, 4164488417365119208890, 2268865228588763261145, 373378359519104211335, 2051155593097076291577,
2970095533409352444320, 2958229750651070732579, 3043880125518408023765, 2991965357676747841 85, 3117927996219499254797, 6909169640585009596480,
5071962138064846781585, 1288140502344787225866, 3032356118637413375 51, 818770321375383600 87, 3109211953888464935 55, 3175814829160874109637,
2202897859238100001556, 2194951328592933224041, 4012875406271587452836, 2333608408032729404 57, 1140298555662181859264, 2191307170290812620810,
2125067020789304958754, 2128984029579628888202, 3401078408850290418478, 1361527880340888688503, 5206866845780504163 68, 2997230225202775392 06,
2966178559834798440522, 3183763726305523651050, 8201102040360873312 5, 1516177972142344898 96, 3113881802687682207084, 4508047609288404957 03,
2198858835824456791215, 2342527700552768547123, 8956745418333166786 7, 1218392584679341183875, 2272645776997689222373, 3048046055040877991843,
2198858835855833656521, 1427770308569222667124, 1074594447185873328537, 1221778338282722402141, 2330904272774271517 21, 1004322426859472368324,
1136520373878254511767, 163483650435403558126, 1479784073464538428 26, 1218127009831051096224, 2121159601518699030746, 3032409155000939218452,
3028106870681572802555, 3032403274587610412 49, 1066511596928148637609, 3106459374703457764883, 1148252221241154579628, 1136393502859669246946,
4013533497198600161187, 2125201061926055672349, 1973853660708293377642, 2133152308166267319380, 1136651925276106331852, 1063001338993930304557,
3032145911750151593614, 1973592819141331245416, 3032145946840388892231, 2264823768338303528977, 1291913915851296692458, 5071698877096369845422,
3187802767279967651890, 3195619990006970523532, 4928034728025848301038, 1357618041762890163863, 1214480361852785330091}
```

Jerry: Whoa there, young feller. I thought you said these were the *short* cycles! If that's short, I'd hate to think what the *long* cycles are like! Let's try one:

```
findCycle[6, 22]
```

```
{2198861220010252001146, 1132610499958970211647, 4020955889935686201037, 3179853870103945439474, 3113620961152109523070, 1973719637289227781077, 3129387028247207997183, 3191312937316026270692,
2962527213885067491805, 2198992788937544523642, 4168400622630886855083, 369466171908284728773, 2206936917804738435418, 2198988055813088311834, 2486055424489005359811, 2191043962098877040673,
3113879400941086206650, 2121422862549938086129, 3175939298244602182200, 3105930521325881561953, 2117259299715228850999, 6064026160345903804710, 1062996623367516958335, 3032674765096371902757,
1989490560779583850517, 4172315176835281948726, 1218129341240288172908, 2268599565810932399633, 5071830481302169246965, 2121425246735733296058, 1066647951819209235771, 3040228797098105194549,
4094482024600816933267, 2121420513548527547942, 1066387127718925686739, 2207070888509999629348, 5226956081707787936057, 2137066879900103115436, 2051545689742877882908, 2350344958432762447985,
2125074261370366152618, 82137891233920223210, 2121025578131031271002, 81611386826369304556, 1206794725645252636753, 997036424135044313339, 2958356604046084699077, 3110237609232570574624,
996768412387158807427, 2280594656550144330762, 1062872154221056126681, 152015046417417516712, 11999911887373067156, 4098652652126107977719, 3044138618115311317292, 1136388717021408632502,
229446216261497951546, 2958753853155128741369, 2198865935668038018367, 2342917762171094959058, 4024736473466222131877, 89821196063601093777, 3114010987460552190651, 2047509032891458584172,
2198729580714227883898, 3408766429274986798442, 3187798051684947948191, 4246095035757119197149, 3950951898949352596847, 6134037356728909736718, 2133152308166263125077, 82006252000654030876,
151883424744947920572, 2128850076466553738690, 1214485130192990496033, 4013004643789626121436, 1062994256805297241040, 3032277568450096369144, 2051548109113045181666, 1132746907657944836843,
2129242539862857210667, 2125335050160765957297, 1981546431912385744438, 2194949032430821966804, 4086920875163324758520, 1214221904377496200481, 2051280114863210929953, 3102023066870899350811,
2195078181987947190538, 4245965763054700051110, 992863377239569192915, 5990500043367093907111, 3947039658593364429254, 4017050872537200511892, 1144081488099989343771, 4242051226442470030364,
4175554257957895181, 2128859560401770219726, 2129113249474117229994, 4931674223415368349301, 2047504299829777074492, 4032422144826750048738, 229314664895022996766, 4017440933998638403000,
3105928172387203782857, 1295562860023037998228, 3179851468325980962345, 3179853887727512543500, 1221780669691959478822, 4168661446605646165682, 148763386664587220373, 233619298341328383585,
2264826117402484574988, 1288004165014552584030, 221502140139468530496, 2043596845280660073129, 2121425246735737490360, 996768429979344851843, 5153300779924722800979, 4028514655250157867981,
1214226672686311918211, 1136781180260827777954, 1225946581528091835052, 2191046293508118311659, 3102154688574733229341, 1140300939847972874892, 4172174053604037156139, 996768429979332268933,
6064413890617759453484, 2125335120560866028746, 152017430665966457248, 1066911212756305112329, 1973851258961693182909, 5149393272693190845198, 5075474709910263520038, 2055197053316167547043,
996773180758728255766, 2210853856194941321900, 3102023084463081200923, 1132476511787043017431, 89560319249508947806, 4164622405662566447233, 4704407666927740630, 1000936743593441685198,
3106064544839060977220, 2051545724895873106432, 1140305708156792786923, 2129113249536870960604, 3032406788438719501154, 1214087916111421633139, 2047501880396851850822, 1357754396591180254200,
2051289616453375574621, 1066781957677453070316, 1078638256563263643021, 152146668246775633673, 86310973313746460946, 2051674962476678088554, 1218394986363183453696, 3176202541777789983388,
2284372838365461126477, 233487694198299489865, 5223177917578796169282, 3121703776194089454166, 205545554594451900180, 2043345557923532197987, 3039838718044493841935, 3253372887490210003884,
1287740868955829960641, 3257679922494841810697, 4098652704871297634267, 2133152343256500423689, 1058828309784801184587, 1509104181931984028225, 3175678439022696080643, 2125464305333748595225,
1062611295061928921556, 3028633322218430797747, 1148115796012756029235, 2051418836347863916413, 1210438954316113223347, 1062601758350141724365, 82008671308046627507, 233487658951156893206,
2195214589655557533339, 3032157832616352941129, 2047506631207637285869, 1144605590760948456297, 3036321412980486101458, 1206397511532311102857, 1066516294930986491199, 5982941295613423030668,
3102286327902146794802, 2125198677708904568632, 2203031847504174568898, 1287874892374882974297, 3342796746075895641282, 2129244906425089510874, 3105932940633278352888, 2268735938419686503427,
2199122044110539744482, 3032011976072373967690, 2970346855982225079293, 4094615995337471769715, 3954993341733154717336, 2966178612768232511690, 2125595891790465042922, 4016921599709265516027,
3947305286092709383236, 3109971946580255562939, 5001824106067282507934, 1140432543865485918784, 1283967490696458896402, 4164883282476650204600, 225799691334395511796, 4931944566666617333504,
1974246194504709503979, 4935720434539358858517, 2198734349179944705366, 4024865746231399202829, 3106062160621909873504, 2047767490366760296689, 3044528732478818997168, 2350340207716124386066,
82135524671692117304, 1066645567602028771931, 1070950236138567263058, 1140566514633505037627, 8355700934218569108, 2194951346216487745154, 2051418906716603899772, 3114013389207152385387,
1213956259285973590694, 5001824106067286702238, 229577837902582293766, 3117793955176891720027, 3047785178226781651568, 311189224666160118971, 2121552082444426427923, 1062604177594797367599,
3959032382676226047174, 2055455528383659498282, 2264835671612314637770, 89955166768858093403, 3253772468102617524466, 86047747466875300089, 1222168417367714814359, 1144339998351844995236,
5071564924077429486126, 2055457947659675229609, 3951219893105060446948, 4086925625942712356747, 2055460314284665454730, 78101287221812788328, 454451320946180234064, 1058825995873602779191,
4172312775057313277294, 1008234632125223237303, 77830821013552045170, 159310585947754976195, 4024743626023582595840, 1136525142218451289103, 1132483664281653945092, 2117515443310721606338,
81874665481175463965, 1214485165345973136650, 1062872154252428797685, 1218131725363325457921, 1066516312554557789527, 1070696529474046791286, 3040358069769147475281, 2129113284721238855131,
1210046438174641066341, 78223372182486798664, 1292043170867390809559, 4094613611151668171180, 1136783582038783866476, 381193233338814557794, 2198727179093147733295, 4032422092144330900016,
1969673496533968866607, 4095400957220303429371, 2962137169890295600979, 5990629280822383039404, 4160578578787124878552, 388625180348492779643, 2272775032107926518297, 2063014276011806136292,
1062994203997366436792, 4932200675109119059619, 4928032361369481210613, 2117510657378334590282, 1144213109866593730125, 2047506648768433882069, 1288267373300618760078, 311182054579363146897,
2125203446111850882277, 229316996272879013841, 4094740464483936795675, 3040228885090408087626, 1357881267515626534500, 155800398382280820804, 1427497545979183249462, 4024736526242780265124,
82006322275263418318, 225536395212923352103, 1969682962971159259269, 6971624367815667701693, 2059760196920189600804, 4090964649262216582560, 3028762612513040182502, 151751803072495101656,
1066650318350035310549, 1058962298050850586108, 2338749465992270483464, 3109972016886237621385, 2199119624740376640027, 2966437087616061239970, 3040487272165588757178, 314835819899244617163,
3179849136948112362364, 3106191398202710661324, 2047633484508512267843, 229448653223847100416, 1136520373846869257855, 1214355892706320304132, 1062604124912369830267, 2047765123773163714088,
167388720704590559340, 2128984029611001559203, 3102023066839518291202, 2117381384644538578937, 1291784713486223887261, 1291911549163548542426, 3028370149210867306444, 1140427810741033901280,
1140164549709782262986, 3110103603311564620865, 74318249199503783419, 4094479640477783842557, 2136801357859739637730, 2133023053087406888759, 1287874857253273004682, 310923614696260061705,
1974112135775764357361, 1004590438670103216241, 1062733379959836618369, 4095006074579356897070, 3044009398220814586891, 3249594670459148448336, 3106064597615623304770, 997031655794830758787,
3195361532594426735926, 2958626964764016460782, 2125727566239480189390, 3109974330671907594043, 3950947130671909550118, 4020829019042612591735, 3032145929185449117202, 3032014325105173954092,
1973458813283087410869, 2346430369106732218907, 2051543323180662359914, 2043599211937027163556, 2962402762299399062046, 4928290853997786535263, 4168534593367524914316, 2047640689873816118965,
2273038257860658694633, 1214482746069965793929, 5005858431415329939771, 3109715873259359612135, 3036060483515376837889, 1288138100692330209955, 3175810025604928378163, 1214219502630896005747,
2051416469754258945202, 2047511452230253211929, 1973458813220337874564, 1217997737191389875100, 4106209050815593613849, 3102157090352706095075, 1981412426022748267373, 1144337614166062368217,
82264779781925218930, 3187537122094314446186, 1140430194926824916907, 4017043719885684286194, 2272775049637346249193, 2970217671209359290028, 4024734054096067416027, 996897702618997684359,
6142113072052820096188, 1210307297333768271464, 1074460441390374835996, 3036185040591386832011, 1206399860565106894955, 4087193602506225773827, 1148252168401851104378, 299194169111307693762,
4932069035781705494158, 3109845128338215848452, 1353712989085889207066, 3257548265669389573947, 3114020559419473595893, 4016789995691735694919, 6975402602376144793831, 2055455545975837154091,
2051167549053498160487, 2125205847827065823099, 2198861167233706450809, 2199119642301177430530, 2962266389816156613774, 2125727531117870219778, 1155808549467765442183, 1214224323716269856723,
1066774805151473665962, 1070952637916540128795, 3040099559580053943037, 4016789978130926515805, 3183763691121143173612, 1066772403436241947927, 1985576024104600099162, 3032409172561744203257,
996636808275502584707, 2203034231689961390217, 3032272765019666487499, 3040358052239727744386, 1144210760896555862938, 2195214607184981458538, 2268738357664321175147, 163612905545645048356,
1059096339062098032786, 4090964631764173716970, 2970478530399854971852, 4172181188569224158597, 2272648161089341253476, 1140561799007108468625, 2125335067721549970586, 2055331041613618979693,
3032409155095078202974, 3035926512747357719043, 1985319898132674447847, 3261324151197079262596, 2962531999786073448253, 4094745250479081736644, 2055326361171577722305, 15912064439340505014,
1969680649059948270962, 6060638092925467359873, 3110237574110964799314, 2966176228456921451935, 3032543178482766934235, 1140432561583196201635, 1058959931425872943900, 5075345472360831208917,
1144213127458775580236, 159442242835973526468, 2121296044402062521985, 2043596845217910536823, 2121296009249067298459, 5001816971039345969169, 5001950959399534355214, 4923868851311321720120,
1210175675692688123547, 1144476353211516145180, 77967263739989266853, 4102825716613764948252, 1140564183161518424641, 147973674065100721586, 1074596831371647566947, 2059499372882663976685,
4168795452558037373354, 1144217913453920521206, 1973588068330566781884, 1435712053219244503666, 989082793771807964203, 4176215461172090322491, 1977627126865819961835, 3187934353799437830197,
4102299265076902758761, 3040228797066732523546, 1070687010385839281025, 1287874839598324841050, 2346301149149490146506, 2954710043871848051282, 1287743270639663841857, 1222168399838299277771,
4176215443579916860989, 4094876889712339540372, 3187537157341440265627, 89696709324937440493, 5005724443180636432034, 77964897209150609160, 4024997315064540157890, 3036058169604182626795,
2121688472551231785913, 1214090265081472083237, 1140298538007237889937, 3261192476748064116124, 1066904077791122304177, 1989354188233583477332, 2272514155387990134062, 2051287232267592947604,
2055326290802854516161, 1132749274251562390961, 2962400395674417225533, 1977631895300164112299, 4020955872374881216230, 1214087898487867112025, 1365569287877569183857, 2280733395658364421246,
1136654362207078615417, 86047729874680867067, 1299994434605624350662, 3939614934352914911113, 4923988569741157072769, 4102564892513481399221, 3102023102055271439643, 988817148617531623803,
1361791071034777208747, 1086058282769511025182, 1284099024376621405153, 2047506666329243061178, 1067038048527764557712, 167393489013410471371, 2055189918413734275198, 3183500465337029937670,
2055326273336171738661, 86047694784456151365, 1140698206643320974601, 2047765141365341369896, 2051679730816883254500, 1214221886785305961762, 1214351124271984542274, 1066382376939529699907,
5990760902588983231453, 4164493150615095464828, 2117517862618114202969, 2125332665943585493459, 3028374900084406472101, 1140296189005810574535, 2121166771668245539124, 1066908810978336440899,
4238536235321041754889, 1210180479280019108931, 3179583474107506798723, 2136801287553757579286, 1222043895476081103373, 1140298538069995814851, 4234370323390770414140, 996500453447204105763,
1977631912860956514194, 4021089895825315289494, 4234238719279122580026, 2125069440190857511425, 2047379812934220706075, 2059102105993176892450, 4016919197962661126988, 5075996410667721334091,
2966441838426829897805, 3327554711178877311815, 240917204371136024065, 992856224713585594257, 3109849879086243358588, 3401080810722389685826, 1357881249954821549695, 4164495569922496450069,
4924388238251736890513, 2268735955980491488235, 3253511626472922633147, 992990213073803340428, 4090567417682613242682, 1140693420679569676151, 2962795260754550384420, 2051421255718031215169,
1062608875597622638277, 1222302370480806741089, 1214083130116285080775, 229316978712061446123, 2051543323117904435002, 988687928691662222404, 3253896954778531641445, 2125208249667805002357,
1140434910459099278600, 4016914482367628840378, 1288133385003171521735, 229187723695967329023, 4024865675862671802380, 303498837679235633102, 2125201044428021195364, 1058694338954019946528,
4160714986423341578835, 1214219555407449944691, 3943132309597367888692, 4168529825058700807981, 2346435119791989221217, 4020824268263233382118, 2954111838969588853222, 3249599403646366779363,
3947563796470080884524, 2202900278608263106009, 2121420443148410699277, 2051280132455396974369, 3032279935137840324876, 2128979261333571095388, 3183629667733475413870, 1148381423606218996221,
2191297633610414871833, 2125198677771654104941, 2059236129412225711805, 2047377393595451244139, 2966049392748232514375, 3036187389592822536019, 3179851468388734692956, 3257679922588980795220,
4172312775057325860203, 89565052436731473132, 1066647951850577712468, 1148517813524737996563, 2129115651346224885951, 2117388572323517401124, 159308219385539453205, 3101898597787183861158,
2424129515420187086302, 1136391118705255096624, 2047640637034500060805, 82006304714437461990, 2051411736598421673784, 1144342382537631816556, 151885844209250009556, 2191046311068914907857,
3109971964046908980316, 5075733184914976574843, 2132893885875333501390, 2268606683340826072806, 299847474105954357571, 3043748574183297351382, 1217866115518928667573, 1218394933618006380061,
2191297616080978363722, 3114010987460564773563, 1070687027978008548228, 1369479091333966127487, 4024994948596459425118, 5071567343322072546450, 12002296167311455907, 1977629475867234694323,
3044136269208035569324, 2043728467047264459481, 1144340051097022068871, 1140298555568034486137, 1210314485106881883867, 446897341658226179089, 3183890579637779692633, 4102694094972680606031,
3032536043517571543167, 12002278637879142103, 1144205957277843817945, 2132762264108737503645, 85916108202228048146, 1280184470140828474685, 376888617421928901870, 2350469410018422489137,
2121159654326634029297, 2958622196329680698923, 5145744310866513958705, 1140439714046413486773, 1070550690679142383091, 3036187354377056804668, 233621682527111010602, 78094046703522102289,
2125069440159468063207, 2047638288001704268704, 307140664540738100045, 81874700602777044968, 1225944232495287654343, 2047377464026953346714, 1000807523730342791626, 1070552986904015759546,
3036194524463853776740, 1070687045601579846555, 1144481139143890578323, 2194815008980383699237, 4238275358538351640043, 225411961313575756979, 2966314967502387811808, 2272906618596015636994,
4017443300592239179906, 3947037309591953891068, 5079384513398033134671, 2125071824502147599663, 2051418853940054155131, 1132356828541567170709, 1144344731539050743349, 1977366320545992037654,
2966444222644006167341, 989338937335919659933, 7045016479218629746794, 3044136286706074240610, 82133175638887936598, 2346564339843374472444, 1066643289063493007321, 2047765123835917444697,
2059236147067173875436, 1074596831434413880468, 1284094344060095997593, 5001687768768412148491, 1292045572582593167473, 2055199437501966951277, 3951085869654617985079, 4168668599194383494949,
6130383679307192175011, 2055323871526813619015, 1136527456066874992373, 2055589534273284392436, 2121166789354587345275, 1144347133317031997693, 2966173844365269420833, 2121554501908736905505,
2047384546152807513797, 1148122966068163553092, 2117647029798810725034, 2132889082256629845003, 2264957738980810992295, 5153171489598744939523, 4094486793035156889432, 3179851538726089422402,
2198858800671478344906, 2346562008339998411240, 3102152339604699556457, 2958626964732631206869, 3106588612252902658912, 2191304750952038964569, 4017050837290066303844, 1140430177334634678184,
159566747229564371867, 2059501739444896276892, 4094745268008505661842, 1210443740154361254878, 155530072785967417322, 1074338338774748467725, 244953931559918440852, 4086667168498800092444,
```

2269126105371461764596, 197802435857094754147, 213276226410873330934, 1066640799324594113610, 3032406806030897156963, 212155446672435642065, 782328913020963400480, 21949442112826901909111, 499777316169331154847, 30440070316899717349904, 30399608381581504928843, 3323383995818163506507, 219508295045366820631, 21175177922807594735521, 20628505608593254059, 2191177191521195638449, 40946136287124731555991, 30361873895614330878059, 12880064789884879428290, 24940019550086807040, 21950830304193998190309, 5071430865411323800917, 15943984105798807820, 3261194874463274862643, 1214478034443560836320, 15174947172601175559984, 1074338373896350048734, 1217995353068332504109, 31050376563224370411090, 197762849355559923261, 39510858697171384298600, 32575482826157142059, 14603570815796981227, 21291132495504895090996, 59025488216847695633492, 32517725523269980109060, 11099743131115198481493, 40170458797948497728, 42500048974365111364306, 78228122993263845104, 21949465954371105535356, 30322847121016000119340, 10625993565094025454516, 27547195278070771152270, 26967948771031134469030, 20540531617900419441620, 19737220917809966600843, 40987819072363535662251, 212533505022351549360, 984914462565511669782110, 31063301723384017368980, 12142147343534529590200, 197345884843682623636396, 226899665038674807510520, 227681882379905058105577, 23503425190939904013910, 30189146284473897790160, 32614557376851683812920, 121435350852053348281200, 22133705093159178637900, 205910685683153080419800, 22649601213197966290314, 39435199518455473389000, 40946184147700176021872, 11482474527754377758161, 16726190249394029306900, 49281592323251327440960, 21211620209516132643026, 985299790839744646512, 507951617019211270041900, 296617857736420139420600, 205558715005611651150500, 78108351755489299600500, 31836134453603091922100, 20435944435968219976110, 401704848882864737705200, 384708241958289893190900, 43119331148759435798003, 310971112254272155021600, 992729331665580598541100, 40908401801785094815170, 22705141727918814322180, 12178637136154441663150, 82006332338004566021500, 147971219557334030421100, 198127370456947634052500, 205532869161219589599600, 317680842150722803439500, 11403009222244057708660, 106664320097704693541500, 197789275449066639884260, 4172571302869973913562300, 30400097175457029240934300, 296604700849967937953100, 500976824990530995540040, 401691925070570591312340, 3947039676154177802670500, 20632751704494318318600, 114043017733146398724900, 114420601011715148749900, 205128249901760830306000, 21212912232539181631840, 21172497805328865505240, 12140926662806808036600, 128084017691343961562800, 21952098384447804868980, 34748654203608649961670, 21255959621305765972800, 40248728282589747612500, 12917847133920974854840, 31875371571310059206020, 10704261159795652849410, 30161897768446413984120, 21991712933311139543460, 39432590751569842601530, 30322823193226271140190, 20514116891601249654000, 217615425687150380210010, 15551477075715310800011, 156488737768246557773, 24131228704346781022750, 15941747446439149521700, 296617866538788954119700, 32617213474686457886772, 24143894037573643477070, 10743312256648873329123, 114043015980529141596000, 30282385099148306062850, 226495773901218366329600, 30364482136303439659350, 11327445412526262212830, 77964861993418432241000, 31099696150765753074340, 30402281475304496995730, 21250718595923848982740, 32572874461604995473131, 10704238021625184649800, 12103073125181361659910, 20475066136154428528470, 15579568275588057549600, 20029097625121069160440, 29586198128812750440150, 226886795596662347252100, 31256006775423711128900, 11482521684018511043790, 12101780950000807201790, 21288476042884472470740, 31091899163066008890100, 31762001223134795058010, 10665139283738151998800, 32516384446835644510814000, 22176301463987312249700, 20553215225254072751310, 78339648668853993030900, 42385386019714089845140, 12878749099984458840080, 43898275631551795340010, 20514212384959719534001000, 12140878994564860924170, 12880065316081491666320, 12067923414280847558240, 12140879136408581412480, 12839627047326950150410, 20514164697856400048110, 11365431796737278384880, 12959553176164513494540, 29584977626175667902780, 31219670137199958385470, 31137549142651888660980, 14180224973147069473020, 20551893597454764861100, 3109979134196468071605000, 40210875116709011391730, 20551922267352395277070800, 20591092233661820447970, 30361849878746446163700, 12182562298196700333930, 31060621078767286035630, 15966629268989251833300, 52194020496432925250500, 29544539178058001926580, 31797246501466991927170, 29742590963068279929740, 59944075153515000434510, 197346600096205784444600, 20516773817527022008497000, 24104644182643733926000, 10669040954146984089199000, 50718257831737794572030100, 15159013028129430439100, 19190860281987596034230, 41646200039787167603320, 10708138673494721879130, 22066736744283076645300, 86177002608449461319, 21991727756761872205408, 21332010705226960237400, 99285618595198401324900, 63102276727336785216, 938649526016921271632160, 30325383925503757523874, 114408387244265565743800, 30323564707946697384200, 21291109005982099598722, 507534305292791856815500, 21250813435526769767918, 21291132495168755298000, 310593528969745504597700, 40208338050063890560060, 12065314822375681024780, 22944861800009814628100, 23387339902256087405170, 32766872021579262744300, 10745944472172585824900, 2128852478213149739122, 21987247947813454507550, 22065512680997180681731700, 21254666542740540280300, 78098854124675204500, 22264816108933705916, 21172885547626998334060, 21252198527062993930090, 29958232099558346480550000, 31758712131529245425800, 11401740688921497129640, 31837565737716769544569000, 20595041236934410231270, 19735880683619478414910, 32575459342601483029640, 20475090681386011800180000, 12842258955324403564550, 11324884678698912447700, 24242564214976327844330, 10666432538163713821840, 22579965624416240747900, 29625320524998696622800, 40870572300230084913750, 11440791215691422974740, 29661762635471587505480, 11446103766933132780510, 10667748051828337545301000, 23336082327384062465100, 15201266238852760482400, 22567041863198056080620, 11367859486324014205991, 21212936426240770713390, 19815345642305732629710, 20514189540028120800045000, 29515511051329654889400, 31758175195697211159933000, 30399703045325745720027000, 19851982764289836375013000, 13617934552205724186750, 10705601570221193791229, 29661785980540479600530, 31837637087113292180260, 12181245377784721652000, 16725948315516663682900, 21216908567370228015390, 21252034108961031617470, 10664213834162177563070, 86176967455490043491, 41646200397781760323300, 219507818201932825014800, 226860431659032419324600, 20438576869310375593968000, 31838953128897016223400, 32613288841567026442310, 22579967377559891559800, 50872089062118413669920, 31799072340482881005770, 22764215922152578680500, 11484379461140427368900, 20473726780631768924440, 23739514462189225279100, 31099427089668069521212000, 31799941010179099071722500, 40285122710643625658540, 15188588441151152193350, 12061437872442193322759000, 20551923025861610084280, 12064022244565671314664000, 86118449833449542100, 21910364447572529479360, 30400971210610020270156000, 99285618949781724568160, 42394093995459892418000, 61299911983814647778350, 41724396636053224673180, 10669064844788704542100, 11405618517204818997420000, 31836297027923190694920, 31836297033791270028954040, 50059924021833448643100, 21172521749521982117700, 20589728505820190602210, 21949489443757563431100, 43082841178464862158760, 45093880197146061318300, 21950782172016901905730, 30399655361296198697740, 50059924021833444864310, 43385362167948030947200, 30360585803373339774806000, 11443423474747755577540, 17104013705442996611700, 20551923025083630630100, 10583065875484348574660, 37715897826536812479300, 22068100449316732147250, 10667748050887031158371700, 31105521880789950721100, 21987295277937665556349100, 42500468676468371725900, 11405642007536968004470, 10667724458853679680, 12223024056515704411330, 41778596985676624966130, 12923111825838382672951000, 22687359207333656688796, 21295086971189780311150, 31834989045935485773606, 21989928421604031409840, 31758053217959332599663000, 30361921052081991224240, 21727986936873461025000, 3113750146341070919160, 197358579421278451050, 21288547920929540511998, 51493324485921568477100, 31094514894920502756500, 10549405981985039823000, 31509535272136642831180000, 11165227051855870046600, 30324034508232395097100, 20472434076423515661315000, 41826716623155424227000, 82003902936477179168000, 31138793834890162234400, 21949944211576829175436000, 21129120572449423798600, 30360533834064035522650000, 74191413522195905466000, 29594929763724218493080, 41683982384450958394580, 33233864327491313995770, 20551946692555907569955000, 40171898593993345412200, 20476335196614991027620, 29626612543496306549875000, 20470862621863694049632010, 22141291022919696523980, 40869232605725702233810, 11416312526304689322584, 13326129370154458345040, 12042853204485221656160, 20479018971611698087900, 51611178950261585685960, 22600631663566433580550900, 197020710075371156419400, 19851375138527360590940, 31094747773710158485000, 12217793206905032163422000, 10666431658554453564010, 74325472062858594340000, 30422509614804830296640, 39955254183314853262610, 11326176702265426212373000, 12258351833325924300810, 12061390013759400718272, 11443375789816770696470, 21370621819286379328530, 21988880030677919626804, 42385362175467843019472, 21291109005982183473311, 31057988820612259214050, 214955148615127991300, 31735404084203004506560, 21015302032658397004010, 42342300845901965364280, 12210124993553575819320, 21982791376711372070760, 24096956595212643026000, 25148438116173945373971000, 31094274421591344350460, 20437350627582244159000, 620781956489403792715, 3113886553467078191650, 21099210026400425440260, 296657105028995195720200, 40947499836035375441480, 31098427793995544865720, 40985258517041424636850, 12101368692612960341860, 21177738813107096092100, 21328666624922466554620, 21179079241730785581700, 213666964822635240242010, 10592184240541740742470, 10702922155489092841530, 31058056796223607215500, 10669111060426132926000, 197007069302334296482000, 30361360240365431256580, 21495921037539540065560, 3061363514191119651980, 490901342936774082684200, 21989880558132952060160, 32497310075806418441240, 10743336056418410196030, 30320170097100288690360, 40209535006066913061680000, 40851290277296854694456000, 500195340138911119870700, 3253377603022471782671, 91601726884955756620160, 21294817740326925431330, 21948173403268754339210, 21250694533571169975450, 30440117824067094313900, 21730536961499910290620, 20476335196649102300880, 29626612540694306549875000, 11064617764844431358289001570, 22107198853610532897579200, 22107198853610532897579200, 21071988855210596992937600, 39504174733103661532350, 22660311585003018439100, 39625320350018414021378, 11636391085383670037210, 32610404849846109397000, 20470548661037181000101000, 22759064814042426010000, 13590176400616227133000, 15579324585428883539180, 22687430939456742963689, 40947450551793797290100, 40286510804789540069820, 15581028966060637650000, 20516316838367876378700, 12050650136559384011300, 106300610727136076987400, 89952764090972360744000, 40984551504617889040300, 31799831482063003912100, 31060597413498430536150, 197588268576187336373100, 22370597449976787329100, 40477553226647242001000, 21197220265497420826000, 13773724817963658384560, 197228539058887077637200, 40984502064234348360161, 12103097167153030489200, 197672710913368276840270, 21370597449976787329110, 40287755320246147024841000, 15188586167592020417100, 12010120832661466898914, 21912976316104100177529, 296643941664863226373100, 21218153611306302415920, 74055023352636816967000, 15592732517459221162970, 296643134577960043690600, 21255982916625726989875, 31838976794198010789171000, 32653631569755117774606, 106704279993853321510549000, 3050462008520003394053400, 31020231020866441106410, 74181894244569784325500, 21988612200010025200114600, 3109979116604284621492, 40171753106405162853106, 82006713100422433201, 22540246964664784758, 12800065492003394053400, 3102023102086644110641, 74181894244569784325500, 21988612200010025200114600

Even in three point type this is a pretty serious cycle! (If you have the electronic version, click <u>here</u> to make this readable.) Just how long are these "short" and "long" cycles?

```
Length[findCycle[5, 22]]
```

95

```
Length[findCycle[6, 22]]
```

1223

So, although in human terms a 95-element cycle might seem long, compared to a 1223-element cycle, it's short.

Theo: Moving right along, what about looking for patterns when we vary the exponent for a given starting point, instead of varying the starting point for a given exponent. For example, what do we find if we always start with 57, and run the exponent from 1 to 10:

```
Table[Min[findCycle[57, e]], {e, 1, 10}]
```

{3, 4, 153, 1138, 9045, 282595, 86874, 8616804, 2274831, 192215803}

We just learned that for an exponent of 10, starting at 57, the minimum number in the cycle with the smallest minimum is 192215803.

Jerry: Let's see that cycle.

```
findCycle[192215803, 10]
```

{192215803, 4570352949, 7277732526, 1200194918, 8048360229, 5695843898,
10275899325, 8349378223, 5917971069, 11095535504, 3526954528,
4651398949, 11606483030, 1195840852, 5654848901, 5716362628,
1547442324, 296496276, 7438493203, 4845276797, 5480281949, 9132916252,
7043862726, 1760734347, 910107174, 4052783478, 2724356996, 7387851701,
3004734071, 567165749, 4193247078, 5127633949, 7327443551, 586698023,
5765026099, 7396508677, 5538708998, 10496859822, 9192334876,
8391419750, 8340659127, 4914341925, 6986540230, 4692332851, 4631926749,
7379133629, 7599163648, 8461591478, 5989072253, 8349378222, 5917913044,
7267965879, 9025435374, 3791007174, 4335317775, 868182721, 3564168947,
4975855653, 4943637775, 4406657199, 7388839181, 8064345046,
1207644578, 1711022300, 282536349, 4631926748, 4966091052, 7105316380,
1426566974, 3962521980, 8117603525, 1436274574, 638388101, 3281809748,
6991593772, 11095595576, 7355572729, 4363568120, 1205607500,
362473700, 626584372, 1488024723, 2432117147, 567108750, 1718689749,
9747517702, 4627500623, 414282899, 9123151651, 3566841904, 4693380404,
4624256227, 415274474, 578911452, 4863582326, 2279350347, 4062669246,
3730748305, 1649683670, 5025507628, 1445982172, 4854866301,
2280337827, 2712555316, 372299399, 14229732999, 14230723551,
303175223, 292420070, 3770311298, 5125595847, 4883113575, 2450656823,
1215315099, 6993160128, 8168303053, 2217892597, 8622029822, 5694739345,
7338256727, 1991519518, 11553626281, 1214266526, 192215803}

Jerry: The numbers are *not* getting smaller ... Didn't you prove that they would always get smaller? Also, what if we arranged these numbers on a number line—would they cluster or be spread out evenly? How many of these numbers start with 1 or 2 or 3? Are the numbers following any pattern by size? Bigger, bigger, smaller? Or what?

Theo: I proved there was an upper limit for exponent 2. I happen to know that I can prove this for any other exponent as well. For exponent 10 the upper limit is a little bigger than for exponent 2, but there is still a limit. I think it's roughly the case that for any exponent, the numbers are going to hover around that many digits. E.g., for exponent 10 you're going to get numbers approximately 10 digits long. Think of a number with **e** digits, all of which are 9. The next step will be:

$$e\,9^e$$

Now, 9^e is a lot like 10^e only smaller: 10^e has e digits, so it's reasonable to think that $e\,9^e$ will also have around e digits.

Jerry: This seems very magical. How many numbers were there in the cycle above?

```
Length[%]
```

124

Isn't it remarkable that these 9- or 10-digit numbers just *happen* to come back in only 124 steps? I can understand how two-digit numbers would repeat in short order, but it seems hard to believe that out of all the possible 9-, 10-, or 11-digit numbers, it would fall on the same one so soon! Can we print out the length of the cycle for each exponent, always starting at 57?

```
Table[Length[findCycle[57, e]], {e, 1, 10}]
```

{2, 9, 2, 8, 23, 4, 57, 26, 94, 124}

Theo: Readers should be made aware that Jerry is having some sort of religious experience. He seems awed by these numbers. It is quite remarkable that the cycle lengths are so short, given how large the numbers are. Statistically, it seems unlikely that out of the billions of 10-digit numbers, you would hit the same one so soon. The answer is that because it doesn't matter what order the digits of a given number are in, many, many numbers all go to the same next step. The size of the number is balanced against the number of permutations of the digits, which is also huge.

This fact could be used to calculate a statistically expected cycle length as a function of exponent: This is left as an exercise for the reader, as is a proper proof that all numbers and all exponents always cycle. Readers may want to keep us informed of their progress with this problem by email to info@mathware.com.

Jerry: I'm *sure* my friend Prof. Gene Nichols will be very pleased with this chapter.

Theo: He's probably never suckered anyone this good before.

Chapter **61**

How do I make hyperlinks in and between notebooks?

There are three main types of hyperlinks:

- links to a particular place in the current document
- links to a different document
- links to a particular place in a different document.

These will be described separately. (It is also possible to make links to destinations on the world wide web; see Chapter 74.)

▪ Links to a particular place in the current document

To make a link to a particular place in a document, you need to give that place a name. In *Mathematica*, this is done using the **Add/Remove Cell Tags...** command in the Find menu. To mark the destination for a hyperlink you plan to create, select the cell bracket of the target cell, and choose the **Add/Remove Cell Tags...** command. You will see the following dialog box:

Type into the uppermost text field the name you want to use to identify this location. The name you pick should describe *what* the target is, not *where* it is. For example, don't use "Section 5", because it may no longer *be* Section 5 if you add a new section in the middle of your document. It's best to use a fairly short (one or two word) tag, something like "Solving Equations", or "Pig Farming in Egalitarian Collectives".

To assign the tag to the selected cell, type Return, or click the Add button.

You are now ready to create a link to this location. Scroll to the location from which you want to make the link, and type the sentence containing the link. For example, you might enter:

> Click here to go to the section on pig farming.

The word "here" will become your link. Select the word "here", then choose **Create Hyperlink...** from the **Input** menu. You will see this dialog:

```
Destination notebook:
  ● Current notebook
  ○ Other notebook or URL:   [ Browse ]

  ┌─────────────────────────────────────┐
  │                                     │
  │                                     │
  └─────────────────────────────────────┘

Destination within notebook:
  ● Entire notebook
  ○ Cells with the tag:
  ┌─────────────────────────────┬─┐   To set up new
  │                             │▲│   tags, use the
  │ Pig Farming in Egalitarian Collectives │ │   Add/Remove
  │                             │ │   Cell Tags
  │                             │ │   command in the
  │                             │▼│   Find menu.
  └─────────────────────────────┴─┘

        [ Help ]  [ Cancel ]  [  OK  ]
```

The list at the bottom will contain all the potential destinations you have defined in this notebook. Click on the one you want, then click OK or type Return. The result will be:

> Click here to go to the section on pig farming.

The blue text and underlining indicates that the word "here" is a hyperlink.

Make a habit of typing complete sentences first and then creating your hyperlinks within them, after you have finished editing your text. (If you don't, and click just to the right of a link and start typing, the new text becomes part of the link, just as that text would become italic if the text to the left were italic. It's also risky editing near a link, because if you accidentally click on it, you'll be whisked off somewhere you didn't mean to go.)

▪ Links to a different document

Making links from one file to another can be a delicate operation, because you have to take into account how the files you are linking to might be moved around in the future. For the purpose of illustration, consider this set of files and folders:

```
┌─┬────────────────── Jerry ──────────────────┬─┐
│ │  Name                    Size  Kind         Lab│
│ ├────────────────────────────────────────────┤ │
│ ▽ □ Brian                    —   folder        ⇧│
│   ▽    □ Trevor              —   folder         │
│         □ EnglishHomework.nb  33K  Mathematica document│
│ ▽ □ David                    —   folder         │
│   ▽    □ Jessica             —   folder         │
│         □ MathHomework.nb    33K  Mathematica document│
│   ▽    □ Rasha               —   folder         │
│         □ ObedienceHomework.nb 33K Mathematica document│
│   ▽    □ Marty               —   folder         │
│         □ KnittingHomework.nb 33K Mathematica document ⇩│
│ ◁│░░░░░░░░░░░░░░░░░░░░░░░░░░░░░░░░░░░░░░│▷│ │
└─┴────────────────────────────────────────────┴─┘
```

This represents a disk named Jerry with two folders, Brian and David, each with subfolders and files. We will be discussing how to make links between these files.

When making a link from one file to another, the first question is whether the reference will be an absolute or relative reference. An absolute reference (called an absolute path name) specifies the name of the disk, and all the folders and sub-folders, and the file itself. For example, an absolute path name to Rasha's `ObedienceHomework.nb` file would be:

Jerry:David:Jessica:Rasha:ObedienceHomework.nb

In this example, file/folder names are separated by colons, which is the convention on the Macintosh. In Windows the path would be:

C:Jerry\David\Jessica\Rasha\ObedienceHomework.nb

while on UNIX it would be:

/Jerry/David/Jessica/Rasha/ObedienceHomework.nb

Such an absolute reference has a serious disadvantage: It will stop working if the disk is renamed, if the files are copied to another disk or moved to another location on the same disk, etc. An absolute reference is a very fragile way to specify a particular file.

If your link is from one of the files within this layout to another, you can instead use a *relative* path from one to the other. For example, if you are starting at Marty's `Knitting-Homework.nb`, you can get to `ObedienceHomework.nb` by the relative path:

::Jessica:Rasha:ObedienceHomework.nb

The `::` notation means "up one level", so this path is saying to start at the folder containing `KnittingHomework.nb`, move up one level (to David), then down into Jessica, from there to Rasha, then to `ObedienceHomework.nb`. This relative link will work regardless of where these files are located, as long as the relative position remains the same.

On Windows, this relative path would be:

`..\Jessica\Rasha\ObedienceHomework.nb`

while on UNIX it would be:

`../Jessica/Rasha/ObedienceHomework.nb`

Because relative links are almost always what you want to use, *Mathematica* automatically suggests a relative path when you make a link from one notebook to another (explained below). Because of this, it's important that you save the notebook you are making the link from *before* bringing up the Create Hyperlink dialog box. Since an Untitled window does not exist anywhere on disk, *Mathematica* does not know where to make the path relative to, and is forced to suggest an absolute path.

As an example, let's form that link from Marty's `KnittingHomework.nb`, to Rasha's `Obedi` `enceHomework.nb`. Open `KnittingHomework.nb` (if you are reading this book in electronic form, these files are all included in a folder called `Jerry`, inside the `ActiveElements` folder. Click here to open `KnittingHomework.nb`).

Begin as you did above, by typing in the text around the link. For example, type:

Here is a link to Rasha's Obedience Homework.

Select the text that is to become the link ("Rasha's Obedience Homework"), then choose **Create Hyperlink...** from the Input menu. You will see the same dialog as before. Click on the **Browse** button: You will be presented with your system's standard Open File dialog box. Choose `ObedienceHomework.nb`. You will now see:

Click OK, and the link will be created:

Here is a link to <u>Rasha's Obedience Homework</u>.

If you prefer, you can type the file name directly into upper text field, or modify the one that *Mathematica* produces after you use the Browse button. For example, you can edit it to be an absolute path name, if this is your preference.

In the dialog box, the path name is shown using the path name delimiter character (slash, backslash, or colon) suitable for the platform the front end is running on. This is not a portable representation of the path name, so when the path name is stored in the notebook it is represented as a **FrontEnd`FileName** object, which does not use any particular path name delimiter character. <u>Chapter</u> 65 discusses the complex issue of platform-independent path names.

▪ Links to a particular place in a different document

Making a link to a particular place within a different document requires a combination of the steps shown above to links within a document, and links to a different document.

First you open the target document (the one the link is going *to*), select the cell or cells that you want to make a specific link to, and use the **Add/Remove Cell Tags...** dialog (see <u>above</u>) to assign a unique name to the cells. Close the target document and open the source document (the one the link will be in). Type in the link, select the text that is to become the link, and open the Create Hyperlink dialog.

Click the Browse button and select the target notebook. You will see the path name to the target in the upper text field; in the bottom of the dialog you will see a list of the destinations you defined in the first step. Click on one of these, then click OK.

You have now created a hyperlink to that named location within the target notebook.

Chapter **62**

Is *Mathematica* "scriptable"?

Yes, but not in the ordinary way.

"Scriptable" means that it is possible to drive a program to perform repetitive actions under the control of a program, or "script". In many cases, this capability was added as a sort of after-thought, glued on in a fairly sloppy way. The programming languages developed specially for scripting (e.g., AppleScript) are generally designed by people who want them to be easy for "ordinary" people to use. They do this by making them "flexible", which is another word for sloppy, imprecise, and disorganized.

For the *Mathematica* front end, we have chosen to use the *Mathematica* language itself as the scripting language. And we have chosen not to glue this capability on, but rather to build the *Mathematica* language into the very foundations of the front end.

Take for example a dialog box that allows you to set attributes of the currently selected text—say its font, size, color, etc. The traditional approach to scripting is to make a scripting interface to this dialog box, which allows you under script control to simulate a user selecting items out of the dialog. This has many disadvantages, because the items in the dialog box are arranged for the convenience of the user; they may make little sense from a programming point of view. The dialog is also likely to be different on different platforms, making scripts non-portable.

In *Mathematica* we started from the opposite direction: How could the text itself be repre-sented as an expression in the *Mathematica* programming language? *Mathematica* uses a generic expression structure to represent all of mathematics; surely it could also represent italic text? In fact, it's quite easy to come up with an expression structure. For example, consider the following cell:

Hello this is *italic* text.

This could be represented in *Mathematica* as:

```
Cell[TextData[{
   "Hello this is ",
   StyleBox["italic",
     FontSlant->"Italic"],
   " text."
}], "Input"]
```

Now, here's the critical point: This cell actually *is* represented this way. It's written out this way in files; you can see (and edit) this text interactively in the front end, and you can write *Mathematica* programs that manipulate expressions in the front end directly by modifying this expression structure.

The font settings dialog box discussed above can be thought of as a user-interface layer glued on top of the underlying expression structure. Scripts need pay no attention to the dialog box, because they can directly address the expression representation.

To start getting used to this idea, take the following cell:

Hello this is *purple italic* text.

Assuming you are reading the electronic edition of this book, please click on the cell bracket containing the cell above, then choose **Show Expression** from the **Format** menu. You will see:

```
Cell[TextData[{
   "Hello this is ",
   StyleBox["purple italic",
     FontSlant->"Italic",
     FontColor->RGBColor[1, 0, 1]],
   " text."
}], "Input"]
```

This is the *Mathematica* expression representing the cell. Click in it. You now have your fingers on the very life pulse of the front end: the expression structure underlying everything you see on the screen. Go ahead, edit it. Try changing the numbers in the RGBColor object, say to RGBColor[1, 0, 0]. Then choose **Show Expression** again, to see the result:

Hello this is *purple italic* text.

You can go back and forth at will between these two representations, formatted and expression; any editing changes you make in one form are automatically reflected in the other. This is a *very* powerful thing to be able to do.

For example, suppose you want to find out what expression structure represents the size of text. Create a cell, select some text in it, choose something from the **Size** submenu of the **Format** menu, then use **Show Expression** to see the expression.

Now that you know about the expression structure, you can start writing *Mathematica* programs to generate cells automatically. The function **CellPrint** lets you generate a cell as output. For example:

CellPrint[Cell["Hello this is a cell", "Text", FontSize -> 24]]

Hello this is a cell

You can write loops:

```
Do[
  CellPrint[Cell["Hello this is a cell", "Text", FontSize -> i]],
  {i, 6, 16, 2}]
```

Hello this is a cell

Hello this is a cell

Hello this is a cell

Hello this is a cell

Hello this is a cell

Hello this is a cell

You can use functions to generate complex contents within one cell:

```
CellPrint[Cell[TextData[Table[i, {i, 1, 10}]], "Text"]]
```

12345678910

In this example, we are using **StyleBox** objects to produce colored text. The size, color, and background of each character is individually set according to the value of **i**.

```
CellPrint[Cell[TextData[
    Table[
        StyleBox[
            ToString[i],
            FontColor -> Hue[i/100.],
            Background -> Hue[Mod[0.5 + i/100., 1]],
            FontSize -> i/2.
        ],
    {i, 1, 60}]], "Output"]]
```

Cells can be collected into larger expressions that represent entire notebooks. For example, here is an expression representing a notebook with two simple cells in it:

```
Notebook[{
    Cell["My title", "Title"],
    Cell["This is a simple notebook", "Text"]
}]
```

The first argument to **Notebook** is a list of cells (it must be a list even if the notebook contains only a single cell). You can use **NotebookPut** the same way you used **CellPrint** above:

```
NotebookPut[Notebook[{
    Cell["My title", "Title"],
    Cell["This is a simple notebook", "Text"]
}]];
```

Because this expression represents an entire notebook document, this command creates a new window to hold the data, rather than placing it after the input expression. **Notebook** expressions, like cells, can take options. You can use all the same options as for cells (the values are applied to all the cells in the notebook), and you can use additional options that are defined only at the **Notebook** level. For example, **WindowSize** specifies (in points) the dimensions of the window.

This command creates a small (200 by 200 pixel) window containing blue text:

```
NotebookPut[Notebook[{
    Cell["My title", "Title"],
    Cell["This is a simple notebook", "Text"]
}, FontColor -> RGBColor[0, 0, 1], WindowSize -> {200, 200}]];
```

Already we have done a number of things that could be thought of as "scripting", but we've done them using ordinary *Mathematica* language functions.

In the next chapter, we list all the individual commands you can use to control the front end.

Chapter **63**

What commands can I use to control the *Mathematica* front end?

There are five ways to interact with the *Mathematica* front end under program control:

- use a high level command

- send a low level packet to the front end

- send a command token to the front end

- get or set an option value

- get the value of a front end global variable.

In this chapter we'll describe how to use each of these methods, and give listings of the relevant functions, packets, tokens, options, and global variables.

Please note that this chapter assumes a higher level of knowledge about programming languages and systems than the rest of this book. If the phrase "...is like a stream object" makes you think of shiny stones, you may not be ready for this chapter.

Important Disclaimer: This chapter (for that matter, this whole book) is *not* a publication of Wolfram Research, Inc., and is *not* an extension of The official *Mathematica* Book. Some of the functions, arguments, and features documented in this chapter are not described anywhere else. There is a good reason for this: Wolfram Research does not officially support or acknowledge them. They are subject to change without warning or remorse. Technical support personnel at Wolfram Research may never have heard of them, and are in any case not going to be willing to help you with them. Some of these features are experimental preludes to more extensive features coming in the future; some are experimental features leading nowhere; and some will prove to be just plain bad design. *C`est la vie.*

These unsupported, unofficial features are marked with a ⚹ (wolf) character to let you know you should be careful with them. Have fun using them, but *please* don't build elaborate programs around them and then get mad when they go away in some future version. It's going to happen, so just remember you have been warned. You'll get no sympathy if you ignore these cautions.

Features *not* marked with a ⚠ are supported, official *Mathematica* features that you can expect to remain a part of *Mathematica* as long as they have a sensible place. (Think of them as having tenure, but if their entire department gets cut, they go.)

■ Using a high level command

A few dozen built-in *Mathematica* commands can be used to drive the front end to open a notebook, move the selection, read/write data to/from a notebook, etc. These functions use **NotebookObject**s to refer to notebooks in the front end. A notebook object is like a stream object; it's a reference to the notebook in the front end, but it does not itself contain any of the data in the notebook.

To get started, you might want to create a new notebook. The following command creates an empty Untitled notebook window, and returns the notebook object representing it:

> **nb = NotebookCreate[]**
>
> - NotebookObject -

FullForm will show you the internal structure of the object:

> **FullForm[nb]**
>
> NotebookObject[
>   FrontEndObject[LinkObject["Mathematica", 1, 1]], 19]

The first argument contains a *MathLink* object, which will always be the same as **$Parent‑Link**. The second is a serial number that uniquely identifies this notebook to the front end; this number will never be used again in a given session. Note that the internal structure of **NotebookObject** is not guaranteed to remain the same in future versions of *Mathematica*. As with any object-oriented system, you should never try to modify or construct **NotebookOb‑jects** yourself: always use notebook functions to manipulate them.

To find out more about a **NotebookObject**, use **NotebookInformation**:

> **NotebookInformation[nb]**
>
> {WindowTitle → Untitled-1, MemoryModificationTime → 3.07424×10^9}

It returns a list of replacement rules that tell you the modification time (in seconds since 1 Jan 1900), the window title, and file name (if it has been saved to disk). If you're worried about any possible Y2K problems with this time mechanism, please see Chapter 59.

If you're tired of your new notebook, you can close it:

NotebookClose[nb]

If you make changes manually to the notebook after creating it, this command will close the notebook without asking whether you wanted to save the changes. This may or may not be what you want; the option **Interactive** controls whether **NotebookClose** puts up the "Do you want to save..." dialog box. To see this work, re-evaluate the **NotebookCreate** above to re-open the notebook, make some changes to it, then evaluate:

NotebookClose[nb, Interactive → True]

Another way of creating a notebook is with **NotebookPut**, which is like the file operation **Put** in that it creates a new notebook containing the information you give it. In the case of **NotebookPut**, the data is a **Notebook[]** expression. (See Chapter 62 for a brief description of the format of **Notebook[]** expressions.)

```
nb =
 NotebookPut[Notebook[{Cell["Hi! I'm a notebook!", "Title"]}]]
```

- NotebookObject -

Again, you can close it:

NotebookClose[nb]

There are several functions that allow you to refer to notebooks that are currently playing a particular role in the front end. Each of these functions returns a **NotebookObject**:

SelectedNotebook[] — the notebook whose title bar is highlighted
EvaluationNotebook[] — the notebook containing the current evaluation
ButtonNotebook[] — the notebook containing the button that initiated this evaluation
InputNotebook[] — the notebook into which typed characters are being placed
ClipboardNotebook[] — the notebook containing the contents of the clipboard
HelpBrowserNotebook[] — the notebook contents of the Help Browser

You can also get a list of all the open notebooks in the front end:

Notebooks[]

{ - NotebookObject -, - NotebookObject -, - NotebookObject - }

This list is usually not very useful in itself, but you can map **NotebookInformation** onto it to get information about the individual notebooks—for example the file names of all the open notebooks:

```
getFileName[n_] := ("FileName" /. NotebookInformation[n]) //.
    {FrontEnd`FileName[dir_, filename_, ___] → filename,
     "FileName" → "Untitled"};

Map[getFileName, Notebooks[]]

{FrontEndCommands.nb, TableOfContents.nb, Untitled}
```

We next give descriptions of the high level commands you can use with **NotebookObject**s.

■ SetSelectedNotebook[*notebookobject*]

Brings the notebook to the front and makes it the currently selected (highlighted) notebook. Exactly what this means is somewhat dependent on the window system you are using. For example, if you are using the X Window System and you have not set click-to-type, this function does nothing (because the highlighted notebook always follows the location of the mouse pointer).

■ NotebookCreate[]
NotebookCreate[*options*]

Creates a new, untitled notebook. If options are specified, they are set at the notebook level.

■ NotebookOpen[*filename*]

Opens a notebook from a file on disk. The filename can be an absolute path name, or a path relative to the current notebook directory. It can be a string (using path name delimiters that are appropriate for the system the front end is running on), or it can be a **FrontEnd`File⸴ Name** object (see Chapter 65).

■ **NotebookLocate[***filename***]**
  NotebookLocate[{*filename***,** *celltag***}]**

NotebookLocate is similar to **NotebookOpen**, except that it can also automatically scroll to a location indicated by a **CellTag** after opening the notebook. (In the future, it will also be able to locate notebooks and other files on the Web by using URL syntax in the *filename* argument.)

This is the command used to implement hyperlinks in the front end.

■ **NotebookClose[***notebookobject***]**

Closes the specified notebook. By default, the notebook is forcibly closed even if it has been modified by the user. With the option **Interactive→True**, the standard "Do you want to save..." dialog will be used.

■ **NotebookSave[***notebookobject***]**
  NotebookSave[*notebookobject***,** *filename***]**

Saves the specified notebook. In the one-argument form, the notebook is saved into the same file it is currently associated with. In the two-argument form, it is saved into a new file. (The two-argument form is required for notebooks that have never been saved, since they have no current file.)

With the option **Interactive→True** a new file name is prompted for, using the "Save As..." dialog box.

■ **NotebookConvert[***oldfilename***]**
  NotebookConvert[*oldfilename***,** *newfilename***]**
  NotebookConvert[*oldfilename***,** *newfilename***,** *newversion***]**

Converts a file from Version 2.2 or earlier to Version 4.0, or vice versa. With just the file name specified, the new file name will be the same as the old except ending in ".nb" instead of ".m". With no version specified, the file will be converted to the most recent version (e.g., 4.0.0 if you are running a 4.0.0 front end, etc.).

The following options can be specified (the default value for all these options is **False**). See Chapter 11 for a more detailed explanation of what each of these options does (they correspond to similarly named items in the dialog box described in that chapter).

Interactive→True
Prompts for a new file name using the "Save As..." dialog box.

InputToStandardForm→True
Converts all Input style cells to **StandardForm** (typeset) notation.

OutputToStandardForm→True
Converts all Output style cells to **StandardForm** (typeset) notation.

PreserveStyleSheet→True
Converts all Input style cells to **StandardForm** (typeset) notation.

GenerateBitmapCaches→True
Generates new bitmap caches for all PostScript graphics cells.

The following options apply when converting from 3.0 or later notebooks to 2.2 or earlier form:

InputToInputForm→True
Converts all Input style cells to linear text InputForm notation.

OutputToOutputForm→True
Converts all Output style cells to plain 2-D text OutputForm notation.

- **NotebookPrint[*notebookobject*]**

Prints out the specified notebook via the current default printer. With the option **Interactive→True**, you get a standard Print dialog box; otherwise all the current printing settings are used.

- **NotebookPut[*notebook*]**
  NotebookPut[*notebook, notebookobject*]

The one-argument form writes the data in *notebook* (which is a notebook *expression*, not a notebook object) into a newly created, Untitled notebook window. The two-argument form completely replaces the contents of *notebookobject* with the data in *notebook*. (This function is the notebook analog of <u>Put</u> for ordinary text files.)

- **NotebookGet[]**
  NotebookGet[*notebookobject***]**

Reads into the kernel the entire contents of the currently selected notebook or the notebook specified by *notebookobject*. Returns a **Notebook[]** expression containing the full data of the notebook (not a **NotebookObject**). (This function is the notebook analog of <u>Get</u> for ordinary text files.)

- **NotebookRead[]**
  NotebookRead[*notebookobject***]**

Reads into the kernel the current selection from the current notebook or the notebook specified by *notebookobject*. If you have one or more cells selected, you will get a **Cell[]** expression or a list of **Cell[]** expressions. If you have a selection inside a single cell, you will get a string, **TextData** expression, or **BoxData** expression, depending on what is selected.

(This function is the notebook analog of <u>Read</u> for ordinary text files. The current selection corresponds to the file position, except that the selection defines a range, rather than just a point, and is not advanced by the function.)

- **NotebookWrite[***notebookobject, data***]**

Replaces the current selection in the specified notebook with *data*, which can be a string, **TextData** expression, **BoxData** expression, **Cell** expression, list of **Cell** expressions, or a whole **Notebook** expression. If the current selection is an insertion point, the data is inserted in that point; otherwise the selected area in the notebook is deleted and the new data written in its place.

The option **AutoScroll**, which can be **True** or **False**, determines whether the notebook is scrolled to make the newly written data visible. The default is **True**.

The option **GeneratedCell**, which can be **True** or **False**, determines whether the option **GeneratedCell** is set in all the cells added to the notebook. **GeneratedCell** is an option that does not affect any behavior in the front end; its only purpose is to indicate whether a cell was created manually by the user, or inserted by a program. The default is **True**.

(This function is the notebook analog of <u>Write</u> for ordinary text files. The current selection corresponds to the file position, except that the selection defines a range, rather than just a point, and is not advanced by the function.)

■ NotebookApply[*notebookobject, data*]

This function is very similar to **NotebookWrite**. The difference is that if the data being written to the notebook contains any \[SelectionPlaceholder] characters (drawn as ■), the data selected in the notebook is substituted in place of the \[SelectionPlaceholder] characters before the new data replaces the selection. The effect is to "wrap" the data around the selection, rather than just replace it.

(**NotebookApply** is the packet used to implement the common paste-template type palette buttons.)

■ CellPrint[*data*]

Similar to **NotebookWrite**, except that the data, which can be a **Cell** expression or a list of **Cell** expressions, is inserted after the input cell in which the command is being executed. (In other words, the cell(s) are inserted in the same place that output from the evaluation would be placed.)

■ NotebookDelete[*notebookobject*]

Deletes the currently selected data from the specified notebook. This is equivalent to the **Clear** menu command in the **Edit** menu.

■ NotebookFind[*notebookobject, searchdata*]
   NotebookFind[*notebookobject, searchdata, direction*]
   NotebookFind[*notebookobject, searchdata, direction, searchelements*]

Finds data in the specified notebook. The current selection is moved to the location where the data was found (just as when you use the **Find** dialog).

If the data is found, the command returns the **NotebookObject** you gave it; otherwise it returns **$Failed**. In addition to the arguments below, the command takes two options:

   IgnoreCase determines if the case of the search data should be considered. If this option is omitted, the current setting from the **Find** dialog is used.

   AutoScroll determines if the notebook should be scrolled to make the found location visible. The default is **True**.

Searchdata can be a string, **TextData** expression, or **BoxData** expression, or one of the following special values:

>   **Automatic** — use the search data from the **Find** dialog box.
>   **Selection** — use the currently selected data as the search data.

Direction can be one of the following:

>   **Next** — next occurrence after the current selection
>   **Previous** — first occurrence before the current selection
>   **All** — all cells containing the search data.

If this argument is omitted, the default is **Next**.

In the case of **All**, the selection will always be at the whole-cell level, while for **Next** and **Previous** the selection will be a range of text or a typeset structure within a single cell.

Searchelements determines what part(s) of the notebook are searched. It can be one of the following, or a list of several:

>   **CellContents** — the text/typeset contents of the cell
>   **CellStyle** — the style name ("Text", "Input", etc.) (only exact matches work)
>   **CellLabel** — the cell's In/Out label (only exact matches work)
>   **CellTags** — the cell's **CellTags** (only exact matches work)

If *searchelements* is omitted, the default is **CellContents**.

■ Examples

These examples will all work sensibly within this chapter; if you have the electronic edition, you can evaluate them right where they are to see what they do.

Find the next occurrence of "Hello" after the current selection:

```
NotebookFind[SelectedNotebook[], "Hello"]
```

Find the first occurrence before the current selection:

```
NotebookFind[SelectedNotebook[], "Hello", Previous]
```

Find all cells that contain the word "Hello":

```
NotebookFind[SelectedNotebook[], "Hello", All]
```

Find all "Text" style cells:

```
NotebookFind[SelectedNotebook[], "Text", All, CellStyle ]
```

Find all the cells to do with **NotebookDelete** (and which therefore have this as a cell tag):

```
NotebookFind[SelectedNotebook[],
  "NotebookDelete", All, CellTags ]
```

Find the first input evaluated in this notebook (which works only if the input cell is still there, and hasn't been re-evaluated; re-evaluation would reassign its cell label):

```
NotebookFind[SelectedNotebook[], "In[1]:=", All, CellLabel ]
```

■ SelectionMove[*notebookobject, direction, unit*]
SelectionMove[*notebookobject, direction, unit, count*]

Moves the current selection by a specified amount, or moves it to a specified location. The option **AutoScroll** determines whether the notebook is automatically scrolled to make the new selection location visible. The default is **True**.

The following listings will probably not make a whole lot of sense until the examples at the end, which will show you how different values fit together to do useful things.

Direction can be one of the following:
    Next — select the next *unit* after the current selection
    Previous — select the first *unit* before the current selection
    After — make the selection an insertion point after the *unit*
    Before — make the selection an insertion point before the *unit*
    All — select the entire *unit*

Unit can be one of the following to move the selection by the specified amount:
    Character — one letter
    Word — a white-space delimited word
    Expression — one sub-expression (typeset cells only)
    TextLine — one line of text
    TextParagraph — same as **TextLine** (a return-delimited paragraph)
    CellContents — the entire contents of the cell
    Cell — the cell as a whole
    CellGroup — the group containing the cell
    Notebook — the entire notebook

Unit can be one of the following to move the selection to a specific point in the notebook, regardless of what the current selection is:
    EvaluationCell — the cell in which this command is being executed
    ButtonCell — the cell, if any, containing the button that initiated the evaluation of this command
    GeneratedCell — the output cells, if any, generated by the evaluation of the cell containing this command

■ Examples

These examples will all work sensibly within this chapter; if you have the electronic edition, you can evaluate them right where they are to see what they do.

Select the next cell after the current selection:

```
SelectionMove[SelectedNotebook[], Next, Cell]
```

Select the next cell after the current selection, then make the selection an insertion point at the end of that cell's contents:

```
SelectionMove[SelectedNotebook[], Next, Cell]
SelectionMove[SelectedNotebook[], After, CellContents]
```

Select a point to the left of the last four words in the next cell after the current selection:

```
SelectionMove[SelectedNotebook[], Next, Cell]
SelectionMove[SelectedNotebook[], After, CellContents]
SelectionMove[SelectedNotebook[], Previous, Word, 4]
```

Select the input cell currently being evaluated:

```
SelectionMove[SelectedNotebook[], All, EvaluationCell]
```

Move the selection above the cell currently being evaluated, then write "BOO" there:

```
SelectionMove[SelectedNotebook[], Before, EvaluationCell]
NotebookWrite[SelectedNotebook[], "BOO"]
```

Generate some output cells, then select them all:

```
Do[Print[i], {i, 1, 5}];
SelectionMove[SelectedNotebook[], All, GeneratedCell]
```

```
1

2

3

4

5
```

■ **SelectionCreateCell[***notebookobject***]**
SelectionCreateCell[*notebookobject, selection***]**

Takes the currently selected data and copies it into a newly created cell, which is inserted below the cell containing the selection. This command can be used to create a record of operations that are applied to the current selection (by duplicating the selection into a new cell before applying the operation).

If the second argument is omitted, the selection will be placed inside the newly created cell, at the very end. The *selection* argument can be used to change what the selection is after the new cell is created:

None — do not change the selection from what it was before the duplication

All — select the entire contents of the new cell

Before — insertion point at the start of the cell

After — insertion point at the end of the cell

Placeholder — the first \[Placeholder] or \[SelectionPlaceholder] character in the new cell, or an insertion point at the end of the cell if there are no placeholders.

■ **SelectionCellCreateCell[***notebookobject***]**
SelectionCellCreateCell[*notebookobject, selection***]**

Similar to **SelectionCreateCell**, except that the entire cell containing the current selection is duplicated, not just the selected data itself. See **SelectionCreateCell** for a description of the *selection* argument.

■ **SelectionEvaluate[***notebookobject***]**
SelectionEvaluate[*notebookobject, selection***]**

Evaluates the currently selected data, and pastes the result back over the selection (replacing what was selected). This is equivalent to the **Evaluate In Place** command in the **Evaluation** submenu of the **Kernel** menu.

■ **SelectionEvaluateCreateCell[***notebookobject***]**
SelectionEvaluateCreateCell[*notebookobject, selection***]**

Evaluates the cell or cells containing the current selection, placing the result in a new cell or cells below the input cell. This is equivalent to normal Shift-Return evaluation in the front end.

Note that this command evaluates the entire contents of the cell, not just the selected portion, unlike **SelectionEvaluate**, which evaluates just the selected expression.

■ **FileBrowse[]**
   FileBrowse[False]

Puts up the standard "Save file" dialog box (first case), or the standard "Open file" dialog (second case). The return value is the full path name of the file selected, or $Failed if Cancel is clicked. The optional argument specifies whether new files are allowed, or only existing ones.

Note: In versions before V3.1 the second form does not work. See the <u>next section</u> for information on how to work around this by sending the `FileBrowse` packet manually to the front end.

■ Sending a low level packet to the front end

All the high level commands described in the section above are implemented by having the kernel send a *MathLink packet* to the front end. (*MathLink* is the communications protocol used for all communication between the front end and kernel; see the `Add-Ons section` in the online help for more information about *MathLink*.)

You can send these packets (and others that do not have any high level command) directly, using the *MathLink* function **LinkWrite**.

There are a few reasons you might want to manually send packets that do have high level equivalents. It's more efficient to send a long sequence of commands in a single transaction, which can't be done with the high level commands. There are some bugs in the implementation of the high level commands that you can work around by sending the packets yourself.

For example, consider this command:

```
SelectionMove[SelectedNotebook[], Next, Cell]
```

The evaluation of **SelectedNotebook[]** causes the kernel to send a packet to the front end requesting the notebook object representing the currently selected notebook. The front end responds by sending the notebook object back to the kernel. Then the kernel sends another packet to the front end to carry out the **SelectionMove** action on the notebook object it just got from the front end. Thus, two round-trips to the front end were required to carry out this single command.

You can achieve the same effect in the front end by writing these packets manually with **LinkWrite** to **$ParentLink** (the link that represents the connection to the front end):

```
LinkWrite[$ParentLink, FrontEnd`SelectionMove[
   FrontEnd`SelectedNotebook[], Next, Cell]]
```

Each high level command is implemented with a packet of the same name, but in the **Front** **End`** context. The packet takes the same arguments as the high level command. In this example, **FrontEnd`SelectedNotebook[]** does not cause an extra round trip to the front end, because it is just a packet name, not a high level command.

Some packets return a value to the front end. In such cases, you must include a **LinkRead** command *in the same cell* as the **LinkWrite**. This is very, very important: If you don't read the data back before the evaluation of the cell finishes, the link between front end and kernel will get out of sync, and will be virtually impossible to restore. The only way out is to kill the kernel (with the **Quit Kernel** submenu in the **Kernel** menu) and start over. For example, here is how you can use the **FileBrowse** packet manually:

```
LinkWrite[$ParentLink, FrontEnd`FileBrowse[False]];
LinkRead[$ParentLink]
```

FrontEndExecute is a high level function designed to make this process convenient; it is simply a wrapper function that calls **LinkWrite[$ParentLink, ...]** for you. You can give it a list of several front end packets, which are sent to the front end in a single transaction. For example, we will create a new cell, select it, then delete it, leaving the notebook unchanged:

```
FrontEndExecute[{
    FrontEnd`NotebookWrite[
        FrontEnd`SelectedNotebook[], "Hello"],
    FrontEnd`SelectionMove[
        FrontEnd`SelectedNotebook[], All, Cell],
    FrontEnd`NotebookDelete[
        FrontEnd`SelectedNotebook[]]
}]
```

Following are descriptions of packets that do not correspond to a high level command:

■ FrontEnd`HelpBrowserLookup[*radiobuttoncategory, item*]
FrontEnd`HelpBrowserLookup[*radiobuttoncategory, item, findtag*]

Looks an item up in the help browser. The first argument, *radiobuttoncategory*, determines which of the six major categories you want to look in. Possible values are:

"RefGuide" — Built-in Functions
"AddOns" — Add-ons
"MainBook" — The *Mathematica* Book
"GettingStarted" — Getting Started/Demos
"OtherInformation" — Other Information
"MasterIndex" — Master index

For example:

```
LinkWrite[$ParentLink,
  FrontEnd`HelpBrowserLookup["RefGuide", "Factor"]]
```

The three-argument form allows you to specify a **CellTag** to be looked up in the data placed in the Help Browser by the first two arguments. This allows you to scroll to a particular place in the help data. For example:

```
LinkWrite[$ParentLink,
  FrontEnd`HelpBrowserLookup["MainBook", "3.2.6", "6.7"]]
```

▪ Value[*globalvariable*]

Returns the value of a front end global variable (see the section "Getting the value of a front end global variable" for a list of available global variables and instructions on how to use this packet).

▪ ToFileName[*filenameobject*]

This packet allows you to ask the front end to turn a **FrontEnd`FileName** object (see Chapter 65) into a platform-specific full path name. If the front end and kernel are running on different computers, or are installed in different locations on the same computer, the information necessary to do this is not available to the kernel, other than by asking the front end through this packet. For example, the following command will tell you the location of the top level installation directory for the front end:

```
FrontEndExecute[
   {FrontEnd`ToFileName[FrontEnd`FileName[{$TopDirectory}]]}],
LinkRead[$ParentLink]
```

⚠ NotebookResetGeneratedCells[]
DontNotebookResetGeneratedCells[]

When you evaluate a cell that has already been evaluated, the new output usually replaces the old. If you watch closely, you will notice that the old output is not deleted until the new output is ready to replace it. If the new output consists of several output cells (e.g., several graphics cells), the old output is deleted when the first new output cell is placed, then subsequent output cells are inserted in order.

If, during the placement of output cells, you send a **NotebookResetGeneratedCells** packet, the front end will consider any previously placed output cells as "old", and the next one will cause them to be deleted. For example, the following commands will produce some printed output, then replace it with a graphic (depending on how fast your computer is, you may have to increase the 10 in the first line to make the process visible):

```
Do[Print["Hello"], {10}];
FrontEndExecute[{NotebookResetGeneratedCells[]}];
Plot[Sin[x], {x, 0, 2 Pi}];
```

DontNotebookResetGeneratedCells is the reverse: It tells the front end to consider any existing output cells as "new", and thereby prevents them from being deleted. If you send this packet before any output is generated, output cells from the previous evaluation of the same cell will be preserved.

⚞ DisplayFlushImagePacket[]

When the front end is receiving PostScript data from the kernel (from a plotting command, for example), it updates the screen only a few times per second (or even less often on a slow computer). This greatly increases the speed at which PostScript can be rendered. If you are sending PostScript to the front end manually (with **LinkWrite[$FrontEnd, Display**⁚ **Packet["…"]]**), and you want to force the front end to display the current state of the graphic *now*, you can send a **DisplayFlushImagePacket**.

⚞ FlushPrintOutputPacket[]

The front end does not display the output from **Print[]** commands immediately. Instead, it buffers output and displays it only about three times per second. This greatly increases the speed at which large volumes of print output can be displayed, and usually is not noticeable to the user. However, if you want to force the front end to display something you printed *now*, you can send a **FlushPrintOutputPacket**.

⚞ ResetMenusPacket[*menus*]

Replaces all the menus in the front end with an entirely new set. The *menus* argument should be an expression in the same form as the contents of MenuSetup.tr, found in SystemFiles/⁚ FrontEnd/TextResources/*platform*/MenuSetup.tr.

Warning: You will almost certainly screw everything up if you try to use this packet. Be prepared to use force many times to kill the front end and start all over again before you get it right.

- **ConvertToPostScriptPacket[***cells***]**
  VerboseConvertToPostScriptPacket[*cells***]**
  ConvertToBitmapPacket[*cells***]**
  VerboseConvertToBitmapPacket[*cells***]**

These packets accept any of the following as input:

A complete **Notebook[]** expression.
A list of **Cell[]** expressions.
A single **Cell[]** expression.
A **BoxData** or **TextData** expression.
A string.

They return either a bitmap object in MGF form or PostScript text representing an image of the data sent as input. They also return information about the bounding box of the image. Non-verbose packets return an expression of the form:

```
{
    graphicsdata,
    {{left, bottom}, {right, top}},
    baseline
}
```

The first argument, *graphicsdata*, is the PostScript or MGF data. The second argument is the bounding box of the image in points. The third argument is the distance in points from the top of the image to the baseline of the text (the position of the bottom of non-descender characters like "x").

The verbose packets return more information, in the following form:

```
{
    graphicsdata,
    {
        Baseline → baseline,
        CellBoundingBox → {{left, right}, {bottom, top}},
        CellElementsBoundingBox → {{left, right}, {bottom, top}},
        ContentsBoundingBox → {{left, right}, {bottom, top}},
        ShrinkWrapBoundingBox → {{left, right}, {bottom, top}}
    }
}
```

The baseline is the same as described above. The four bounding boxes are:

CellBoundingBox — the overall area from the left of the window to the right of the cell bracket

CellElementsBoundingBox — the area of all the parts of the cell, including CellLabel, cell bracket, CellFrameLabel, etc.

ContentsBoundingBox — the area of the cell's primary data (text, typeset, or graphic)

ShrinkWrapBoundingBox — the area exactly enclosing anything that is actually drawn in the image

These different kinds of bounding boxes are useful for different purposes. Often several of them will be the same. The following functions will let you experiment with these packets. The two Test functions generate output cells containing the PostScript or Bitmap images.

```
GetPostScriptOfCells[cell_] :=
  (LinkWrite[$ParentLink,
     VerboseConvertToPostScriptPacket[cell]];
   LinkRead[$ParentLink])

GetBitmapOfCells[cell_] :=
  (LinkWrite[$ParentLink,
     VerboseConvertToBitmapPacket[cell]];
   LinkRead[$ParentLink])

TestGetPostScriptOfCells[cell_] :=
Module[{data},
    data = GetPostScriptOfCells[cell];
    CellPrint[Cell[First[data],"Graphics"]];
]

TestGetBitmapOfCells[cell_] :=
Module[{data, bb},
    data = GetBitmapOfCells[cell];
    bb = ContentsBoundingBox /. data[[2]];
    CellPrint[Cell[First[data],"Graphics",
    ImageSize->
      {bb[[1,2]]-bb[[1,1]], bb[[2,2]]-bb[[2,1]]}]];
]
```

⚹ SetNotebookStatusLine[*notebook*, *text*]

Set the text in the status line at the bottom of the specified notebook window. For example:

```
FrontEndExecute[{FrontEnd`SetNotebookStatusLine[
    FrontEnd`SelectedNotebook[], "Hello"]}]
```

■ SelectionAnimate[*time*]
SelectionAnimate[*notebook*, *time*]

Animate the selected cells for the specified number of seconds. For example, here we create a series of graphics cells, select them, then animate them for 5 seconds:

```
Do[Plot[Sin[n x], {x, 0, 2 Pi}], {n, 1, 2, 0.1}];
SelectionMove[SelectedNotebook[], All, GeneratedCell];
FrontEndExecute[{FrontEnd`SelectionAnimate[5.0]}]
```

You can also include the option **AnimationDisplayTime** to specify the time in seconds to display each individual frame. Here is the same animation displayed slowly for 30 seconds:

```
Do[Plot[Sin[n x], {x, 0, 2 Pi}], {n, 1, 2, 0.1}];
SelectionMove[SelectedNotebook[], All, GeneratedCell];
FrontEndExecute [{FrontEnd`SelectionAnimate [30.0,
    AnimationDisplayTime -> 0.2}]
```

✍ AddEvaluatorNames[*evaluators*]

Adds new evaluators to the submenus in the **Kernel** menu that list them. This packet takes a list of replacement rules where the left hand side is the evaluator name and the right hand side is a list of rules specifying properties of the evaluator. The format is the same as for the **EvaluatorNames** option (see Chapter 64 for a description of this option).

✍ AddMenuCommands[*aftercommand*, *commands*]

Adds new menu commands to the front end menus. The first argument specifies the location in the menus where the new commands should be added. It is a command token (see next section). For example, to add a new command after the **Cell Size Statistics...** command in the **Cell** menu, use "NotebookStatisticsDialog", which is the token for that command.

The second argument is a list of the command(s) to be added (it must be a list even if it contains only a single element). The format is the same as the format of the main menu set up file, MenuSetup.tr, found in SystemFiles/FrontEnd/TextResources/*platform*/ MenuSetup.tr.

✍ AddDefaultFontProperties[*fontlist*]

Adds new default font information. The *fontlist* is a list in the same format as the **Default FontProperties** option (see Chapter 64 for a description of this option).

⚕ SpeakTextPacket[*text*]

Asks the front end to speak the given text (which should be a text string). This packet works only on Macintosh and Windows, and only if you have suitable text-to-speech system software installed.

■ DisplayPacket[*postscript*]
DisplayEndPacket[*postscript*]

The first `DisplayPacket` creates a new PostScript graphics cell containing the given Post-Script text. The front end then accepts any number of additional `DisplayPacket`s, incorporating the additional PostScript into the current graphics cell. A `DisplayEndPacket` finishes the graphic.

Because PostScript text is rendered as the front end receives it, you can use multiple `Display` `Packet`s to draw incrementally rendered images that appear during an ongoing calculation. The only problem is, you have to generate the PostScript text yourself, rather than using *Mathematica* graphics primitives.

■ Forward[*evaluatorname, data*]

Forwards data from one evaluator to another. The first argument specifies the name of the evaluator to which the data should be sent. The front end simply takes the data and re-transmits it to the specified evaluator. This allows one kernel to communicate with another, without either kernel knowing where the other is actually located. It also allows a kernel to communicate with any other *MathLink*-based program, such as an external graphics rendering or data collection system.

While it is always possible to make these connections directly, using the front end as an intermediary can sometimes greatly simplify the process of making the connection.

■ EvaluatorStart[*name*]
EvaluatorQuit[*name*]
EvaluatorInterrupt[*name*]
EvaluatorAbort[*name*]
EnterSubsession[*name*]
ExitSubsession[*name*]

Each performs the specified operation on the evaluator whose name is given.

■ Sending a command token to the front end

In addition to the several dozen high level commands and packets understood by the front end, there are several hundred simple *command tokens*. These are the tokens that define the actions carried out by menu commands. They are different from the higher level commands and packets in that they do not have complex argument structures, and generally each does just one simple thing; most are intended to implement a single menu command.

These tokens can be executed with a **FrontEndToken** packet, which is sent to the front end with **FrontEndExecute** (or equivalently with **LinkWrite**). For example, the following command opens up the About Box:

```
FrontEndExecute[{FrontEndToken["AboutBoxDialog"]}]
```

Some tokens (e.g., **"Save"**, which implements the **Save** command in the **File** menu) operate on a particular notebook. If you use the one-argument form of **FrontEndToken**, the token is applied to the currently selected notebook. If you want to apply it to a different notebook, you can use the two-argument form, with the first argument being a **NotebookObject**. For example, the following command saves the notebook containing the current evaluation, whether it is the front (selected) notebook or not:

```
FrontEndExecute[{FrontEndToken[
        FrontEnd`EvaluationNotebook[],
        "Save"
]}]
```

(Of course, this is only for illustrative purposes; you would normally use **NotebookSave[** **EvaluationNotebook[]]** to do this.)

Some tokens require a parameter to specify a variation of their behavior. For example, the **"CopySpecial"** token, which implements all the items in the **Copy As** submenu in the **Edit** menu, requires a parameter to specify the format the data should be copied in. This is done with the three-argument form of **FrontEndToken**. For example, the following command copies the selection to the clipboard in the form of a PostScript graphic:

```
FrontEndExecute[{FrontEndToken[
        FrontEnd`SelectedNotebook[],
        "CopySpecial",
        "PostScript"
]}]
```

If you want to include a parameter of this sort, you must also include the notebook object as the first argument. If you include only the token and the parameter, you will get an error message when executing the command.

Following is a complete current list of all the tokens supported in V4.0.1. Be warned that this list is far from static. Future versions of the front end will include more tokens; while every effort will be made to continue supporting any existing token forever, if a feature is removed from the front end (for only the best of reasons), the corresponding token will also be discontinued. Tokens marked with the ⚠ symbol are especially likely to be changed in future versions.

▪ Opening dialog boxes

"AboutBoxDialog" — open About Box

"ExplainBeepDialog" — open "Why the Beep?" dialog

"PasswordDialog" — open the password/registration dialog

"CellTagsEditDialog" — open Add/Remove Cell Tags dialog box

"CreateHyperlinkDialog" — open Create Hyperlink dialog box

"CreateCounterBoxDialog" — open Create Automatic Numbering Object dialog box

"CreateValueBoxDialog" — open Create Value Display Object dialog box

"OptionsDialog" — open the Option Inspector

⚠ **"ViewPointSelectorDialog"** — open the 3-D Viewpoint Selector dialog

"ColorSelectorDialog" — open the system's standard Color Selector dialog

"RecordSoundDialog" — open the system's standard Record Sound dialog

"CreateGridBoxDialog" — open the Create Table/Matrix/Palette dialog

"FileNameDialog" — open the Get File Path dialog

"FontPanel" — open the system's standard Font dialog (Windows and NeXT only)

"ColorsPanel" — open the color selected for a color well (NeXT only)

"HelpDialog" — open the Help Browser

"SelectionHelpDialog" — look up the currently selected text in the help browser

"FEintroHelpDialogCom" — open the Startup Help dialog box

"NotebookStatisticsDialog" — open the Cell Size Statistics dialog

"XInfoDialog" — open the X-Windows System specific information dialog

"GraphicsCoordinatesDialog" — open the dialog that explains how to get coordinates from graphics

"ModifyEvaluatorNames" — open the dialog for adding/removing/editing evaluators

"ModifyNotebooksMenu" — open dialog for adding/removing/editing the contents of the Notebooks submenu of the File menu

"ModifyFontSubstitutions" — open dialog for editing the list of font substitutions

"ModifyDefaultFontProperties" — open dialog for editing the list of defaults for FontProperties

"ModifyBoxFormFormatTypes" — open dialog for editing the list of FormatTypes that are typeset box forms

"FontColorDialog" — open the dialog for choosing a color for the currently selected text

"BackgroundDialog" — open the dialog for choosing a background color for the currently selected text or cell

"FontSizeDialog" — open the dialog for choosing a font size for the currently selected text

"ModifyKeyboardAliases" — open the dialog for editing the list of keyboard aliases

"SpellCheckerDialog" — open the spell checker dialog box

▪ Application level operations

"RebuildHelpIndex" — rebuild the Help Browser categories and Master Index

"FrontEndHide" — hide the application (NeXT only)

"AllWindowsFront" — bring all *Mathematica* windows in front of any non-*Mathematica* windows (NeXT only)

"MacintoshOpenDeskAccessory" — open a desk accessory. This token requires a parameter, the name of the desk accessory you want to open.

▪ File/notebook operations

"New" — create new Notebook window
"Open" — open the Open File dialog box
"Close" — close front window, with "Do you want to save?" dialog if needed
"Save" — save the front window, or open Save As dialog if Untitled
"SaveRename" — open Save As dialog
"SaveRenameSpecial" — save the selected notebook in a specified non-notebook file format. This token requires a parameter, which may be one of the following:

> "V20Notebook" — a pre-V3 format notebook file
> "Text" — plain text in $SystemCharacterEncoding
> "InputText" — plain ASCII text
> "Package" — plain ASCII text with any cells that do not have the options Cell
Evaluatable→True and InitializationCell→True in kernel comments
> "CellExpression" — one or more Cell[] expressions
> "NotebookExpression" — a Notebook[] expression
> "CompleteNotebook" — a Notebook[] expression plus all the comments, file
outline cache, etc., that are part of a notebook file
> "PostScript" — PostScript graphic image
> "EPS" — Encapsulated PostScript graphic image
> "Illustrator" — Adobe Illustrator compatible graphic image
> "PICT" — Macintosh PICT format graphic, individual drawing commands
> "PICTBitmap" — Macintosh PICT format graphic containing one bitmap drawing
command
> "PICTEmbeddedPS" — Macintosh PICT format with one bitmap and embedded
PostScript
> "MGF" — *Mathematica* Graphics Format (bitmap)
> "PICS" — Sequence of PICT resources
> "QuickTime" — Apple QuickTime animation
> "RTF" — Rich Text Format
> "EMF" — Enhanced Metafile (Windows only)
> "WMF" — Windows Metafile (Windows only)
> "TIFF" — Tagged Image File Format
> "WAV" — Wave (Windows only)

"NotebookMail" — mail notebook (Windows only)
"NotebookMailSelection" — mail selected text (Windows only)
"OpenSpecial" — open Open Special dialog
"OpenSelection" — use selected text as file name to open
"Import" — open the system standard Open File dialog. The contents of the selected file will be inserted at the current selection/insertion point
"SystemPrintOptionsDialog" — open system's Page Setup dialog
"PrintOptionsDialog" — open *Mathematica* print options dialog
"HeadersFootersDialog" — open headers/footers dialog
"PrintDialog" — open Print Job dialog
"PrintSelectionDialog" — open Print Job dialog for printing the selection
"FrontEndQuit" — quit front end, asking to save files if needed
"FrontEndQuitNonInteractive" — quit front end without asking anything
"StackWindows" — arrange windows in the same positions they would be in if they were newly created windows opened in the order they are currently stacked in

"TileWindowsWide" — arrange windows to make them all visible, preferring width over height

"TileWindowsTall" — arrange windows to make them all visible, preferring height over width

"WindowMiniaturize" — miniaturize the selected notebook window (NeXT and Windows only)

"NotebookReleaseHold" — convert all automatic objects (**CounterBox**, **ValueBox**) into plain text reflecting their current values

■ Text/editing operations

"Undo" — undo last action, if possible

"Cut" — cut selected text to clipboard

"Copy" — copy selected text to clipboard

"Paste" — paste clipboard over selection

"PasteApply" — paste clipboard over selection, substituting selection into any \[Selection-Placeholder] characters in the clipboard data

"PasteApplyNoAutoScroll" — same, but don't autoscroll to make selection visible

"Clear" — delete selected text

"PasteDiscard" — delete selected text without putting it in the undo buffer

"PasteDiscardNoAutoScroll" — same, but don't autoscroll to make selection visible

"SelectionSaveSpecial" — save the selected data to a file in a specified format. This token requires a parameter: see next token for a list of possible values.

"CopySpecial" — copy the selected data to the clipboard in a specified format. This token requires a parameter, which may be one of the following:

    "V20Notebook" — a pre-V3 format notebook file

    "Text" — plain text in $SystemCharacterEncoding

    "StyledText" — text with font information in platform-specific clipboard format

    "InputText" — plain ASCII text

    "Package" — plain ASCII text with any cells that do not have the options Cell Evaluatable→True and InitializationCell→True in kernel comments

    "CellExpression" — one or more Cell[] expressions

    "NotebookExpression" — a Notebook[] expression

    "CompleteNotebook" — a Notebook[] expression plus all the comments, file outline cache, etc., that are part of a notebook file

    "PostScript" — PostScript graphic image

    "EPS" — Encapsulated PostScript graphic image

    "Illustrator" — Adobe Illustrator compatible graphic image

    "PICT" — Macintosh PICT format graphic, individual drawing commands

    "PICTBitmap" — Macintosh PICT format graphic containing one bitmap drawing command

    "PICTEmbeddedPS" — Macintosh PICT format with one bitmap and embedded PostScript

    "MGF" — *Mathematica* Graphics Format (bitmap)

    "PICS" — sequence of PICT resources

    "QuickTime" — Apple QuickTime animation

    "RTF" — Rich Text Format

`"EMF"` — Enhanced Metafile (Windows only)

`"WMF"` — Windows Metafile (Windows only)

`"TIFF"` — Tagged Image File Format

`"WAV"` — Wave (Windows only)

`"Style"` — set the currently selected text or cells to have a particular style. This token requires a parameter, the style to be set.

`"SelectAll"` — select all cells in the notebook

`"InsertObject"` — open the system dialog to insert an OLE object (Windows only)

`"CreateInlineCell"` — create an inline cell: If the selection is in a text cell, a typeset cell is created; in V3.1 and later, if the selection is in a typeset cell a text cell is created

`"InsertRawExpression"` — open a dialog box that allows you to type in an arbitrary box expression, which will then be inserted at the current insertion point

`"Balance"` — extend the current selection to include the next pair of matching parentheses, brackets, or curly brackets

`"Indent"` — indent the selected line(s) by one tab

`"DeleteIndent"` — remove one tab from each selected line

`"SimilarCellBelow"` — create a new cell below the selected one; the new cell has the same style and all the same options as the selected one. The selection is placed in the newly created cell

`"DuplicatePreviousInput"` — insert at the current insertion point a copy of the nearest Input style cell above the current selection

`"DuplicatePreviousOutput"` — insert at the current insertion point a copy of the nearest Output style cell above the current selection

`"Linebreak"` — insert a linebreak/return character

`"ShortNameDelimiter"` — insert a ⁝ character (usually associated with the ESC key)

`"Tab"` — move to the next `\[Placeholder]` or `\[SelectionPlaceholder]` character, if one is present; otherwise insert a Tab character

`"DeletePrevious"` — delete character to the left of the insertion point

`"DeleteNext"` — delete character to the right of the insertion point

`"DeletePreviousWord"` — delete word to the left of the insertion point

`"DeleteNextWord"` — delete word to the right of the insertion point

`"DeleteLineBeginning"` — delete characters from the insertion point to the beginning of the line

`"DeleteLineEnd"` — delete characters from the insertion point to the end of the line

`"DeletePreviousExpression"` — delete sub-expression to the left of the insertion point

`"DeleteNextExpression"` — delete sub-expression to the right of the insertion point

`"DeleteParagraphBeginning"` — delete characters from the insertion point to the beginning of the paragraph (defined by a hard return)

`"DeleteParagraphEnd"` — delete characters from the insertion point to the end of the paragraph (defined by a hard return)

`"DeleteCellBeginning"` — delete characters from the insertion point to the beginning of the cell

`"DeleteCellEnd"` — delete characters from the insertion point to the end of the cell

`"InsertChar"` — insert a character at the current insertion point. This token requires a parameter, the character to be inserted. The character is assumed to be in the character encoding of the font at the insertion point.

`"InsertUnicodeChar"` — insert a character at the current insertion point. This token requires a parameter, the character to be inserted. The character is assumed to be in Unicode encoding.

■ Typeset structure editing

"Fraction" — create a `FractionBox` and fill the numerator with the current selection, or with the sub-expression to the left of the selection if it is an insertion point

"Radical" — create a `SqrtBox` and fill the base with the current selection, or with a placeholder if the selection is an insertion point

"Superscript" — create a `SuperscriptBox` and fill the base with the current selection, or with the sub-expression to the left of the selection if it is an insertion point

"Subscript" — create a `SubscriptBox` and fill the base with the current selection, or with the sub-expression to the left of the selection if it is an insertion point

"Otherscript" — move to the "other" script position; if the selection is in a superscript, move to the subscript; if the selection is in a subscript, move to the superscript; if the selection is in an overscript, move to the underscript; if the selection is in an underscript, move to the overscript

"Above" — create an `OverscriptBox` and fill the base with the current selection, or with the sub-expression to the left of the selection if it is an insertion point

"Below" — create an `UnderscriptBox` and fill the base with the current selection, or with the sub-expression to the left of the selection if it is an insertion point

"NewColumn" — add a new column to an existing `GridBox`, or create a `GridBox` if none exists

"NewRow" — add a new row to an existing `GridBox`, or create a `GridBox` if none exists

"NudgeLeft" — add an `AdjustmentBox`, or modify an existing one, to shift the selected expression one point to the left

"NudgeRight" — add an `AdjustmentBox`, or modify an existing one, to shift the selected expression one point to the right

"NudgeUp" — add an `AdjustmentBox`, or modify an existing one, to shift the selected expression one point up

"NudgeDown" — add an `AdjustmentBox`, or modify an existing one, to shift the selected expression one point down

"RemoveAdjustments" — remove any `AdjustmentBoxes` in the selected expression

"Make2D" — parse any linear syntax in the selection and substitute the corresponding typeset boxes

"ReplaceParent" — take the currently selected sub-expression and use it to replace the next expression level up. Any other children of the parent expression are deleted.

"DeleteInvisible" — similar to `"ReplaceParent"` except remove one layer of invisible (formatting) box. Box types removed are: `StyleBox`, `LineWrapBox`, `ErrorBox`, `Adjust`- `mentBox`, `TagBox`, `InterpretationBox`, and `FormBox`.

■ Cell operations

"CellSplit" — split cell into 2 or 3 cells at the current selection

"CellMerge" — merge the selected cells into a single cell

"CellGroup" — group the currently selected cells (works only if automatic grouping is turned off)

"CellUngroup" — ungroup the currently selected cells (works only if automatic grouping is turned off)

"OpenCloseGroup" — open the selected group(s) if they are closed, or close them if they are open. This command affects only the outermost level of selected groups, not subgroups.

"SelectionOpenAllGroups" — open all groups and subgroups in the current selection

"SelectionCloseAllGroups" — close all groups and subgroups in the current selection

"FixCellHeight" — assign a CellSize option to the currently selected cells to fix their height at the height they currently have

"FixCellWidth" — assign a CellSize option to the currently selected cells to fix their width at the width they currently have

"ToggleGrayBox" — set or unset the options CellFrame and Background to give the selected cells a gray box, or remove it if they already have one

"CellLabelsToTags" — for all the selected cells, creates a CellTag for each cell matching that cell's CellLabel

"ToggleShowExpression" — convert all the selected cells to Cell[] expression form, or convert them back to display form if they are already in expression form

"SelectionConvert" — convert the selected cells to a new format type. If the conversion is between two *Mathematica* syntax forms (e.g. InputForm to StandardForm, Standard·Form to TraditionalForm, etc.), the data for each cell is sent to the kernel to be re-formatted in the new format type. This token requires a parameter to specify the new format type. Possible values are:

>"InputForm" — linear text
>"OutputForm" — old-style 2-D text format
>"StandardForm", "TraditionalForm", other typeset format type — typeset format
>"PostScript" — PostScript graphic
>"PICT" — Macintosh PICT format graphic, individual drawing commands
>"PICTBitmap" — Macintosh PICT format graphic containing one bitmap drawing

command
>"PICTEmbeddedPS" — Macintosh PICT format with one bitmap and embedded

PostScript
>"QuickTime" — Apple QuickTime animation
>"Metafile" — Windows Metafile format

"SelectionDisplayAs" — redisplay the selected cells in a new format type. This operation seems similar to "SelectionConvert", but is actually quite different. The data is never sent to the kernel to be re-formatted; instead it is just reinterpreted locally in the new form. This token requires a parameter to specify the new format type. Possible values are:

>"InputForm" — linear text
>"OutputForm" — old-style 2D text format
>"StandardForm", "TraditionalForm", other typeset format type — typeset format

■ Buttons and palettes

"CreateButtonBox" — wrap a ButtonBox around the current selection. This token requires a parameter to specify the ButtonStyle option to be used by the new button.

"CreateCustomButtonBox" — wrap a ButtonBox around the current selection, then open the Edit Button Box dialog

"EditButtonBoxDialog" — open the Edit Button Box dialog

"GeneratePalette" — create a palette window containing a copy of the currently selected cells (works only if the selection is in a non-palette notebook)

"GenerateNotebook" — create a new notebook window containing a copy of the contents of the currently selected (frontmost) palette window (works only if the selected window is a palette notebook)

■ Graphics

"SoundPlay" — play all sounds in the current selected cells, in order

"GraphicsRender" — re-render all selected graphics

"GenerateImageCaches" — render all graphics in the notebook that need rendering, and save the notebook after rendering each one

"GraphicsOriginalSize" — restore all selected graphics to their default size

"SelectionAnimate" — animate the selected graphics

"GraphicsAlign" — open the Align Selected Graphics dialog box

■ Evaluation

"DeleteGeneratedCells" — delete all output in the selected notebook (Output, Graphics, Message, Print, etc., style cells—any cell with the option GeneratedCell→True)

"EvaluateCells" — evaluate the selected input cells, putting the output from each into new cells below the input cell

"EvaluateNextCell" — if the current selection is an input cell, evaluate it; otherwise move the selection to the next input cell. By using this command repeatedly, you can evaluate each input in a notebook in order, pausing to look at each one before evaluating it.

"Evaluate" — evaluate the selection in-place. The output is pasted over the input, replacing it

"SubsessionEvaluateCells" — interrupt the current evaluation, initiate a kernel Dialog session, evaluate the selected cells in that dialog, then resume the main evaluation

"EvaluateCells:Reminder" — like "EvaluateCells" but first puts up a dialog reminding users that they could use Shift-Return instead (this token is sometimes used for the menu command while Shift-Return itself uses "EvaluateCells")

"EvaluateNextCell:Reminder" — like "EvaluateNextCell" but first puts up a dialog reminding users that they could use Shift-Enter instead

"Evaluate_Reminder" — same as "Evaluate" but first puts up a dialog reminding users that they could use Command-Return instead

"SubsessionEvaluateCells:Reminder" — like "SubsessionEvaluateCells" but first puts up a dialog reminding users that they could use Shift-Option-Return instead

"RemoveFromEvaluationQueue" — prevent the evaluation of any selected cells currently scheduled to be evaluated but not yet actually being processed by the kernel

"EvaluateNotebook" — evaluate all the input cells in the current notebook

"EvaluateInitialization" — evaluate all the initialization cells in the current notebook

"CompleteSelection" — send the current selection (or the token to the left of the selection if the selection is an insertion point) to the kernel to get a list of possible completions, then put the completions in a popup menu. In V3.1 and later, if the characters to the left of the selected token are "\[", the completions are instead pulled from the table of character long names; if the character to the left is ⁚, the completions are pulled from the table of short names.

"TemplateSelection" — send the current selection (or the token to the left of the selection if the selection is an insertion point) to the kernel to get an example of the use of the function. If the selected token is not unique, a popup menu of possible completions is presented first.

"EvaluatorStart" — start the specified evaluator. This packet requires a parameter, which can be the name of the evaluator or Automatic if you want the default evaluator.

"EvaluatorQuit" — kill the specified evaluator. This packet requires a parameter, which can be the name of the evaluator or Automatic if you want the default evaluator.

"EvaluatorInterrupt" — interrupt the specified evaluator, resulting in the kernel interrupt dialog box. This packet requires a parameter, which can be the name of the evaluator or Automatic if you want the default evaluator.

"EvaluatorAbort" — abort the current evaluation in the specified evaluator. This packet requires a parameter, which can be the name of the evaluator or Automatic if you want the default evaluator.

"EnterSubsession" — initiate a subsession in the specified evaluator. This packet requires a parameter, which can be the name of the evaluator or Automatic if you want the default evaluator.

"ExitSubsession" — terminate a subsession in the specified evaluator. This packet requires a parameter, which can be the name of the evaluator or Automatic if you want the default evaluator.

⚠ **"SelectTerminalWindow"** — open a terminal window to the machine specified by a particular evaluator name. This packet requires a parameter, the evaluator name. The evaluator must be one that specifies a connection to a remote UNIX host. (Note that, despite the packet's name, it does *not* select an already existing terminal window. It always opens a new one.)

"SelectGeneratedCells" — select all the output cells generated by the currently running evaluation

■ Navigation/selection

"HyperlinkGoBack" — return to the last point a hyperlink was clicked on

"SelectionScroll" — scroll to bring the top of the current selection near the top of the window, if it is not currently visible

"OpenSelectionParents" — open any groups that contain cells that are currently selected

"ScrollPageUp" — scroll up by one page

"ScrollPageDown" — scroll down by one page

"ScrollLineUp" — scroll up by one line

"ScrollLineDown" — scroll down by one line

"ScrollNotebookStart" — scroll to top of notebook

"ScrollNotebookEnd" — scroll to end of notebook

"MovePrevious" — move the insertion point left by one character

"MoveNext" — move the insertion point right by one character

"MovePreviousWord" — move the insertion point left by one word

"MoveNextWord" — move the insertion point right by one word

"MovePreviousLine" — move the insertion point up by one line

"MoveNextLine" — move the insertion point down by one line

"MovePreviousExpression" — move the insertion point left by one sub-expression

"MoveNextExpression" — move the insertion point right by one sub-expression

"MovePreviousParagraph" — move the insertion point up by one paragraph (defined by a hard-return)

"MoveNextParagraph" — move the insertion point down by one paragraph (defined by a hard-return)

"MovePreviousCell" — move the insertion point up by one cell

"MoveNextCell" — move the insertion point down by one cell

"MoveLineBeginning" — move the insertion point to the start of the current line

"MoveLineEnd" — move the insertion point to the end of the current line

"MoveExpressionBeginning" — move the insertion point to the start of the current sub-expression

"MoveExpressionEnd" — move the insertion point to the end of the current sub-expression

"MoveParagraphBeginning" — move the insertion point to the start of the current paragraph (defined by a hard-return)

"MoveParagraphEnd" — move the insertion point to the end of the current paragraph (defined by a hard-return)

"MoveCellBeginning" — move the insertion point to the start of the current cell

"MoveCellEnd" — move the insertion point to the end of the current cell

"MoveNextPlaceHolder" — select the next \[Placeholder] or \[SelectionPlace᠌ holder] character after the end of the current selection (does not go beyond the current cell)

"MovePreviousPlaceHolder" — select the first \[Placeholder] or \[Selection᠌ Placeholder] character before the end of the current selection (does not go beyond the current cell)

"SelectPrevious" — extend the selection by one character to the left

"SelectNext" — extend the selection by one character to the right

"SelectPreviousWord" — extend the selection by one word to the left

"SelectNextWord" — extend the selection by one word to the right

"SelectPreviousLine" — extend the selection by one line up

"SelectNextLine" — extend the selection by one line down

"SelectLineBeginning" — extend the selection to the beginning of the line

"SelectLineEnd" — extend the selection to the end of the line

"SelectPreviousExpression" — extend the selection by one sub-expression to the left

"SelectNextExpression" — extend the selection by one sub-expression to the right

"SelectParagraphEnd" — extend the selection to the beginning of the paragraph (defined by a hard return)

"SelectParagraphBeginning" — extend the selection to the end of the paragraph (defined by a hard return)

"SelectCellBeginning" — extend the selection to the beginning of the cell

"SelectCellEnd" — extend the selection to the end of the cell

"ExpandSelection" — extend the selection to include the next higher level sub-expression (typeset cells only)

"FirstChildOfSelection" — select the first sub-expression that is part of the current selection

▪ Find/replace

"FindDialog" — open the Find dialog box

"SelectionSetFind" — enter the current selection as the find string

"Replace" — paste the replace string over the current selection

"ReplaceFind" — paste the replace string over the current selection then find next occurrence of find string

"ReplaceAll" — replace all occurrences of find string with replace string

"CreateIndexDialog" — open the Make Index dialog box

"CellTagsFind" — search for a keyword in the CellTags of all the cells in the notebook. This token requires a parameter, the keyword to search for.

"FindNextMisspelling" — select the next misspelled word

▪ Styles and style sheets

"EditStyleDefinitions" — edit the style definitions for the current notebook. If the notebook has private definitions the style notebook is just opened. If the notebook uses a shared style sheet, you first get a dialog asking whether you want to edit the shared styles or import a private copy.

"ClearCellOptions" — open the dialog asking whether you want to remove all options from the selection, or from the selection and all sub-objects within the selection

"RestoreDefaultStyles" — put up dialog asking whether you want to switch the notebook back to default styles (Default.nb is the shared style sheet for the notebook)

"PlainFont" — remove from the current selection any setting of the FontWeight, Font-Slant, FontTracking, and FontVariations options

"StyleOther" — open the dialog box allowing you to enter a style name to be applied to the current selection

"StyleDefinitionsOther" — open standard system Open File dialog box to select a style sheet for the current notebook

▪ Experimental/unsupported tokens

⚠ **"SelectionSpeak"** — speak the currently selected text, using text-to-speech system software (Macintosh and Windows only; requires special system software)

⚠ **"SelectionSpeakSummary"** — speak a shortened description of the current selection using text-to-speech system software (Macintosh and Windows only; requires special system software)

▪ Getting or setting an option value

Many things in the front end are controlled by option settings, including some that you might not associate with options. Anything that is a parameter, setting, or preference, is an option. Options can be associated with the front end as a whole (preference settings), with a notebook, with a cell, or with individual words and characters within a cell.

Any option can be set at a level higher than the level it is defined at. For example, the **Font-Color** option, which controls the color of text, is defined at the level of individual characters, but it can be set for a whole cell, a whole notebook, or globally for the entire front end. When an option is set at a high level, its value is inherited by all the items below it. (See Chapter 54 for more information about the style inheritance mechanism.)

To set options associated with the front end, evaluate:

```
SetOptions[$FrontEnd, options]
```

For example, to change the color of all text in all notebooks (except for text that has an individually specified color), evaluate:

```
SetOptions[$FrontEnd, FontColor -> RGBColor[1, 0, 0]];
```

■ Getting the value of a front end global variable

The front end supports a number of global variables, similar to the $-variables in the kernel. For example, in the kernel **$TopDirectory** gives the path name of the kernel's main installation directory:

> **$TopDirectory**

> Rebecca:Apps:Mathematica 4.0

The front end has an analogous variable, also called **$TopDirectory**, but, conceptually, in the **FrontEnd`** context. In V3.1 and later, you can access these values directly just by evaluating the symbols, for example:

> **FrontEnd`$TopDirectory**

> FrontEnd`FileName[{$RootDirectory, "Rebecca", "Omega2
>   .3"}, CharacterEncoding -> "MacintoshRoman"]

See Chapter 65 for a description of the **FrontEnd`FileName** object. (The kernel uses a more primitive, non-portable representation of files names, though this may change in future versions.)

Notice that in the example above the two directories are not the same. This is because, on the machine this example was run on, the front end and kernel are installed in different locations. This is perfectly OK, if somewhat unusual.

In versions before V3.1, you can get the value of front end globals manually, using the **Value** packet. Here is a utility function that does this for you:

```
Attributes[GetFrontEndGlobal] = {HoldAll};
GetFrontEndGlobal[var_] :=
  (LinkWrite[$ParentLink, FrontEnd`Value[
      ToString[HoldForm[var]]]]; LinkRead[$ParentLink])
```

It gives the same value as above:

> **GetFrontEndGlobal[FrontEnd`$TopDirectory]**

> FrontEnd`FileName[{$RootDirectory, "Rebecca", "Omega2
>   .3"}, CharacterEncoding -> "MacintoshRoman"]

Here is a list of the global variables supported by the front end:

$UserName — the login name of the user running the front end
$MachineName — the network name of the machine on which the front end is running
$Version — the platform and 2-digit version number
$FullVersion — the platform and 4-digit version number
$VersionNumber — the 2-digit version number as a decimal number
$System — the type of computer system

$ReleaseNumber — the second digit of the version number

$MinorReleaseNumber — the third digit of the version number

$CreationDate — the date the front end was compiled

$MachineID — a unique number computed from the properties of the system

$MachineType — the general type of hardware

$OperatingSystem — the name of the operating system

$ProcessorType — the name/model number of the CPU

$ProgramName — the name of the front end application program

$SystemID — a short form of $MachineType.

$TopDirectory — the main directory containing all the *Mathematica* application files

$PreferencesDirectory — the directory containing user preference settings files

$LaunchDirectory — the directory from which *Mathematica* was launched (often the same as $TopDirectory)

$HomeDirectory — the user's home directory, or the system preferences directory on systems that do not support separate user home directories

$InitialDirectory — the current directory when the front end was started. Usually the same as $TopDirectory.

$SoftwareExpirationDate — the date, if any, at which this version of the front end becomes invalid and non-functional

$SoftwareExpirationDateString — a string giving the above date plus a label

$LicenseExpirationDate — the date, if any, at which the password currently in use will stop working

$LicenseExpirationDateString — a string giving the above date plus a label

$ExpirationDate — the earlier of $SoftwareExpirationDate or $LicenseExpirationDate

$ExpirationString — a string giving the above date plus a label

PageCellTags — the union of all the cell tags on the current page (valid only inside a ValueBox, and only when printing)

FileName — the file name of the current notebook

PathName — the full path name of the current notebook

MemoryInUse — the amount of memory currently being used by the front end

FreeMemory — the amount of memory still available for use by the front end (Macintosh only)

ClipboardMemoryInUse — the amount of memory used by the current contents of the clipboard)

Date — the current date as numbers (day, month, and year)

DateLong — the current date and names and numbers

Time — the current time (hours, minutes, and seconds)

Year — the current year

ShortYear — the current 2-digit year

Month — the number of the current month

MonthName — the name of the current month

ShortMonthName — the 3-letter abbreviation of the current month name

Day — the number of the current day

DayName — the name of the current day

ShortDayName — the 3-letter abbreviation of the current day name

Hour — the current hour

Minute — the current minute

Second — the current second

Chapter **64**

What options can I use to control the *Mathematica* front end?

In V4.0, about 700 individual options control some aspect of the appearance or behavior of objects in the front end. To find the documentation for a particular option, open the Help Browser, click on the "Other Information" button near the top, then type in the name of the option. Click on the "Front End Options" item in the first list column: You will get a categorized list of all the options to browse. Users of the electronic edition of this book can click this Front End Options hyperlink to go directly there.

A good way to become familiar with the options available in the front end is to open the Option Inspector and browse through the categories and subcategories. Many options have names that make further explanation fairly superfluous (e.g., **FontSize**). To find out what possible values an option can take, look at the icon to the right of each option. If it's a check box, the option is a Boolean (True/False) option. If it's a pull-down menu, click on it to see the possible values. If it's a funny looking icon that the authors think looks like a miniature dialog box, click on it to get a dialog box in which you can specify a value (it might be a color selector dialog, an open-file dialog, or a specialized dialog for a particular option).

For more information on using the Option Inspector, see Chapter 55.

Chapter **65**

How do I use file names in programs?

How to use file names might not sound like a topic for a whole chapter, but difficulties quickly mount. (Don't Panic; the punchline is that almost all of these difficulties are handled automatically by *Mathematica*. Unless you are creating complex programs containing file names with non-Roman letters—and plan to transfer them to a different brand of computer—you do not need to read this chapter.)

As motivation, consider an interconnected set of notebooks (such as a book)—a number of files in different directories with hyperlinks in and between the notebooks in the set. These hyperlinks of course contain file names. (See Chapter 61 for a discussion of hyperlinks.) If the files are not all in the same directory, then the hyperlinks must also contain directory names. The traditional method of recording the location of a file within a certain directory or directories is with a *full path name*, where directory and file names a combined in one string with a delimiter character separating each directory or file name component of the path.

The most obvious difficulty is the delimiter character, because all major branches of the computer world have picked different delimiter characters (**/** in UNIX, **** in Windows, and **:** in Macintosh).

Consider copying this collection of notebooks from the Macintosh on which it was created to a Windows system. If the hyperlinks are to continue working, the file and directory names must be recorded in a way that is platform-independent.

While there are many possible ways around the delimiter problem, the most obvious *Mathematica*-style solution is to use an expression to break the path into individual components, eliminating the need for a delimiter character. For file names representing notebooks in the front end, the format is:

> **FrontEnd`FileName[{"*dir1*", "*dir2*", …}, "*filename*"]**

Although quite verbose, this format provides an extremely clean specification of a path and is particularly easy to manipulate using ordinary *Mathematica* commands, since the individual elements of the path can be addressed as elements of a list.

To represent file names of files in the kernel, you can use the same format with the **ToFile** **Name** command. This returns a platform-specific file name appropriate for whatever platform you are currently running on. The return value can then be passed to any of the kernel's file manipulation commands.

```
ToFileName[{"dir1", "dir2"}, "filename"]
```

```
:dir1:dir2:filename
```

Another area of disagreement among platforms is how they represent absolute vs. relative path names. For example, on UNIX a leading **/** indicates an absolute path, while on Macintosh a leading **:** indicates a relative path. In *Mathematica*, there are instead symbols that represent the root directory and the current directory. These symbols are used as the first element of a directory list to indicate explicitly whether the path is absolute or relative.

The following symbols can be used:

$RootDirectory — the root of the file system
$TopDirectory — the directory containing the main *Mathematica* files
$HomeDirectory — your home directory (UNIX and NT systems only)
Directory[] — the current directory (for hyperlinks, the directory containing the notebook where the hyperlink button appears)
ParentDirectory[] — the parent of current directory
ParentDirectory[*dir***]** — the parent of the specified directory

Here is an absolute path:

```
FrontEnd`FileName[{$RootDirectory, "dir1", "dir2"}, "filename"]
```

A relative path:

```
FrontEnd`FileName[{Directory[], "dir1", "dir2"}, "filename"]
```

A path that starts at the current directory, goes up two levels in the hierarchy, then down into another directory:

```
FrontEnd`FileName[
  {ParentDirectory[ParentDirectory[]], "dir"}, "filename"]
```

A path that refers to a file in a directory that is at the same level as the directory containing the main *Mathematica* files:

```
FrontEnd`FileName[
  {ParentDirectory[$TopDirectory], "dir"}, "filename"]
```

On Windows systems, **$RootDirectory** doesn't actually translate into anything in the ultimate file name. Instead, it is a signal that what follows is either a drive letter or a UNC (Universal Naming Convention) name of a network share. For example:

```
FrontEnd`FileName[{$RootDirectory, "C:", "dir"}, "filename"]

FrontEnd`FileName[
  {$RootDirectory, "\\\\machine\\share", "dir"}, "filename"]
```

Note in particular that you have to double the ordinary number of backslashes in the network disk name. This is because inside a quoted string, backslash is an escape character, and if you want to represent an actual backslash, you have to use ****.

Another complication arises if file names contain anything other than plain ASCII Roman letters (e.g., accented characters, Kanji). Such file names may be represented differently on different platforms. For example, the file name "GröbnerExamples.nb" will employ different character codes to represent the ö character depending on what platforms it is on.

When a file with a name containing such an accented character is copied from one platform to another the character code contained in the file name will not be translated, so the file name appearing in the Finder/File Manager will be incorrect on the new platform.

In *Mathematica*, all characters are represented by Unicode character codes, which are *not* platform dependent. The expression

```
FrontEnd`FileName[
  {ParentDirectory[$TopDirectory], "dir"}, "GröbnerExamples.nb"]
```

will continue to represent the character ö correctly regardless of what platform it is on.

You might think that if you transfer both the file and this expression representing it, you might break the connection, because while the expression remains correct, the file name itself changes.

The answer lies in how *Mathematica* translates the Unicode characters in the expression into the character codes communicated to the operating system when referring to this file. To do this translation, it must consult a particular mapping between Unicode and file system character codes (called an encoding table).

To preserve the connection between expression and file, the **FrontEnd`FileName** object must record not only the Unicode character code of the accented characters, but also what encoding table should be used to translate the Unicode into character codes passed to the system. You can use an option to do this (this option is added automatically when you use, for example, the **Create Hyperlink...** menu command):

```
FileName`FrontEnd[{"dir1", "dir2"},
  "GröbnerExamples.nb", CharacterEncoding -> "MacintoshRoman"]
```

This expression will correctly locate a file named GröbnerBasis.nb on a Macintosh, and it will correctly locate a file that *was* called GröbnerBasis.nb before it was copied to a Windows machine, but which is displayed in Windows with a completely different character in place of the ö. This allows the hyperlink to continue working.

Of course, if you fix the file name manually to use the proper character, you will also have to modify the file name expression manually.

In general, all this complexity is hidden behind the fact that it just works. The front end automatically constructs **FrontEnd`FileName** objects anywhere a file name is recorded in a notebook document (hyperlinks, style sheets, etc.). This means that hyperlinks are automatically portable across platforms, and at worst need to be modified only if the file names themselves are manually modified (to correct character encodings) after copying.

Chapter **66**

I'd rather not see complex numbers. Can you help me?

Jerry: Many math teachers that I have spoken to have complained that symbolic algebra programs sometimes do too much. An example is solving the equation $x^2 = -1$. A teacher of first year algebra often wants the students to learn that there is no solution for such an equation.

Theo: Such a teacher should perhaps first consider a new line of work.

Jerry: Nasty, nasty.

Theo: Well, it just makes life harder for everyone when people try to live in a fantasy world where there are only real numbers.

Jerry: Now that you're a parent of, what, 16 children, I can use an analogy for you: You would certainly want to protect your child from falling off the edge of a steep cliff. Some teachers feel that exposing young students to complex numbers too early is in the same category.

Theo: More like not telling them about the existence of steep cliffs, thereby improving the odds that when they first see one they will fall off it straightaway.

Jerry: I'm sure everyone is fascinated by the philosophical discussion, but why can't *Mathematica* respond the way these teachers want it to?

Theo: Because it's mathematically impossible and violates some of the most basic laws of man and nature, that's why. For example, by divine law, quartics have four solutions:

```
Solve[x⁴ == 16, x] // TableForm
```

$x \to -2$
$x \to -2\,\mathrm{I}$
$x \to 2\,\mathrm{I}$
$x \to 2$

Also, as Moses said on the mount, you can't make a plot of the cube root if the plot domain includes negative numbers:

```
Plot[∛x, {x, -5, 5}];
```

Plot::plnr : $x^{1/3}$ is not a machine-size real number at x = -5..

Plot::plnr : $x^{1/3}$ is not a machine-size real number at x = -4.59433.

Plot::plnr : $x^{1/3}$ is not a machine-size real number at x = -4.15191.

General::stop : Further output of
        Plot::plnr will be suppressed during this calculation.

There is no visible left branch of this curve, because the principal value of the cube root of a negative number is complex:

```
N[∛-8]
```

1. + 1.73205 I

Jerry: Many teachers will expect the curve above to have a left branch to it which is a mirror image about the origin.

Theo: Well, if you insist, a passable simulation can be attempted. In fact, there is a built-in package, which you should never use, that implements this. To load it, execute:

```
Needs["Miscellaneous`RealOnly`"];
```

(Note that the two single quotes used here are "back quotes" usually found on the same key with ~. They are *not* the single quotes found on the double-quote key.)

After loading this package we find, thankfully, that quartics still have four solutions. But to shield the eyes of the innocent, two of them are blanked out:

```
Solve[x⁴ == 16, x] // TableForm
```

Nonreal::warning : Nonreal number encountered.

```
x → -2
x → 2
x → Nonreal
x → Nonreal
```

Furthermore, against all mathematical convention, the principal values of roots are negative numbers, where possible:

$$N\left[\sqrt[3]{-8}\right]$$

-2.

which in turn makes it possible to make this plot:

$$Plot\left[\sqrt[3]{x}, \{x, -5, 5\}\right];$$

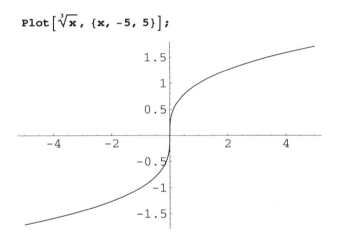

Jerry: Good! So people now have a choice. That's big of you.

Theo: Actually, it was George Beck who wrote the package. Don't blame me.

Chapter **67**

The Units Calculator

Mathematica's ability to handle units of measure is such an advantage that you may soon come to prefer *Mathematica* over your calculator even for simple numerical arithmetic.

Load *Mathematica's* standard unit conversion package with the following command:

Needs["Miscellaneous`Units`"]

(Note that the two single quotes used here are "back quotes" usually found on the same key with ~. They are *not* the single quotes found on the double-quote key.)

Include units in your *Mathematica* input pretty much as you would write them, though remember that as with other built-in *Mathematica* functions, all standard unit names must be capitalized. And, to avoid trouble, stick to the singular form of unit names. For example, while the package accepts **Feet** or **Foot**, it takes only **Acre**, not **Acres**.

For example, to calculate an area, we enter:

12 Foot × 16 Foot

192 Foot^2

(The × sign is an alternate character for multiplication in *Mathematica*. It is equivalent to * or space, and can be entered by typing ⎡ESC⎤*⎡ESC⎤. You need not use × when multiplying terms that include units, but they seem to look particularly nice when you do.)

To calculate the distance traveled in a certain time, multiply the speed by the time:

$$85 \; \frac{\text{Meter}}{\text{Second}} \times 10 \; \text{Second}$$

850 Meter

In these examples, *Mathematica* has not done anything special with the unit names; it has treated them as arbitrary symbols. It will work with any units you like, sensible or otherwise:

$$10 \, \textbf{duck} \times 85 \, \frac{\textbf{egg}}{\textbf{duck Year}}$$

$$\frac{850 \, \text{egg}}{\text{Year}}$$

Notice how *Mathematica* has meaningfully and cleverly cancelled **duck**, retaining **egg** and **Year**. Notice also that we didn't capitalize **egg** and **duck**, indicating that they are user-defined symbols, not built-in.

Mathematica's ability to handle units is very useful in many symbolic calculations. If at the end of a calculation you don't have the units you expected (e.g., a volume when you expected an area), you know that you have probably made a mistake somewhere along the way, or that your calculation does not match physical reality.

Beyond simply keeping track of units, the **Units** package also allows conversions among a very large number of standard units of measure. The **Convert** function converts both simple and compound units.

    Convert[60.0 Mile, Foot]

    316800. Foot

$$\textbf{Convert}\left[60.0 \, \frac{\textbf{Mile}}{\textbf{Hour}}, \frac{\textbf{Foot}}{\textbf{Second}}\right]$$

$$\frac{88. \, \text{Foot}}{\text{Second}}$$

(The formatting of the output is not ideal, but the meaning is clear.)

We have made a small palette for you that automates use of the Units package. Click here to open the palette. (Unfortunately, this palette is too complex for its source to be listed in the printed version of this book. If you don't have the electronic edition of this book, you can purchase it at http://www.mathware.com/BeginnersGuide.)

The palette will look something like this:

▷	**Length**
▷	**Area**
▷	**Volume**
▷	**Speed**
▷	**Weight**
▷	**Time**
▷	**Angle**
▷	**Numbers of things**

Open one of the sections in the palette by clicking the triangle to the left of its name. Let's try
Length:

▽	**Length**			
	Inch	Foot	Yard	Mile
	Centi Meter		Meter	Kilo Meter
	LightYear	Parsec	Furlong	Fathom

▷	**Area**
▷	**Volume**
▷	**Speed**
▷	**Weight**
▷	**Time**

Now, start by typing a number into your working notebook window:

    42.7

Click on a unit of length from the palette, say Mile:

    42.7 Mile

Mathematica assigns the unit to the number you entered. Now, click another unit of length,
say Foot:

    42.7 Mile → 225456. Foot

If you already have a unit specified, your input is converted to the new unit you clicked on. You can keep going; your cell is automatically duplicated each time, so you don't lose previous results.

42.7 Mile → 225456. Foot

225456. Foot → 68719. Meter

68719. Meter → 2.70547 × 10^6 Inch

2.70547 × 10^6 Inch → 37576. Fathom

37576. Fathom → 7.26378 × 10^{-12} LightYear

Chapter **68**

Surfaces of Revolution

Jerry: Many teachers, when shown a graphing program, ask if it can make surfaces of revolution. They want to specify a 2-D graph, specify an axis it should rotate about, and then see the resulting surface.

Theo: Fortunately, *Mathematica* can do this. First, you need to load a package, by evaluating the following command:

> **Needs["Graphics`SurfaceOfRevolution`"]**

(Note that the two single quotes used here are "back quotes" usually found on the same key with ~. They are *not* the single quotes found on the double-quote key.)

This package defines **SurfaceOfRevolution**. Here are some examples:

> **SurfaceOfRevolution[x², {x, 0, 1}];**

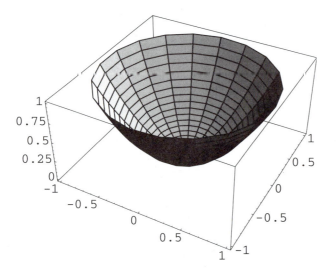

```
SurfaceOfRevolution[x², {x, 0, 5}];
```

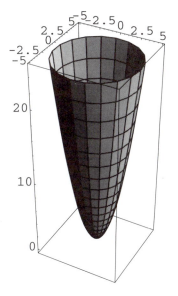

Mathematica by default rotates around the *z*-axis. Here is the same example with the default shown explicitly:

```
SurfaceOfRevolution[x², {x, 0, 1}, RevolutionAxis → {0, 0, 1}];
```

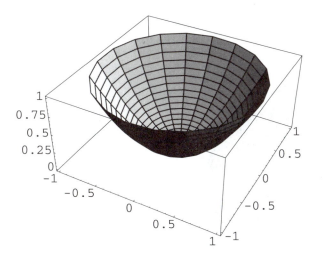

Since **{0,0,1}** told *Mathematica* to rotate about the *z*-axis you may want to guess what happens with **{1,0,0}**:

SurfaceOfRevolution[x², {x, 0, 1}, RevolutionAxis → {1, 0, 0}];

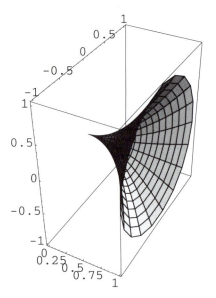

What about **{0,1,0}**?

SurfaceOfRevolution[x², {x, 0, 1}, RevolutionAxis → {0, 1, 0}];

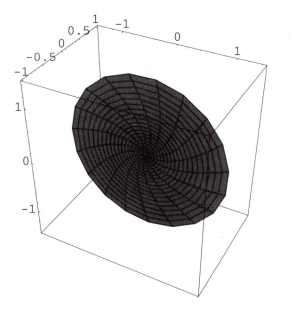

This is a bit hard to make out. It appears flat, but is it really? Let's look at it from a different viewpoint, from along the x-axis:

```
SurfaceOfRevolution[x², {x, 0, 1},
   RevolutionAxis → {0, 1, 0}, ViewPoint → {3, 0, 0}];
```

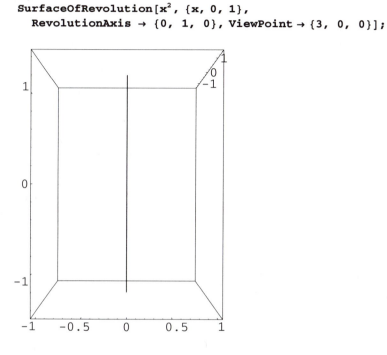

From this angle, all we see is a line, indicating that this must be a flat surface.

What's going on? **SurfaceOfRevolution** takes a function, which it plots in the *x-z* plane (not the *x-y* plane, which would be horizontal). It then rotates this plot around, by default, the z-axis. The **RevolutionAxis** option specifies an (*x, y, z*) vector about which to do the revolution.

It can be quite confusing trying to visualize the axis of revolution relative to a plot in the *x-z* plane. Here is a program that draws the surface of revolution together with the original 2-D plot drawn in red and the axis of revolution drawn in blue: You do not need to understand this program which is included only for the curious or those wishing to make their own plots. (If you try to type this program in, you will almost certainly make a mistake. Get the electronic edition of this book from http://www.mathware.com/BeginnersGuide and you will not need to type it in.)

```
AnnotatedSurfaceOfRevolution[
   f_, {x_, xmin_, xmax_}, options___] :=
Module[{surfacePlot, linePlot, axisPlot, axis, plotRange},
   axis =
    RevolutionAxis /. {options} /. Options[SurfaceOfRevolution];
   surfacePlot = SurfaceOfRevolution[f, {x, xmin, xmax},
      options, DisplayFunction → Identity];
   linePlot = Graphics3D[{Thickness[0.02], RGBColor[1, 0, 0],
      Line[Table[{x, 0, f}, {x, xmin, xmax, (xmax - xmin)/30}]]}];
   axisPlot = Graphics3D[{Thickness[0.02],
      RGBColor[0, 0, 1], Line[{-100 axis, 100 axis}]}];
   plotRange = FullOptions[surfacePlot, PlotRange];

   Show[surfacePlot, linePlot, axisPlot,
    PlotRange → plotRange, DisplayFunction → $DisplayFunction]
]
```

Here is the example from above:

```
AnnotatedSurfaceOfRevolution[
   x^2, {x, 0, 1}, RevolutionAxis → {1, 0, 0}];
```

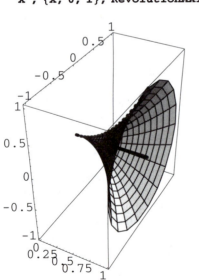

The following plot makes much clearer where the flat surface came from:

```
AnnotatedSurfaceOfRevolution[
    x², {x, 0, 1}, RevolutionAxis → {0, 1, 0}];
```

If you have *Mathematica*, you may want to try out your own examples at this point. If you're reading the electronic edition, click in any example above, modify it, and re-evaluate.

To make the relationship between axis and generating plot even more clear, we have prepared an animation. The function below will allow you to create your own.

```
onePlot[f_, range_, r_, axis_] := AnnotatedSurfaceOfRevolution[
    f, range, PlotRange → {{-r, r}, {-r, r}, {-r, r}},
    RevolutionAxis → axis, Boxed → False, Axes → None];
MakeRevolutionAnimation[f_, range_, r_, steps_] := (
    Do[onePlot[f, range, r, {1 - i, -i, 0}], {i, 0, 1, 1. / steps}];
    Do[onePlot[f, range, r, {0, -1 + i, i}], {i, 0, 1, 1. / steps}];
    Do[onePlot[f, range, r, {i, 0, 1 - i}], {i, 0, 1, 1. / steps}];
    )
```

Here is the animation. The original 2-D function is drawn in red, and the axis of revolution is drawn as a thick blue line. In the electronic edition, double-click on the image to animate it. In the printed edition we have substituted a few frames from the animation (unfortunately, it is not nearly so easy to understand what is happening from these still frames as from the animation).

In this animation, the axis of revolution starts out along the x-axis (1, 0, 0), then swings around to the negative y-axis (0, −1, 0), then up the z-axis (0, 0, 1), and finally back down to the x-axis.

`MakeRevolutionAnimation[x`^{2}`, {x, 0, 1}, 1.5, 10]`

Readers of the paper version can get this animation by purchasing the electronic edition from http://www.mathware.com/BeginnersGuide. Electronic edition readers: Notice how the red line stays stationary, and the surface passes through it at all times.

It is also possible to rotate parametrically defined functions, for example a Lissajous figure:

`ParametricPlot[{Cos[t] + 2, Sin[3 t]}, {t, 0, 2 `π`}];`

Here is the result of rotating this figure about the z-axis:

```
SurfaceOfRevolution[{Cos[t] + 2, Sin[3 t]},
   {t, 0, 2 π}, PlotPoints → {40, 50}];
```

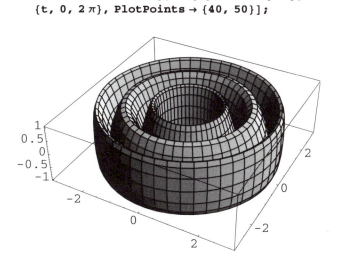

This result is not entirely clear. To see what is happening, here is an animation showing progressively how the surface is built up:

```
Do[SurfaceOfRevolution[{Cos[t] + 2, Sin[3 t]}, {t, 0, 2 π},
   {θ, 0, n}, PlotRange → {{-3, 3}, {-3, 3}, {-1, 1}}, Boxed → False,
   Axes → None, PlotPoints → {40, 50 n/(2 π)}], {n, 2 π/10, 2 π, 2 π/10}]
```

 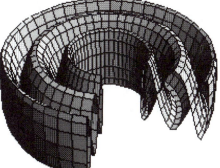

Theo: Doing these animation, particularly the earlier one with the shifting axis of revolution, has caused me to finally understand surfaces of revolution. Before computers, making animations like these would have taken weeks of work by a skilled animator. Before *Mathematica*, it would have taken weeks of work by a skilled programmer. Does this mean that until recently few people properly understood surfaces of revolution? Probably so.

Jerry: "Dance Squared" and "Notes on a Triangle" are wonderful animations from the National Film Board of Canada, produced about 35 years ago with the old technology. Surely the people who made these animations learned much more than those who only viewed the results. The readers of this book should view the animations above, many times, and then go on to make their own. Learning is not a passive thing.

Theo: Here are a few variations to get you started, but it doesn't count unless you actually modify the examples, and make your own plots.

```
Do[SurfaceOfRevolution[{Cos[t] + 2, Sin[3 t]}, {t, 0, n},
  {θ, 0, 2 π}, PlotRange → {{-3, 3}, {-3, 3}, {-1, 1}},
  Boxed → False, Axes → None,
  PlotPoints → {Floor[40 n/(2 π)], 50}], {n, (2 π)/30, 2 π, (2 π)/30}]
```

```
MultipleSurfaceOfRevolutionPlot[f_, range_, r_] := Show[
   {
    onePlot[f, range, r, {1, 0, 0}, DisplayFunction → Identity],
    onePlot[f, range, r, {0, -1, 0}, DisplayFunction → Identity],
    onePlot[f, range, r, {0, 0, 1}, DisplayFunction → Identity]
    },
   DisplayFunction → $DisplayFunction];
```

```
MultipleSurfaceOfRevolutionPlot[Sin[x], {x, 0, 2 π}, 7];
```

Chapter **69**

Can *Mathematica* show me the steps?

This common question from math educators has only one answer:

> What steps?
> Do you really want to see them?

In a few cases, there really are sensible internal steps you can watch happening. For a good example, see the end of Chapter 27, which demonstrates how to print out all the intermediate steps taken during the process of numerically approximating the solution to an equation using *Mathematica*'s **FindRoot** command.

However, for most symbolic calculations that *Mathematica* carries out, the steps it takes internally will bear little or no relationship to what anyone outside the computational symbolic algebra research community would expect. For example, most integrals are first transformed into their Gröbner basis representation, thereby losing touch with reality almost immediately.

What math educators generally mean by "the steps" is what a human would do if the human were carrying out a particular algorithm manually. It is unlikely that *Mathematica* uses this same algorithm internally, so seeing the steps *Mathematica* takes would be a profoundly unsatisfying experience.

However, it is possible to program *Mathematica* to solve problems using any particular algorithm, and to report the steps along the way. For example, in this chapter we demonstrate a program that causes *Mathematica* to show the steps in one way of expanding polynomials and solving linear equations. This program completely replaces *Mathematica's* basic arithmetic operations of addition, multiplication, and power with "manual" versions. It then implements functions to selectively distribute, commute, and associate terms one step at a time.

This program is included in the Implementation section at the end of this chapter. It is not shown in the printed form of the book because it is too long and would be impractical to type in. (To get an electronic version of this book, visit this book's home page at: http://www.mathware.com/BeginnersGuide.) When you evaluate the examples below, the program will be loaded automatically.

Here is a polynomial, expanded step-by-step:

`ShowExpand[x (x + 3)]`

$$x \cdot (x + 3)$$

$$x \cdot x + x \cdot 3$$

$$x^2 + 3 \cdot x$$

$x^2 + 3x$

The program prints the original input, shows step-by-step how the terms are multiplied together, and at the end prints the final result with italic variables. (Notice how x^2 is written as x·x first, to make clear where this term came from—something that would ordinarily never be shown by *Mathematica*; it would be simplified into x^2 without comment. However, the fact that this is the ordinary behavior of *Mathematica* in no way means it is its only *possible* behavior.)

If you're reading this in electronic form on a color screen, you will also notice that the variables are colored to indicate their origin. The two x's, for example, are different colors, so you can follow a particular x through the steps. When they are combined into x^2, the color is a blending of the two colors.

A slightly bigger example:

`ShowExpand[(x + 5) (x + 7)]`

$$(x + 5) \cdot (x + 7)$$

$$x \cdot (x + 7) + 5 \cdot (x + 7)$$

$$x \cdot x + x \cdot 7 + 5 \cdot x + 5 \cdot 7$$

$$x^2 + 7 \cdot x + 5 \cdot x + 35$$

$$x^2 + 12 \cdot x + 35$$

$x^2 + 12x + 35$

If the "same" example is entered in a different order, we see a different sequence:

ShowExpand[(5 + x) (x + 7)]

$$(5 + x) \cdot (x + 7)$$

$$5 \cdot (x + 7) + x \cdot (x + 7)$$

$$5 \cdot x + 5 \cdot 7 + x \cdot x + x \cdot 7$$

$$5 \cdot x + 35 + x^2 + 7 \cdot x$$

$$12 \cdot x + 35 + x^2$$

$$x^2 + 12\,x + 35$$

Notice how the terms are always kept in the order in which they were entered; in "ordinary" *Mathematica*, polynomials are kept in a standard order. In our version of *Mathematica*, only the very last output puts the terms into standard order.

Because the program is written in an open-ended, general way, it is possible to carry out a large range of examples, including complex ones that require a large number of steps. To conserve paper, we restrict ourselves to only a slightly larger example:

ShowExpand[(a + b) (a + b) (a + b)]

$$(a +) \cdot (a + b) \cdot (a + b)$$

$$(a \cdot (a + b) + \cdot (a + b)) \cdot (a + b)$$

$$a \cdot (a + b) \cdot (a + b) + \cdot (a + b) \cdot (a + b)$$

$$(a \cdot a + a \cdot b) \cdot (a + b) + (\cdot a + \cdot b) \cdot (a + b)$$

$$a \cdot a \cdot (a + b) +$$
$$\quad a \cdot b \cdot (a + b) + \cdot a \cdot (a + b) + \cdot b \cdot (a + b)$$

$$a \cdot (a \cdot a + a \cdot b) + a \cdot (b \cdot a + b \cdot b) +$$
$$\cdot (a \cdot a + a \cdot b) + \cdot (b \cdot a + b \cdot b)$$

$$a \cdot a \cdot a + a \cdot a \cdot b + a \cdot b \cdot a + a \cdot b \cdot b +$$
$$\cdot a \cdot a + \cdot a \cdot b + \cdot b \cdot a + \cdot b \cdot b$$

$$a^3 + a^2 \cdot b +$$
$$a^2 \cdot b + b^2 \cdot a + a^2 \cdot + b^2 \cdot a + b^2 \cdot a + b^3$$

$$a^3 + 3 \cdot a^2 \cdot b + 3 \cdot b^2 \cdot a + b^3$$

$$a^3 + 3\,b\,a^2 + 3\,b^2\,a + b^3$$

This process can get out of hand very quickly: the number of steps increases as the factorial of the exponent, quickly exhausting the capacity of most computers. Meltdown occurs around exponent 6 or 7.

This factorial explosion makes clear one reason why *Mathematica* does not generally use such simplistic algorithms. Its built-in **Expand** function handles such problems almost trivially. The following example is done before your finger leaves the Return key:

Expand[(a + b)⁷]

$$a^7 + 7\,a^6\,b + 21\,a^5\,b^2 + 35\,a^4\,b^3 + 35\,a^3\,b^4 + 21\,a^2\,b^5 + 7\,a\,b^6 + b^7$$

Mathematica can evaluate even *much* larger examples in a matter of seconds:

Expand[(a + b)¹⁰⁰]

Obviously, **ShowExpand** is not a function you would want to use if you actually had a polynomial to expand, but it is a fine educational tool for showing students how people, not computers, multiply polynomials.

Jerry: So, computers can show people how people do math. First <u>people show computers how people do math</u>, then <u>people show computers better ways to do math that people can't do</u>, then <u>computers show people how computers do math</u>, and finally <u>people show computers how to show people how people do math</u>.

Theo: Moving right along, the following examples show step-by-step how to solve linear equations in one variable:

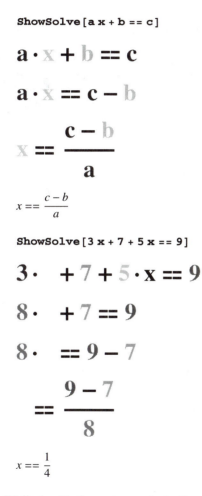

```
ShowSolve[a x + b == c]
```

$$a \cdot x + b == c$$

$$a \cdot x == c - b$$

$$x == \frac{c - b}{a}$$

$$x == \frac{c-b}{a}$$

```
ShowSolve[3 x + 7 + 5 x == 9]
```

$$3 \cdot \quad + 7 + 5 \cdot x == 9$$

$$8 \cdot \quad + 7 == 9$$

$$8 \cdot \quad == 9 - 7$$

$$== \frac{9 - 7}{8}$$

$$x == \frac{1}{4}$$

Jerry: Well, the *Mathematica* snobs in the crowd may poo-poo these functions, but I think **ShowExpand** and **ShowSolve** are two of the most exciting functions I've seen in a long time! Why couldn't they have been done years ago? I've been asking for *some* program to do this forever, and all I ever got was "You don't want to see the real steps", and "Of course we could write a program to show the steps you want, but it's so trivial we couldn't be bothered".

Theo: These functions are a good example of the kind of thing that is so easy it never gets done. The people (*Mathematica* experts) for whom it is easy consider it a childish programming exercise that could trivially be done by someone else. The someone else's don't find it quite so easy after all, because when you get down to it, it is a bit tricky to get it to work properly. So, programs like this rarely get written.

A few such functions actually have been written. For example, *Mathematica* includes a demo file written by George Beck that does step-by-step differentiation (click <u>here</u>, or look up "Step-by-Step Differentiation" in the Getting Started/Demos category in the help browser).

Jerry: Suppose a reader wants to do something else step-by-step, like adding fractions, or integration by parts. Can she program *Mathematica* to do that too?

Theo: Yes, provided she is willing to take the time, or find someone else to do it. Using the framework provided by the program below, a person familiar with programming *Mathematica* could write her own step-by-step functions. Of course, doing so requires her to thoroughly understand, step-by-step, how to do what she's asking the function to do, which is very much more than just being able to do it for a few examples.

■ Implementation (Electronic version only)

Chapter **70**

Will it rot my students' brains if they use *Mathematica*?

Jerry: I have young students who reach for their calculators to get the answer to 5×6.

5 × 6

30

My response, when I see that, is to explain that such behavior is socially unacceptable, sort of like picking your nose. Many people will see this and think the student must be brain damaged. It's a social problem, not a mathematical one.

Theo: I agree that the problem lies with the other people more than with the students. The most profound engine of civilization is the inability of a larger and larger fraction of the population to do the basic things needed to survive. Many people fail to realize this.

Jerry: I don't understand that statement *at all*. It must be very significant.

Theo: In a society where everyone knows how to hunt, grow food, and make shelter, and knows these things well enough to survive, no one has time for much of anything else—even for perfecting one or the other of these basic skills. In early tribal societies, some people were undoubtedly better at one thing than another, to the point where they would probably have had a hard time outside the group. The best arrow makers probably weren't very good at weaving shoes, and would have had a lot of blisters without some help from the shoe weavers.

Few people would argue that people who are bad at weaving shoes are somehow inadequate, but it's surprising how strongly people feel this way about "modern" skills such as the ability to add well.

Technology's greatest contribution is to permit people to be incompetent at a larger and larger range of things. Only by embracing such incompetence is the human race able to progress.

Irate bystander: So, you're saying civilization progresses by having technology relieve everyone of the need to learn skills, so we can choose to be incompetent idiots barely able to feed ourselves. Is this really progress? Isn't the result of too much technology an aimless, pathetic populace just moving from one senseless pastime to another? What else could explain professional wrestling and the $180 sneaker!

Theo: I didn't say incompetence is a *sufficient* condition for progress. I do say it is a *necessary* one. If you want to move beyond endless drudgery, you have to have technology (or slaves, servants, or a spouse) to free you from the otherwise all-consuming task of survival. Technology is the least-objectionable way of generating free time, in my opinion. Of course, some people will use their free time more responsibly than others.

Jerry: People are very attached to the value of *their* skills. They believe that the skills of their generation should be preserved, with new skills added on.

Theo: Such an attitude represents a tremendous degree of disrespect of our forepersons. It was really, *really* hard to be a cave person. The skills needed to live comfortably in, say, northern Europe in 20,000 BCE were extremely complex. They required then and would require now the full range of human intelligence.

To think that a modern human should be able to do everything that previous generations have been able to do (hunt, speak Latin, do square roots by hand, etc.), and also have any time left over to learn *anything* new (microbiology, email, calculus), is basically insulting to all those previous generations, since it implies that they under-employed their intelligence. It is also quite false.

Jerry: I think it matters that students spend their time thinking and learning. People seem happiest if they are good at something. But I agree it doesn't matter whether they learn all the same things their parents learned. Not learning Latin is a problem only if you need to speak to Latin people on a regular basis, or if people will make fun of you on the playground. Not learning to add is a problem only if you have to add regularly, or if people will make fun of you for using a calculator to do

```
5 + 7
```

```
12
```

Theo: Well, you probably *do* think people should learn to add. Adding is not that hard, and it's a fairly practical skill in the day-to-day world.

Jerry: In the old days (before television), being able to add up a long column of numbers without making any mistakes was a valuable skill. People would pay you a living wage to do nothing but add numbers well. Not today.

Theo: Today, it's nice to be able to add small numbers, and larger numbers in a pinch, but the specific mental tricks and habits needed to get the right answer consistently when adding lots of numbers are just not helpful. Not being able to do this does not represent a failure of the intellect, any more than not knowing which fields in your neighborhood have the best rabbit hunting: both were, at one time, failings that would get you laughed at.

Jerry: But, you'd agree that being able to *estimate* the sum of a column of numbers is valuable. I would spend more time learning to do *that* well than working to reduce my error rate in doing exact sums.

Theo: And yet, in schools you find worksheets with 100 addition problems that are supposed to be done *correctly*, with points taken off for errors. What a waste of time.

Irate bystander: Oh, now I get it. You're one of those romantic educational know-nothings who think it's not necessary to learn anything in particular, as long as you learn "critical thinking skills" and have good self esteem. Yuck.

Theo: *No*, and let me make this very clear. No one can learn to think without having something to think about. If you try to teach someone *how* to think in the abstract, you are not going to get anywhere. If you try to make education "easy", by removing the content, you are cheating your students out of the most important thing you have to offer: the chance to do something *hard*. Only by mastering a difficult body of knowledge can a child develop into a confident, thinking adult. The point is, it doesn't necessarily have to be the *same* difficult body of knowledge that the child's parents learned.

And while we're on the topic of romantic educational know-nothings, let me just say that if you think you can improve your students' self esteem by letting them "succeed" at various insipid educational games, you are kidding yourself. Kids are *much* smarter than that. There is nothing more demoralizing to most children than being put through an educational program they know they can't fail at. Instead of teaching them self esteem, it teaches them that you expect so little of them that you have contrived special extra-stupid lessons for their benefit. Don't think for a *minute* they don't know what's going on.

If you start a lesson off by telling the students "This is going to be easy", you are simultaneously telling them "We had to make this easy because we don't think you're capable of doing anything hard". And when the lesson is over, the only sense of accomplishment they can feel is that they did something easy. So what?

Learning is hard work. If you are not working hard, you are not learning. Period. Kids love hard work, as long as they see where it's going and why. Instead of killing that energy by giving them something *easy*, we should foster it by giving them something *really hard*. We should tell them it's hard. We should give them the chance to do something meaningful.

Jerry: Readers should be aware that Theo is the father of one three year old and a couple-odd babies, while I am the father of four adults. It is well known that people at the beginning of the child rearing process have much stronger opinions than those who have completed at least two children. However, in this case I have to agree with Theo.

His viewpoint is nicely supported by Joseph Mitchell's story in his wonderful book *Up in the Old Hotel* about a bridge-building disaster which killed a number of young members of the Mohawk nation. People believed this disaster would drive the Mohawks away, but instead it had the opposite effect. The tragedy confirmed that working on high steel is serious, dangerous work, worthy of the efforts of young Mohawk men. Mohawks have gone on to erect the steel of a high proportion of all the high-rise buildings and bridges on the North American continent since 1910.

We seem to agree in general principles but how do we put them into action. If we want our children to learn some things that are hard, how do we decide which hard things are-- or are not--worth their effort?

Theo: It's not easy, and of course it changes every day. The one sure wrong answer is: The same thing we learned as children.

Therapy can probably help, if you feel you must insist that your child learn the multiplication tables up to 12 by 12 because *you* had to, and you would be embarrassed if her grandma finds out. If you want her to learn it because you really think it's something that will help *her* in her life, fine, there's nothing wrong with that. Examine your motives. Look around at our society. Be open-minded.

Jerry: I forget, what was the point of this chapter? Have we said anything yet?

Theo: The point of this chapter is to tell people that if they think *Mathematica* might be harmful to the process of education, they need to reconsider their fundamental belief structure. Just like the breech-loading rifle, or the pocket calculator, modern tools such as *Mathematica* change (maybe a little, maybe a lot) the kinds of things that *ought* to be learned. Some things that used to be important are not anymore, and some new things have become important.

Jerry: How about a short list? After *Mathematica*:

> **Less Important**
> Guessing factors for polynomials
> Knowing many tricks for integration
> Being careful when copying over expressions many times
> Finding roots of complex equations
> Knowing how to do matrix row operations
> Knowing how to avoid dropping minus signs
> Memorizing specific rules for derivatives of such functions as tangent and secant
> Memorizing multiple angle formulas for trig functions

> **More Important**
> Translating statements about problems in natural language into statements in
>   mathematical or procedural language
> Learning how to experiment with math
> Knowing which integrals should best be done numerically
> Knowing how to work backwards or to use numerical methods to check symbolic
>   results for plausibility
> Knowing how to use techniques from programming
> Understanding recursion and how to use it practically
> Knowing which functions are discontinuous and where they are discontinuous
> Knowing how to mix math and programming

Theo: So, won't people be in trouble if they don't know how to do these traditional, now less important, things? What if they have to function without computers some day?

Jerry: Well, I guess they'll just all die.

I have trouble taking this criticism seriously. How many microprocessors are there per person in the US? Too many to count. Very few of us are more than 100 meters from a computer most of the time.

Theo: I would have to agree. If you are worried that your child will suffer by not learning to solve a polynomial by hand, I would suggest worrying more about not learning how to skin a rabbit, or how to start a stalled car. Of all the failures of education likely to get your child into trouble, manual polynomial solving is not high on the list.

Jerry: Readers who think the topic of this chapter is unimportant are mistaken. Computer use in our schools today can only be described as pathetically limited. Attitudes we have discussed here are a serious factor. Maybe ten years ago one could argue that computers did not belong in the classroom. They were too expensive, good software was not available, and they were too difficult to operate. But today, a math classroom without a computer is a joke. Yet the number of math teachers who use computers regularly with their students is *very* small. In same cases, teachers have computers in the classroom, but by the time they are finished teaching all the old lessons, there is no time left over for using the computers. Try to tell them to *cut out* some of the old topics, and war breaks out. In that conflict, parents and teachers are often on the same side, outnumbering the voices for change. Misuse of computers is easy and a problem but *no* use is presently a bigger problem.

Chapter **71**

Will it rot my students' brains if they use other educational software?

Theo: Yes.

Jerry: But wait, didn't we just write a whole chapter about how great it was for students to forget everything their parents ever learned and use *Mathematica* instead?

Theo: Well, yes, but we were talking about one particular piece of software being used by relatively advanced students to replace manual computation, a very narrow set of skills.

It is interesting to note that many teachers and parents feel that using calculators to avoid learning multiplication tables, or using *Mathematica* to avoid learning integration, is an educational failure. Yet they don't seem to have a problem with using software that retards development of far more fundamental aspects of the student's humanity, such as creativity, enthusiasm, love of learning, and empathy.

Jerry: What? Have you gone completely off the deep end?

Theo: Yes, in this chapter we will be firmly off the deep end.

The sad fact is that 95% of all "educational software" and 95% of all educational use of computers is, for lack of a better word, crap. I'm not claiming that *Mathematica* is the only good educational software in the world. But you have to look far and wide to find the few others.

Jerry: Why do you say it's mostly crap? And if you're right, how did educational software get to be so bad?

Theo: It's bad because thousands of earnest and dedicated software engineers are working hard to make it that way. Bringing to bear all their skills in commercial software design, the best programmers in the industry have created an impressive body of absolutely worthless educational software. Worse than worthless, much of it is downright scary in its effects.

Jerry: How about some specific examples. So far this is sounding like a pretty categorical attack on the competition by someone with a vested interest in one particular product.

Theo: Let's start with something I'm sure most people would agree has little educational value, the video game. We'll discuss later how video games are related to educational software.

To understand the effects of video games, one needs to go back to debriefings conducted by the U.S. Army after WWII. Interviewing soldiers returning from battle, researchers discovered a very disturbing fact. A significant number of soldiers had been face to face with an enemy soldier, rifle in hand, enemy in their sights, gun not jammed, and had *not fired*. Something deep in their being, some sort of innate humanity, had prevented them from actually pulling the trigger.

Needless to say, this was very disturbing to the military. They began a research effort to figure out what to do about this problem. They discovered that in the heat of battle, under the incredible physical and psychological stress of being faced with another human being you were supposed to kill, the higher mental functions were largely absent. Under such conditions, the mind reverts to much simpler modes of operation, to deeply wired, almost instinctive behaviors. In other words, no amount of target practice at bullseye targets and classroom lectures about how you're supposed to kill the enemy had much effect when it counted.

Over the following decades and wars, the Army learned that the way to get soldiers to reliably pull the trigger was to use very basic, repetitive operant conditioning, along the lines of standard behaviorist theory. Now, behaviorism provides a very poor model for how humans act in everyday life, but it turns out to be a pretty good model for how humans act when they are under stress and have to act quickly, and are responding primarily to fear. Under stress, fearful people do what they have been conditioned to do.

The Army's solution was to replace dry target practice with realistic training grounds, complete with pop-up targets, loud noises, smoke, stress, the works. The goal was to condition the soldiers: If it moves, shoot it *now*, don't think about it. Repetition, repetition, repetition: Target pops up, you shoot. Target pops up, you shoot. Do that often enough, and, research shows, next time you see something pop up, you are more likely to shoot it, even if it's a real human in a real battle. This is not just a theory, it is documented by exit interviews from soldiers in later wars: The Army got what it wanted. (What armies do, and how that is similar to video games, is forcefully presented in the book *On Killing* by David Grossman, a former military officer (Little Brown, 1995)).

Now, what does this have to do with video games? The answer should be obvious by now to anyone who's ever seen one. The whole point is, if it moves, shoot it. Again and again and again.

Jerry: Well yes, but it's aliens and other fantasy figures they are shooting at, not people. Does it really carry over?

Theo: Yes it does. (And by the way, it's not all aliens; many video games have photo-realistic people complete with recognizable human faces, and blood splatters. You stick your handgun in their face at point blank range and pull the trigger.) Intellectually, no one would confuse a video game with real life, but we're not talking about an intellectual situation. We're talking about a scared kid with a Saturday night special in his hand seeing a member of a rival gang move his hand around in his coat. That kid is thinking at an operant conditioning level; what matters more than anything else is how many times in the past he has pulled the trigger. In reality or in a video game, it doesn't make that much difference. For a good discussion of the current consensus opinion on the effects of violence on TV and in movies and video games, see the book *Mayhem* by Sissela Bok (Perseus Books, 1998).

If you think watching violent TV is bad, video games are much, much worse. TV is a passive medium, requiring no participation from the viewer. A kid watching a murder on TV may not be benefiting much from it, and maybe he's learning a certain degree of callousness, but at least he is not being conditioned to pull the trigger. He is just watching. In the video game, *he is* the murderer, *he pulls* the trigger, *he participates* in the violence.

When soldiers are trained to kill, it is with a certain amount of context, with an effort to teach honor, duty, self restraint, and the difference between civilian and military life. When a 12-year-old kid comes out of his bedroom after spending three hours actively participating in the killing of people, what context has he had? what debriefing does he get?

I should mention that most of this chapter was written before the recent outbreak of kids shooting their classmates at school. To what degree video games contributed to those incidence is of course subject to endless debate, but the public does seem to have been alerted to the topic. There are even reports of, for example, Disney resorts removing violent video games that include humans as targets. A fine move, but obviously mainly symbolic. As long as parents pay to have killing arcades installed in their kid's bedrooms, the harm will be done.

Jerry: I am alarmed. (Reader: I've read Grossman's book, and Theo is right, we should be alarmed.)

But what do violent video games have to do with educational software?

Theo: Video games are at one end of a continuum. Educational software doesn't usually have the same kind of violence, and it tries to be "positive". But the fact is that it's written by the same people, and more importantly, it's often judged by the same criteria, as video games and other types of entertainment software.

When software engineers design educational software, there are a few things they take for granted, and reviewers of educational software appear to agree with them:

- Software should be "easy to use". That means you shouldn't have to read a manual before starting to use it; you should be able to click on just about anything on the screen and have it work; you should be able to figure out how to use the program just by flipping through the menus and trying things that seem relevant. In short, you should be able to use the software by trial and error.

- Users should never feel at a loss for what to do next. The software should lead them seamlessly from one stage to the next, with no moments of confusion or uncertainty.

- Software should engage and keep its users' attention with colorful graphics, sounds, animations, whatever it takes. Software without these elements is judged to be boring and of inferior quality to the better grades of multi-media educational software.

- Good performance should be rewarded with a treat, such as a clever animation or a game that can be played for a while.

Obvious, right? Any software that lacks these characteristics is routinely trashed in reviews. It is called "hard to use", "boring", or "unmotivating". We are told repeatedly that kids prefer flashy graphics software.

Well, kids prefer TV over homework, late movies instead of sleep, and chocolate coated sugar bombs for breakfast. Have we all forgotten what education is supposed to be about? Shouldn't education be about preparing children to lead successful, fulfilling lives? Here are a few self-evident facts about children and learning:

- Children need to know certain facts, but acquiring them is not the main point of learning, especially not in the earlier grades. Mainly children need to have effective habits of mind and an ability to think analytically. They also need to be self-motivated, because in real life there isn't always someone there to provide external motivation (unless they join the army).

- The hardest things to teach are the skill of solving problems with incomplete information, the skill of figuring out which problems need solving in the first place, and the skill of finding and bringing together the resources needed to solve a problem.

- Children are primed to want to learn. They start out valuing learning and accomplishment above anything else in the world. If you see a child uninterested in learning, it is overwhelmingly likely that the child was made that way by something in the child's world: Children do not start out that way. (Of course there are always exceptions, but they are just that: exceptions.)

Let's go through our list of features of "good quality software" and see how each feature affects these learning goals. (Many of these points are made very effectively in the fine book *Failure to Connect* by Jane M. Healy, Simon & Schuster 1998.)

- Software should be "easy to use".
  Life is not "easy to use". Children quickly learn that the best and most effective way to handle typical educational software is to click as fast as you can on anything you can find on the screen until something works. It's really not worthwhile to read the bothersome text; understanding the material just slows you down. Since the software is "high quality", it will always do something, help you out, not be judgmental; pretty soon you'll hit the right icon and get to the next level.

Extensive use of this sort of software supports and develops shallow thinking habits. It discourages careful analytic thought. It is dysfunctional. Real life is not a multiple choice test. In real life there are points off for making wrong choices.

- The user should never feel at a loss for what to do next.
  In life, it's *rarely* clear what to do next. Uncertainty is one of the defining characteristics of life; one of the most important things a good education can give a child is the ability to sift through seemly limitless options and make wise choices. It's usually not even clear when a choice is there to be made, let alone what the alternatives are.

  Extensive use of sanitized, candyland software develops a weak, passive mode of thinking. Children reared with software that never lets them get lost often seem lost and helpless when faced with the confusing mess of the real world. Jane M. Healy gives many illustrations of this effect in her book *Failure to Connect*.

  Now, it's possible that children have always been helpless and confused in the real world, but this sort of software isn't helping things. Sure, some kids will come out fine, and yes, some kids would never have come out fine. But what about the ones in between who would have developed into thoughtful, capable adults but for their exposure to this sort of software? How many is too many?

- Software should engage and keep the user's attention.
  Good performance should be rewarded with a treat.
  These two are without a doubt the most damaging attributes of most educational software. It is absolutely tragic that, by rewarding learning with stupid tricks and games, such software devalues the learning itself. Children who would gladly learn for the sake of learning are, quickly and devestatingly, turned into children who demand rewards for learning.

Now, I know a lot of people will say, "Oh, kids today need to be entertained or they will lose interest!" Well, sorry, but that's no excuse for pandering. Kids in your neighborhood may be zoned-out video addicts, and maybe some of them are beyond help, but do not delude yourself into thinking you are helping the situation by giving in and giving them what they want. You are the adult here, and it is your responsibility to work with them to recapture their innate love of learning. It may not be easy, and you will probably fail with some or most of them (and you certainly will fail with many of those whose parents aren't helping). But you have to try: It is part of being an adult, just like not giving your kids candy every time they ask for it, and not giving them edutainment when they need education.

Jerry: Well, I can see you feel strongly about this. It must be nice to be so sure of things.

I think there's quite a bit of software out there that is valid and valuable. Perhaps we can help people see the difference. I assume that your attack on "easy to use" software doesn't mean you think good software should be intentionally hard to use?

Theo: I think that learning is *intrinsically* hard. Educational software that students just get through without working hard has not succeeded in making learning easy, it has simply replaced learning with entertainment.

Imagine taking your kids to a fun movie, having a good time, eating ice cream. No harm in that. But should you tell them that they are having an important educational experience? Should you tell them that they have *accomplished* something by sitting through the whole movie? What a horrible devaluation of accomplishment that would be! What's the point of actually working hard to reach success, if your parents and teachers will praise you for joking around and eating ice cream?

That's exactly what most educational software is: A stupid, insipid movie that keeps your kids entertained for an hour or two while the teacher plans a bake sale to replace the music budget that was spent on computers. Kids don't learn anything, but worse they are being taught that it's not necessary to work hard to achieve success.

Software should not be *unnecessarily* hard to use, but neither should it shy away from or disguise the inherent richness of the subject matter. It should be open-ended, deep, and capable of doing senseless things if asked.

Jerry: Why should software be able to do senseless things? What's the point in that?

Theo: Let's take a specific case. Give me an example of a program you like.

Jerry: Geometry programs like Geo1, Geometer's Sketchpad, Cabri, and Cyclone let students make constructions with lines and circles, then discover relationships among the elements. Students of mine have acquired a deeper understanding of geometry, trigonometry, and algebra from programs like these than they did from traditional textbook approaches alone. Contrary to your description of mindless multiple choice quiz programs, these programs have let my students build anything they like, then manipulate it freely.

Theo: Exactly! If students decide to build a completely useless geometrical construction, the program won't stop them. It lets them discover for themselves that their construction is uninteresting. This is very important: By allowing freedom to go off in the wrong direction, the software is giving students the opportunity to learn.

Jerry: Maybe I'm starting to see what you mean. As the saying goes, you learn from your mistakes. Software that prevents you from making mistakes limits what you can learn.

Theo: Exactly. I'm not saying that educational software should encourage mistakes, or have outright flaws, such as buttons that are confusingly labeled and crash the program. But I am saying that programs should be rich enough to allow both right and wrong paths to be followed, and followed in a more than superficial way.

Software can be divided into page-turning vs. simulation-based. Page-turning software, which is very common, allows the student to following only certain pre-determined paths through screens that have been laid out in advance by the authors. Breaking out onto more creative paths is impossible, because there is nothing to break out into: It's a closed box.

Simulation software in contrast has a set of rules and algorithms (the laws of physics; sociological models; geometrical relationships; etc.). It is able to apply these rules to a fairly open-ended set of inputs. Simulation software is inherently more difficult to write; not surprisingly there is little of it out there. In fact, good simulations are so difficult to create that one could almost name all the examples that have ever been done. Page-turning software is incredibly easy to make, and there are countless thousands of titles available, virtually all of very low quality.

Interestingly, while violent video games may be evil, they are largely simulation-based. No page-turning software could hold anyone's attention for the hundreds of hours that video games capture our children. In a good video game, you have a huge world to roam about in, complete with back alleys, multiple levels, and great detail in all the parts. The only problem is that you have to keep killing people to see the next back alley. Oh well, if people get in your way, killing them is OK, right?

Jerry: OK, OK, let's not get started on that again. Now, by that definition, *Mathematica* is simulation software, as is most of the educational software I like. But this kind of software is much harder on the teachers. Students are constantly going off on tangents and asking questions about what they've done.

At some schools, teachers (and maybe administrators) would rather use software that the students can use for an hour without needing a teacher. From their point of view, what's the point of spending your school's entire music, PE, and after-school programs budget on a shiny new computer lab, if you just have to hire new teachers to baby-sit the students? For that kind of money, shouldn't it be "automatic"?

Finding and training teachers able to work with students using untamed, open-ended software is very hard. Potential teachers may be computer-phobic, or may not want to be put in the position of answering questions instead of lecturing. It's much harder to answer students' open-ended questions than it is to spill out a prepared lecture. They may not always know the answers to all the questions; from time to time, a student might actually end up knowing more than the teacher does about something.

Theo: I think we can all agree that it would be sad to see classroom teaching replaced by computer lab brain damage, just because school administrations don't know what they are doing. It would be far better not to bother with the computers in the first place, if they're not going to be used in ways that help people learn.

Skeptical Bystander: It's all well and good to support the discovery method of learning, but we all know that if you just throw students in a lab with open-ended software and wait for them to discover the great laws of the universe, most of them *won't*. Sometimes it's necessary to tell them to read one page, then the next page, then the next. And what about learning multiplication tables or the reverse declination of irregular French pronouns? Isn't there a place for drill-and-practice, page turning software?

Theo: Yes, there is a place for well-designed drill and practice software. If you have a group of highly motivated, mature students who wish to learn a defined body of knowledge (say, The Knowledge—all the streets and cul-de-sacs of London—so they can pass the London taxi driver exam), they can do this very effectively using page-turning, quiz-giving, flash-card-simulating software.

Drill and practice software is used quite effectively in industry, in the military, and by students of medicine, law, and other fields that require a lot of memorization. It's not flashy, and it doesn't have any video games at the end as a reward (the learning itself is the reward, as it should be).

But this software has almost nothing in common with the "educational software" we've been ranting about. It differs in these ways:

- Good drill and practice software has no externalized reward: Learning is the reward. As discussed above, providing a video game or animation at the end is exactly like rewarding the eating of vegetables with ice cream. It devalues the vegetables and increases the attractiveness of the ice cream. It doesn't work at the dinner table, and it doesn't work in teaching either.

- Good drill and practice software spends the vast majority of its time on teaching, practice, and evaluation. Bad educational software spends far too much time on the (harmful) reward. Jane Healy's book cites examples of software in which the students spend *more* time playing the reward game than they do in the learning portion of the program.

Life, and classroom time, is simply too valuable to waste this way.

Chapter **72**

Will my students spend more time learning *Mathematica* than mathematics?

They certainly could, and for some of them that might not be a bad thing at all. Some of them will probably spend more time learning to play the banjo than learning mathematics, and that might not be such a bad thing either. There are all kinds of people in the world, and for some of them the joy of programming in *Mathematica* will prove to be more compelling than the study of mathematics.

The better question is, will *Mathematica* be an impediment to learning math, instead of an aid? In its raw form, *Mathematica* certainly can be a bit confusing. For those who would not enjoy the process of learning about *Mathematica* itself, courseware (in the form of notebooks) prepared specially for a particular subject can make *Mathematica* available for learning math.

Because of the programmability of *Mathematica*, enhanced in V3 and above by palettes and the math typesetting system, it is possible to prepare variations of *Mathematica* that are much easier for a particular set of users to learn.

Let's imagine a student who has learned how to do expansion of polynomials by hand (see Chapter 69). Now a new game is possible: Given the expression $(a + b)^3$ and the resulting expansion $a^3 + 3\,b\,a^2 + 3\,b^2\,a + b^3$, can the student see a connection between the input and the output? If the answer is yes, can she write out the expansion of $(a + b)^4$ without *Mathematica*'s help?

One approach is to show the student one example:

> **Expand[(a + b) ^ 3]**
>
> $a^3 + 3\,a^2\,b + 3\,a\,b^2 + b^3$

Then tell the student to type Command-L (Copy Input from Above), select the number three in the new input cell, type a new number, and type Shift-Return. Many students will have no trouble doing this, and the result will be a nice record of what they tried out, something like:

> **Expand[(a + b) ^ 4]**
>
> $a^4 + 4\,a^3\,b + 6\,a^2\,b^2 + 4\,a\,b^3 + b^4$

```
Expand[(a + b) ^ 5]
```

$$a^5 + 5 a^4 b + 10 a^3 b^2 + 10 a^2 b^3 + 5 a b^4 + b^5$$

```
Expand[(a + b) ^ -7]
```

$$\frac{1}{(a + b)^7}$$

Teacher, teacher, it didn't work!

Well, Addison, maybe you could try **ExpandAll**:

```
ExpandAll[(a + b) ^ -7]
```

$$\frac{1}{a^7 + 7 a^6 b + 21 a^5 b^2 + 35 a^4 b^3 + 35 a^3 b^4 + 21 a^2 b^5 + 7 a b^6 + b^7}$$

Very quickly, opportunities for learning present themselves.

But what if there isn't a teacher to present the first example, or to suggest **ExpandAll**? One solution is to prepare a small notebook to show one or two initial examples, and encourage experimentation. It might look like this:

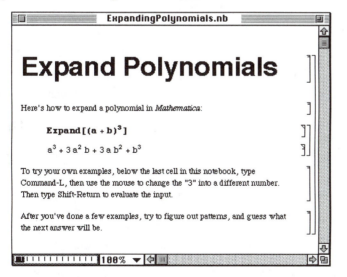

What if this is too complicated? Is it possible to give the student a notebook with things that just *work* without anyone, teacher or student, knowing any *Mathematica* syntax? Leaving aside the question of whether this is desirable, the answer is yes. For example, here is a button that will demonstrate polynomial expansion completely automatically:

```
Start
```

Click on this button, and it spits out the following cell, containing an example and two buttons:

$$\uparrow \downarrow \qquad (a + b)^2 \; \longrightarrow \; a^2 + 2\,a\,b + b^2$$

Click on the up (or down) button, and you get a new example above (or below) the original one, with the exponent increased (or decreased) by one. We clicked the up button twice:

$$\uparrow \downarrow \qquad (a + b)^4 \; \longrightarrow \; a^4 + 4\,a^3\,b + 6\,a^2\,b^2 + 4\,a\,b^3 + b^4$$

$$\uparrow \downarrow \qquad (a + b)^3 \; \longrightarrow \; a^3 + 3\,a^2\,b + 3\,a\,b^2 + b^3$$

$$\uparrow \downarrow \qquad (a + b)^2 \; \longrightarrow \; a^2 + 2\,a\,b + b^2$$

The advantage of this method is that it takes the student pretty much no time to get started. The disadvantage is that it's a closed system. The student has explored binomials, but has not learned anything that would allow independent exploration of trinomials. Showing students the **Expand** command would allow many of them to generalize the input and go off in other directions.

In this example, it's a toss-up whether the initial student convenience is worth the downside of a closed system—students could so easily learn a very small amount of useful *Mathematica* syntax, and then be able to go off in other directions on their own.

■ Implementation

This function implements the up/down polynomial-expanding button. The function creates an output cell containing two buttons and an expanding example. The buttons are pre-programmed to call the same function that created them, but with the exponent one unit higher or lower. Thus the buttons are self-propagating.

```
more[n_, dir_] := (
        SelectionMove[
      SelectedNotebook[ ], All, ButtonCell];
        SelectionMove[
      SelectedNotebook[ ], dir, Cell];
   NotebookWrite[
     SelectedNotebook[], {Cell[BoxData[ToBoxes[SequenceForm[
                              Button["↑",
      ButtonFunction :> ( more[n + 1, Before] &),
      ButtonEvaluator -> Automatic,
      Active -> True], Button["↓",
      ButtonFunction :> ( more[n - 1, After] &),
      ButtonEvaluator -> Automatic,
      Active -> True], "   ",
          (a + b)^n, " → ", ExpandAll[(a + b)^n]]]], "Output"]}];);
```

Chapter 73

Can *Mathematica* make math relevant to my students?

Jerry: No! But maybe it can help? A recently published calculus book includes a table giving the depth of water in Bombay on an hourly basis. Subsequent discussion leads to a curve-fitting experience that results in a picture of the data points and a cosine curve. We then read about a local surfer who wonders how fast the tide is coming in at 8 in the morning. This situation is used to discuss rate of change, on the assumption that the youth of today will find it engaging.

Theo: As a former youth of today, I can say that's a bit lame.

Jerry: In math, as in novels, you have to write what you know. Otherwise it sounds phony, like the example of surfers in Bombay. Have you ever had an experience where math was useful to *you*?

Theo: Why yes! Just last summer I used math to save an entire dinner party from sinking.

I decided that my house really needed a floating deck out the bedroom door. (Fortunately, this desire was facilitated by the presence of a lake.)

I decided early on that the two most important properties of my deck would be:
  a) does not sink
  b) does not flip over.

Jerry: Fascinating. I can see all kinds of math, such as how many fat people fit on a deck, and how many more thin people fit than fat? How cold is the water? How thick is the deck?

Theo: The first question is related to sinking. Recalling Archimedes's famous *eureka* realization that a floating object displaces an equal weight of water, we want to know how much will the people weigh, and what volume of water will their weight displace? Most of the people I know weigh about 200 pounds, and I don't think I'd want more than about 20 of them at my house at any one time. So the maximum weight of the people on my deck is approximately:

$$20 \, \text{Person} \times 200 \, \frac{\text{Pound}}{\text{Person}}$$

4000 Pound

I happen to know that the weight of one cubic centimeter of water is one gram. Styrofoam suitable for the floating of decks is not sold in cubic centimeters, so we'll need to do some unit conversions.

$$\textbf{Needs}[\texttt{"Miscellaneous`Units`"}]$$

$$\textbf{Convert}\left[1\ \frac{\textbf{Gram}}{(\textbf{Centi Meter})^3},\ \frac{\textbf{Pound}}{\textbf{Foot}^3}\right]$$

$$\frac{62.428\ \texttt{Pound}}{\texttt{Foot}^3}$$

(Some readers may have been taught that water weighs $64\ \frac{\text{Pounds}}{\text{Foot}^3}$. Is it *only* our proofreader, or are there other readers with this same misinformation? Or was it salt water? British water? Heavy water? We will be accepting votes on the correct weight of water at http://www.mathware.com/BeginnersGuide, from which the electronic edition of this book is also available.)

Dividing this into the weight of people, we get the number of cubic feet of displacement the deck needs, not counting the weight of the deck itself:

$$\frac{20\ \textbf{Person} \times 200\ \frac{\text{Pound}}{\text{Person}}}{62.428\ \frac{\text{Pound}}{\text{Foot}^3}}$$

$$64.0738\ \texttt{Foot}^3$$

(As an amusing sideline, if you consider that people are pretty much made of water, this is also approximately the volume of the people themselves. We could have arrived at the same figure by sinking them in the lake and measuring the rise in water level.)

Jerry: OK, that's the people. Now how did you calculate the weight of your deck itself?

Theo: Decks are made of wood, Trex, and Styrofoam, the densities of which are known. Using a preliminary plan for the deck, I added up the weight of all the boards. For example, a 16-foot 2×12:

$$\textbf{WoodDensity} = 37\ \frac{\textbf{Pound}}{\textbf{Foot}^3};$$

$$\frac{1.5\ \textbf{Inch}}{12\ \frac{\text{Inch}}{\text{Foot}}} \times \frac{11.5\ \textbf{Inch}}{12\ \frac{\text{Inch}}{\text{Foot}}} \times 16\ \textbf{Foot} \times \textbf{WoodDensity}$$

$$70.9167\ \texttt{Pound}$$

Jerry: So a 2×12 is really a 1.5×11.5? Hm. Even so, one such board 16 feet long (not 15' 11.5") weighs about 70 pounds: No wonder carpenters are burly.

Theo: Without boring the readers with exactly how many boards I needed, my deck weighs about 4228 pounds (including all the structural lumber, Trex decking, Styrofoam, trim, and railing). So my calculation for total displacement of the fully loaded deck was:

$$\frac{4228 \text{ Pound} + 20 \text{ Person} \times 200 \frac{\text{Pound}}{\text{Person}}}{62.428 \frac{\text{Pound}}{\text{Foot}^3}}$$

131.8 Foot^3

To make this all float, I knew I would need an equal volume of Styrofoam flotation. My deck was going to measure 12'×18', so I next calculated how thick a layer of Styrofoam under the decking would give this volume:

$$\frac{131.8 \text{ Foot}^3}{16 \text{ Foot} \times 20 \text{ Foot}}$$

0.411875 Foot

Convert[%, Inch]

4.9425 Inch

Now, I could have built a deck with 5 inches of Styrofoam, but as I have experience with the interaction of math and the real world I quickly realized that 9.5 inches would be better. Doubling the minimum flotation gives us a comfortable margin of safety. Conveniently, 9.5 inches of Styrofoam neatly fills out the height of the 2×10 lumber I used to frame the deck. Working backwards, I calculated the exact number of people I would have to invite onto the deck in order to sink it. The total displacement was:

$$\textbf{Convert[9.5 Inch, Foot]} \times 16 \text{ Foot} \times 20 \text{ Foot} \times 62.428 \frac{\textbf{Pound}}{\textbf{Foot}^3}$$

15815.1 Pound

Subtracting the weight of the deck and dividing by the weight of a person:

$$\frac{\% - 4228 \text{ Pound}}{200 \frac{\text{Pound}}{\text{Person}}}$$

57.9355 Person

So, the 59th person would sink the deck. Was my safety factor enough? Well, I next calculated that if 58 people were on a 16×20 deck, each would have to fit into:

$$\frac{16 \text{ Foot} \times 20 \text{ Foot}}{58. \text{ Person}}$$

$$5.51724 \frac{\text{Foot}^2}{\text{Person}}$$

To visualize this, I wanted to see how big a square this was:

$\sqrt{\%}$

$$2.34888 \sqrt{\frac{\text{Foot}^2}{\text{Person}}}$$

So each person gets only a 2.3 foot square to stand in (not counting the area taking up by railings, table, chairs, Jerry Uhl's beer, etc.). This is pretty tight, especially if they all weigh 200 pounds. (Some people may find the square root of **Person** to be a curious concept. Think of it as the average of the front-to-back and side-to-side measurements of **Person**. Multiplied together, we get the total measure of the man.)

Jerry: Your deck example *seems* relevant. The problem for the world is that it was relevant to you, but maybe not to the next person. Each of us will have to find our own relevant math problems. Maybe we can use our web site http://www.mathware.com/BeginnersGuide to collect examples from our readers. We'll allow only math that has resulted in a real thing in the real world. Real numbers only.

Theo: Great idea! By the way, what we did above was pretty simple arithmetic, but we made good use of *Mathematica*'s ability to handle units, something calculators can't do. Without the units, we would have been a lot more likely to make a mistake (such as confusing an area with a volume, or forgetting to include the density of wood properly). See Chapter 67 for more on using units in *Mathematica*.

Jerry: The computer also makes an good place to store the calculation and experiment with different numbers (what if your friends went on diets?).

Theo: Actually I carried out a number of more complex calculations to determine the lateral stability of my deck; it's no good to have a deck that's floating, but upside down. In the end, my deck was built on land exactly according to the calculations above. No experiments were done to verify them. With the help of a retired undertaker and my neighbor Gerdes's tractor, my deck was dumped ceremoniously into the lake, has been tested on numerous festive occasions, and *has not sunk*. Obviously a triumph for mathematics and *Mathematica*!

And it's worth mentioning, now that we've reached V4, that the deck is still floating.

Chapter **74**

How do I make hyperlinks to the Web?

A *Mathematica* hyperlink can take you automatically to a particular web site, if you have a web browser installed and working on your system. *Mathematica* is not itself a web browser, but is able to cooperate with the browser of your choice. (For information on how to create links in and between notebooks on your local disk, see <u>Chapter</u> 61).

Here is a link to the home page for this book: <u>www.mathware.com/BeginnersGuide</u>. Click on it, and *Mathematica* will attempt to locate a browser on your computer. If one is installed, *Mathematica* will usually be able to find it automatically; if not, you will get a standard Open File dialog asking you to locate your browser.

After opening your web browser, *Mathematica* will instruct the browser to look up the site specified in the hyperlink.

To create such a hyperlink in *Mathematica*, it is usually easiest to begin by typing the whole sentence containing the link. For example, you might type:

> Click here to see my favorite site.

Next, select the word or words you want to turn into a link, for example the word "here". Choose **Create Hyperlink...** from the **Input** menu. In the upper text field, type in (or copy/paste) the full web address, including the `"http://"` or `"news://"`, etc. part. Click OK. The result is a web hyperlink, like this one:

> Click <u>here</u> to see my favorite site.

If you want to see how this hyperlink is represented in *Mathematica*, click on the cell bracket of the cell containing the link, and choose **Show Expression** from the **Format** menu. You will see:

```
Cell[TextData[{
  "Click ",
  ButtonBox["here",
    ButtonData:>{
      URL[ "http://hella.stm.it/market/bretagna/home.]
      None},
    ButtonStyle->"Hyperlink"],
  " to see my favorite site."
}], "Text"]
```

The target is a URL[] object containing the web address. Note that the **Create Hyperlink...** dialog box recognizes web prefixes like http:, etc., and automatically wraps them in URL[].

Chapter **75**

Does this book have a Home Page?

Yes, this book has a home page at <u>http://www.mathware.com/BeginnersGuide</u>.

The full text of this book is available at this site in electronic form as a set of *Mathematica* notebooks.

If you are not reading this book on screen, you are missing a lot:

- Any time you see underlined text in the book, you are looking at a hyperlink that will take you to something interesting. In the electronic version, you can click on it. In the paper version, clicking is futile.

- You may feel the urge to try out or modify the examples you see in this book. If you have *Mathematica* and the electronic edition, you can easily modify our examples without having to type them in from scratch. Because some of the examples make use of fairly lengthy function definitions, this is a big advantage of the electronic edition.

- The electronic edition includes palettes and larger program examples not reproduced in the printed book.

- The electronic edition includes a fully searchable electronic index, automatically merged with indices to the *Mathematica* book and to all the other documentation that came with your copy of *Mathematica*.

- Graphics are in full color in the electronic edition. Some graphics are far more intelligible in color.

- Sounds can be heard and animations can be animated if you have the electronic edition. Readers of the paper edition must use their imagination. For example, the animation demonstrating a moving axis of revolution in <u>Chapter</u> 68 is quite stunningly educational. An even better example, too complex to include in the printed edition, is included as a QuickTime animation in the electronic edition. Click <u>here</u> to open it if you have a Macintosh or a Windows machine with Quick-Time support.

If you visit the home page above, you will be instructed how to download the complete set of notebook files for a fee.

Chapter **76**

What *Mathematica* resources are available on the World Wide Web?

The main Wolfram Research web site is at http://www.wolfram.com. From there you can get to many Wolfram Research services. A list of third-party web sites can be found at http://www.wolfram.com/community/links/.

This book has a home page at http://www.mathware.com/BeginnersGuide. There you will find corrections, additions, supplementary chapters, and the full text of this book in electronic form, as a set of *Mathematica* notebooks.

An interesting site that uses *Mathematica* is http://integrals.com. It allows you to carry out just about any indefinite integral you like from your web browser. (Of course, if you have a copy of *Mathematica* yourself it's probably easier to use that, but if you ever find yourself stuck on a desert island without *Mathematica*, the web site might come in handy.)

Because studies show that the average lifetime of a web address, before it becomes invalid, is 42 days, we are not going to attempt to list additional, more specific, web addresses. The web sites above will lead you to currently active sites.

Chapter **77**

How do I do statistics?

Dozens of statistics programs are available for almost all brands of computers. At one end of the spectrum are simple inexpensive programs used by students to draw shaky conclusions from their data. At the other end are sophisticated expensive programs used by professional sociologists to draw shaky conclusions from *their* data.

How does *Mathematica's* ability to handle statistics compare to these programs? *Mathematica* can read files of data in almost any text format (many other programs require the data to be in one of a fixed set of formats). *Mathematica* can carry out most of the statistical analyses that the better special-purpose programs can. It can draw most of the same plots that they can. Perhaps the biggest advantage of using *Mathematica* to do your statistics is that you always have the whole of *Mathematica* available, not just the statistical portions. If you need to solve an equation on the side, you can. *Mathematica* is also able to carry out a variety of symbolic statistical analyses that data-based numerical programs can't approach.

However, because *Mathematica* is a general-purpose system, it does not have many special features designed specifically for doing statistics. This can make it somewhat harder to get started than with a program that does only statistics. But, the good overall design of *Mathematica* can be an advantage over the often primitive design of many statistics programs.

If you decide that you want to use *Mathematica* to do statistics, how does it work? You must load *Mathematica's* standard statistics package (included in all versions), using the following command:

    Needs["Statistics`Master`"]

(Note that the two single quotes used here are "back quotes" usually found on the same key with ~. They are *not* the single quotes found on the double-quote key.)

Loading this package gives you access to *Mathematica's* approximately 185 standard statistical functions. Obviously we can't describe all of them here (they are described in the <u>Guide to Standard Mathematica Packages</u> that comes with each copy of *Mathematica*).

Next you'll need to get some data to work with. See <u>Chapter</u> 79 for information about how to read in external data files, and <u>Chapter</u> 23 for information about how to pick out rows and columns from tables of data.

For this chapter, we'll just type in some not completely random numbers and assign them to a variable we will call **theData**:

```
theData = {1.6597, 2.8722, 3.8955, 4.2325, 5.7835, 6.4807,
     7.1861, 8.6568, 9.6286, 10.7319, 10.6251, 9.2095, 8.4716,
     7.8621, 6.2796, 5.6767, 4.8754, 3.9759, 2.3209, 1.8559};
```

Let's discuss descriptive statistics. The following analyses of our data are given without further discussion. The function names correspond to the traditional names used in statistics (demonstrating once again the value of using fully spelled-out names):

Mean[theData]

6.11401

Median[theData]

6.03155

GeometricMean[theData]

5.34876

HarmonicMean[theData]

4.5124

RootMeanSquare[theData]

6.72815

StandardDeviation[theData]

2.88132

Variance[theData]

8.30199

Skewness[theData]

0.0359457

Kurtosis[theData]

1.84603

Three report functions give you collections of the measures above (and others):

LocationReport[theData]

{Mean → 6.11401, HarmonicMean → 4.5124, Median → 6.03155}

DispersionReport[theData]

{Variance → 8.30199, StandardDeviation → 2.88132,
 SampleRange → 9.0722, MeanDeviation → 2.39919,
 MedianDeviation → 2.28805, QuartileDeviation → 2.31425}

ShapeReport[theData]

{Skewness → 0.0359457,
 QuartileSkewness → 0.0943718, KurtosisExcess → -1.15397}

Confidence intervals of several sorts can be computed. For example, here is the 95% confidence interval for the mean:

MeanCI[theData]

{4.76551, 7.46251}

If you want a different confidence level, you can use the following form:

MeanCI[theData, ConfidenceLevel → 0.75]

{5.34949, 6.87853}

Quite a few more measures are available; we've shown just a few. Click here for a complete list.

Mathematica can operate with several continuous and discrete distributions. For example, let us specify the "normal" distribution with a mean (center) of 6.11 and a standard deviation of 2.88:

NormalDistribution[6.11, 2.88]

NormalDistribution[6.11, 2.88]

This object does not, in itself, do anything; it is meaningful only in combination with other statistical functions. For example, we can ask for the mean of this distribution:

Mean[NormalDistribution[6.11, 2.88]]

6.11

As expected, its mean is the one we specified. Its kurtosis requires an actual calculation:

Kurtosis[NormalDistribution[6.11, 2.88]]

  3

If we want to make a picture or table of our distribution, we need the actual function that generates it. The **PDF** function (which stands for **P**robability **D**istribution **F**unction) gives us this function:

normalFunction = PDF[NormalDistribution[6.11, 2.88], x]

$0.138522 \, E^{-0.0602816 \, (-6.11+x)^2}$

• The first argument is the description of the distribution.
• The second argument gives our choice of variable name.

We can plot this function:

Plot[normalFunction, {x, 0, 12}];

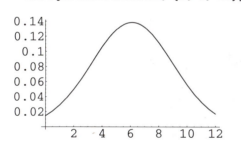

Or we can make a table of values:

theData = Table[{x, N[normalFunction]}, {x, 0, 12}] // TableForm

0	0.0145936
1	0.0287014
2	0.050036
3	0.0773218
4	0.105916
5	0.128606
6	0.138421
7	0.132063
8	0.111686
9	0.0837259
10	0.0556365
11	0.0327717
12	0.0171111

A couple of dozen other continuous distributions are available: Click here for a complete list. Click here for information on discrete distributions.

Mathematica can make several common statistical plots and charts if we load another package, using the following command:

```
Needs["Graphics`Graphics`"]
```

(Note that the two single quotes used here are "back quotes" usually found on the same key with ~. They are *not* the single quotes found on the double-quote key.)

Now we can make the following plots of our data (the labels in these plots are the index numbers of each data point within our list of data):

```
chartData = {1.6597, 2.8722, 0.8955,
    1.2325, 5.7835, 15.4807, 7.1861, 8.6568, 30.7319};
```

```
BarChart[chartData];
```

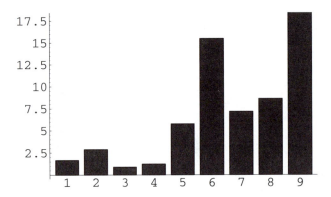

PieChart[chartData];

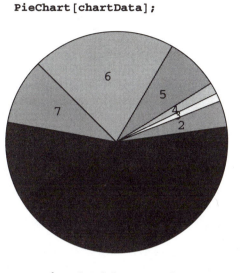

TextListPlot[chartData];

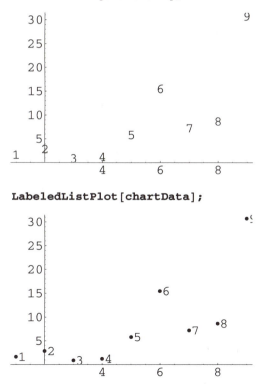

LabeledListPlot[chartData];

As with other *Mathematica* graphics commands, there are countless options that change details of the plots. These are all described in the *Guide to Standard Packages*.

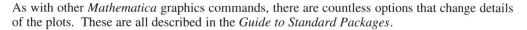

Chapter **78**

How do I fit a curve to data?

The list of pairs below gives the population of the earth over the last 10 decades, starting in 1900; the first element in each pair is the year since 1900 and the second is the population in billions:

```
population =
   {{0, 1.59}, {10, 1.70}, {20, 1.81}, {30, 2.02}, {40, 2.25},
    {50, 2.59}, {60, 3.01}, {70, 3.61}, {80, 4.48}, {90, 5.33}};
```

We will plot these points using **ListPlot**, joining the points with straight lines. (**ListPlot** is explained in more detail in <u>Chapter</u> 42.)

```
dataPlot = ListPlot[population, PlotJoined → True];
```

We might want to find a smooth function that approximates this plot. For example, the following command will find the best-fitting third-order polynomial:

```
fitFunction = Fit[population, {1, x, x², x³}, x]
```

$$1.59155 + 0.0101523\,x - 4.02098 \times 10^{-6}\,x^2 + 3.96076 \times 10^{-6}\,x^3$$

- The first argument is the data to fit.
- The second argument is a list of functions to fit.
- The third argument names the independent variable.

The second argument to **Fit** is a list of functions that will be combined linearly to form the fit function. In the example above, the listed functions are combined like this:

$$a\,1 + b\,x + c\,x^2 + d\,x^3$$

The job of **Fit** is to choose the coefficients **a**, **b**, **c**, and **d** that give us the best possible fit. (This task is called *linear regression* because the coefficients being fit are all linearly related to the fit function. Non-linear regression is much more complicated and will not be discussed here.)

After *Mathematica* has found a function that fits, we can plot it. (**Plot** is discussed in more detail in Chapter 31):

```
fitPlot =
    Plot[fitFunction, {x, 0, 100}, PlotStyle → Dashing[{0.01}]];
```

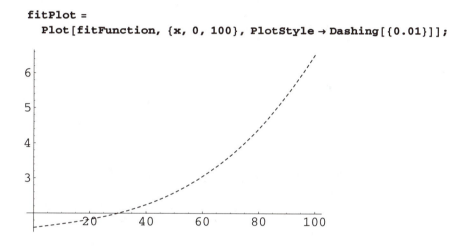

To see how good the fit is, we can show both plots together:

```
Show[{dataPlot, fitPlot}];
```

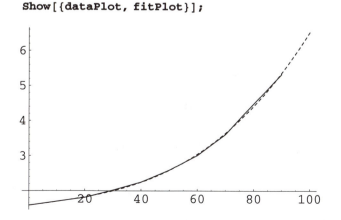

Notice that we have plotted the fit function one decade beyond the end of the data, illustrating *extrapolation*, the most common use of curve fitting. Our example also illustrates the danger of extrapolating beyond the reasonable range of validity; the extrapolated curve predicts a population of about 6.6 billion in the year 2000, compared to current best estimates of 6.2 billion.

In the example above we fit to a polynomial. Polynomials are commonly used when you have no idea what the data *should* look like; they are generic functions that work reasonably well anywhere. In this case, however, it is widely recognized that populations grow more or less exponentially, so we might want to try a fitting function of the form:

$$a\ E^{b\,x}$$

Here **a** and **b** are constants to be determined by **Fit**. In this example, **b** is in a nonlinear position. But, as we noted above, **Fit** works only when the constants are in linear positions.

Fortunately, we can use a trick: we can fit the log of this function to the log of the data. If we take the log of the function, we get:

$$Log[a] + b\,x$$

Now **a** is nonlinearly related to the function, but we can make up a new constant, **loga**, which is linear:

$$loga + b\,x$$

If we fit this function to the log of the data, we will get an answer in the form we want.

To proceed, we need a new table, similar to **population** but with the **Log** of the second element of each data pair. There are several ways to create this table. The following is not the most efficient but is probably the least confusing.

First we define a function, **logOfSecondElement**, which, when applied to a list of two elements, returns a list in which the second element has been replaced by its **Log** (see Chapter 7 and Chapter 58 for more information on defining functions).

```
logOfSecondElement[{x_, y_}] := {x, Log[y]}
```

Next we apply (map) this function to each element in the **population** list:

```
logPopulation = Map[logOfSecondElement, population]
```

```
{{0, 0.463734}, {10, 0.530628}, {20, 0.593327},
 {30, 0.703098}, {40, 0.81093}, {50, 0.951658},
 {60, 1.10194}, {70, 1.28371}, {80, 1.49962}, {90, 1.67335}}
```

Now we can fit one constant plus a second constant times **x** to this new data:

```
Fit[logPopulation, {1, x}, x]
```

```
0.34869 + 0.0136113 x
```

So our constant **loga** is 0.34869, and our constant **b** is 0.0136113. Translating back into the original form of the desired function, we get:

$$\texttt{fitFunction2} = E^{0.34869} E^{0.0136113\,x}$$

$$1.41721\, E^{0.0136113\,x}$$

In terms of our original equation, the constant **a** is 1.41721.

We can plot this function:

```
fitPlot2 =
   Plot[fitFunction2, {x, 0, 100}, PlotStyle → Dashing[{0.01}]];
```

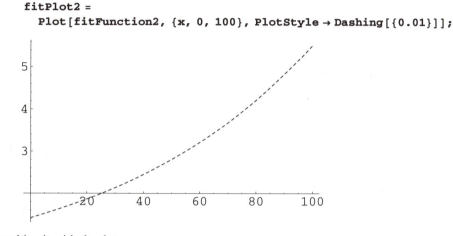

and combine it with the data:

```
Show[{dataPlot, fitPlot2}];
```

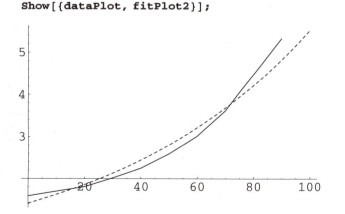

We have learned that population growth is not, after all, described by a simple exponential.

Sadly, a great deal of curve fitting is done without sufficient thought, as we just did above. It's like statistics: A little knowledge can get you into a lot of trouble. Readers are encouraged *not* to use the **Fit** function unless they are qualified to do so by at least two semesters of college statistics, or by mastering at least three books on the subject. (This book doesn't count.)

Chapter **79**

How do I import data into *Mathematica*?

If you want to use *Mathematica* to analyze just about any sort of real-world data, chances are you will need to start by importing the data into *Mathematica* from wherever you got it. In V4, a new, general-purpose data-importing function has been introduced. It is able to handle, often completely automatically, ASCII text, tabular data, various binary data formats, and a wide range of image formats. The mechanism is extensible; it is expected that new formats will be added based on user requests.

To import data you need only one command: **Import**. You give **Import** the name of the file you want to import, and if necessary some options to narrow down how the importing should be done, and it returns your data in *Mathematica* form. Often you will not need to specify any options, because **Import** is able to determine the format of the data automatically.

For example, suppose you had the following text in a file called "mydata.dat":

```
Time     Voltage
1.0      4.2
2.0      5.6
3.0      6.9
4.0      4.8
5.0      3.9
6.0      2.4
```

To import it, just give **Import** the file name. Based on the fact that the file ends in ".dat", **Import** assumes it's a space- and/or tab-delimited text file containing one or more columns of data. It imports it as a list of lists (one sublist for each line in the file).

```
mydata = Import["mydata.dat"]
```

```
{{Time, Voltage}, {1., 4.2}, {2., 5.6},
 {3., 6.9}, {4., 4.8}, {5., 3.9}, {6., 2.4}}
```

You can use **TableForm** to display this list as a table: It will look pretty much like the original file.

    mydata // TableForm

```
Time      Voltage
1.        4.2
2.        5.6
3.        6.9
4.        4.8
5.        3.9
6.        2.4
```

At this point we should take a short detour to discuss file names and locations. In this example we gave **Import** just a plain file name; in order for *Mathematica* to find the file, it had to be located in one of the directories listed on *Mathematica*'s default search path. The exact set of directories that will be searched depends on a lot of things, but it typically includes the directory containing *Mathematica* itself, your home directory (on Unix systems), etc. To see the list for your setup, evaluate **$Path**:

    $Path

```
{Rebecca:System Folder:Preferences:Mathematica:4.0:Kernel,
 Rebecca:System Folder:Preferences:Mathematica:
    4.0:AddOns:Autoload, Rebecca:System Folder:
    Preferences:Mathematica:4.0:AddOns:Applications,
 :, Rebecca:FE:2.3:AddOns:StandardPackages,
 Rebecca:FE:2.3:AddOns:StandardPackages:StartUp,
 Rebecca:FE:2.3:AddOns:Autoload,
 Rebecca:FE:2.3:AddOns:Applications,
 Rebecca:FE:2.3:AddOns:ExtraPackages,
 Rebecca:FE:2.3:SystemFiles:Graphics:Packages,
 Rebecca:FE:2.3:Configuration:Kernel}
```

You can also give **Import** a full path name (in the syntax appropriate to your platform). If you're going to be importing a lot of files from the same directory, you can add a new directory to **$Path** using **AppendTo**; for example:

    AppendTo[$Path, "Rebecca:AllMyData:"];

Note that whether you use **:** or **/** or **** to separate directory names depends on the platform on which you are running *Mathematica*. It is also possible to use *Mathematica*'s own platform-independent **ToFileName** syntax. File names in *Mathematica* are described at great length in Chapter 65.

Perhaps *most* usefully, you can ask to have an open file dialog box put up to let you pick a file interactively:

```
mydata = Import[Experimental`FileBrowse[False]];
```

Note that some day **FileBrowse** won't be "experimental" anymore, and the command above may need to be modified.

Now back to the data. The original file contains column headings, which have been imported as strings. In order to do most sorts of further analysis on the data, you'll need to remove these headings from the data. The command Drop can be used to remove the first row (which contains the headings):

```
mydata = Drop[mydata, 1]
```

$$\{\{1., 4.2\}, \{2., 5.6\}, \{3., 6.9\}, \{4., 4.8\}, \{5., 3.9\}, \{6., 2.4\}\}$$

Now you can, for example, fit a curve to the data and plot it:

```
fitCurve = Fit[mydata, {1, x, x^2}, x];
Plot[fitCurve, {x, 1, 6}, Epilog →
    {PointSize[0.04], Map[Point, mydata]}, PlotRange → All];
```

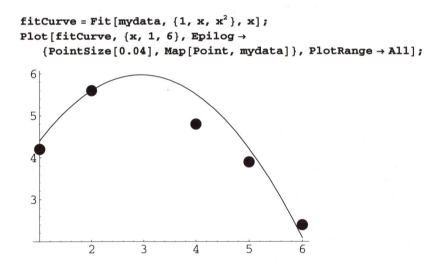

At this point, you may want to read Chapter 23, which contains some very useful information about how to deal with rows and columns in a table of data. It tells you such things as how to extract a single column of data, a range of rows, or an arbitrary sub-matrix. These methods can be used to remove undesirable rows or columns, restrict your analysis to subsets of the data, etc. For more information about fitting curves and making plots like this, see Chapter 78.

▪ How does **Import** decide what to do?

When you ask to import data from a file, *Mathematica* has to decide certain things about the file. It is a text file? Is it a binary file? Is it an image? If it's a text file, does it contain separate columns of data? Are the elements text, numbers, dollar amounts, or what?

Mathematica tries to do as much as it can automatically, but it can't read your mind (not before V14.0, to be introduced in late September 2012). In the meantime there are three steps you can take to help *Mathematica* make the right choices.

First, **Import** looks at the end of the file name for one of the conventional file extensions (for example, ".jpg" for JPEG image files). We'll mention some of these extensions in the sections below, but for a complete listing you should refer to the online documentation for **Import**.

Second, if the file extension does not give **Import** enough information to properly import the file, you can include a second argument specifying the file format. For example:

```
data = Import["MyPicture", "JPEG"];
```

will import a JPEG image file, even though the file name does not end in ".jpg".

Third, if the file type alone is not enough to determine exactly how you want the data imported, **Import** supports options that allow you to control the details of how the data in the file will be interpreted. A few options apply to all file formats, but most of the options are specific to a particular file type (since they would not make sense for other formats).

The details of these options are beyond the scope of this book; the reader is encouraged to look at the online documentation for **Import**. Most of the detail information about options is contained in the "Further Information" section at the very end of the online documentation (click the triangle next to the heading to open up the section).

■ How *doesn't* Import decide what to do?

There are two pieces of information about a file that **Import** might look at to determine its type, but does not. (Both of these limitations may be addressed in future versions of *Mathematica*).

- **Import** does not look at the file type information maintained by the Macintosh file system. If you have Macintosh files that do not use the standard file extensions, you'll need to include the second argument to **Import** as discussed above.

- **Import** does not attempt to examine the data in the file to determine its type (for example by looking at the first four bytes of the file, which for many types of files contain characteristic values).

The way in which the data will be imported is completely determined by the file extension, the second argument to **Import** if present, and any options you include in the command.

▪ Importing data from text files

Text files present the most complex challenge for importing, because there isn't just one kind of text file. There are files that contain paragraphs of text, files that contain lists of various sorts delimited by various delimiters, and files that contain tables (rows and columns) of elements delimited by various delimiters.

The first common case is text files that contain actual *text*, such as sentences in some language. If **Import** is given a file ending in ".txt", or "Text" as a second argument, it will import the file as a single big quoted string. You can then use the *Mathematica* string manipulation commands (e.g. **StringReplace**, etc.) to have your way with the file.

The next common case is text files that contain rows and columns of data with each row on one line (terminated with a carriage return, newline, or linefeed character) and the columns separated by spaces or tabs. If **Import** is given a file ending in ".dat", or "Table" as a second argument, it will return a matrix containing the rows and columns of items. (See the example at the beginning of this chapter.) **Import** will attempt to handle each element of the table appropriately based on whether it's a number, a string (like a column heading), a dollar amount, or a mathematical expression.

For text files that are more highly structured, there are many options to help control exactly how the importing is done. The issues break down into how to decide where the boundaries between elements are, and how to import elements of each type. It is beyond the scope of this book to go into these options, so we refer the reader to the online documentation for **Import**.

▪ Importing binary files

Two standard binary data formats are supported: HDF (for ".hdf" files) and MAT (for ".mat" files). More formats are expected to be supported in future versions.

There isn't too much to say about binary formats, since in general the details of how the data is stored are determined by the definition of the format, and there isn't such a range of arbitrary variation as in text files. The online documentation for **Import** (in the Further Information section) lists specific options that can be used with these binary formats.

▪ Importing images

The two basic kinds of image formats are: Bitmap and complicated. Bitmap images are fairly easy to import, because they can always be represented by 2-dimensional matrices of numbers (plus perhaps a color table for index color bitmaps). More complicated image formats contain tokens that represent lines, arcs, text in different fonts, patterns, *and* bitmaps.

▪ Bitmap formats

Import supports all the major bitmap formats (JPEG, GIF, TIFF, BMP, PNG, PPM, etc.), and for each of these it supports pretty much the full range of sub-cases (different bit depths, compression types, etc.). To get a complete listing, look at the online documentation for **Import**, or if you just want a list of the names, try:

```
$ImportFormats

{AIFF, AU, BMP, Dump, EPS, EPSI, EPSTIFF,
 Expression, GIF, HDF, JPEG, Lines, List, MAT, MGF,
 MPS, PBM, PGM, PNM, PPM, PSImage, RawBitmap, SND,
 Table, Text, TIFF, UnicodeText, WAV, Words, XBitmap}
```

Depending on exactly what version of *Mathematica* you have, and whether you have add-on import modules installed, the list you get may differ from this one.

Bitmaps are imported as **Graphics** objects with the actual bitmap data contained in a **Raster** object. If this sounds confusing, it is a little bit, but it makes a lot of sense once you understand it. Fortunately, we have a chapter that explains this structure and shows how to use it: see Chapter 45.

Import can import animated GIFs, resulting in a list of **Graphics** objects. (Note that some animated GIFs contain only partial images for some frames: These will not be imported properly in V4.)

▪ Non-bitmap formats

Non-bitmap-format images, sometimes referred to as vector graphics formats, can be imported, but generally only with a certain loss of fidelity. These formats typically contain a large number of types of graphics primitives (lines, fills, points, text, bitmaps, gradients, etc.). Not all of these primitives can be represented in *Mathematica*'s graphics language, and those that can sometimes have slightly different meanings in *Mathematica* than in the original file. For example, it simply isn't possible to represent, in *Mathematica* graphics syntax, all the subtleties of a PostScript linecap command.

At present, the only supported non-bitmap graphics format is PostScript (files ending in ".ps", ".eps", and ".epsi"). The result of importing a PostScript graphic is a **Graphics** object containing a mixture of **Line**, **Text**, **Polygon**, etc., graphics primitives.

Import does not at present support Macintosh PICT files, but it is possible to use the front end to do basically the same thing. Use Copy/Paste to place the PICT graphic in a Notebook, click on it to select the graphic, then choose **InputForm** from the **Convert To...** submenu of the **Cell** menu. The graphic will be replaced with a **Graphics** expression containing a list of graphics primitives, in the same format as **Import** would give.

■ Importing Sounds

Various sound files can be imported: The result is a **Sound** expression containing a **Sampled- Sound** expression, which contains the actual sample values. See the online documentation for **Import** for a list of the sound formats supported, and the documentation for **Sound** and **SampledSound** for more information about these formats. (For a quick introduction to generating sounds in *Mathematica*, see Chapter 43.)

Chapter **80**

How do I export data from *Mathematica*?

Complementing the powerful **Import** command described in the <u>previous</u> chapter is the similarly powerful **Export** command. To a first approximation, **Export** can export about the same set of formats as **Import** can import. That means it can export ASCII text, text tables, binary data formats, various graphics formats, and sounds.

Let's use the same example as in the previous chapter, but in reverse. Say we have typed in the following table of data in *Mathematica*, and we want to export it as a tab-separated ASCII text file.

$$
\text{mydata} = \begin{pmatrix}
\text{"Time"} & \text{"Voltage"} \\
1. & 4.2 \\
2. & 5.6 \\
3. & 6.9 \\
4. & 4.8 \\
5. & 3.9 \\
6. & 2.4
\end{pmatrix} ;
$$

To export this data, we give **Export** a file name and the data:

```
Export["mydata.dat", mydata];
```

Based on the ".dat" file ending, **Export** decides to export the data as a tab-delimited text file. To see the result you can either open "mydata.dat" in the text editor of your choice, or you can use the somewhat obscure **!!** notation to display the contents of a text file in *Mathematica*.

```
!! mydata.dat

Time    Voltage
1.      4.2
2.      5.6
3.      6.9
4.      4.8
5.      3.9
6.      2.4
```

As with **Import**, you can give **Export** a full path name to place the file in a particular directory, or you can ask to have a save-file dialog put up allowing you to pick the file name interactively:

Export[Experimental`FileBrowse[True], mydata];

Be sure to include the appropriate file ending, or **Export** won't know what format to use. File names in *Mathematica* are described at great length in Chapter 65.

As with **Import**, if you don't want to use the standard file endings for the format you are exporting, you can use a third argument to specify the format. For example, the command below allows you to pick any file name you like and will always export as a tab-delimited table:

Export[Experimental`FileBrowse[True], mydata, "Table"];

It should be noted that if you have very large tables of data, using **Export** is much faster than the other ways of writing files from *Mathematica*. This is mainly because **Export** does not attempt to do any line-wrapping of expressions: All the elements in a particular row of the table go on one line.

Of course there are many options you can use to control the behavior of **Export**; refer to the online documentation for the full details.

■ Exporting images

You can export *Mathematica*-generated graphics in any of the standard graphics formats. For example, you can make a plot:

myplot = Plot[Sin[x], {x, 0, 2 π}];

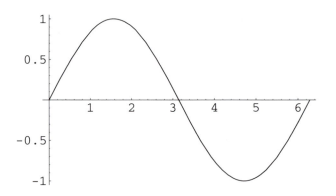

and then export the plot to a JPEG file:

```
Export["myplot.jpg", myplot]
```

```
myplot.jpg
```

You can combine these commands and use the option **DisplayFunction→Identity** to prevent the graphic from being drawn in the front end:

```
Export["myplot.jpg",
 Plot[Sin[x], {x, 0, 2 π}, DisplayFunction → Identity]]
```

```
myplot.jpg
```

Most graphics formats support a bewildering array of variations (for example, the JPEG format supports a "quality" parameter which determines the degree of compression used to reduce the file size). These parameters can be controlled using the **ConversionOptions** option to **Export**. The full details, which are different for each graphics format, are described in the online help for **Export** (in the Further Information section near the bottom).

Animated GIFs (popular for use on the Web) can be generated by giving **Export** a list of graphics, and specifying GIF as the export format.

Unfortunately, QuickTime animations are not supported by the V4 **Export** command (they may be in the future). In the meantime, the Macintosh front end is able to create QuickTime animations. Follow the instructions in <u>Chapter</u> 44 to create an animation, then click on the cell bracket containing all the graphics cells (and only the graphics cells). Choose **QuickTime** from the **Cell** menu, **Convert To** submenu. You will be asked to choose a file name (and various other parameters): The exported QuickTime animation will be placed in the file you specify (you will also get a cell in the Notebook containing the animation, but it is not necessary to further export this cell; the file contains the entire animation).

■ Export text and typeset expressions as images

It is possible to export typeset mathematical expressions, or paragraphs of text, as images. To do this, you give **Export** what is called the box-form of the expression you want exported. It is somewhat beyond the scope of this book to go into detail about what this means, but fortunately you don't really need to know much about it to use the feature.

To export an expression in the default typeset notation (StandardForm, which is displayed in the monospaced Courier font), use Export as follows:

$$\texttt{myintegral} = \int \frac{1}{1-x^3}\, dx$$

$$\frac{\text{ArcTan}\left[\frac{1+2x}{\sqrt{3}}\right]}{\sqrt{3}} - \frac{1}{3}\,\text{Log}[-1+x] + \frac{1}{6}\,\text{Log}[1+x+x^2]$$

Export["myintegral.gif", ToBoxes[myintegral]]

`myintegral.gif`

If you want to export the somewhat more attractive **TraditionalForm** notation

myintegral // TraditionalForm

$$\frac{\tan^{-1}\left(\frac{2x+1}{\sqrt{3}}\right)}{\sqrt{3}} - \frac{1}{3}\log(x-1) + \frac{1}{6}\log(x^2+x+1)$$

use the following command:

Export["myintegral.gif", ToBoxes[myintegral, TraditionalForm]]

`myintegral.gif`

The advanced reader may be interested to know that **Export** can also handle **Cell[]** and **Notebook[]** expressions, but this is well beyond what we can describe here. **Export** is also able to export in HTML and TₑX formats, but except under unusual circumstances it's easier to use the menu items provided for this purpose.

References

In the first edition of this book we printed a list of the books about and using *Mathematica*—a mistake, because the list was out of date before the book reached bookstores. This time we provide a list of web addresses where current lists can be found. (Note that according to an authoritative recent study the average lifetime of a web address is 42 days, so this list itself may not last very long. We are confident that the major sites, at least, will exist well into next month.)

Electronic edition of this book:
http://www.mathware.com/BeginnersGuide

General *Mathematica* information:
http://www.wolfram.com (US)
http://www.wolfram.co.uk (UK)
http://www.wolfram.co.jp (Japan)

Books about *Mathematica*:
http://www.wolfram.com/bookstore

Application packages:
www.wolfram.com/mathsource/
www.wolfram.com/applications/index.html

Links to *Mathematica*-related sites:
www.wolfram.com/community/links/

Index

(Our indexing has been described as unprofessional by no fewer that two separate reviewers of previous editions of this book. So don't get your hopes up.)